A POCKETFUL

OF PLAYS

VINTAGE

DRAMA

A POCKETFUL

OF PLAYS

VINTAGE

DRAMA

DAVID MADDEN

Louisiana State University

HARCOURT BRACE COLLEGE PUBLISHERS

*Fort Worth   Philadelphia   San Diego   New York   Orlando   Austin   San Antonio
Toronto   Montreal   London   Sydney   Tokyo*

PUBLISHER	*Ted Buchholz*
EDITOR IN CHIEF	*Christopher P. Klein*
EXECUTIVE EDITOR	*Michael A. Rosenberg*
ASSISTANT EDITOR	*Tina Winslow*
PROJECT EDITOR	*Laura J. Hanna*
PRODUCTION MANAGER	*Jane Tyndall Ponceti*
ART DIRECTORS	*Melinda Welch/Nick Welch*

Address for Editorial Correspondence: Harcourt Brace College Publishers, 301 Commerce Street, Suite 3700, Fort Worth, TX 76102.

Address for Orders: Harcourt Brace & Company, 6277 Sea Harbor Drive, Orlando, FL 32887-6777. 1-800-782-4479, or 1-800-433-0001 (in Florida).

Printed in the United States of America

ISBN: 0-15-502543-0

Library of Congress Catalog Card Number: 95-79364

5 6 7 8 9 0 1 2 3 4   039   10 9 8 7 6 5 4 3 2 1

CONTENTS

A POCKETFUL

OF PLAYS

VINTAGE

DRAMA

Susan Glaspell, 1882–1948

Trifles (1916)

CHARACTERS

George Henderson, *county attorney*
Henry Peters, *sheriff*
Lewis Hale, *a neighboring farmer*
Mrs. Peters
Mrs. Hale

SCENE.

The kitchen in the now abandoned farmhouse of John Wright, a gloomy kitchen, and left without having been put in order—unwashed pans under the sink, a loaf of bread outside the breadbox, a dish towel on the table— other signs of incompleted work. At the rear the outer door opens and the Sheriff comes in followed by the County Attorney and Hale. The Sheriff and Hale are men in middle life, the County Attorney is a young man; all are much bundled up and go at once to the stove. They are followed by two women—the Sheriff's wife first; she is a slight wiry woman, a thin nervous face. Mrs. Hale is larger and would ordinarily be called more comfortable looking, but she is disturbed now and looks fearfully about as she enters. The women have come in slowly, and stand close together near the door.

COUNTY ATTORNEY: *(rubbing his hands)* This feels good. Come up to the fire, ladies.

MRS. PETERS: *(after taking a step forward)* I'm not—cold.

SHERIFF: *(unbuttoning his overcoat and stepping away from the stove as if to mark the beginning of official business)* Now, Mr. Hale, before we move things about, you explain to Mr. Henderson just what you saw when you came here yesterday morning.

COUNTY ATTORNEY: By the way, has anything been moved? Are things just as you left them yesterday?

5 SHERIFF: *(looking about)* It's just the same. When it dropped below zero last night I thought I'd better send Frank out this morning to make a fire for us—no use getting pneumonia with a big case on, but I told him not to touch anything except the stove—and you know Frank.

COUNTY ATTORNEY: Somebody should have been left here yesterday.

1

SHERIFF: Oh—yesterday. When I had to send Frank to Morris Center for that man who went crazy—I want you to know I had my hands full yesterday. I knew you could get back from Omaha by today and as long as I went over everything here myself—

COUNTY ATTORNEY: Well, Mr. Hale, tell just what happened when you came here yesterday morning.

HALE: Harry and I had started to town with a load of potatoes. We came along the road from my place and as I got here I said, "I'm going to see if I can't get John Wright to go in with me on a party telephone." I spoke to Wright about it once before and he put me off, saying folks talked too much anyway, and all he asked was peace and quiet—I guess you know about how much he talked himself; but I thought maybe if I went to the house and talked about it before his wife, though I said to Harry that I didn't know as what his wife wanted made much difference to John—

10 **COUNTY ATTORNEY:** Let's talk about that later, Mr. Hale. I do want to talk about that, but tell now just what happened when you got to the house.

HALE: I didn't hear or see anything; I knocked at the door, and still it was all quiet inside. I knew they must be up, it was past eight o'clock. So I knocked again, and I thought I heard somebody say, "Come in." I wasn't sure, I'm not sure yet, but I opened the door—this door (*Indicating the door by which the two women are still standing.*) and there in that rocker—(*Pointing to it.*) sat Mrs. Wright.

They all look at the rocker.

COUNTY ATTORNEY: What—was she doing?

HALE: She was rockin' back and forth. She had her apron in her hand and was kind of—pleating it.

COUNTY ATTORNEY: And how did she—look?

15 **HALE:** Well, she looked queer.

COUNTY ATTORNEY: How do you mean—queer?

HALE: Well, as if she didn't know what she was going to do next. And kind of done up.

COUNTY ATTORNEY: How did she seem to feel about your coming?

HALE: Why, I don't think she minded—one way or other. She didn't pay much attention. I said, "How do, Mrs. Wright, it's cold, ain't it?" And she said, "Is it?"—and went on kind of pleating at her apron. Well, I was surprised; she didn't ask me to come up to the stove, or to set down, but just sat there, not even looking at me, so I said, "I want to see John." And then she—laughed. I guess you would call it a laugh. I thought of Harry and the team outside, so I said a little sharp: "Can't I see John?" "No," she says, kind o' dull like. "Ain't he home?" says I. "Yes," says she, "he's home." "Then why can't I see him?" I asked her, out of patience. "'Cause he's dead," says she. "*Dead?*" says I. She just nodded her head, not getting a bit excited, but rockin' back and forth. "Why—where is he?" says I, not knowing what to say. She just pointed upstairs—like that (*Himself pointing to the room* *above.).* I got up, with the idea of going up there. I walked from there to here—then I says, "Why, what did he die of?" "He died of a rope round his neck," says she, and just went on pleatin' at her apron. Well, I went out and called Harry. I thought I might—need help. We went upstairs and there he was lyin'—

20   **COUNTY ATTORNEY:**   I think I'd rather have you go into that upstairs, where you can point it all out. Just go on now with the rest of the story.

    HALE: Well, my first thought was to get that rope off. It looked . . . *(Stops, his face twitches.)* . . . but Harry, he went up to him, and he said, "No, he's dead all right, and we'd better not touch anything." So we went back down stairs. She was still sitting that same way. "Has anybody been notified?" I asked. "No," says she, unconcerned. "Who did this, Mrs. Wright?" said Harry. He said it businesslike—and she stopped pleatin' of her apron. "I don't know," she says. "You don't *know?*" says Harry. "No," says she. "Weren't you sleepin' in the bed with him?" says Harry. "Yes," says she, "but I was on the inside." "Somebody slipped a rope round his neck and strangled him and you didn't wake up?" says Harry. "I didn't wake up," she said after him. We must 'a looked as if we didn't see how that could be, for after a minute she said, "I sleep sound." Harry was going to ask her more questions but I said maybe we ought to let her tell her story first to the coroner, or the sheriff, so Harry went fast as he could to Rivers' place, where there's a telephone.

    COUNTY ATTORNEY: And what did Mrs. Wright do when she knew that you had gone for the coroner?

    HALE: She moved from that chair to this one over here *(Pointing to a small chair in the corner.)* and just sat there with her hands held together and looking down. I got a feeling that I ought to make some conversation, so I said I had come in to see if John wanted to put in a telephone, and at that she started to laugh, and then she stopped and looked at me—scared. *(The County Attorney, who has had his notebook out, makes a note.)* I dunno, maybe it wasn't scared. I wouldn't like to say it was. Soon Harry got back, and then Dr. Lloyd came, and you, Mr. Peters, and so I guess that's all I know that you don't.

    COUNTY ATTORNEY: *(looking around)* I guess we'll go upstairs first—and then out to the barn and around there. *(To the Sheriff.)* You're convinced that there was nothing important here—nothing that would point to any motive.

25   **SHERIFF:**   Nothing here but kitchen things.

The County Attorney, after again looking around the kitchen, opens the door of a cupboard closet. He gets up on a chair and looks on a shelf. Pulls his hand away, sticky.

    COUNTY ATTORNEY: Here's a nice mess.

The women draw nearer.

MRS. PETERS: *(to the other woman)* Oh, her fruit; it did freeze. *(To the County Attorney.)* She worried about that when it turned so cold. She said the fire'd go out and her jars would break.

SHERIFF: Well, can you beat the women! Held for murder and worryin' about her preserves.

COUNTY ATTORNEY: I guess before we're through she may have something more serious than preserves to worry about.

30 HALE: Well, women are used to worrying over trifles.

The two women move a little closer together.

COUNTY ATTORNEY: *(with the gallantry of a young politician)* And yet, for all their worries, what would we do without the ladies? *(The women do not unbend. He goes to the sink, takes a dipperful of water from the pail and pouring it into a basin, washes his hands. Starts to wipe them on the roller towel, turns it for a cleaner place.)* Dirty towels! *(Kicks his foot against the pans under the sink.)* Not much of a housekeeper, would you say, ladies?

MRS. HALE: *(stiffly)* There's a great deal of work to be done on a farm.

COUNTY ATTORNEY: To be sure. And yet *(With a little bow to her)* I know there are some Dickson county farmhouses which do not have such roller towels.

He gives it a pull to expose its full length again.

MRS. HALE: Those towels get dirty awful quick. Men's hands aren't always as clean as they might be.

35 COUNTY ATTORNEY: Ah, loyal to your sex, I see. But you and Mrs. Wright were neighbors. I suppose you were friends, too.

MRS. HALE: *(shaking her head)* I've not seen much of her of late years. I've not been in this house—it's more than a year.

COUNTY ATTORNEY: And why was that? You didn't like her?

MRS. HALE: I liked her all well enough. Farmers' wives have their hands full, Mr. Henderson. And then—

COUNTY ATTORNEY: Yes—?

40 MRS. HALE: *(looking about)* It never seemed a very cheerful place.

COUNTY ATTORNEY: No—it's not cheerful. I shouldn't say she had the homemaking instinct.

MRS. HALE: Well, I don't know as Wright had, either.

COUNTY ATTORNEY: You mean that they didn't get on very well?

MRS. HALE: No, I don't mean anything. But I don't think a place'd be any cheerfuller for John Wright's being in it.

45 COUNTY ATTORNEY: I'd like to talk more of that a little later. I want to get the lay of things upstairs now.

He goes to the left, where three steps lead to a stair door.

SHERIFF: I suppose anything Mrs. Peters does'll be all right. She was to take in some clothes for her, you know, and a few little things. We left in such a hurry yesterday.

COUNTY ATTORNEY: Yes, but I would like to see what you take, Mrs. Peters, and keep an eye out for anything that might be of use to us.

MRS. PETERS: Yes, Mr. Henderson.

The women listen to the men's steps on the stairs, then look about the kitchen.

MRS. HALE: I'd hate to have men coming into my kitchen, snooping around and criticizing.

She arranges the pans under sink which the County Attorney had shoved out of place.

50 **MRS. PETERS:**   Of course it's no more than their duty.

MRS. HALE: Duty's all right, but I guess that deputy sheriff that came out to make the fire might have got a little of this on. *(Gives the roller towel a pull.)* Wish I'd thought of that sooner. Seems mean to talk about her for not having things slicked up when she had to come away in such a hurry.

MRS. PETERS: *(who has gone to a small table in the left rear corner of the room, and lifted one end of a towel that covers a pan)* She had bread set.

Stands still.

MRS. HALE: *(eyes fixed on a loaf of bread beside the breadbox, which is on a low shelf at the other side of the room. Moves slowly toward it.)* She was going to put this in there. *(Picks up loaf, then abruptly drops it. In a manner of returning to familiar things.)* It's a shame about her fruit. I wonder if it's all gone. *(Gets up on the chair and looks.)* I think there's some here that's all right, Mrs. Peters. Yes—here; *(Holding it toward the window)* this is cherries, too. *(Looking again.)* I declare I believe that's the only one. *(Gets down, bottle in her hand. Goes to the sink and wipes it off on the outside.)* She'll feel awful bad after all her hard work in the hot weather. I remember the afternoon I put up my cherries last summer.

She puts the bottle on the big kitchen table, center of the room. With a sigh, is about to sit down in the rocking-chair. Before she is seated realizes what chair it is; with a slow look at it, steps back. The chair which she has touched rocks back and forth.

MRS. PETERS: Well, I must get those things from the front room closet. *(She goes to the door at the right, but after looking into the other room, steps back.)* You coming with me, Mrs. Hale? You could help me carry them.

They go in the other room; reappear, Mrs. Peters carrying a dress and skirt, Mrs. Hale following with a pair of shoes.

55 **MRS. PETERS:** My, it's cold in there.

She puts the clothes on the big table, and hurries to the stove.

MRS. HALE: *(examining her skirt)* Wright was close. I think maybe that's why she kept so much to herself. She didn't even belong to the Ladies Aid. I suppose she felt she couldn't do her part, and then you don't enjoy things when you feel shabby. She used to wear pretty clothes and be lively, when she was Minnie Foster, one of the town girls singing in the choir. But that—oh, that was thirty years ago. This all you was to take in?

MRS. PETERS: She said she wanted an apron. Funny thing to want, for there isn't much to get you dirty in jail, goodness knows. But I suppose just to make her feel more natural. She said they was in the top drawer in this cupboard. Yes, here. And then her little shawl that always hung behind the door. *(Opens stair door and looks.)* Yes, here it is.

Quickly shuts door leading upstairs.

MRS. HALE: *(abruptly moving toward her)* Mrs. Peters?
MRS. PETERS: Yes, Mrs. Hale?
60 **MRS. HALE:** Do you think she did it?
MRS. PETERS: *(in a frightened voice)* Oh, I don't know.
MRS. HALE: Well, I don't think she did. Asking for an apron and her little shawl. Worrying about her fruit.
MRS. PETERS: *(starts to speak, glances up, where footsteps are heard in the room above. In a low voice.)* Mr. Peters says it looks bad for her. Mr. Henderson is awful sarcastic in a speech and he'll make fun of her sayin' she didn't wake up.
MRS. HALE: Well, I guess John Wright didn't wake when they was slipping that rope under his neck.
65 **MRS. PETERS:** No, it's strange. It must have been done awful crafty and still. They say it was such a—funny way to kill a man, rigging it all up like that.
MRS. HALE: That's just what Mr. Hale said. There was a gun in the house. He says that's what he can't understand.
MRS. PETERS: Mr. Henderson said coming out that what was needed for the case was a motive; something to show anger, or—sudden feeling.
MRS. HALE: *(who is standing by the table)* Well, I don't see any signs of anger around here. *(She puts her hand on the dish towel which lies on the table, stands looking down at table, one half of which is clean, the other half messy.)* It's wiped to here. *(Makes a move as if to finish work, then turns and looks at loaf of bread outside the breadbox. Drops towel. In that voice of coming back to familiar things.)* Wonder how they are finding things upstairs. I hope she had it a little more red-up[1] up there.

---

[1] (slang) spruced up.

You know, it seems kind of *sneaking.* Locking her up in town and then coming out here and trying to get her own house to turn against her!

MRS. PETERS: But Mrs. Hale, the law is the law.

70 **MRS. HALE:** I s'pose 'tis. (*Unbuttoning her coat.*) Better loosen up your things, Mrs. Peters. You won't feel them when you go out.

Mrs. Peters takes off her fur tippet, goes to hang it on hook at back of room, stands looking at the under part of the small corner table.

MRS. PETERS: She was piecing a quilt.

She brings the large sewing basket and they look at the bright pieces.

MRS. HALE: It's log cabin pattern. Pretty, isn't it? I wonder if she was goin' to quilt it or just knot it?

Footsteps have been heard coming down the stairs. The Sheriff enters followed by Hale and the County Attorney.

SHERIFF: They wonder if she was going to quilt it or just knot it!

The men laugh; the women look abashed.

COUNTY ATTORNEY: (*rubbing his hands over the stove*) Frank's fire didn't do much up there, did it? Well, let's go out to the barn and get that cleared up.

The men go outside.

75 **MRS. HALE:** (*resentfully*) I don't know as there's anything so strange, our takin' up our time with little things while we're waiting for them to get the evidence. (*She sits down at the big table smoothing out a block with decision.*) I don't see as it's anything to laugh about.

MRS. PETERS: (*apologetically*) Of course they've got awful important things on their minds.

Pulls up a chair and joins Mrs. Hale at the table.

MRS. HALE: (*examining another block*) Mrs. Peters, look at this one. Here, this is the one she was working on, and look at the sewing! All the rest of it has been so nice and even. And look at this! It's all over the place! Why, it looks as if she didn't know what she was about!

After she has said this they look at each other, then start to glance back at the door. After an instant Mrs. Hale has pulled at a knot and ripped the sewing.

MRS. PETERS: Oh, what are you doing, Mrs. Hale?

MRS. HALE: (*mildly*) Just pulling out a stitch or two that's not sewed very good. (*Threading a needle.*) Bad sewing always made me fidgety.

80 **MRS. PETERS:** (*nervously*) I don't think we ought to touch things.

MRS. HALE: I'll just finish up this end. *(Suddenly stopping and leaning forward.)* Mrs. Peters?

MRS. PETERS: Yes, Mrs. Hale?

MRS. HALE: What do you suppose she was so nervous about?

MRS. PETERS: Oh—I don't know. I don't know as she was nervous. I sometimes sew awful queer when I'm just tired. *(Mrs. Hale starts to say something, looks at Mrs. Peters, then goes on sewing.)* Well, I must get these things wrapped up. They may be through sooner than we think. *(Putting apron and other things together.)* I wonder where I can find a piece of paper, and string.

85 **MRS. HALE:**   In that cupboard, maybe.

MRS. PETERS: *(looking in cupboard)* Why, here's a birdcage. *(Holds it up.)* Did she have a bird, Mrs. Hale?

MRS. HALE: Why, I don't know whether she did or not—I've not been here for so long. There was a man around last year selling canaries cheap, but I don't know as she took one; maybe she did. She used to sing real pretty herself.

MRS. PETERS: *(glancing around)* Seems funny to think of a bird here. But she must have had one, or why would she have a cage? I wonder what happened to it.

MRS. HALE: I s'pose maybe the cat got it.

90 **MRS. PETERS:**   No, she didn't have a cat. She's got that feeling some people have about cats—being afraid of them. My cat got in her room and she was real upset and asked me to take it out.

MRS. HALE: My sister Bessie was like that. Queer, ain't it?

MRS. PETERS: *(examining the cage)* Why, look at this door. It's broke. One hinge is pulled apart.

MRS. HALE: *(looking too)* Looks as if someone must have been rough with it.

MRS. PETERS: Why, yes.

She brings the cage forward and puts it on the table.

95 **MRS. HALE:**   I wish if they're going to find any evidence they'd be about it. I don't like this place.

MRS. PETERS: But I'm awful glad you came with me, Mrs. Hale. It would be lonesome for me sitting here alone.

MRS. HALE: It would, wouldn't it? *(Dropping her sewing.)* But I tell you what I do wish, Mrs. Peters. I wish I had come over sometimes when *she* was here. I—*(Looking around the room)*—wish I had.

MRS. PETERS: But of course you were awful busy, Mrs. Hale—your house and your children.

MRS. HALE: I could've come. I stayed away because it weren't cheerful—and that's why I ought to have come. I—I've never liked this place. Maybe because it's down in a hollow and you don't see the road. I dunno what it is but it's a lonesome place and always was. I wish I had come over to see Minnie Foster sometimes. I can see now—

Shakes her head.

100 **MRS. PETERS:** Well, you mustn't reproach yourself, Mrs. Hale. Somehow we just don't see how it is with other folks until—something comes up.

MRS. HALE: Not having children makes less work—but it makes a quiet house, and Wright out to work all day, and no company when he did come in. Did you know John Wright, Mrs. Peters?

MRS. PETERS: Not to know him; I've seen him in town. They say he was a good man.

MRS. HALE: Yes—good; he didn't drink, and kept his word as well as most, I guess, and paid his debts. But he was a hard man, Mrs. Peters. Just to pass the time of day with him—*(Shivers.)* Like a raw wind that gets to the bone. *(Pauses, her eye falling on the cage.)* I should think she would 'a wanted a bird. But what do you suppose went with it?

MRS. PETERS: I don't know, unless it got sick and died.

She reaches over and swings the broken door, swings it again. Both women watch it.

105 **MRS. HALE:** You weren't raised round here, were you? *(Mrs. Peters shakes her head.)* You didn't know—her?

MRS. PETERS: Not till they brought her yesterday.

MRS. HALE: She—come to think of it, she was kind of like a bird herself— real sweet and pretty, but kind of timid and—fluttery. How—she—did— change. *(Silence; then as if struck by a happy thought and relieved to get back to everyday things.)* Tell you what, Mrs. Peters, why don't you take the quilt in with you? It might take up her mind.

MRS. PETERS: Why, I think that's a real nice idea, Mrs. Hale. There couldn't possibly be any objection to it, could there? Now, just what would I take? I wonder if her patches are in here—and her things.

They look in the sewing basket.

MRS. HALE: Here's some red. I expect this has got sewing things in it. *(Brings out a fancy box.)* What a pretty box. Looks like something some-body would give you. Maybe her scissors are in here. *(Opens box. Sud-denly puts her hand to her nose.)* Why—*(Mrs. Peters bends nearer, then turns her face away.)* There's something wrapped up in this piece of silk.

110 **MRS. PETERS:** Why, this isn't her scissors.

MRS. HALE: *(lifting the silk)* Oh, Mrs. Peters—it's—

Mrs. Peters bends closer.

MRS. PETERS: It's the bird.

MRS. HALE: *(jumping up)* But, Mrs. Peters—look at it! Its neck! Look at its neck! It's all—other side *too.*

MRS. PETERS: Somebody—wrung—its—neck.

Their eyes meet. A look of growing comprehension, of horror. Steps are heard outside. Mrs. Hale slips box under quilt pieces, and sinks into her chair. Enter Sheriff and County Attorney. Mrs. Peters rises.

115 **COUNTY ATTORNEY:** *(as one turning from serious things to little pleasantries)* Well, ladies, have you decided whether she was going to quilt it or knot it?

MRS. PETERS: We think she was going to—knot it.

COUNTY ATTORNEY: Well, that's interesting, I'm sure. *(Seeing the birdcage.)* Has the bird flown?

MRS. HALE: *(putting more quilt pieces over the box)* We think the—cat got it.

COUNTY ATTORNEY: *(preoccupied)* Is there a cat?

Mrs. Hale glances in a quick covert way at Mrs. Peters.

120 **MRS. PETERS:** Well, not *now.* They're superstitious, you know. They leave.

COUNTY ATTORNEY: *(to Sheriff Peters, continuing an interrupted conversation)* No sign at all of anyone having come from the outside. Their own rope. Now let's go up again and go over it piece by piece. *(They start upstairs.)* It would have to have been someone who knew just the—

Mrs. Peters sits down. The two women sit there not looking at one another, but as if peering into something and at the same time holding back. When they talk now it is in the manner of feeling their way over strange ground, as if afraid of what they are saying, but as if they can not help saying it.

MRS. HALE: She liked the bird. She was going to bury it in that pretty box.

MRS. PETERS: *(in a whisper)* When I was a girl—my kitten—there was a boy took a hatchet, and before my eyes—and before I could get there—*(Covers her face an instant)* If they hadn't held me back I would have—*(Catches herself, looks upstairs where steps are heard, falters weakly)*—hurt him.

MRS. HALE: *(with a slow look around her)* I wonder how it would seem never to have had any children around. *(Pause.)* No, Wright wouldn't like the bird—a thing that sang. She used to sing. He killed that, too.

125 **MRS. PETERS:** *(moving uneasily)* We don't know who killed the bird.

MRS. HALE: I knew John Wright.

MRS. PETERS: It was an awful thing was done in this house that night, Mrs. Hale. Killing a man while he slept, slipping a rope around his neck that choked the life out of him.

MRS. HALE: His neck. Choked the life out of him.

Her hand goes out and rests on the birdcage.

MRS. PETERS: *(with rising voice)* We don't know who killed him. We don't know.

130 **MRS. HALE:** *(her own feeling not interrupted)* If there'd been years and years of nothing, then a bird to sing to you, it would be awful—still, after the bird was still.

MRS. PETERS: *(something within her speaking)* I know what stillness is. When we homesteaded in Dakota, and my first baby died—after he was two years old, and me with no other then—

MRS. HALE: *(moving)* How soon do you suppose they'll be through, looking for the evidence?

MRS. PETERS: I know what stillness is. *(Pulling herself back.)* The law has got to punish crime, Mrs. Hale.

MRS. HALE: *(not as if answering that)* I wish you'd seen Minnie Foster when she wore a white dress with blue ribbons and stood up there in the choir and sang. *(A look around the room.)* Oh, I *wish* I'd come over here once in a while! That was a crime! That was a crime! Who's going to punish that?

135 **MRS. PETERS:** *(looking upstairs)* We mustn't—take on.

MRS. HALE: I might have known she needed help! I know how things can be—for women. I tell you, it's queer, Mrs. Peters. We live close together and we live far apart. We all go through the same things—it's all just a different kind of the same thing. *(Brushes her eyes; noticing the bottle of fruit, reaches out for it.)* If I was you I wouldn't tell her her fruit was gone. Tell her it *ain't.* Tell her it's all right. Take this in to prove it to her. She—she may never know whether it was broke or not.

MRS. PETERS: *(takes the bottle, looks about for something to wrap it in; takes petticoat from the clothes brought from the other room, very nervously begins winding this around the bottle. In a false voice)* My, it's a good thing the men couldn't hear us. Wouldn't they just laugh! Getting all stirred up over a little thing like a—dead canary. As if that could have anything to do with—with—wouldn't they *laugh!*

The men are heard coming downstairs.

MRS. HALE: *(under her breath)* Maybe they would—maybe they wouldn't.

COUNTY ATTORNEY: No, Peters, it's all perfectly clear except a reason for doing it. But you know juries when it comes to women. If there was some definite thing. Something to show—something to make a story about—a thing that would connect up with this strange way of doing it—

The women's eyes meet for an instant. Enter Hale from outer door.

140 **HALE:** Well, I've got the team around. Pretty cold out there.

COUNTY ATTORNEY: I'm going to stay here a while by myself. *(To the Sheriff.)* You can send Frank out for me, can't you? I want to go over everything. I'm not satisfied that we can't do better.

SHERIFF: Do you want to see what Mrs. Peters is going to take in?

The County Attorney goes to the table, picks up the apron, laughs.

COUNTY ATTORNEY: Oh, I guess they're not very dangerous things the ladies have picked out. *(Moves a few things about, disturbing the quilt pieces which cover the box. Steps back.)* No, Mrs. Peters doesn't need supervising. For that matter, a sheriff's wife is married to the law. Ever think of it that way, Mrs. Peters?

MRS. PETERS: Not—just that way.

145 **SHERIFF:** *(chuckling)* Married to the law. *(Moves toward the other room.)* I just want you to come in here a minute, George. We ought to take a look at these windows.

COUNTY ATTORNEY: *(scoffingly)* Oh, windows!

SHERIFF: We'll be right out, Mr. Hale.

Hale goes outside. The Sheriff follows the County Attorney into the other room. Then Mrs. Hale rises, hands tight together, looking intensely at Mrs. Peters, whose eyes make a slow turn, finally meeting Mrs. Hale's. A moment Mrs. Hale holds her, then her own eyes point the way to where the box is concealed. Suddenly Mrs. Peters throws back quilt pieces and tries to put the box in the bag she is wearing. It is too big. She opens box, starts to take bird out, cannot touch it, goes to pieces, stands there helpless. Sound of a knob turning in the other room. Mrs. Hale snatches the box and puts it in the pocket of her big coat. Enter County Attorney and Sheriff.

COUNTY ATTORNEY: *(facetiously)* Well, Henry, at least we found out that she was not going to quilt it. She was going to—what is it you call it, ladies?

MRS. HALE: *(her hand against her pocket)* We call it—knot it, Mr. Henderson.

CURTAIN

Questions That Suggest How to See and Hear a Printed Play in the Theater of Your Mind

Susan Glaspell's one-act play "Trifles" appears first in this anthology to provide you with good examples for each of the following questions.

1. Have you imagined *a theater in your head*—auditorium (place to listen) and a stage (place to see) filled with an audience—with yourself as director? [Arch or arena stage]

2. Do you have in mind the *playwright's other plays* and *the times* in which this play was first produced?

3. Have you imagined the literal and implied significance of the *title?*

4. Have you noted the ages and relationships of the *characters?*

5. What is the time and place *setting* of the play?

6. What are the most important features of the playwright's description of the *set?*

7. Have you imagined the *design of the set?*

8. Have you become confused because you did not read the playwright's *stage directions* carefully?

9. Do you see clearly where the *entrances* onto the set are located?

10. Do you imagine the effects upon the audience of the *entrances* and *exits* of the characters?

11. As director of the theater in your head, have you *cast the play* with actors and actresses you have seen on stage or screen?

12. As director, have you imagined the *costumes* and their significance?

13. What given *situation* is revealed early in the play?

14. How does that *situation change* as the play progresses?

15. Why do the *characters do and say* what they do and say?

16. With what *attributes or characteristics* does the playwright endow each character?

17. Who is the *protagonist* and what are his or her motivations and problem?

18. Have you traced a *series of causes and effects* throughout the play?

19. In what *conflict* is the protagonist caught up?

20. What *revelations* does the protagonist experience?

21. How does the *protagonist change* as the action progresses?

22. What is the *plot* of the play and how is it structured?

23. At what point was your *interest* most aroused?

24. Where in the *structure* of the play does the first major *turning point occur?*

25. What *action* are you watching?

26. What are the causes of *tension and suspense?*

27. What are the stages of the development of the *dialog* you are listening to?

28. What is the function of *exposition* in dialog of previous action?

29. What *types of characters* are being presented?

30. What *types of functions* do the characters have in the play?

31. How do the *minor characters* parallel or enhance facets of the major characters?

32. What *comparisons and contrasts* do you see and hear about the characters?

33. Which *actions* most effectively *reveal character?*

34. Which *speeches* most effectively *reveal character?*

35. What is the function of *props* (objects used by the characters), from moment to moment, in the play?

36. What is the function of *on-stage* or *offstage sound effects?*

37. What is the function of *characters who never appear* but about whom the other characters speak?

38. How does an action on stage relate dramatically to an *action offstage?*

39. What makes the *openings of scenes and acts* effective?

40. Have you imagined the effect upon the audience of the way the scenes or the *acts climax?*

41. In what sense does a *new scene* begin every time any character enters or exits?

42. Does the playwright employ the device of *foreshadowing?*

43. What effects does the playwright achieve by employing the device of *repetition?*

44. Does the playwright create a pattern of *motifs or symbols* throughout the play?

45. Does the playwright create *irony* (verbal or dramatic)?

46. What effect does the *external context* (created by events occurring before or referred to during the action of the play) have upon the various elements in the play?

47. How does the *internal context* (created cumulatively as the play develops) enable the playwright to create implications that the audience catches even though the characters may not?

48. How does the *immediate context* (at any given moment) enable the playwright to create implications that the audience catches even though the characters may not?

49. What *type of play* is the one you are reading?

50. In what ways does one *play differ* from another?

51. Have you noted any *changes in the set* from scene to scene or act to act?

52. Have you noticed any special *lighting directions* and imagined their effects?

53. What overall *theatrical image* are you looking at?

54. What are the stages in the *development of* that *theatrical image?*

55. What *overall conception* holds this play together as an experience in theater?

56. What is the play about (what is the *theme*)?

57. What *meaning* may be derived from what the play is about?

58. Does the playwright deliberately create *ambiguities* in the play?

59. Now that you have watched and listened to the play in your head, why do you want to see and hear it in a real theater?

Your responses to these questions may prove, on first reading, difficult or bewildering. On second reading, at least on reviewing your highlighting and notes, answers may come quite readily and surprisingly clearly.

Sophocles, c. 496–406 B.C.

Oedipus the King* (c. 430 B.C.)

translated by Thomas Gould

CHARACTERS

Oedipus,[1] *The King of Thebes*
Priest of Zeus, *Leader of the Suppliants*
Creon, *Oedipus's Brother-in-law*
Chorus, *a Group of Theban Elders*
Choragos, *Spokesman of the Chorus*
Tiresias, *a blind Seer or Prophet*
Jocasta, *The Queen of Thebes*
Messenger, *from Corinth, once a Shepherd*
Herdsman, *once a Servant of Laius*
Second Messenger, *a Servant of Oedipus*

MUTES

Suppliants, *Thebans seeking Oedipus's help*
Attendants, *for the Royal Family*
Servants, *to lead Tiresias and Oedipus*
Antigone, *Daughter of Oedipus and Jocasta*
Ismene, *Daughter of Oedipus and Jocasta*

The action takes place during the day in front of the royal palace in Thebes. There are two altars (left and right) on the proscenium and several steps leading down to the orchestra. As the play opens, Thebans of various ages who have come to beg Oedipus for help are sitting on these steps and in part of the orchestra. These suppliants are holding branches of laurel or olive which have strips of wool[2] wrapped around them. Oedipus enters from the palace (the central door of the skene).

---

*Note that individual lines are numbered in the following play. When a line is shared by two or more characters, it is counted as one line.   [1]*Oedipus:* The name means "swollen foot." It refers to the mutilation of Oedipus's feet done by his father, Laius, before the infant was sent to Mount Cithaeron to be put to death by exposure.   [2]*wool:* Branches wrapped with wool are traditional symbols of prayer or supplication.

Prologue

OEDIPUS: My children, ancient Cadmus'[3] newest care,
    why have you hurried to those seats, your boughs
    wound with the emblems of the suppliant?
    The city is weighed down with fragrant smoke,
5   with hymns to the Healer[4] and the cries of mourners.
    I thought it wrong, my sons, to hear your words
    through emissaries, and have come out myself,
    I, Oedipus, a name that all men know.

(Oedipus addresses the Priest.)

    Old man—for it is fitting that you speak
10   for all—what is your mood as you entreat me,
    fear or trust? You may be confident
    that I'll do anything. How hard of heart
    if an appeal like this did not rouse my pity!
PRIEST: You, Oedipus, who hold the power here,
15   you see our several ages, we who sit
    before your altars—some not strong enough
    to take long flight, some heavy in old age,
    the priests, as I of Zeus,[5] and from our youths
    a chosen band. The rest sit with their windings
20   in the markets, at the twin shrines of Pallas,[6]
    and the prophetic embers of Ismēnos.[7]
    Our city, as you see yourself, is tossed
    too much, and can no longer lift its head
    above the troughs of billows red with death.
25   It dies in the fruitful flowers of the soil,
    it dies in its pastured herds, and in its women's
    barren pangs. And the fire-bearing god[8]
    has swooped upon the city, hateful plague,
    and he has left the house of Cadmus empty.
30   Black Hades[9] is made rich with moans and weeping.
    Not judging you an equal of the gods,
    do I and the children sit here at your hearth,
    but as the first of men, in troubled times
    and in encounters with divinities.

---

[3]*Cadmus:* Oedipus's great-great grandfather (although he does not know this) and the founder of Thebes.   [4]*Healer:* Apollo, god of prophecy, light, healing, justice, purification, and destruction.   [5]*Zeus:* father and king of the gods.   [6]*Pallas:* Athena, goddess of wisdom, arts, crafts, and war.   [7]*Ismēnos:* a reference to the temple of Apollo near the river Ismēnos in Thebes. Prophecies were made here by "reading" the ashes of the altar fires. [8]*fire-bearing god:* contagious fever viewed as a god.   [9]*Black Hades:* refers to both the underworld where the spirits of the dead go and the god of the underworld.

35 You came to Cadmus' city and unbound
the tax we had to pay to the harsh singer,[10]
did it without a helpful word from us,
with no instruction; with a god's assistance
you raised up our life, so we believe.
40 Again now Oedipus, our greatest power,
we plead with you, as suppliants, all of us,
to find us strength, whether from a god's response,
or learned in some way from another man.
I know that the experienced among men
45 give counsels that will prosper best of all.
Noblest of men, lift up our land again!
Think also of yourself; since now the land
calls you its Savior for your zeal of old,
oh let us never look back at your rule
50 as men helped up only to fall again!
Do not stumble! Put our land on firm feet!
The bird of omen was auspicious then,
when you brought that luck; be that same man again!
The power is yours; if you will rule our country,
55 rule over men, not in an empty land.
A towered city or a ship is nothing
if desolate and no man lives within.
OEDIPUS: Pitiable children, oh I know, I know
the yearnings that have brought you. Yes, I know
60 that you are sick. And yet, though you are sick,
there is not one of you so sick as I.
For your affliction comes to each alone,
for him and no one else, but my soul mourns
for me and for you, too, and for the city.
65 You do not waken me as from a sleep,
for I have wept, bitterly and long,
tried many paths in the wanderings of thought,
and the single cure I found by careful search
I've acted on: I sent Menoeceus' son,

---

[10]*harsh singer:* the Sphinx, a monster with a woman's head, a lion's body, and wings. The "tax" that Oedipus freed Thebes from was the destruction of all the young men who failed to solve the Sphinx's riddle and were subsequently devoured. The Sphinx always asked the same riddle: "What goes on four legs in the morning, two legs at noon, and three legs in the evening, and yet is weakest when supported by the largest number of feet?" Oedipus discovered the correct answer—man, who crawls in infancy, walks in his prime, and uses a stick in old age—and thus ended the Sphinx's reign of terror. The Sphinx destroyed herself when Oedipus answered the riddle. Oedipus's reward for freeing Thebes of the Sphinx was the throne and the hand of the recently widowed Jocasta.

70   Creon, brother of my wife, to the Pythian
      halls of Phoebus,[11] so that I might learn
      what I must do or say to save this city.
      Already, when I think what day this is,
      I wonder anxiously what he is doing.
75   Too long, more than is right, he's been away.
      But when he comes, then I shall be a traitor
      if I do not do all that the god reveals.
   PRIEST: Welcome words! But look, those men have signaled
      that it is Creon who is now approaching!
80 OEDIPUS: Lord Apollo! May he bring Savior Luck,
      a Luck as brilliant as his eyes are now!
   PRIEST: His news is happy, it appears. He comes,
      forehead crowned with thickly berried laurel.[12]
   OEDIPUS: We'll know, for he is near enough to hear us.

(Enter Creon along one of the parados.)

85   Lord, brother in marriage, son of Menoeceus!
      What is the god's pronouncement that you bring?
   CREON: It's good. For even troubles, if they chance
      to turn out well, I always count as lucky.
   OEDIPUS: But what was the response? You seem to say
90   I'm not to fear—but not to take heart either.
   CREON: If you will hear me with these men present,
      I'm ready to report—or go inside.

(Creon moves up the steps toward the palace.)

   OEDIPUS: Speak out to all! The grief that burdens me
      concerns these men more than it does my life.
95 CREON: Then I shall tell you what I heard from the god.
      The task Lord Phoebus sets for us is clear:
      drive out pollution sheltered in our land,
      and do not shelter what is incurable.
   OEDIPUS: What is our trouble? How shall we cleanse ourselves?
100 CREON: We must banish or murder to free ourselves
      from a murder that blows storms through the city.
   OEDIPUS: What man's bad luck does he accuse in this?
   CREON: My Lord, a king named Laius ruled our land
      before you came to steer the city straight.
105 OEDIPUS: I know. So I was told—I never saw him.

---

[11]*Pythian . . . Phoebus:* the temple of Phoebus Apollo's oracle or prophet at Delphi.
[12]*laurel:* Creon is wearing a garland of laurel leaves, sacred to Apollo.

CREON: Since he was murdered, you must raise your hand
    against the men who killed him with their hands.
OEDIPUS: Where are they now? And how can we ever find
    the track of ancient guilt now hard to read?
110 CREON: In our own land, he said. What we pursue,
    that can be caught; but not what we neglect.
OEDIPUS: Was Laius home, or in the countryside—
    or was he murdered in some foreign land?
CREON: He left to see a sacred rite, he said;
115   He left, but never came home from his journey.
OEDIPUS: Did none of his party see it and report—
    someone we might profitably question?
CREON: They were all killed but one, who fled in fear,
    and he could tell us only one clear fact.
120 OEDIPUS: What fact? One thing could lead us on to more
    if we could get a small start on our hope.
CREON: He said that bandits chanced on them and killed him—
    with the force of many hands, not one alone.
OEDIPUS: How could a bandit dare so great an act—
125   unless this was a plot paid off from here!
CREON: We thought of that, but when Laius was killed,
    we had no one to help us in our troubles.
OEDIPUS: It was your very kingship that was killed!
    What kind of trouble blocked you from a search?
130 CREON: The subtle-singing Sphinx asked us to turn
    from the obscure to what lay at our feet.
OEDIPUS: Then I shall begin again and make it plain.
    It was quite worthy of Phoebus, and worthy of you,
    to turn our thoughts back to the murdered man,
135   and right that you should see me join the battle
    for justice to our land and to the god.
    Not on behalf of any distant kinships,
    it's for myself I will dispel this stain.
    Whoever murdered him may also wish
140   to punish me—and with the selfsame hand.
    In helping him I also serve myself.
    Now quickly, children: up from the altar steps,
    and raise the branches of the suppliant!
    Let someone go and summon Cadmus' people:
145   say I'll do anything.

(Exit an Attendant along one of the parados.)

                Our luck will prosper
  if the god is with us, or we have already fallen.

PRIEST: Rise, my children; that for which we came,
      he has himself proclaimed he will accomplish.
      May Phoebus, who announced this, also come
150   as Savior and reliever from the plague.

*(Exit Oedipus and Creon into the palace. The Priest and the Suppliants
exit left and right along the parados. After a brief pause, the Chorus [in-
cluding the Choragos] enters the orchestra from the parados.)*

Parados

STROPHE 1[13]

CHORUS: Voice from Zeus,[14] sweetly spoken, what are you
      that have arrived from golden
      Pytho[15] to our shining
      Thebes? I am on the rack, terror
155   shakes my soul.
      Delian Healer,[16] summoned by "iē!"
      I await in holy dread what obligation, something new
      or something back once more with the revolving years,
          you'll bring about for me.
160   Oh tell me, child of golden Hope,
          deathless Response!

ANTISTROPHE 1

      I appeal to you first, daughter of Zeus,
          deathless Athena,
          and to your sister who protects this land,
165   Artemis,[17] whose famous throne is the whole circle
          of the marketplace,
      and Phoebus, who shoots from afar: iō!
      Three-fold defenders against death, appear!
      If ever in the past, to stop blind ruin
170   sent against the city,
      you banished utterly the fires of suffering,
          come now again!

---

[13]*Strophe, Antistrophe:* probably refer to the direction in which the Chorus danced while
reciting specific stanzas. Strophe may have indicated dance steps to stage left, antistrophe to
stage right.   [14]*Voice from Zeus:* a reference to Apollo's prophecy. Zeus taught Apollo how
to prophesy.   [15]*Pytho:* Delphi.   [16]*Delian Healer:* Apollo.   [17]*Artemis:* goddess of vir-
ginity, childbirth, and hunting.

STROPHE 2

Ah! Ah! Unnumbered are the miseries
I bear. The plague claims all
175 our comrades. Nor has thought found yet a spear
by which a man shall be protected. What our glorious
earth gives birth to does not grow. Without a birth
from cries of labor
     do the women rise.
180 One person after another
     you may see, like flying birds,
faster than indomitable fire, sped
to the shore of the god that is the sunset.[18]

ANTISTROPHE 2

And with their deaths unnumbered dies the city.
185 Her children lie unpitied on the ground,
spreading death, unmourned.
Meanwhile young wives, and gray-haired mothers with them,
on the shores of the altars, from this side and that,
suppliants from mournful trouble,
190   cry out their grief.
A hymn to the Healer shines,
     the flute a mourner's voice.
Against which, golden goddess, daughter of Zeus,
     send lovely Strength.

STROPHE 3

195 Causing raging Ares[19]—who,
     armed now with no shield of bronze,
burns me, coming on amid loud cries—
to turn his back and run from my land,
with a fair wind behind, to the great
200   hall of Amphitritē,[20]
or to the anchorage that welcomes no one,
Thrace's troubled sea!
If night lets something get away at last,
     it comes by day.

---

[18]*god . . . sunset:* Hades, god of the underworld.   [19]*Ares:* god of war and destruction.
[20]*Amphitritē:* the Atlantic Ocean.

205 Fire-bearing god . . .
    you who dispense the might of lightning,
    Zeus! Father! Destroy him with your thunderbolt!

(Enter Oedipus from the palace.)

ANTISTROPHE 3

    Lycēan Lord![21] From your looped
      bowstring, twisted gold,
210 I wish indomitable missiles might be scattered
    and stand forward, our protectors; also fire-bearing
    radiance of Artemis, with which
      she darts across the Lycian mountains.
    I call the god whose head is bound in gold,
215 with whom this country shares its name,
    Bacchus,[22] wine-flushed, summoned by "euoi!,"
      Maenads' comrade,
    to approach ablaze
      with gleaming . . .
220 pine, opposed to that god-hated god.

Episode 1

OEDIPUS: I hear your prayer. Submit to what I say
    and to the labors that the plague demands
    and you'll get help and a relief from evils.
    I'll make the proclamation, though a stranger
225 to the report and to the deed. Alone,
    had I no key, I would soon lose the track.
    Since it was only later that I joined you,
    to all the sons of Cadmus I say this:
    whoever has clear knowledge of the man
230 who murdered Laius, son of Labdacus,
    I command him to reveal it all to me—
    nor fear if, to remove the charge, he must
    accuse himself: his fate will not be cruel—
    he will depart unstumbling into exile.
235 But if you know another, or a stranger,
    to be the one whose hand is guilty, speak:
    I shall reward you and remember you.
    But if you keep your peace because of fear,
    and shield yourself or kin from my command,

---

[21]*Lycēan Lord:* Apollo.   [22]*Bacchus:* Dionysus, god of fertility and wine.

240 hear you what I shall do in that event:
I charge all in this land where I have throne
and power, shut out that man—no matter who—
both from your shelter and all spoken words,
nor in your prayers or sacrifices make
245 him partner, nor allot him lustral[23] water.
All men shall drive him from their homes: for he
is the pollution that the god-sent Pythian
response has only now revealed to me.
In this way I ally myself in war
250 with the divinity and the deceased.[24]
And this curse, too, against the one who did it,
whether alone in secrecy, or with others:
may he wear out his life unblest and evil!
I pray this, too: if he is at my hearth
255 and in my home, and I have knowledge of him,
may the curse pronounced on others come to me.
All this I lay to you to execute,
for my sake, for the god's, and for this land
nor ruined, barren, abandoned by the gods.
260 Even if no god had driven you to it,
you ought not to have left this stain uncleansed,
the murdered man a nobleman, a king!
You should have looked! But now, since, as it happens,
It's I who have the power that he had once,
265 and have his bed, and a wife who shares our seed,
and common bond had we had common children
(had not his hope of offspring had bad luck—
but as it happened, luck lunged at his head);
because of this, as if for my own father,
270 I'll fight for him, I'll leave no means untried,
to catch the one who did it with his hand,
for the son of Labdacus, of Polydōrus,
of Cadmus before him, and of Agēnor.[25]
This prayer against all those who disobey:
275 the gods send out no harvest from their soil,
nor children from their wives. Oh, let them die
victims of this plague, or of something worse.
Yet for the rest of us, people of Cadmus,
we the obedient, may Justice, our ally,
280 and all the gods, be always on our side!

[23]*lustral:* purifying.   [24]*the deceased:* Laius.   [25]*Son . . . Agēnor:* refers to Laius by citing his genealogy.

CHORAGOS: I speak because I feel the grip of your curse:
the killer is not I. Nor can I point
to him. The one who set us to this search,
Phoebus, should also name the guilty man.

285 **OEDIPUS:** Quite right, but to compel unwilling gods—
no man has ever had that kind of power.

CHORAGOS: May I suggest to you a second way?

OEDIPUS: A second or a third—pass over nothing!

CHORAGOS: I know of no one who sees more of what

290 Lord Phoebus sees than Lord Tiresias.
My Lord, one might learn brilliantly from him.

OEDIPUS: Nor is this something I have been slow to do.
At Creon's word I sent an escort—twice now!
I am astonished that he has not come.

295 **CHORAGOS:** The old account is useless. It told us nothing.

OEDIPUS: But tell it to me. I'll scrutinize all stories.

CHORAGOS: He is said to have been killed by travelers.

OEDIPUS: I have heard, but the one who did it no one sees.

CHORAGOS: If there is any fear in him at all,

300 he won't stay here once he has heard that curse.

OEDIPUS: He won't fear words: he had no fear when he did it.

*(Enter Tiresias from the right, led by a Servant and two of Oedipus's
Attendants.)*

CHORAGOS: Look there! There is the man who will convict him!
It's the god's prophet they are leading here,
one gifted with the truth as no one else.

305 **OEDIPUS:** Tiresias, master of all omens—
public and secret, in the sky and on the earth—
your mind, if not your eyes, sees how the city
lives with a plague, against which Thebes can find
no Saviour or protector, Lord, but you.

310 For Phoebus, as the attendants surely told you,
returned this answer to us: liberation
from the disease would never come unless
we learned without a doubt who murdered Laius—
put them to death, or sent them into exile.

315 Do not begrudge us what you may learn from birds
or any other prophet's path you know!
Care for yourself, the city, care for me,
care for the whole pollution of the dead!
We're in your hands. To do all that he can

320 to help another is man's noblest labor.

TIRESIAS: How terrible to understand and get
no profit from the knowledge! I knew this,
but I forgot, or I had never come.

OEDIPUS: What's this? You've come with very little zeal.
325 **TIRESIAS:** Let me go home! If you will listen to me,
You will endure your troubles better—and I mine.
OEDIPUS: A strange request, not very kind to the land
that cared for you—to hold back this oracle!
TIRESIAS: I see your understanding comes to you
330 inopportunely. So that won't happen to me . . .
OEDIPUS: Oh, by the gods, if you understand about this,
don't turn away! We're on our knees to you.
TIRESIAS: None of you understands! I'll never bring
my grief to light—I will not speak of yours.
335 **OEDIPUS:** You know and won't declare it! Is your purpose
to betray us and to destroy this land!
TIRESIAS: I will grieve neither of us. Stop this futile
cross-examination. I'll tell you nothing!
OEDIPUS: Nothing? You vile traitor! You could provoke
340 a stone to anger! You still refuse to tell?
Can nothing soften you, nothing convince you?
TIRESIAS: You blamed anger in me—you haven't seen.
The kind that lives with you, so you blame me.
OEDIPUS: Who wouldn't fill with anger, listening
345 to words like yours which now disgrace this city?
TIRESIAS: It will come, even if my silence hides it.
OEDIPUS: If it will come, then why won't you declare it?
TIRESIAS: I'd rather say no more. Now if you wish,
respond to that with all your fiercest anger!
350 **OEDIPUS:** Now I am angry enough to come right out
with this conjecture: you, I think, helped plot
the deed; you did it—even if your hand,
cannot have struck the blow. If you could see,
I should have said the deed was yours alone.
355 **TIRESIAS:** Is that right! Then I charge you to abide
by the decree you have announced: from this day
say no word to either these or me,
for you are the vile polluter of this land!
OEDIPUS: Aren't you appalled to let a charge like that
360 come bounding forth? How will you get away?
TIRESIAS: You cannot catch me. I have the strength of truth.
OEDIPUS: Who taught you this? Not your prophetic craft!
TIRESIAS: You did. You made me say it. I didn't want to.
OEDIPUS: Say what? Repeat it so I'll understand.
365 **TIRESIAS:** I made no sense? Or are you trying me?
OEDIPUS: No sense I understood. Say it again!
TIRESIAS: I say you are the murderer you seek.
OEDIPUS: Again that horror! You'll wish you hadn't said that.
TIRESIAS: Shall I say more, and raise your anger higher?

370 **OEDIPUS:**   Anything you like! Your words are powerless.
  TIRESIAS: You live, unknowing, with those nearest to you
    in the greatest shame. You do not see the evil.
  OEDIPUS: You won't go on like that and never pay!
  TIRESIAS: I can if there is any strength in truth.
375 **OEDIPUS:**   In truth, but not in you! You have no strength,
    blind in your ears, your reason, and your eyes.
  TIRESIAS: Unhappy man! Those jeers you hurl at me
    before long all these men will hurl at you.
  OEDIPUS: You are the child of endless night; it's not
380   for me or anyone who sees to hurt you.
  TIRESIAS: It's not my fate to be struck down by you.
    Apollo is enough. That's his concern.
  OEDIPUS: Are these inventions Creon's or your own?
  TIRESIAS: No, your affliction is yourself, not Creon.
385 **OEDIPUS:**   Oh success!—in wealth, kingship, artistry,
    in any life that wins much admiration—
    the envious ill will stored up for you!
    to get at my command, a gift I did not
    seek, which the city put into my hands,
390   my loyal Creon, colleague from the start,
    longs to sneak up in secret and dethrone me.
    So he's suborned this fortuneteller—schemer!
    deceitful beggar-priest!—who has good eyes
    for gains alone, though in his craft he's blind.
395   Where were your prophet's powers ever proved?
    Why, when the dog who chanted verse[26] was here,
    did you not speak and liberate this city?
    Her riddle wasn't for a man chancing by
    to interpret; prophetic art was needed,
400   but you had none, it seems—learned from birds
    or from a god. I came along, yes I,
    Oedipus the ignorant, and stopped her—
    by using thought, not augury from birds.
    And it is I whom you now wish to banish,
405   so you'll be close to the Creontian throne.
    You—and the plot's concocter—will drive out
    pollution to your grief: you look quite old
    or you would be the victim of that plot!
  CHORAGOS: It seems to us that this man's words were said
410   in anger, Oedipus, and yours as well.
    Insight, not angry words, is what we need,
    the best solution to the god's response.

[26]*dog . . . verse:* the Sphinx.

TIRESIAS: You are the king, and yet I am your equal
in my right to speak. In that I too am Lord.
415   for I belong to Loxias,[27] not you.
I am not Creon's man. He's nothing to me.
Hear this, since you have thrown my blindness at me:
Your eyes can't see the evil to which you've come,
nor where you live, nor who is in your house.
420   Do you know your parents? Not knowing, you are
their enemy, in the underworld and here.
A mother's and a father's double-lashing
terrible-footed curse will soon drive you out.
Now you can see, then you will stare into darkness.
425   What place will not be harbor to your cry,
or what Cithaeron[28] not reverberate
when you have heard the bride-song in your palace
to which you sailed? Fair wind to evil harbor!
Nor do you see how many other woes
430   will level you to yourself and to your children.
So, at my message, and at Creon, too,
splatter muck! There will never be a man
ground into wretchedness as you will be.
OEDIPUS: Am I to listen to such things from him!
435   May you be damned! Get out of here at once!
Go! Leave my palace! Turn around and go!

(Tiresias begins to move away from Oedipus.)

TIRESIAS: I wouldn't have come had you not sent for me.
OEDIPUS: I did not know you'd talk stupidity,
or I wouldn't have rushed to bring you to my house.
440   TIRESIAS: Stupid I seem to you, yet to your parents
who gave you natural birth I seemed quite shrewd.
OEDIPUS: Who? Wait! Who is the one who gave me birth?
TIRESIAS: This day will give you birth,[29] and ruin too.
OEDIPUS: What murky, riddling things you always say!
445   TIRESIAS: Don't you surpass us all at finding out?
OEDIPUS: You sneer at what you'll find has brought me greatness.
TIRESIAS: And that's the very luck that ruined you.
OEDIPUS: I wouldn't care, just so I saved the city.
TIRESIAS: In that case I shall go. Boy, lead the way!
450   OEDIPUS: Yes, let him lead you off. Here, underfoot,
you irk me. Gone, you'll cause no further pain.

---

[27]*Loxias:* Apollo.   [28]*Cithaeron:* reference to the mountain on which Oedipus was to be
exposed as an infant.   [29]*give you birth:* that is, identify your parents.

TIRESIAS: I'll go when I have said what I was sent for.
Your face won't scare me. You can't ruin me.
I say to you, the man whom you have looked for
455   as you pronounced your curses, your decrees
on the bloody death of Laius—he is here!
A seeming stranger, he shall be shown to be
a Theban born, though he'll take no delight
in that solution. Blind, who once could see,
460   a beggar who was rich, through foreign lands
he'll go and point before him with a stick.
To his beloved children, he'll be shown
a father who is also brother; to the one
who bore him, son and husband; to his father,
465   his seed-fellow and killer. Go in
and think this out; and if you find I've lied,
say then I have no prophet's understanding!

(Exit Tiresias, led by a Servant. Oedipus exits into the palace with his Attendants.)

Stasimon 1

STROPHE 1

CHORUS: Who is the man of whom the inspired
rock of Delphi[30] said
470   he has committed the unspeakable
with blood-stained hands?
Time for him to ply a foot
mightier than those of the horses
of the storm in his escape;
475   upon him mounts and plunges the weaponed
son of Zeus,[31] with fire and thunderbolts,
and in his train the dreaded goddesses
of Death, who never miss.

ANTISTROPHE 1

The message has just blazed,
480   gleaming from the snows
of Mount Parnassus: we must track
everywhere the unseen man.

---

[30]*rock of Delphi:* Apollo's oracle at Delphi.   [31]*son of Zeus:* Apollo.

He wanders, hidden by wild
forests, up through caves
485   and rocks, like a bull,
anxious, with an anxious foot, forlorn.
He puts away from him the mantic[32] words come from earth's
navel,[33] at its center, yet these live
forever and still hover round him.

STROPHE 2

490   Terribly he troubles me,
       the skilled interpreter of birds![34]
I can't assent, nor speak against him.
       Both paths are closed to me.
I hover on the wings of doubt,
495   not seeing what is here nor what's to come.
What quarrel started in the house of Labdacus[35]
or in the house of Polybus,[36]
       either ever in the past
       or now, I never
500 heard, so that . . . with this fact for my touchstone
I could attack the public
       fame of Oedipus, by the side of the Labdaceans
an ally, against the dark assassination.

ANTISTROPHE 2

No, Zeus and Apollo
505   understand and know things
mortal; but that another man
       can do more as a prophet than I can—
for that there is no certain test,
       though, skill to skill,
510 one man might overtake another.
No, never, not until
       I see the charges proved,
when someone blames him shall I nod assent.
For once, as we all saw, the winged maiden[37] came
515 against him: he was seen then to be skilled,
       proved, by that touchstone, dear to the people. So,
never will my mind convict him of the evil.

---

[32]*mantic:* prophetic.   [33]*earth's navel:* Delphi.   [34]*interpreter of birds:* Tiresias. The
Chorus is troubled by his accusations.   [35]*house of Labdacus:* the line of Laius.   [36]*Polybus:* Oedipus's foster father.   [37]*winged maiden:* the Sphinx.

Episode 2

(Enter Creon from the right door of the skene and speaks to the Chorus.)

CREON: Citizens, I hear that a fearful charge
is made against me by King Oedipus!
520   I had to come. If, in this crisis,
he thinks that he has suffered injury
from anything that I have said or done,
I have no appetite for a long life—
bearing a blame like that! It's no slight blow
525   the punishment I'd take from what he said:
it's the ultimate hurt to be called traitor
by the city, by you, by my own people!
CHORAGOS: The thing that forced that accusation out
could have been anger, not the power of thought.
530 CREON: But who persuaded him that thoughts of mine
had led the prophet into telling lies?
CHORAGOS: I do not know the thought behind his words.
CREON: But did he look straight at you? Was his mind right
when he said that I was guilty of this charge?
535 CHORAGOS: I have no eyes to see what rulers do.
But here he comes himself out of the house.

(Enter Oedipus from the palace.)

OEDIPUS: What? You here? And can you really have
the face and daring to approach my house
when you're exposed as its master's murderer
540   and caught, too, as the robber of my kingship?
Did you see cowardice in me, by the gods,
or foolishness, when you began this plot?
Did you suppose that I would not detect
your stealthy moves, or that I'd not fight back?
545   It's your attempt that's folly, isn't it—
tracking without followers or connections,
kingship which is caught with wealth and numbers?
CREON: Now wait! Give me as long to answer back!
Judge me for yourself when you have heard me!
550 OEDIPUS: You're eloquent, but I'd be slow to learn
from you, now that I've seen your malice toward me.
CREON: That I deny. Hear what I have to say.
OEDIPUS: Don't you deny it! You are the traitor here!
CREON: If you consider mindless willfulness
555   a prized possession, you are not thinking sense.
OEDIPUS: If you think you can wrong a relative
and get off free, you are not thinking sense.

CREON: Perfectly just, I won't say no. And yet
　　　what is this injury you say I did you?
560 OEDIPUS: Did you persuade me, yes or no, to send
　　　someone to bring that solemn prophet here?
CREON: And I still hold to the advice I gave.
OEDIPUS: How many years ago did your King Laius . . .
CREON: Laius! Do what? Now I don't understand.
565 OEDIPUS: Vanish—victim of a murderous violence?
CREON: That is a long count back into the past.
OEDIPUS: Well, was this seer then practicing his art?
CREON: Yes, skilled and honored just as he is today.
OEDIPUS: Did he, back then, ever refer to me?
570 CREON: He did not do so in my presence ever.
OEDIPUS: You did inquire into the murder then.
CREON: We had to, surely, though we discovered nothing.
OEDIPUS: But the "skilled" one did not say this then? Why not?
CREON: I never talk when I am ignorant.
575 OEDIPUS: But you're not ignorant of your own part.
CREON: What do you mean? I'll tell you if I know.
OEDIPUS: Just this: if he had not conferred with you
　　　he'd not have told about my murdering Laius.
CREON: If he said that, you are the one who knows.
580 　　But now it's fair that you should answer me.
OEDIPUS: Ask on! You won't convict me as the killer.
CREON: Well then, answer. My sister is your wife?
OEDIPUS: Now there's a statement that I can't deny.
CREON: You two have equal power in this country?
585 OEDIPUS: She gets from me whatever she desires.
CREON: And I'm a third? The three of us are equals?
OEDIPUS: That's where you're treacherous to your kinship!
CREON: But think about this rationally, as I do.
　　　First look at this: do you think anyone
590 　prefers the anxieties of being king
　　　to untroubled sleep—if he has equal power?
　　　I'm not the kind of man who falls in love
　　　with kingship. I am content with a king's power.
　　　And so would any man who's wise and prudent.
595 　I get all things from you, with no distress;
　　　as king I would have onerous duties, too.
　　　How could the kingship bring me more delight
　　　than this untroubled power and influence?
　　　I'm not misguided yet to such a point
600 　that profitable honors aren't enough.
　　　As it is, all wish me well and all salute;
　　　those begging you for something have me summoned,

for their success depends on that alone.
Why should I lose all this to become king?
605   A prudent mind is never traitorous.
Treason's a thought I'm not enamored of;
nor could I join a man who acted so.
In proof of this, first go yourself to Pytho[38]
and ask if I brought back the true response.
610   Then, if you find I plotted with that portent
reader,[39] don't have me put to death by your vote
only—I'll vote myself for my conviction.
Don't let an unsupported thought convict me!
It's not right mindlessly to take the bad
615   for good or to suppose the good are traitors.
Rejecting a relation who is loyal
is like rejecting life, our greatest love.
In time you'll know securely without stumbling,
for time alone can prove a just man just,
620   though you can know a bad man in a day.
CHORAGOS: Well said, to one who's anxious not to fall.
Swift thinkers, Lord, are never safe from stumbling.
OEDIPUS: But when a swift and secret plotter moves
against me, I must make swift counterplot.
625   If I lie quiet and await his move,
he'll have achieved his aims and I'll have missed.
CREON: You surely cannot mean you want me exiled!
OEDIPUS: Not exiled, no. Your death is what I want!
CREON: If you would first define what envy is . . .
630 OEDIPUS: Are you still stubborn? Still disobedient?
CREON: I see you cannot think!
OEDIPUS: For me I can.
CREON: You should for me as well!
OEDIPUS: But you're a traitor!
CREON: What if you're wrong?
OEDIPUS: Authority must be maintained.
CREON: Not if the ruler's evil.
OEDIPUS: Hear that, Thebes!
635 CREON: It is my city too, not yours alone!
CHORAGOS: Please don't, my Lords! Ah, just in time, I see
Jocasta there, coming from the palace.
With her help you must settle your quarrel.

(Enter Jocasta from the palace.)

---

[38]*Pytho:* Delphi.   [39]*portent reader:* Apollo's oracle or prophet.

JOCASTA: Wretched men! What has provoked this ill-
640   advised dispute? Have you no sense of shame,
    with Thebes so sick, to stir up private troubles?
    Now go inside! And Creon, you go home!
    Don't make a general anguish out of nothing!
CREON: My sister, Oedipus your husband here
645   sees fit to do one of two hideous things:
    to have me banished from the land—or killed!
OEDIPUS: That's right: I caught him, Lady, plotting harm
    against my person—with a malignant science.
CREON: May my life fail, may I die cursed, if I
650   did any of the things you said I did!
JOCASTA: Believe his words, for the god's sake, Oedipus,
    in deference above all to his oath
    to the gods. Also for me, and for these men!

Kommos[40]

STROPHE 1

CHORUS: Consent, with will and mind,
655   my king, I beg of you!
OEDIPUS: What do you wish me to surrender?
CHORUS: Show deference to him who was not feeble in time past
    and is now great in the power of his oath!
OEDIPUS: Do you know what you're asking?
CHORUS: Yes.
OEDIPUS: Tell me then.
660 **CHORUS:**   Never to cast into dishonored guilt, with an unproved
    assumption, a kinsman who has bound himself by curse.
OEDIPUS: Now you must understand, when you ask this,
    you ask my death or banishment from the land.

STROPHE 2

CHORUS: No, by the god who is the foremost of all gods,
665   the Sun! No! Godless,
        friendless, whatever death is worst of all,
    let that be my destruction, if this
        thought ever moved me!
    But my ill-fated soul
670   this dying land

---

[40]*Kommos:* a dirge or lament sung by the Chorus and one or more of the chief characters.

wears out—the more if to these older troubles
she adds new troubles from the two of you!
OEDIPUS: Then let him go, though it must mean my death,
or else disgrace and exile from the land.

675   My pity is moved by your words, not by his—
he'll only have my hate, wherever he goes.
CREON: You're sullen as you yield; you'll be depressed
when you've passed through this anger. Natures like yours
are hardest on themselves. That's as it should be.

680 **OEDIPUS:**   Then won't you go and let me be?
CREON: I'll go.
Though you're unreasonable, they know I'm righteous.

(Exit Creon.)

ANTISTROPHE 1

CHORUS: Why are you waiting, Lady?
Conduct him back into the palace!
JOCASTA: I will, when I have heard what chanced.

685 **CHORUS:**   Conjectures—words alone, and nothing based on thought.
But even an injustice can devour a man.
JOCASTA: Did the words come from both sides?
CHORUS: Yes.
JOCASTA: What was said?
CHORUS: To me it seems enough! enough! the land already troubled,
that this should rest where it has stopped.

690 **OEDIPUS:**   See what you've come to in your honest thought,
in seeking to relax and blunt my heart?

ANTISTROPHE 2

CHORUS: I have not said this only once, my Lord.
That I had lost my sanity,
     without a path in thinking—

695   be sure this would be clear
     if I put you away
who, when my cherished land
     wandered crazed
with suffering, brought her back on course.

700   Now, too, be a lucky helmsman!
JOCASTA: Please, for the god's sake, Lord, explain to me
the reason why you have conceived this wrath?

OEDIPUS: I honor you, not them,[41] and I'll explain
    to you how Creon has conspired against me.
705 JOCASTA: All right, if that will explain how the quarrel started.
    OEDIPUS: He says I am the murderer of Laius!
    JOCASTA: Did he claim knowledge or that someone told him?
    OEDIPUS: Here's what he did: he sent that vicious seer
    so he could keep his own mouth innocent.
710 JOCASTA: Ah then, absolve yourself of what he charges!
    Listen to this and you'll agree, no mortal
    is ever given skill in prophecy.
    I'll prove this quickly with one incident.
    It was foretold to Laius—I shall not say
715 by Phoebus himself, but by his ministers—
    that when his fate arrived he would be killed
    by a son who would be born to him and me.
    And yet, so it is told, foreign robbers
    murdered him, at a place where three roads meet.
720 As for the child I bore him, not three days passed
    before he yoked the ball-joints of its feet,[42]
    then cast it, by others' hands, on a trackless mountain.
    That time Apollo did not make our child
    a patricide, or bring about what Laius
725 feared, that he be killed by his own son.
    That's how prophetic words determined things!
    Forget them. The things a god must track
    he will himself painlessly reveal.
    OEDIPUS: Just now, as I was listening to you, Lady,
730 what a profound distraction seized my mind!
    JOCASTA: What made you turn around so anxiously?
    OEDIPUS: I thought you said that Laius was attacked
    and butchered at a place where three roads meet.
    JOCASTA: That is the story, and it is told so still.
735 OEDIPUS: Where is the place where this was done to him?
    JOCASTA: The land's called Phocis, where a two-forked road
    comes in from Delphi and from Daulia.
    OEDIPUS: And how much time has passed since these events?
    JOCASTA: Just prior to your presentation here
740 as king this news was published to the city.
    OEDIPUS: Oh, Zeus, what have you willed to do to me?
    JOCASTA: Oedipus, what makes your heart so heavy?
    OEDIPUS: No, tell me first of Laius' appearance,
    what peak of youthful vigor he had reached.

[41]*them:* the Chorus.   [42]*ball-joints of its feet:* the ankles.

745 **JOCASTA:**   A tall man, showing his first growth of white.
He had a figure not unlike your own.

OEDIPUS: Alas! It seems that in my ignorance
I laid those fearful curses on myself.

JOCASTA: What is it, Lord? I flinch to see your face.

750 **OEDIPUS:**   I'm dreadfully afraid the prophet sees.
But I'll know better with one more detail.

JOCASTA: I'm frightened too. But ask: I'll answer you.

OEDIPUS: Was his retinue small, or did he travel
with a great troop, as would befit a prince?

755 **JOCASTA:**   There were just five in all, one a herald.
There was a carriage, too, bearing Laius.

OEDIPUS: Alas! Now I see it! But who was it,
Lady, who told you what you know about this?

JOCASTA: A servant who alone was saved unharmed.

760 **OEDIPUS:**   By chance, could he be now in the palace?

JOCASTA: No, he is not. When he returned and saw
you had the power of the murdered Laius,
he touched my hand and begged me formally
to send him to the fields and to the pastures,

765   so he'd be out of sight, far from the city.
I did. Although a slave, he well deserved
to win this favor, and indeed far more.

OEDIPUS: Let's have him called back in immediately.

JOCASTA: That can be done, but why do you desire it?

770 **OEDIPUS:**   I fear, Lady, I have already said
too much. That's why I wish to see him now.

JOCASTA: Then he shall come; but it is right somehow
that I, too, Lord, should know what troubles you.

OEDIPUS: I've gone so deep into the things I feared

775   I'll tell you everything. Who has a right
greater than yours, while I cross through this chance?
Polybus of Corinth was my father,
my mother was the Dorian Meropē.
I was first citizen, until this chance

780   attacked me—striking enough, to be sure,
but not worth all the gravity I gave it.
This: at a feast a man who'd drunk too much
denied, at the wine, I was my father's son.
I was depressed and all that day I barely

785   held it in. Next day I put the question
to my mother and father. They were enraged
at the man who'd let this fiction fly at me.
I was much cheered by them. And yet it kept
grinding into me. His words kept coming back.

790   Without my mother's or my father's knowledge
      I went to Pytho. But Phoebus sent me away
      dishonoring my demand. Instead, other
      wretched horrors he flashed forth in speech.
      He said that I would be my mother's lover,
795   show offspring to mankind they could not look at,
      and be his murderer whose seed I am.[43]
      When I heard this, and ever since, I gauged
      the way to Corinth by the stars alone,
      running to a place where I would never see
800   the disgrace in the oracle's words come true.
      But I soon came to the exact location
      where, as you tell of it, the king was killed.
      Lady, here is the truth. As I went on,
      when I was just approaching those three roads,
805   a herald and a man like him you spoke of
      came on, riding a carriage drawn by colts.
      Both the man out front and the old man himself[44]
      tried violently to force me off the road.
      The driver, when he tried to push me off,
810   I struck in anger. The old man saw this, watched
      me approach, then leaned out and lunged down
      with twin prongs[45] at the middle of my head!
      He got more than he gave. Abruptly—struck
      once by the staff in this my hand—he tumbled
815   out, head first, from the middle of the carriage.
      And then I killed them all. But if there is
      a kinship between Laius and this stranger,
      who is more wretched than the man you see?
      Who was there born more hated by the gods?
820   For neither citizen nor foreigner
      may take me in his home or speak to me.
      No, they must drive me off. And it is I
      who have pronounced these curses on myself!
      I stain the dead man's bed with these my hands,
825   by which he died. Is not my nature vile?
      Unclean?—if I am banished and even
      in exile I may not see my own parents,
      or set foot in my homeland, or else be yoked
      in marriage to my mother, and kill my father,
830   Polybus, who raised me and gave me birth?

---

[43]*be . . . am:* that is, murder my father.   [44]*old man himself:* Laius.   [45]*lunged . . . prongs:*
Laius strikes Oedipus with a two-pronged horse goad, or whip.

If someone judged a cruel divinity
did this to me, would he not speak the truth?
You pure and awful gods, may I not ever
see that day, may I be swept away
835   from men before I see so great and so
calamitous a stain fixed on my person!

CHORAGOS: These things seem fearful to us, Lord, and yet,
until you hear it from the witness, keep hope!

OEDIPUS: That is the single hope that's left to me,
840   to wait for him, that herdsman—until he comes.

JOCASTA: When he appears, what are you eager for?

OEDIPUS: Just this: if his account agrees with yours
then I shall have escaped this misery.

JOCASTA: But what was it that struck you in my story?

845 OEDIPUS: You said he spoke of robbers as the ones
who killed him. Now: if he continues still
to speak of many, then I could not have killed him.
One man and many men just do not jibe.
But if he says one belted man, the doubt
850   is gone. The balance tips toward me. I did it.

JOCASTA: No! He told it as I told you. Be certain.
He can't reject that and reverse himself.
The city heard these things, not I alone.
But even if he swerves from what he said,
855   he'll never show that Laius' murder, Lord,
occurred just as predicted. For Loxias
expressly said my son was doomed to kill him.
The boy—poor boy—he never had a chance
to cut him down, for he was cut down first.
860   Never again, just for some oracle
will I shoot frightened glances right and left.

OEDIPUS: That's full of sense. Nonetheless, send a man
to bring that farm hand here. Will you do it?

JOCASTA: I'll send one right away. But let's go in.
865   Would I do anything against your wishes?

(Exit Oedipus and Jocasta through the central door into the palace.)

Stasimon 2

STROPHE 1

CHORUS: May there accompany me
the fate to keep a reverential purity in what I say,
in all I do, for which the laws have been set forth
and walk on high, born to traverse the brightest,

870   highest upper air; Olympus[46] only
is their father, nor was it
mortal nature
that fathered them, and never will
oblivion lull them into sleep;
875   the god in them is great and never ages.

ANTISTROPHE 1

The will to violate, seed of the tyrant,
if it has drunk mindlessly of wealth and power,
without a sense of time or true advantage,
mounts to a peak, then
880   plunges to an abrupt . . . destiny,
where the useful foot
is of no use. But the kind
of struggling that is good for the city
I ask the god never to abolish.
885   The god is my protector: never will I give that up.

STROPHE 2

But if a man proceeds disdainfully
    in deeds of hand or word
and has no fear of Justice
    or reverence for shrines of the divinities
890   (may a bad fate catch him
    for his luckless wantonness!),
if he'll not gain what he gains with justice
and deny himself what is unholy,
or if he clings, in foolishness, to the untouchable
895   (what man, finally, in such an action, will have strength
enough to fend off passion's arrows from his soul?),
if, I say, this kind of
    deed is held in honor—
why should I join the sacred dance?

ANTISTROPHE 2

900   No longer shall I visit and revere
    Earth's navel,[47] the untouchable,

---

[46]*Olympus:* Mount Olympus, home of the gods, treated as a god.   [47]*Earth's navel:* Delphi.

nor visit Abae's[48] temple,
　　or Olympia,[49]
if the prophecies are not matched by events
905　　　for all the world to point to.
No, you who hold the power, if you are rightly called
Zeus the king of all, let this matter not escape you
and your ever-deathless rule,
for the prophecies to Laius fade . . .
910　and men already disregard them;
nor is Apollo anywhere
　　glorified with honors.
Religion slips away.

Episode 3

*(Enter Jocasta from the palace carrying a branch wound with wool and a
jar of incense. She is attended by two women.)*

JOCASTA:　Lords of the realm, the thought has come to me
915　to visit shrines of the divinities
with suppliant's branch in hand and fragrant smoke.
For Oedipus excites his soul too much
with alarms of all kinds. He will not judge
the present by the past, like a man of sense.
920　He's at the mercy of all terror-mongers.

(Jocasta approaches the altar on the right and kneels.)

Since I can do no good by counseling,
Apollo the Lycēan!—you are the closest—
I come a suppliant, with these my vows,
for a cleansing that will not pollute him.
925　For when we see him shaken we are all
afraid, like people looking at their helmsman.

*(Enter a Messenger along one of the parados. He sees Jocasta at the altar
and then addresses the Chorus.)*

MESSENGER:　I would be pleased if you would help me, stranger.
Where is the palace of King Oedipus?
Or tell me where he is himself, if you know.
930　**CHORUS:**　This is his house, stranger. He is within.
This is his wife and mother of his children.

---

[48]*Abae:* a town in Phocis where there was another oracle of Apollo.　　[49]*Olympia:* site of
the oracle of Zeus.

MESSENGER: May she and her family find prosperity,
    if, as you say, her marriage is fulfilled.
JOCASTA: You also, stranger, for you deserve as much
935   for your gracious words. But tell me why you've come.
    What do you wish? Or what have you to tell us?
MESSENGER: Good news, my Lady, both for your house and
    husband.
JOCASTA: What is your news? And who has sent you to us?
MESSENGER: I come from Corinth. When you have heard my
    news
940   you will rejoice, I'm sure—and grieve perhaps.
JOCASTA: What is it? How can it have this double power?
MESSENGER: They will establish him their king, so say
    the people of the land of Isthmia.[50]
JOCASTA: But is old Polybus not still in power?
945 **MESSENGER:** He's not, for death has clasped him in the tomb.
JOCASTA: What's this? Has Oedipus' father died?
MESSENGER: If I have lied then I deserve to die.
JOCASTA: Attendant! Go quickly to your master,
    and tell him this.

(Exit an Attendant into the palace.)

               Oracles of the gods!
950   Where are you now? The man whom Oedipus
    fled long ago, for fear that he should kill him—
    he's been destroyed by chance and not by him!

(Enter Oedipus from the palace.)

OEDIPUS: Darling Jocasta, my beloved wife,
    Why have you called me from the palace?
955 **JOCASTA:** First hear what this man has to say. Then see
    what the god's grave oracle has come to now!
OEDIPUS: Where is he from? What is this news he brings me?
JOCASTA: From Corinth. He brings news about your father:
    that Polybus is no more! that he is dead!
960 **OEDIPUS:** What's this, old man? I want to hear you say it.
MESSENGER: If this is what must first be clarified,
    please be assured that he is dead and gone.
OEDIPUS: By treachery or by the touch of sickness?
MESSENGER: Light pressures tip agéd frames into their sleep.
965 **OEDIPUS:** You mean the poor man died of some disease.
MESSENGER: And of the length of years that he had tallied.

---

[50]*land of Isthmia:* Corinth, which was on an isthmus.

OEDIPUS: Aha! Then why should we look to Pytho's vapors,[51]
or to the birds that scream above our heads?[52]
If we could really take those things for guides,

970   I would have killed my father. But he's dead!
He is beneath the earth, and here am I,
who never touched a spear. Unless he died
of longing for me and I "killed" him that way!
No, in this case, Polybus, by dying, took

975   the worthless oracle to Hades with him.

JOCASTA: And wasn't I telling you that just now?

OEDIPUS: You were indeed. I was misled by fear.

JOCASTA: You should not care about this anymore.

OEDIPUS: I must care. I must stay clear of my mother's bed.

980 **JOCASTA:**   What's there for man to fear? The realm of chance
prevails. True foresight isn't possible.
His life is best who lives without a plan.
This marriage with your mother—don't fear it.
How many times have men in dreams, too, slept

985   with their own mothers! Those who believe such things
mean nothing endure their lives most easily.

OEDIPUS: A fine, bold speech, and you are right, perhaps,
except that my mother is still living,
so I must fear her, however well you argue.

990 **JOCASTA:**   And yet your father's tomb is a great eye.

OEDIPUS: Illuminating, yes. But I still fear the living.

MESSENGER: Who is the woman who inspires this fear?

OEDIPUS: Meropē, Polybus' wife, old man.

MESSENGER: And what is there about her that alarms you?

995 **OEDIPUS:**   An oracle, god-sent and fearful, stranger.

MESSENGER: Is it permitted that another know?

OEDIPUS: It is. Loxias once said to me
I must have intercourse with my own mother
and take my father's blood with these my hands.

1000   So I have long lived far away from Corinth.
This has indeed brought much good luck, and yet,
to see one's parents' eyes is happiest.

MESSENGER: Was it for this that you have lived in exile?

OEDIPUS: So I'd not be my father's killer, sir.

1005 **MESSENGER:**   Had I not better free you from this fear,
my Lord? That's why I came—to do you service.

OEDIPUS: Indeed, what a reward you'd get for that!

---

[51]*Pytho's vapors:* the prophecies of the oracle at Delphi.   [52]*birds . . . heads:* the prophecies derived from interpreting the flights of birds.

MESSENGER: Indeed, this is the main point of my trip,
   to be rewarded when you get back home.
1010 OEDIPUS: I'll never rejoin the givers of my seed![53]
MESSENGER: My son, clearly you don't know what you're doing.
OEDIPUS: But how is that, old man? For the gods' sake, tell me!
MESSENGER: If it's because of them you won't go home.
OEDIPUS: I fear that Phoebus will have told the truth.
1015 MESSENGER: Pollution from the ones who gave you seed?
OEDIPUS: That is the thing, old man, I always fear.
MESSENGER: Your fear is groundless. Understand that.
OEDIPUS: Groundless? Not if I was born their son.
MESSENGER: But Polybus is not related to you.
1020 OEDIPUS: Do you mean Polybus was not my father?
MESSENGER: No more than I. We're both the same to you.
OEDIPUS: Same? One who begot me and one who didn't?
MESSENGER: He didn't beget you any more than I did.
OEDIPUS: But then, why did he say I was his son?
1025 MESSENGER: He got you as a gift from my own hands.
OEDIPUS: He loved me so, though from another's hands?
MESSENGER: His former childlessness persuaded him.
OEDIPUS: But had you bought me, or begotten me?
MESSENGER: Found you. In the forest hallows of Cithaeron.
1030 OEDIPUS: What were you doing traveling in that region?
MESSENGER: I was in charge of flocks which grazed those mountains.
OEDIPUS: A wanderer who worked the flocks for hire?
MESSENGER: Ah, but that day I was your savior, son.
OEDIPUS: From what? What was my trouble when you took me?
1035 MESSENGER: The ball-joints of your feet might testify.
OEDIPUS: What's that? What makes you name that ancient trouble?
MESSENGER: Your feet were pierced and I am your rescuer.
OEDIPUS: A fearful rebuke those tokens left for me!
MESSENGER: That was the chance that names you who you are.
1040 OEDIPUS: By the gods, did my mother or my father do this?
MESSENGER: That I don't know. He might who gave you to me.
OEDIPUS: From someone else? You didn't chance on me?
MESSENGER: Another shepherd handed you to me.
OEDIPUS: Who was he? Do you know? Will you explain!
1045 MESSENGER: They called him one of the men of—was it Laius?
OEDIPUS: The one who once was king here long ago?
MESSENGER: That is the one! The man was shepherd to him.
OEDIPUS: And is he still alive so I can see him?
MESSENGER: But you who live here ought to know that best.

---

[53]*givers of my seed:* that is, my parents. Oedipus still thinks Meropē and Polybus are his parents.

1050 **OEDIPUS:**   Does any one of you now present know
　　　　　about the shepherd whom this man has named?
　　　　　Have you seen him in town or in the fields? Speak out!
　　　　　The time has come for the discovery!
　　CHORAGOS: The man he speaks of, I believe, is the same
1055　as the field hand you have already asked to see.
　　　　　But it's Jocasta who would know this best.
　　OEDIPUS: Lady, do you remember the man we just
　　　　　now sent for—is that the man he speaks of?
　　JOCASTA: What? The man he spoke of? Pay no attention!
1060　His words are not worth thinking about. It's nothing.
　　OEDIPUS: With clues like this within my grasp, give up?
　　　　　Fail to solve the mystery of my birth?
　　JOCASTA: For the love of the gods, and if you love your life,
　　　　　give up this search! My sickness is enough.
1065 **OEDIPUS:**   Come! Though my mothers for three generations
　　　　　were in slavery, you'd not be lowborn!
　　JOCASTA: No, listen to me! Please! Don't do this thing!
　　OEDIPUS: I will not listen; I will search out the truth.
　　JOCASTA: My thinking is for you—it would be best.
1070 **OEDIPUS:**   This "best" of yours is starting to annoy me.
　　JOCASTA: Doomed man! Never find out who you are!
　　OEDIPUS: Will someone go and bring that shepherd here?
　　　　　Leave her to glory in her wealthy birth!
　　JOCASTA: Man of misery! No other name
1075　shall I address you by, ever again.

(Exit Jocasta into the palace after a long pause.)

　　CHORAGOS: Why has your lady left, Oedipus,
　　　　　hurled by a savage grief? I am afraid
　　　　　disaster will come bursting from this silence.
　　OEDIPUS: Let it burst forth! However low this seed
1080　of mine may be, yet I desire to see it.
　　　　　She, perhaps—she has a woman's pride—
　　　　　is mortified by my base origins.
　　　　　But I who count myself the child of Chance,
　　　　　the giver of good, shall never know dishonor.
1085　She is my mother,[54] and the months my brothers
　　　　　who first marked out my lowness, then my greatness.
　　　　　I shall not prove untrue to such a nature
　　　　　by giving up the search for my own birth.

---

[54]*She . . . mother:* Chance is my mother.

Stasimon 3

STROPHE

CHORUS: If I have mantic power
1090   and excellence in thought,
        by Olympus,
            you shall not, Cithaeron, at tomorrow's
        full moon,
        fail to hear us celebrate you as the countryman
1095   of Oedipus, his nurse and mother,
        or fail to be the subject of our dance,
            since you have given pleasure
        to our king.
        Phoebus, whom we summon by "iē!,"
1100   may this be pleasing to you!

ANTISTROPHE

        Who was your mother, son?
        which of the long-lived nymphs
        after lying with Pan,[55]
            the mountain roaming . . . Or was it a bride
1105   of Loxias?[56]
        For dear to him are all the upland pastures.
        Or was it Mount Cyllēnē's lord,[57]
        or the Bacchic god,[58]
            dweller of the mountain peaks,
1110   who received you as a joyous find
        from one of the nymphs of Helicon,
        the favorite sharers of his sport?

Episode 4

OEDIPUS: If someone like myself, who never met him,
        may calculate—elders, I think I see
1115   the very herdsman we've been waiting for.
        His many years would fit that man's age,
        and those who bring him on, if I am right,
        are my own men. And yet, in real knowledge,
        you can outstrip me, surely: you've seen him.

---

[55]*Pan:* god of shepherds and woodlands, half man and half goat.   [56]*Loxias:* Apollo.
[57]*Mount Cyllēnē's lord:* Hermes, messenger of the gods.   [58]*Bacchic god:* Dionysus.

(Enter the old Herdsman escorted by two of Oedipus's Attendants. At first, the Herdsman will not look at Oedipus.)

1120 CHORAGOS: I know him, yes, a man of the house of Laius,
         a trusty herdsman if he ever had one.
      OEDIPUS: I ask you first, the stranger come from Corinth:
         is this the man you spoke of?
      MESSENGER: That's he you see.
      OEDIPUS: Then you, old man. First look at me! Now answer:
1125   did you belong to Laius' household once?
      HERDSMAN: I did. Not a purchased slave but raised in the palace.
      OEDIPUS: How have you spent your life? What is your work?
      HERDSMAN: Most of my life now I have tended sheep.
      OEDIPUS: Where is the usual place you stay with them?
1130 HERDSMAN: On Mount Cithaeron. Or in that district.
      OEDIPUS: Do you recall observing this man there?
      HERDSMAN: Doing what? Which is the man you mean?
      OEDIPUS: This man right here. Have you had dealings with him?
      HERDSMAN: I can't say right away. I don't remember.
1135 MESSENGER: No wonder, master. I'll bring clear memory
         to his ignorance. I'm absolutely sure
         he can recall it, the district was Cithaeron,
         he with a double flock, and I, with one,
         lived close to him, for three entire seasons,
1140   six months along, from spring right to Arcturus.[59]
         Then for the winter I'd drive mine to my fold,
         and he'd drive his to Laius' pen again.
         Did any of the things I say take place?
      HERDSMAN: You speak the truth, though it's from long ago.
1145 MESSENGER: Do you remember giving me, back then,
         a boy I was to care for as my own?
      HERDSMAN: What are you saying? Why do you ask me that?
      MESSENGER: There, sir, is the man who was that boy!
      HERDSMAN: Damn you! Shut your mouth! Keep your silence!
1150 OEDIPUS: Stop! Don't you rebuke his words.
         Your words ask for rebuke far more than his.
      HERDSMAN: But what have I done wrong, most royal master?
      OEDIPUS: Not telling of the boy of whom he asked.
      HERDSMAN: He's ignorant and blundering toward ruin.
1155 OEDIPUS: Tell it willingly—or under torture.
      HERDSMAN: Oh god! Don't—I am old—don't torture me!
      OEDIPUS: Here! Someone put his hands behind his back!
      HERDSMAN: But why? What else would you find out, poor man?

---

[59]*Arcturus:* a star that is first seen in September in the Grecian sky.

OEDIPUS: Did you give him the child he asks about?

1160 **HERDSMAN:** I did. I wish that I had died that day!

OEDIPUS: You'll come to that if you don't speak the truth.

HERDSMAN: It's if I speak that I shall be destroyed.

OEDIPUS: I think this fellow struggles for delay.

HERDSMAN: No, no! I said already that I gave him.

1165 **OEDIPUS:** From your own home, or got from someone else?

HERDSMAN: Not from my own. I got him from another.

OEDIPUS: Which of these citizens? What sort of house?

HERDSMAN: Don't—by the gods!—don't, master, ask me more!

OEDIPUS: It means your death if I must ask again.

1170 **HERDSMAN:** One of the children of the house of Laius.

OEDIPUS: A slave—or born into the family?

HERDSMAN: I have come to the dreaded thing, and I shall say it.

OEDIPUS: And I to hearing it, but hear I must.

HERDSMAN: He was reported to have been—his son.

1175   Your lady in the house could tell you best.

OEDIPUS: Because she gave him to you?

HERDSMAN: Yes, my lord.

OEDIPUS: What was her purpose?

HERDSMAN: I was to kill the boy.

OEDIPUS: The child she bore?

HERDSMAN: She dreaded prophecies.

OEDIPUS: What were they?

HERDSMAN: The word was that he'd kill his parents.

1180 **OEDIPUS:** Then why did you give him up to this old man?

HERDSMAN: In pity, master—so he would take him home,
to another land. But what he did was save him
for this supreme disaster. If you are the one
he speaks of—know your evil birth and fate!

1185 **OEDIPUS:** Ah! All of it was destined to be true!
Oh light, now may I look my last upon you,
shown monstrous in my birth, in marriage monstrous,
a murderer monstrous in those I killed.

(Exit Oedipus, running into the palace.)

Stasimon 4

STROPHE 1

CHORUS: Oh generations of mortal men,
1190   while you are living, I will
appraise your lives at zero!
What man
comes closer to seizing lasting blessedness
than merely to seize its semblance,

1195   and after living in this semblance, to plunge?
       With your example before us,
       with your destiny, yours,
           suffering Oedipus, no mortal
       can I judge fortunate.

ANTISTROPHE 1

1200   For he,[60] outranging everybody,
       shot his arrow[61] and became the lord
           of wide prosperity and blessedness,
       oh Zeus, after destroying
       the virgin with the crooked talons,[62]
1205   singer of oracles; and against death,
       in my land, he arose a tower of defense.
       From which time you were called my king
       and granted privileges supreme—in mighty
       Thebes the ruling lord.

STROPHE 2

1210   But now—whose story is more sorrowful than yours?
       Who is more intimate with fierce calamities,
       with labors, now that your life is altered?
       Alas, my Oedipus, whom all men know:
       one great harbor[63]—
1215   one alone sufficed for you,
       as son and father,
       when you tumbled,[64] plowman[65] of the woman's chamber.
       How, how could your paternal
           furrows, wretched man,
1220   endure you silently so long.

ANTISTROPHE 2

       Time, all-seeing, surprised you living an unwilled life
       and sits from of old in judgment on the marriage, not a marriage,
       where the begetter is the begot as well.
       Ah, son of Laius . . . ,

---

[60]*he:* Oedipus.   [61]*shot his arrow:* took his chances; made a guess at the Sphinx's riddle.
[62]*virgin . . . talons:* the Sphinx.   [63]*one great harbor:* metaphorical allusion to Jocasta's
body.   [64]*tumbled:* were born and had sex.   [65]*plowman:* plowing is used here as a sexual metaphor.

1225 would that—oh, would that
I had never seen you!
I wail, my scream climbing beyond itself
from my whole power of voice. To say it straight:
from you I got new breath—
1230 but I also lulled my eye to sleep.[66]

Exodos

(Enter the Second Messenger from the palace.)

SECOND MESSENGER: You who are first among the citizens,
what deeds you are about to hear and see!
What grief you'll carry, if, true to your birth,
you still respect the house of Labdacus!
1235 Neither the Ister nor the Phasis river
could purify this house, such suffering
does it conceal, or soon must bring to light—
willed this time, not unwilled. Griefs hurt worst
which we perceive to be self-chosen ones.
1240 **CHORAGOS:**   They were sufficient, the things we knew before,
to make us grieve. What can you add to those?
SECOND MESSENGER: The thing that's quickest said and quickest
heard:
our own, our royal one, Jocasta's dead.
CHORAGOS: Unhappy queen! What was responsible?
1245 **SECOND MESSENGER:**   Herself. The bitterest of these events
is not for you, you were not there to see,
but yet, exactly as I can recall it,
you'll hear what happened to that wretched lady.
She came in anger through the outer hall,
1250 and then she ran straight to her marriage bed,
tearing her hair with the fingers of both hands.
Then, slamming shut the doors when she was in,
she called to Laius, dead so many years,
remembering the ancient seed which caused
1255 his death, leaving the mother to the son
to breed again an ill-born progeny.
She mourned the bed where she, alas, bred double—
husband by husband, children by her child.
From this point on I don't know how she died,
1260 for Oedipus then burst in with a cry,
and did not let us watch her final evil.

---

[66]*I . . . sleep:* I failed to see the corruption you brought.

Our eyes were fixed on him. Wildly he ran
to each of us, asking for his spear
and for his wife—no wife: where he might find
1265 the double mother-field, his and his children's.
He raved, and some divinity then showed him—
for none of us did so who stood close by.
With a dreadful shout—as if some guide were leading—
he lunged through the double doors; he bent the hollow
1270 bolts from the sockets, burst into the room,
and there we saw her, hanging from above,
entangled in some twisted hanging strands.
He saw, was stricken, and with a wild roar
ripped down the dangling noose. When she, poor woman,
1275 lay on the ground, there came a fearful sight:
he snatched the pins of worked gold from her dress,
with which her clothes were fastened: these he raised
and struck into the ball-joints of his eyes.[67]
He shouted that they would no longer see
1280 the evils he had suffered or had done,
see in the dark those he should not have seen,
and know no more those he once sought to know.
While chanting this, not once but many times
he raised his hand and struck into his eyes.
1285 Blood from his wounded eyes poured down his chin,
not freed in moistening drops, but all at once
a stormy rain of black blood burst like hail.
These evils, coupling them, making them one,
have broken loose upon both man and wife.
1290 The old prosperity that they had once
was true prosperity, and yet today,
mourning, ruin, death, disgrace, and every
evil you could name—not one is absent.
CHORAGOS: Has he allowed himself some peace from all this grief?
1295 SECOND MESSENGER: He shouts that someone slide the bolts and show
to all the Cadmeians the patricide,
his mother's—I can't say it, it's unholy—
so he can cast himself out of the land,
not stay and curse his house by his own curse.
1300 He lacks the strength, though, and he needs a guide,
for his is a sickness that's too great to bear.
Now you yourself will see: the bolts of the doors
are opening. You are about to see
a vision even one who hates must pity.

---

[67]*ball-joints of his eyes:* his eyeballs. Oedipus blinds himself in both eyes at the same time.

(Enter the blinded Oedipus from the palace, led in by a household Servant.)

1305   **CHORAGOS:**   Terrifying suffering for men to see,
      more terrifying than any I've ever
      come upon. Oh man of pain
      what madness reached you? Which god from far off,
      surpassing in range his longest spring,
1310   struck hard against your god-abandoned fate?
      Oh man of pain,
      I cannot look upon you—though there's so much
      I would ask you, so much to hear,
      so much that holds my eyes—
1315   such is the shudder you produce in me.
  OEDIPUS: Ah! Ah! I am a man of misery.
      Where am I carried? Pity me! Where
      is my voice scattered abroad on wings?
         Divinity, where has your lunge transported me?
1320   **CHORAGOS:**   To something horrible, not to be heard or seen.

Kommos

STROPHE 1

OEDIPUS: Oh, my cloud
      of darkness, abominable, unspeakable as it attacks me,
      not to be turned away, brought by an evil wind!
      Alas!
1325   Again alas! Both enter me at once:
      the sting of the prongs,[68] the memory of evils!
  CHORUS: I do not marvel that in these afflictions
      you carry double griefs and double evils.

ANTISTROPHE 1

OEDIPUS: Ah, friend,
1330   so you at least are there, resolute servant!
      Still with a heart to care for me, the blind man.
      Oh! Oh!
      I know that you are there. I recognize
      even inside my darkness, that voice of yours.
1335   **CHORUS:**   Doer of horror, how did you bear to quench
      your vision? What divinity raised your hand?

---

[68]*prongs:* refers to both the whip that Laius used and the two gold pins Oedipus used to blind himself.

STROPHE 2

OEDIPUS: It was Apollo there, Apollo, friends,
who brought my sorrows, vile sorrows to their perfection,
these evils that were done to me.
1340   But the one who struck them with his hand,
that one was none but I, in wretchedness.
For why was I to see
when nothing I could see would bring me joy?
CHORUS: Yes, that is how it was.
1345 OEDIPUS: What could I see, indeed,
or what enjoy—what greeting
is there I could hear with pleasure, friends?
Conduct me out of the land
as quickly as you can!
1350   Conduct me out, my friends,
the man utterly ruined,
supremely cursed,
the man who is by gods
the most detested of all men!
1355 CHORUS: Wretched in disaster and in knowledge:
oh, I could wish you'd never come to know!

ANTISTROPHE 2

OEDIPUS: May he be destroyed, whoever freed the savage shackles
from my feet when I'd been sent to the wild pasture,
whoever rescued me from murder
1360   and became my savior—
a bitter gift:
if I had died then,
I'd not have been such grief to self and kin.
CHORUS: I also would have had it so.
1365 OEDIPUS: I'd not have returned to be my father's
murderer; I'd not be called by men
my mother's bridegroom.
Now I'm without a god,
child of a polluted parent,
1370   fellow progenitor with him
who gave me birth in misery.
If there's an evil that
surpasses evils, that
has fallen to the lot of Oedipus.
1375 CHORAGOS: How can I say that you have counseled well?
Better not to be than live a blind man.

OEDIPUS: That this was not the best thing I could do—
don't tell me that, or advise me any more!
Should I descend to Hades and endure
1380   to see my father with these eyes? Or see
my poor unhappy mother? For I have done,
to both of these, things too great for hanging.
Or is the sight of children to be yearned for,
to see new shoots that sprouted as these did?
1385   Never, never with these eyes of mine!
Nor city, nor tower, nor holy images
of the divinities! For I, all-wretched,
most nobly raised—as no one else in Thebes—
deprived myself of these when I ordained
1390   that all expel the impious one—god-shown
to be polluted, and the dead king's son![69]
Once I exposed this great stain upon me,
could I have looked on these with steady eyes?
No! No! And if there were a way to block
1395   the source of hearing in my ears, I'd gladly
have locked up my pitiable body,
so I'd be blind and deaf. Evils shut out—
that way my mind could live in sweetness.
Alas, Cithaeron,[70] why did you receive me?
1400   Or when you had me, not killed me instantly?
I'd not have had to show my birth to mankind.
Polybus, Corinth, halls—ancestral,
they told me—how beautiful was your ward,
a scar that held back festering disease!
1405   Evil my nature, evil my origin.
You, three roads, and you, secret ravine,
you oak grove, narrow place of those three paths
that drank my blood[71] from these hands, from him
who fathered me, do you remember still
1410   the things I did to you? When I'd come here,
what I then did once more? Oh marriages! Marriages!
You gave us life and when you'd planted us
you sent the same seed up, and then revealed
fathers, brothers, sons, and kinsman's blood,
1415   and brides, and wives, and mothers, all the most
atrocious things that happen to mankind!

---

[69]*I . . . son:* Oedipus refers to his own curse against the murderer as well as his sins of patricide and incest.   [70]*Cithaeron:* the mountain on which the infant Oedipus was supposed to be exposed.   [71]*my blood:* that is, the blood of my father, Laius.

One should not name what never should have been.
Somewhere out there, then, quickly, by the gods,
cover me up, or murder me, or throw me
1420   to the ocean where you will never see me more!

(Oedipus moves toward the Chorus and they back away from him.)

Come! Don't shrink to touch this wretched man!
Believe me, do not be frightened! I alone
of all mankind can carry these afflictions.

(Enter Creon from the palace with Attendants.)

CHORAGOS: Tell Creon what you wish for. Just when we need him
1425   he's here. He can act, he can advise you.
He's now the land's sole guardian in your place.
OEDIPUS: Ah! Are there words that I can speak to him?
What ground for trust can I present? It's proved
that I was false to him in everything.
1430 **CREON:**   I have not come to mock you, Oedipus,
nor to reproach you for your former falseness.
You men, if you have no respect for sons
of mortals, let your awe for the all-feeding
flames of lordy Hēlius[72] prevent
1435   your showing unconcealed so great a stain,
abhorred by earth and sacred rain and light.
Escort him quickly back into the house!
If blood kin only see and hear their own
afflictions, we'll have no impious defilement.
1440 **OEDIPUS:**   By the gods, you've freed me from one terrible fear,
so nobly meeting my unworthiness:
grant me something—not for me; for you!
CREON: What do you want that you should beg me so?
OEDIPUS: To drive me from the land at once, to a place
1445   where there will be no man to speak to me!
CREON: I would have done just that—had I not wished
to ask first of the god what I should do.
OEDIPUS: His answer was revealed in full—that I,
the patricide, unholy, be destroyed.
1450 **CREON:**   He said that, but our need is so extreme,
it's best to have sure knowledge what must be done.
OEDIPUS: You'll ask about a wretched man like me?
CREON: Is it not time you put your trust in the god?

---

[72]*Hēlius:* the sun.

OEDIPUS: But I bid you as well, and shall entreat you.
1455   Give her who is within what burial
you will—you'll give your own her proper rites;
but me—do not condemn my fathers' land
to have me dwelling here while I'm alive,
but let me live on mountains—on Cithaeron
1460   famed as mine, for my mother and my father,
while they yet lived, made it my destined tomb,
and I'll be killed by those who wished my ruin!
And yet I know: no sickness will destroy me,
nothing will: I'd never have been saved
1465   when left to die unless for some dread evil.
Then let my fate continue where it will!
As for my children, Creon, take no pains
for my sons—they're men and they will never lack
the means to live, wherever they may be—
1470   but my two wretched, pitiable girls,
who never ate but at my table, never
were without me—everything that I
would touch, they'd always have a share of it—
please care for them! Above all, let me touch
1475   them with my hands and weep aloud my woes!
Please, my Lord!
Please, noble heart! Touching with my hands,
I'd think I held them as when I could see.

(Enter Antigone and Ismene from the palace with Attendants.)

What's this?
1480   Oh gods! Do I hear, somewhere, my two dear ones
sobbing? Has Creon really pitied me
and sent to me my dearest ones, my children?
Is that it?
CREON: Yes, I prepared this for you, for I knew
1485   you'd feel this joy, as you have always done.
OEDIPUS: Good fortune, then, and, for your care, be guarded
far better by divinity than I was!
Where are you, children? Come to me! Come here
to these my hands, hands of your brother, hands
1490   of him who gave you seed, hands that made
these once bright eyes to see now in this fashion.

(Oedipus embraces his daughters.)

He, children, seeing nothing, knowing nothing,
he fathered you where his own seed was plowed.
I weep for you as well, though I can't see you,

1495   imagining your bitter life to come,
the life you will be forced by men to live.
What gatherings of townsmen will you join,
what festivals, without returning home
in tears instead of watching holy rites?

1500   And when you've reached the time for marrying,
where, children, is the man who'll run the risk
of taking on himself the infamy
that will wound you as it did my parents?
What evil is not here? Your father killed

1505   his father, plowed the one who gave him birth,
and from the place where he was sown, from there
he got you, from the place he too was born.
These are the wounds: then who will marry you?
No man, my children. No, it's clear that you

1510   must wither in dry barrenness, unmarried.

(Oedipus addresses Creon.)

Son of Menoeceus! You are the only father
left to them—we two who gave them seed
are both destroyed: watch that they don't become
poor, wanderers, unmarried—they are your kin.

1515   Let not my ruin be their ruin, too!
No, pity them! You see how young they are,
bereft of everyone, except for you.
Consent, kind heart, and touch me with your hand!

(Creon grasps Oedipus's right hand.)

You, children, if you had reached an age of sense,

1520   I would have counseled much. Now, pray you may live
always where it's allowed, finding a life
better than his was, who gave you seed.

CREON: Stop this now. Quiet your weeping. Move away, into the house.

OEDIPUS: Bitter words, but I obey them.

CREON: There's an end to all things.

1525 **OEDIPUS:** I have first this request.

CREON: Tell me. I shall judge when
I will hear it.

OEDIPUS: Banish me from my homeland.

CREON: You must ask that of the god.

OEDIPUS: But I am the gods' most hated man!

CREON: Then you will soon get
what you want.

OEDIPUS: Do you consent?

CREON: I never promise when, as now, I'm
   ignorant.

1530 **OEDIPUS:**   Then lead me in.

CREON: Come. But let your hold fall from your
   children.

OEDIPUS: Do not take them from me, ever!

CREON: Do not wish to keep all of
   the power.
   You had power, but that power did not follow you through life.

*(Oedipus's daughters are taken from him and led into the palace by At-
tendants. Oedipus is led into the palace by a Servant. Creon and the other
Attendants follow. Only the Chorus remains.)*

CHORUS: People of Thebes, my country, see: here is that Oedipus—
   he who "knew" the famous riddle, and attained the highest power,
1535   whom all citizens admired, even envying his luck!
   See the billows of wild troubles which he has entered now!
   Here is the truth of each man's life: we must wait, and see his end,
   scrutinize his dying day, and refuse to call him happy
   till he has crossed the border of his life without pain.

(Exit the Chorus along each of the parados.)

—— Oedipus ———————————————————————

James M. Clay and *Daniel Krempel (from* The Theatrical Image)

In 1954 at the Canadian Shakespeare Festival in Stratford, Ontario, *Oedipus
Rex* was presented in the translation of Yeats. The open stage, the more than
halfway encircling auditorium, its steep rake, even the rather general lighting—all would probably have seemed sufficiently "right" to Sophocles. The
festival atmosphere of the production was also beautifully in accord with the
circumstances for which the play was written. The elaborate civic-sponsored
festival in the Athens of Sophocles' day could boast of drawing visitors from
all over the Greek-speaking world, and so, too, could this Stratford festival
claim to have attracted worldwide attention, even in its very first year.
   In this, its second year, the electric excitement and justifiable Canadian
pride was still running high. One could feel it in the daily shoptalk of the
town, and at the theatre the opening ceremonies brought this feeling home
with great force: first, a series of trumpet flourishes; then, in good Elizabethan tradition, a cannon roar reverberating through the bankside park to
signal the performance; and finally, the audience standing, singing "God

Save The Queen." This was no ordinary, dismissive nod to patriotic custom; the singing was strong, for through it—at once solemnly and enthusiastically—the intense local and national pride of Canada found a means of expression. This was clearly an important moment, perhaps one of the great cultural achievements of the English-speaking world, and even the Americans in the audience, for whom the melody also has such familiar emotional value, felt a privileged membership in this enterprise of high daring and merit. Thus, both in the wraparound seating and in audience spirit, this was a *community* festivity to a degree that plays no part in ordinary playgoing. And nothing could have been more favorable for the performance of this ancient play.

With the citizens of Canada now gathered comfortably about the playing space, the lights drain into a moment of expectant darkness, and then refill the bowl of the theatre to materialize the citizens of Thebes. They have somehow come from us, the surrounding crowd, and are converging on the forestage in the hope that Oedipus will appear. Many of the supplicants bear censers from which an astonishing pall of smoke boils up, hangs for a time like a veil . . . only to lift and reveal a shining figure, gold from foot to crown, entering from the permanent colonnade at the rear of the stage. This is Oedipus the King.

The chorus, all in masks, is costumed in earth colors, rough-textured, voluminous robes, which give them, individually and collectively, a shapeless anonymity. The masks are extreme stylizations of sorrowing and of peasant homeliness, and run strongly toward the grotesque. By contrast, the king stands out sharply, a burnished lamp among old rags. He is larger than life, his sandals are thicksoled, his fingers lengthened, his costume padded, and his head made massive by an all-enclosing mask. The crown is made of curving thin spikes—like thorns.

The chorus intones its lines in a half-sung, half-spoken manner; likewise, the delivery of Oedipus is formal recitation rather than conversational reaction.

Now Tiresias appears—a startling figure all in white. At first glance his mask seems to be that of a skull, bone white with gaping black sockets for eyes, but the nose is long and sharp, very beak-like. In fact, the fingers are talons; the feet, whenever one can glimpse them beneath the floor-length robe, are clothed in a suggestion of feathers and claws; and the long necklace is made of eggshells. Perhaps the birds of augury, which this prophet uses to foretell the future, have been the source of the costume image.

The ensuing scene becomes lively. The quality of incantation, so characteristic of the speaking up to this point, begins to diminish during the give and take of the violent argument between king and prophet. In his passion, the blind old seer mistakenly believes Oedipus to be standing opposite him, plunges in that direction, and topples from the stage, being saved only at the last second by the arms of the chorus. Worked up to an even greater pitch, he collapses and delivers his final "curse" from the floor, on his back, one arm pointing heavenward.

Creon and Jocasta too are enveloped in masks and costumes which exaggerate their proportions. The Queen is the color of slightly tarnished silver; Creon is bronze. After the argument with Creon, the cadenced, chant-like delivery becomes more prominent again, and the performance continues with its oddly detached atmosphere. Dimly, on the far side of the platform, one can see the audience, quiet, deeply absorbed.

As the tragedy develops, moments become more and more lyrical in treatment, and at one point, the chorus breaks into full song, singing a mournful lament for their king.

For his final scene, the blind Oedipus emerges from the palace in a thick, dark dull red robe. His head and shoulders are covered by a heavy black net, and the effect, while strange, is a powerful one. The scene with the children is also singular: they circle slowly around him, in a slow, funereal dance, while the lines are all but sung.

At the end, the nearly two thousand spectators sit spellbound for a few moments. Under the mood of this performance no one dares race for the exit before the curtain call.

That the concept for this production of Oedipus was at least partly a ritual-based idea was clear in the performance. The cantorial delivery, the hymns, the symbolic veil of blindness—all contributed to the impression of a performed litany. And the director, Tyrone Guthrie, had written in more than one article that he saw Oedipus as a kind of Christ figure: the legendary Greek was a miracle-working savior of his people, had his own Gethsemane of agony and doubt, and his final self-sacrifice. Thus, the tragedy was to be performed like a mass, with the actors commemorating the sacrifice of Oedipus in ritual recitation, without trying to convince the audience that a real event was taking place. Now whatever one may think of this production, one thing needs pointing up as a frame of reference in evaluating it: this 2,000-year-old play was given a successful professional performance, one which consistently held large popular audiences, and judging from the final response, one which made a deep and moving impression. To this important extent, at least, it was an effective translation.

What remains to be asked is whether the idea that "this play is like a mass" was complimentary to the tragedy's commanding metaphor of light and darkness, and whether the image chosen was well executed.

The first question requires some thought about the playwright's intentions in terms of "religion." For the Greeks religion seems to have been radically different from anything we have been accustomed to since the Judaic-Christian tradition conquered Western culture. In Greece priests had a role in life so minor that they are scarcely mentioned in the literature; there was no authoritarian church, no bible, and no rigid catechism embodying religious doctrine. The rigorous enjoyment of an athletic, singing, or theatre contest was for the Greeks an affirmation of the exciting forces at work in the universe, and hence these things were a form of religious expression. In thinking of Sophocles writing a mass-like play, it is well to recall that this playwright lived in a culture for which such expressions as "God loving" and

"God fearing" simply did not exist, and at ceremonies where a priest did officiate, he did not even wear a specially distinctive costume. If the typical Athenian would not have agreed that "Man is the measure of all things," nevertheless he did not by any means represent the opposite, or spiritual, point of view. Thus, the enormous zest for occasions in which human accomplishment could be thrillingly realized—in contests especially, even contests in the writing of tragedy.

Consistent with this, the plays themselves, no matter how serious and spiritual, typically have for their climactic scenes vivid debating matches between two splendidly matched antagonists. The arguments between Oedipus and Tiresias, and again with Creon, are typical of the Greek love of human prowess exhibiting itself through public rivalry and contention. And it is precisely in such scenes that the Stratford production concept seemed not to fit the play.

In the big, head-on clashes, the performance eased out of its templelike tone into the here-and-now sound of good, hot argument—a quality which seems inherent in the way these scenes are written, despite their formal structure. This is not to say that the disparity in playing style was terribly distracting, but if, as this book contends, a good production image should work easily and consistently without requiring special adjustments, then this fluctuation between ceremony and real verbal conflict was symptomatic of something wrong. Nor was this the only thing about the interpretation which called itself into question.

As one might guess, when Tiresias nearly fell off the stage and when he delivered a religious passage, an oracular revelation of doom, lying flat on his back—these things, coming as they did after a strong churchlike impression had been established—were jarring and distracting. Nor was it clear just why the truth-seeing blind man was so forcefully represented as a bird. The device was intriguing, but it made him seem less an awesome prophet than a spook. As it was performed it seemed to have little to do with the kind of religious ritual suggested by the preceding action.

To be sure, many elements of the production worked well for the play. Just as the radiance of Christ was symbolized in some medieval productions by overlaying the actor's face and hands with gold, Oedipus all in gold was a striking, effective device, and both the symbolism and fascinating unreality of this kind of costuming provided a dramatic yet ceremonial detachment which conveyed an exalted feeling of solemnity—certainly an appropriate emotion for this great tragedy. And the chanting, the hymns, some of the other symbolic devices such as the veil of blindness, these things keenly communicated the terrible dignity and seriousness of the script.

In sum, the analogy with Christian ritual seemed to bring to life crucial aspects of Sophocles' work but to need setting aside at certain moments, particularly in the big scenes whose excitement depends on direct human confrontation. One is tempted to say that therefore the image chosen, being only partly successful, was wrong. But one wonders what the effect would have been if the verbal duels had also been handled in a thoroughly ritualistic way. This would have given the performance greater consistency, though whether this kind of change would have resulted in a more accurate and dramatic translation of the tragedy is very much open to question.

As for how well the production concept was executed, the rather disturbing behavior of Tiresias, his characterization as a supernatural man-bird, the fact that the Herdsman looked for all the world like a sheep—such things are hard to justify in terms of the analogy with ritual commemoration. It is interesting that in the program note for this production, written by the director, no mention was made of the ritual idea, but rather the entire discussion of meaning was concerned with pointing out the light-dark symbolism as a key to the play's nonliteral significance.

Since it is rather easy to find things in this production concept which suggest that it was not in sufficient harmony with the commanding image Sophocles used, one wonders why the live performances had the impressive effect which they so obviously did. This brings us back to the point made at the beginning—for undoubtedly a large part of the successful impact of this production lay in its close parallel with the community-centered assumptions of the original performance. In this area the playwright's idea of theatre and audience was realized to a degree which one has to have experienced by seeing the Stratford performances to appreciate fully. The festival spirit of the city, the audience's proud and deep sense of "family," the community-concept floor plan of the theatre—all these worked together in such measure as to make this particular effort to translate *Oedipus Rex* a quite memorable event.

William Shakespeare, 1564–1616

Hamlet Prince of Denmark* (c. 1600)

CHARACTERS

Claudius, *King of Denmark*
Hamlet, *son to the former and nephew to the present King*
Polonius, *Lord Chamberlain*
Horatio, *friend to Hamlet*
Laertes, *son to Polonius*
Voltimand ⎤
Cornelius ⎥
Rosencrantz ⎬ *courtiers*
Guildenstern ⎥
Osric ⎦
A Gentleman
A Priest
Francisco, *a soldier*
Marcellus ⎤ *officers*
Bernardo ⎦
Reynaldo, *servant to Polonius*
Players
Two Clowns, *grave-diggers*
Fortinbras, *Prince of Norway*
A Captain
English Ambassadors
Ghost of Hamlet's Father
Gertrude, *Queen of Denmark and mother of Hamlet*
Ophelia, *daughter to Polonius*
Lords, Ladies, Officers, Soldiers, Sailors, Messengers, and other
    Attendants

*Note that individual lines are numbered in the following play. When a line is shared by one or more characters, it is counted as one line.

Act I

SCENE I

Elsinore. A platform before the castle.

(Francisco at his post. Enter to him Bernardo.)

BERNARDO: Who's there?
FRANCISCO: Nay, answer me: stand, and unfold yourself.
BERNARDO: Long live the king!
FRANCISCO: Bernardo?
BERNARDO: He.
FRANCISCO: You come most carefully upon your hour.
5 **BERNARDO:** 'Tis now struck twelve; get thee to bed, Francisco.
FRANCISCO: For this relief much thanks: 'tis bitter cold,
And I am sick at heart.
BERNARDO: Have you had quiet guard?
FRANCISCO: Not a mouse stirring.
BERNARDO: Well, good-night.
10 If you do meet Horatio and Marcellus,
The rivals of my watch, bid them make haste.
FRANCISCO: I think I hear them.—Stand, ho! Who is there?

(Enter Horatio and Marcellus.)

HORATIO: Friends to this ground.
MARCELLUS: And liegemen to the Dane.
15 **FRANCISCO:** Give you good-night.
MARCELLUS: O, farewell, honest soldier:
Who hath reliev'd you?
FRANCISCO: Bernardo has my place.
Give you good-night.

(Exit.)

MARCELLUS: Holla! Bernardo!
BERNARDO: Say.
What, is Horatio there?
HORATIO: A piece of him.
BERNARDO: Welcome, Horatio:—welcome, good Marcellus.
20 **MARCELLUS:** What, has this thing appear'd again to-night?
BERNARDO: I have seen nothing.
MARCELLUS: Horatio says 'tis but our fantasy,
And will not let belief take hold of him
Touching this dreaded sight, twice seen of us:
25 Therefore I have entreated him along
With us to watch the minutes of this night;

That, if again this apparition come
He may approve our eyes and speak to it.
HORATIO: Tush, tush, 'twill not appear.
BERNARDO: Sit down awhile,
30   And let us once again assail your ears,
That are so fortified against our story,
What we two nights have seen.
HORATIO: Well, sit we down,
And let us hear Bernardo speak of this.
BERNARDO: Last night of all,
35   When yon same star that's westward from the pole
Had made his course to illume that part of heaven
Where now it burns, Marcellus and myself,
The bell then beating one,—
MARCELLUS: Peace, break thee off; look where it comes again!

(Enter Ghost, armed.)

40 **BERNARDO:**   In the same figure, like the king that's dead.
MARCELLUS: Thou art a scholar; speak to it, Horatio.
BERNARDO: Looks it not like the king? mark it, Horatio.
HORATIO: Most like:—it harrows me with fear and wonder.
BERNARDO: It would be spoke to.
MARCELLUS: Question it, Horatio.
45 **HORATIO:**   What art thou, that usurp'st this time of night,
Together with that fair and warlike form
In which the majesty of buried Denmark
Did sometimes march? by heaven I charge thee, speak!
MARCELLUS: It is offended.
BERNARDO: See, it stalks away!
50 **HORATIO:**   Stay! speak, speak! I charge thee, speak!

(Exit Ghost.)

MARCELLUS: 'Tis gone, and will not answer.
BERNARDO: How now, Horatio! you tremble and look pale:
Is not this something more than fantasy?
What think you on't?
55 **HORATIO:**   Before my God, I might not this believe
Without the sensible and true avouch
Of mine own eyes.
MARCELLUS: Is it not like the king?
HORATIO: As thou art to thyself:
Such was the very armor he had on
60   When he the ambitious Norway combated;

So frown'd he once when, in an angry parle,[1]
He smote the sledded Polacks on the ice.
'Tis strange.

MARCELLUS: Thus twice before, and just at this dead hour,
65   With martial stalk hath he gone by our watch.

HORATIO: In what particular thought to work I know not;
But, in the gross and scope of my opinion,
This bodes some strange eruption to our state.

MARCELLUS: Good now, sit down, and tell me, he that knows,
70   Why this same strict and most observant watch
So nightly toils the subject of the land;
And why such daily cast of brazen cannon,
And foreign mart for implements of war;
Why such impress of shipwrights, whose sore task
75   Does not divide the Sunday from the week;
What might be toward, that this sweaty haste
Doth make the night joint-laborer with the day:
Who is't that can inform me?

HORATIO: That can I;
At least, the whisper goes so. Our last king,
80   Whose image even but now appear'd to us,
Was, as you know, by Fortinbras of Norway,
Thereto prick'd on by a most emulate pride,
Dar'd to the combat; in which our valiant Hamlet,—
For so this side of our known world esteem'd him,—
85   Did slay this Fortinbras; who, by a seal'd compact,
Well ratified by law and heraldry,
Did forfeit, with his life, all those his lands.
Which he stood seiz'd of,[2] to the conqueror:
Against the which, a moiety competent[3]
90   Was gagéd[4] by our king; which had return'd
To the inheritance of Fortinbras,
Had he been vanquisher; as by the same cov'nant,
And carriage of the article design'd,
His fell to Hamlet. Now, sir, young Fortinbras,
95   Of unimproved mettle hot and full,
Hath in the skirts of Norway, here and there,
Shark'd up a list of landless resolutes,
For food and diet, to some enterprise
That hath a stomach in't: which is no other,—

---

[1]Parley, or conference.   [2]Possessed.   [3]A sufficient portion of his lands.   [4]Engaged or pledged.

100   As it doth well appear unto our state,—
       But to recover of us by strong hand,
       And terms compulsatory, those foresaid lands
       So by his father lost: and this, I take it,
       Is the main motive of our preparations,
105   The source of this our watch, and the chief head
       Of this post-haste and romage[5] in the land.
     BERNARDO: I think it be no other, but e'en so:
       Well may it sort that this portentous figure
       Comes armed through our watch; so like the king
110   That was and is the question of these wars.
     HORATIO: A mote it is to trouble the mind's eye.
       In the most high and palmy state of Rome,
       A little ere the mightiest Julius fell,
       The graves stood tenantless, and the sheeted dead
115   Did squeak and gibber in the Roman streets:
       As, stars with trains of fire and dews of blood,
       Disasters in the sun; and the moist star,
       Upon whose influence Neptune's empire stands,
       Was sick almost to doomsday with eclipse:
120   And even the like precurse of fierce events,—
       As harbingers preceding still the fates,
       And prologue to the omen coming on,—
       Have heaven and earth together demonstrated
       Unto our climature and countrymen.—
125   But, soft, behold! lo, where it comes again!

   (Re-enter Ghost.)

       I'll cross it, though it blast me.—Stay, illusion!
       If thou hast any sound or use of voice,
       Speak to me:
       If there be any good thing to be done,
130   That may to thee do ease, and grace to me,
       Speak to me:
       If thou art privy to thy country's fate,
       Which, happily,[6] foreknowing may avoid,
       O, speak!
135   Or if thou has uphoarded in thy life
       Extorted treasure in the womb of earth,
       For which, they say, you spirits oft walk in death,

   (Cock crows.)

---

[5]General activity.   [6]Haply, or perhaps.

Speak of it:—stay, and speak!—Stop it, Marcellus.
MARCELLUS: Shall I strike at it with my partisan?[7]
140 **HORATIO:**   Do, if it will not stand.
BERNARDO: 'Tis here!
HORATIO: 'Tis here!
MARCELLUS: 'Tis gone!

(Exit Ghost.)

We do it wrong, being so majestical,
To offer it the show of violence;
For it is, as the air, invulnerable,
145   And our vain blows malicious mockery.
BERNARDO: It was about to speak when the cock crew.
HORATIO: And then it started like a guilty thing
Upon a fearful summons. I have heard,
The cock, that is the trumpet to the morn,
150   Doth with his lofty and shrill-sounding throat
Awake the god of day; and at his warning,
Whether in sea or fire, in earth or air,
The extravagant and erring spirit hies
To his confine: and of the truth herein
155   This present object made probation.[8]
MARCELLUS: It faded on the crowing of the cock.
Some say that ever 'gainst that season comes
Wherein our Saviour's birth is celebrated,
The bird of dawning singeth all night long:
160   And then, they say, no spirit can walk abroad;
The nights are wholesome; then no planets strike,
No fairy takes, nor witch hath power to charm;
So hallow'd and so gracious is the time.
HORATIO: So have I heard, and do in part believe.
165   But, look, the morn, in russet mantle clad,
Walks o'er the dew of yon high eastern hill:
Break we our watch up: and, by my advice,
Let us impart what we have seen to-night
Unto young Hamlet; for, upon my life,
170   This spirit, dumb to us, will speak to him:
Do you consent we shall acquaint him with it,
As needful in our loves, fitting our duty?
MARCELLUS: Let's do't, I pray; and I this morning know
Where we shall find him most conveniently.

(Exeunt.)

---

[7]Pike.   [8]Proof.

Scene II

Elsinore. A room of state in the castle.

(Enter the King, Queen, Hamlet, Polonius, Laertes, Voltimand, Cornelius, Lords, and Attendants.)

KING: Though yet of Hamlet our dear brother's death
The memory be green; and that it us befitted
To bear our hearts in grief, and our whole kingdom
To be contracted in one brow of woe;
5   Yet so far hath discretion fought with nature
That we with wisest sorrow think on him,
Together with remembrance of ourselves.
Therefore our sometime sister, now our queen,
The imperial jointress of this warlike state,
10   Have we, as 'twere with defeated joy,—
With one auspicious and one dropping eye,
With mirth and funeral, and with dirge in marriage,
In equal scale weighing delight and dole,—
Taken to wife: nor have we herein barr'd
15   Your better wisdoms, which have freely gone
With this affair along:—for all, our thanks.
Now follows that you know, young Fortinbras,
Holding a weak supposal of our worth,
Or thinking by our late dear brother's death
20   Our state to be disjoint and out of frame,
Colleagued with the dream of his advantage,
He hath not fail'd to pester us with message,
Importing the surrender of those lands
Lost by his father, with all bonds of law,
25   To our most valiant brother. So much for him.—
Now for ourself, and for this time of meeting:
Thus much the business is:—we have here writ
To Norway, uncle of young Fortinbras,—
Who, impotent and bed-rid, scarcely hears
30   Of this his nephew's purpose,—to suppress
His further gait herein; in that the levies,
The lists, and full proportions, are all made
Out of his subject:—and we here despatch
You, good Cornelius, and you, Voltimand,
35   For bearers of this greeting to old Norway;
Giving to you no further personal power
To business with the king more than the scope
Of these dilated articles allow.
Farewell; and let your haste commend your duty.

40 **CORNELIUS** and **VOLTIMAND:**   In that and all things will we show our
    duty.
    KING: We doubt it nothing: heartily farewell.

(Exeunt Voltimand and Cornelius.)

    And now, Laertes, what's the news with you?
    You told us of some suit; what is't, Laertes?
    You cannot speak of reason to the Dane,
45   And lose your voice: what wouldst thou beg, Laertes,
    That shall not be my offer, nor thy asking?
    The head is not more native to the heart,
    The hand more instrumental to the mouth,
    Than is the throne of Denmark to thy father.
50   What wouldst thou have, Laertes?
    LAERTES: Dread my lord,
    Your leave and favor to return to France;
    From whence though willingly I came to Denmark,
    To show my duty in your coronation;
    Yet now, I must confess, that duty done,
55   My thoughts and wishes bend again toward France.
    And bow them to your gracious leave and pardon.
    KING: Have you your father's leave? What says Polonius?
    POLONIUS: He hath, my lord, wrung from me my slow leave
    By laborsome petition; and at last
60   Upon his will I seal'd my hard consent:
    I do beseech you, give him leave to go.
    KING: Take thy fair hour, Laertes; time be thine,
    And thy best graces spend it at thy will!—
    But now, my cousin Hamlet, and my son,—
65 **HAMLET:**   *(Aside)* A little more than kin, and less than kind.
    KING: How is it that the clouds still hang on you?
    HAMLET: Not so, my lord; I am too much i' the sun.
    QUEEN: Good Hamlet, cast thy nighted color off,
    And let thine eye look like a friend on Denmark.
70   Do not for ever with thy vailed[1] lids
    Seek for thy noble father in the dust:
    Thou know'st 'tis common,—all that live must die,
    Passing through nature to eternity.
    HAMLET: Ay, madam, it is common.
    QUEEN: If it be,
75   Why seems it so particular with thee?

[1]Downcast.

HAMLET: Seems, madam! nay, it is; I know not seems.
'Tis not alone my inky cloak, good mother,
Nor customary suits of solemn black,
Nor windy suspiration of forc'd breath,
80 No, nor the fruitful river in the eye,
Nor the dejected 'havior of the visage,
Together with all forms, moods, shows of grief,
That can denote me truly: these, indeed, seem;
For they are actions that a man might play:
85 But I have that within which passeth show;
These but the trappings and the suits of woe.

KING: 'Tis sweet and cómmendable in your nature, Hamlet,
To give these mourning duties to your father:
But, you must know, your father lost a father;
90 That father lost, lost his; and the survivor bound,
In filial obligation, for some term
To do obsequious sorrow: but to persever
In obstinate condolement is a course
Of impious stubbornness; 'tis unmanly grief:
95 It shows a will most incorrect to heaven;
A heart unfortified, a mind impatient;
An understanding simple and unschool'd:
For what we know must be, and is as common
As any the most vulgar thing to sense,[2]
100 Why should we, in our peevish opposition,
Take it to heart? Fie! 'tis a fault to heaven,
A fault against the dead, a fault to nature,
To reason most absurd; whose common theme
Is death of fathers, and who still[3] hath cried,
105 From the first corse till he that died to-day,
This must be so. We pray you, throw to earth
This unprevailing woe; and think of us
As of a father: for let the world take note
You are the most immediate to our throne;
110 And with no less nobility of love
Than that which dearest father bears his son
Do I impart toward you. For your intent
In going back to school in Wittenberg,
It is most retrograde to our desire:
115 And we beseech you bend you to remain
Here, in the cheer and comfort of our eye,
Our chiefest courtier, cousin, and our son.

[2]Anything that is very commonly seen or heard.   [3]Ever, or always.

QUEEN: Let not thy mother lose her prayers, Hamlet:
I pray thee, stay with us; go not to Wittenberg.
120 **HAMLET:**   I shall in all my best obey you, madam.
KING: Why, 'tis a loving and a fair reply:
Be as ourself in Denmark.—Madam, come;
This gentle and unforc'd accord of Hamlet
Sits smiling to my heart: in grace whereof,
125 No jocund health that Denmark drinks to-day
But the great cannon to the clouds shall tell;
And the king's rouse[4] the heavens shall bruit[5] again,
Re-speaking earthly thunder. Come away.

(Exeunt all but Hamlet.)

HAMLET: O, that this too too solid flesh would melt,
130 Thaw, and resolve itself into a dew!
Or that the Everlasting had not fix'd
His canon 'gainst self-slaughter! O God! O God!
How weary, stale, flat, and unprofitable
Seem to me all the uses of this world!
135 Fie on't! O fie! 'tis an unweeded garden,
That grows to seed; things rank and gross in nature
Possess it merely. That it should come to this!
But two months dead!—nay, not so much, not two:
So excellent a king; that was, to this,
140 Hyperion[6] to a satyr: so loving to my mother,
That he might not beteem the winds of heaven
Visit her face too roughly. Heaven and earth!
Must I remember? why, she would hang on him
As if increase of appetite had grown
145 By what it fed on: and yet, within a month,—
Let me not think on't,—Frailty, thy name is woman!—
A little month; or ere those shoes were old
With which she follow'd my poor father's body
Like Niobe, all tears;—why she, even she,—
150 O God! a beast, that wants discourse of reason,
Would have mourn'd longer,—married with mine uncle,
My father's brother; but no more like my father
Than I to Hercules: within a month;
Ere yet the salt of most unrighteous tears
155 Had left the flushing in her galled eyes,
She married:—O, most wicked speed, to post
With such dexterity to incestuous sheets!

---

[4]Drink.   [5]Echo.   [6]The Greek sun god, the brightest and most beautiful of the gods.

It is not, nor it cannot come to good;
But break, my heart,—for I must hold my tongue!

(Enter Horatio, Marcellus, and Bernardo.)

160 **HORATIO:**   Hail to your lordship!
HAMLET: I am glad to see you well:
Horatio,—or I do forget myself.
HORATIO: The same, my lord, and your poor servant ever.
HAMLET: Sir, my good friend; I'll change that name with you:
And what make you from Wittenberg, Horatio?—Marcellus?
165 **MARCELLUS:**   My good lord,—
HAMLET: I am very glad to see you.—Good even, sir.—
But what, in faith, make you from Wittenberg?
HORATIO: A truant disposition, good my lord.
HAMLET: I would not hear your enemy say so;
170   Nor shall you do mine ear that violence,
To make it truster of your own report
Against yourself: I know you are no truant.
But what is your affair in Elsinore?
We'll teach you to drink deep ere you depart.
175 **HORATIO:**   My lord, I came to see your father's funeral.
HAMLET: I pray thee, do not mock me, fellow-student;
I think it was to see my mother's wedding.
HORATIO: Indeed, my lord, it follow'd hard upon.
HAMLET: Thrift, thrift, Horatio! the funeral-bak'd meats
180   Did coldly furnish forth the marriage tables.
Would I had met my dearest foe[7] in heaven
Ere I had ever seen that day, Horatio!—
My father,—methinks I see my father.
HORATIO: Where, my lord?
HAMLET: In my mind's eye, Horatio.
185 **HORATIO:**   I saw him once; he was a goodly[8] king.
HAMLET: He was a man, take him for all in all,
I shall not look upon his like again.
HORATIO: My lord, I think I saw him yester-night.
HAMLET: Saw who?
190 **HORATIO:**   My lord, the king your father.
HAMLET: The king my father!
HORATIO: Season your admiration[9] for awhile
With an attent ear, till I may deliver,
Upon the witness of these gentlemen,
This marvel to you.
HAMLET: For God's love, let me hear.

[7]Worst enemy.   [8]Handsome.   [9]Astonishment.

195 **HORATIO:**   Two nights together had these gentlemen,
       Marcellus and Bernardo, in their watch,
       In the dead vast and middle of the night,
       Been thus encounter'd. A figure like your father,
       Arm'd at all points exactly, cap-a-pe,[10]
200   Appears before them, and with solemn march
       Goes slow and stately by them: thrice he walk'd
       By their oppress'd[11] and fear-surprised eyes,
       Within his truncheon's length; whilst they, distill'd
       Almost to jelly with the act of fear,
205   Stand dumb, and speak not to him. This to me
       In dreadful secrecy impart they did;
       And I with them the third night kept the watch:
       Where, as they had deliver'd, both in time,
       Form of the thing, each word made true and good,
210   The apparition comes: I knew your father;
       These hands are not more like.
    HAMLET: But where was this?
    MARCELLUS: My lord, upon the platform where we watch'd.
    HAMLET: Did you not speak to it?
    HORATIO: My lord, I did;
       But answer made it none: yet once methought
215   It lifted up its head, and did address
       Itself to motion, like as it would speak:
       But even then the morning cock crew loud,
       And at the sound it shrunk in haste away,
       And vanish'd from our sight.
    HAMLET: 'Tis very strange.
220 **HORATIO:**   As I do live, my honor'd lord, 'tis true;
       And we did think it writ down in our duty
       To let you know of it.
    HAMLET: Indeed, indeed, sirs, but this troubles me.
       Hold you the watch to-night?
225 **MARCELLUS** and **BERNARDO:**   We do, my lord.
    HAMLET: Arm'd, say you?
    MARCELLUS and **BERNARDO:**   Arm'd, my lord.
    HAMLET: From top to toe?
    MARCELLUS and **BERNARDO:**   My lord, from head to foot.
230 **HAMLET:**   Then saw you not his face?
    HORATIO: O yes, my lord; he wore his beaver up.
    HAMLET: What, look'd he frowningly?
    HORATIO: A countenance more in sorrow than in anger.
    HAMLET: Pale or red?

---

[10]*Cap-a-pie,* from head to toe.   [11]Overwhelmed.

235 **HORATIO:**   Nay, very pale.
    HAMLET: And fix'd his eyes upon you?
    HORATIO: Most constantly.
    HAMLET: I would I had been there.
    HORATIO: It would have much amaz'd you.
    HAMLET: Very like, very like. Stay'd it long?
    HORATIO: While one with moderate haste might tell[12] a hundred.
240 **MARCELLUS** and **BERNARDO:**   Longer, longer.
    HORATIO: Not when I saw't.
    HAMLET: His beard was grizzled,—no?
    HORATIO: It was, as I have seen it in his life,
        A sable silver'd.
    HAMLET: I will watch to-night;
        Perchance 'twill walk again.
    HORATIO: I warrant it will.
245 **HAMLET:**   If it assume my noble father's person
        I'll speak to it, though hell itself should gape
        And bid me hold my peace. I pray you all,
        If you have hitherto conceal'd this sight,
        Let it be tenable in your silence still;
250   And whatsoever else shall hap to-night,
        Give it an understanding, but no tongue:
        I will requite your loves. So, fare ye well:
        Upon the platform, 'twixt eleven and twelve,
        I'll visit you.
    ALL: Our duty to your honor.
255 **HAMLET:**   Your loves, as mine to you: farewell.

(Exeunt Horatio, Marcellus, and Bernardo.)

        My father's spirit in arms; all is not well;
        I doubt some foul play: would the night were come!
        Till then sit still, my soul: foul deeds will rise,
        Though all the earth o'erwhelm them, to men's eyes.

(Exit.)

SCENE III

A room in Polonius' house.

(Enter Laertes and Ophelia.)

    LAERTES: My necessaries are embark'd: farewell:
        And, sister, as the winds give benefit,

[12]Count.

And convoy[1] is assistant, do not sleep,
But let me hear from you.
OPHELIA: Do you doubt that?
5 **LAERTES:**   For Hamlet, and the trifling of his favor,
Hold it a fashion and a toy in blood:
A violet in the youth of primy nature,
Forward, not permanent, sweet, not lasting,
The perfume and suppliance of a minute;
10   No more.
OPHELIA: No more but so?
LAERTES: Think it no more:
For nature, crescent,[2] does not grow alone
In thews and bulk; but as this temple[3] waxes,
The inward service of the mind and soul
Grows wide withal. Perhaps he loves you now;
15   And now no soil nor cautel[4] doth besmirch
The virtue of his will: but you must fear,
His greatness weigh'd, his will is not his own;
For he himself is subject to his birth:
He may not, as unvalu'd persons do,
20   Carve for himself; for on his choice depends
The safëty and the health of the whole state;
And therefore must his choice be circumscrib'd
Unto the voice and yielding of that body
Whereof he is the head. Then if he says he loves you,
25   It fits your wisdom so far to believe it
As he in his particular act and place
May give his saying deed; which is no further
Than the main[5] voice of Denmark goes withal.
Then weigh what loss your honor may sustain
30   If with too credent ear you list his songs,
Or lose your heart, or your chaste treasure open
To his unmaster'd importunity.
Fear it, Ophelia, fear it, my dear sister;
And keep within the rear of your affection,
35   Out of the shot and danger of desire.
The chariest maid is prodigal enough
If she unmask her beauty to the moon:
Virtue itself scrapes not calumnious strokes:
The canker galls the infants of the spring
40   Too oft before their buttons be disclos'd;
And in the morn and liquid dew of youth

[1]Means of conveyance.   [2]Growing.   [3]Body.   [4]Deceit.   [5]Strong, or mighty.

Contagious blastments are most imminent.
Be wary, then; best safety lies in fear:
Youth to itself rebels, though none else near.

45 **OPHELIA:** I shall the effect of this good lesson keep
As watchman to my heart. But, good my brother,
Do not, as some ungracious pastors do,
Show me the steep and thorny way to heaven;
Whilst like a puff'd and reckless libertine,
50 Himself the primrose path of dalliance treads,
And recks not his own rede.[6]

LAERTES: O, fear me not.
I stay too long:—but here my father comes.

(Enter Polonius.)

A double blessing is a double grace;
Occasion smiles upon a second leave.

55 **POLONIUS:** Yet here, Laertes! aboard, aboard, for shame!
The wind sits in the shoulder of your sail,
And you are stay'd for. There,—my blessing with you!

(Laying his hand on Laertes' head.)

And these few precepts in thy memory
See thou ch.arácter.[7] Give thy thoughts no tongue,
60 Nor any unproportion'd thought his act.
Be thou familiar, but by no means vulgar.
The friends thou hast, and their adoption tried,
Grapple them to thy soul with hoops of steel;
But do not dull thy palm with entertainment
65 Of each new-hatch'd, unfledg'd comrade. Beware
Of entrance to a quarrel; but, being in,
Bear't that the opposèd may beware of thee.
Give every man thine ear, but few thy voice:
Take each man's censure,[8] but reserve thy judgment.
70 Costly thy habit as thy purse can buy,
But not express'd in fancy; rich, not gaudy:
For the apparel oft proclaims the man;
And they in France of the best rank and station
Are most select and generous chief in that.
75 Neither a borrower nor a lender be:
For a loan oft loses both itself and friend;
And borrowing dulls the edge of husbandry.
This above all,—to thine own self be true;

---

[6]Counsel.   [7]Engrave in your mind.   [8]Opinion.

And it must follow, as the night the day,
80 Thou canst not then be false to any man.
Farewell: my blessing season this in thee!
LAERTES: Most humbly do I take my leave, my lord.
POLONIUS: The time invites you; go, your servants tend.[9]
LAERTES: Farewell, Ophelia; and remember well
85 What I have said to you.
OPHELIA: 'Tis in my memory lock'd,
And you yourself shall keep the key of it.
LAERTES: Farewell. *(Exit.)*
POLONIUS: What is't, Ophelia, he hath said to you?
OPHELIA: So please you, something touching the Lord Hamlet.
90 **POLONIUS:** Marry, well bethought:
'Tis told me he hath very oft of late
Given private time to you; and you yourself
Have of your audience been most free and bounteous:
If it be so,—as so 'tis put on me,
95 And that in way of caution,—I must tell you,
You do not understand yourself so clearly
As it behoves my daughter and your honor.
What is between you? give me up the truth.
OPHELIA: He hath, my lord, of late made many tenders
100 Of his affection to me.
POLONIUS: Affection! pooh! you speak like a green girl,
Unsifted in such perilous circumstance.
Do you believe his tenders,[10] as you call them?
OPHELIA: I do not know, my lord, what I should think.
105 **POLONIUS:** Marry, I'll teach you: think yourself a baby;
That you have ta'en these tenders for true pay,
Which are not sterling. Tender yourself more dearly;
Or,—not to crack the wind of the poor phrase,
Wronging it thus,—you'll tender me a fool.
110 **OPHELIA:** My lord, he hath impórtun'd me with love
In honorable fashion.
POLONIUS: Ay, fashion you may call it; go to, go to.
OPHELIA: And hath given countenance to his speech, my lord,
With almost all the holy vows of heaven.
115 **POLONIUS:** Ay, springes to catch woodcocks. I do know,
When the blood burns, how prodigal the soul
Lends the tongue vows: these blazes, daughter,
Giving more light than heat,—extinct in both,
Even in their promise, as it is a-making,—

[9]Wait.   [10]Offers.

120   You must not take for fire. From this time
    Be somewhat scanter of your maiden presence;
    Set your entreatments at a higher rate
    Than a command to parley. For Lord Hamlet,
    Believe so much in him, that he is young;
125   And with a larger tether may he walk
    Than may be given you: in few, Ophelia,
    Do not believe his vows; for they are brokers,[11]—
    Not of that die which their investments show,
    But mere implorators of unholy suits,
130   Breathing like sanctified and pious bawds,
    The better to beguile. This is for all,—
    I would not, in plain terms, from this time forth,
    Have you so slander any moment leisure
    As to give words or talk with the Lord Hamlet.
135   Look to't, I charge you; come your ways.
    OPHELIA: I shall obey, my lord.

(Exeunt.)

SCENE **IV**

The platform.

(Enter Hamlet, Horatio, and Marcellus.)

HAMLET: The air bites shrewdly; it is very cold.
HORATIO: It is a nipping and an eager air.
HAMLET: What hour now?
HORATIO: I think it lacks of twelve.
MARCELLUS: No, it is struck.
5 **HORATIO:**   Indeed? I heard it not: then it draws near the season
    Wherein the spirit held his wont to walk.

(A flourish of trumpets, and ordnance shot off within.)

    What does this mean, my lord?
HAMLET: The king doth wake to-night, and takes his rouse,
    Keeps wassail, and the swaggering upspring[1] reels;
10   And, as he drains his draughts of Rhenish down,
    The kettle-drum and trumpet thus bray out
    The triumph of his pledge.[2]
HORATIO: Is it a custom?
HAMLET: Ay, marry, is't:
    But to my mind,—though I am native here,

---

[11]Procurers.   [1]A dance.   [2]The glory of his toasts.

15 And to the manner born,—it is a custom
More honor'd in the breach than the observance.
This heavy-headed revel east and west
Makes us traduc'd and tax'd of other nations:
They clepe us drunkards, and with swinish phrase
20 Soil our addition;³ and, indeed, it takes
From our achievements, though perform'd at height,
The pith and marrow of our attribute.
So oft it chances in particular men
That, for some vicious mole of nature in them,
25 As in their birth,—wherein they are not guilty,
Since nature cannot choose his origin,—
By the o'ergrowth of some complexion,
Oft breaking down the pales and forts of reason;
Or by some habit, that too much o'erleavens
30 The form of plausive⁴ manners;—that these men,—
Carrying, I say, the stamp of one defect,
Being nature's livery or fortune's star,—
Their virtues else,—be they as pure as grace,
As infinite as man may undergo,—
35 Shall in the general censure take corruption
From that particular fault: the dram of evil
Doth all the noble substance of a doubt
To his own scandal.

HORATIO: Look, my lord, it comes!

(Enter Ghost.)

HAMLET: Angels and ministers of grace defend us!—
40 Be thou a spirit of health or goblin damn'd,
Bring with thee airs from heaven or blasts from hell,
Be thy intents wicked or charitable,
Thou com'st in such a questionable shape
That I will speak to thee: I'll call thee Hamlet,
45 King, father, royal Dane: O, answer me!
Let me not burst in ignorance; but tell
Why thy canóniz'd bones, hearsèd in death,
Have burst their cerements; why the sepulchre,
Wherein we saw thee quietly in-urn'd,
50 Hath op'd his ponderous and marble jaws
To cast thee up again! What may this mean,
That thou, dead corse, again in còmplete steel,
Revisit'st thus the glimpses of the moon,
Making night hideous and we⁵ fools of nature

³Reputation.   ⁴Pleasing.   ⁵Us.

55   So horridly to shake our disposition
      With thoughts beyond the reaches of our souls?
      Say, why is this? wherefore? what should we do?

(Ghost beckons Hamlet.)

HORATIO: It beckons you to go away with it,
      As if it some impartment did desire
60   To you alone.
MARCELLUS: Look, with what courteous action
      It waves you to a more removed ground:
      But do not go with it.
HORATIO: No, by no means.
HAMLET: It will not speak; then will I follow it.
HORATIO: Do not, my lord.
HAMLET: Why, what should be the fear?
65   I do not set my life at a pin's fee;
      And for my soul, what can it do to that,
      Being a thing immortal as itself?
      It waves me forth again;—I'll follow it.
HORATIO: What if it tempt you toward the flood, my lord.
70   Or to the dreadful summit of the cliff
      That beetles o'er his base into the sea,
      And there assume some other horrible form,
      Which might deprive your sovereignty of reason,
      And draw you into madness? think of it:
75   The very place puts toys of desperation,
      Without more motive, into every brain
      That looks so many fathoms to the sea
      And hears it roar beneath.
HAMLET: It waves me still.—
      Go on; I'll follow thee.
80 **MARCELLUS:**   You shall not go, my lord.
HAMLET: Hold off your hands.
HORATIO: Be rul'd; you shall not go.
HAMLET: My fate cries out,
      And makes each petty artery in this body
      As hardy as the Némean lion's[6] nerve.—

(Ghost beckons.)

      Still am I call'd;—unhand me, gentlemen;—*(Breaking from them)*
85   By heaven, I'll make a ghost of him that lets[7] me.
      I say, away!—Go on; I'll follow thee.

(Exeunt Ghost and Hamlet.)

---

[6]The fierce lion that Hercules was called upon to slay as one of his "twelve labors."   [7]Hinders.

HORATIO: He waxes desperate with imagination.
MARCELLUS: Let's follow; 'tis not fit thus to obey him.
HORATIO: Have after.—To what issue will this come?
90 **MARCELLUS:**   Something is rotten in the state of Denmark.
HORATIO: Heaven will direct it.
MARCELLUS: Nay, let's follow him.

(Exeunt.)

SCENE V

A more remote part of the platform.

(Enter Ghost and Hamlet.)

HAMLET: Where wilt thou lead me? speak, I'll go no further.
GHOST: Mark me.
HAMLET: I will.
GHOST: My hour is almost come,
   When I to sulphurous and tormenting flames
   Must render up myself.
HAMLET: Alas, poor ghost!
5 **GHOST:**   Pity me not, but lend thy serious hearing
   To what I shall unfold.
HAMLET: Speak; I am bound to hear.
GHOST: So art thou to revenge, when thou shalt hear.
HAMLET: What?
GHOST: I am thy father's spirit;
10   Doom'd for a certain term to walk the night,
   And, for the day, confin'd to waste in fires
   Till the foul crimes[1] done in my days of nature
   Are burnt and purg'd away. But that I am forbid
   To tell the secrets of my prison-house,
15   I could a tale unfold whose lightest word
   Would harrow up thy soul; freeze thy young blood;
   Make thy two eyes, like stars, start from their spheres;
   Thy knotted and combined locks to part,
   And each particular hair to stand on end,
20   Like quills upon the fretful porcupine:
   But this eternal blazon[2] must not be
   To ears of flesh and blood.—List, list, O, list!—
   If thou didst ever thy dear father love,—
HAMLET: O God!

---

[1]Rather, sins or faults.   [2]Disclosure of information concerning the other world.

25 **GHOST:**   Revenge his foul and most unnatural murder.
    HAMLET: Murder!
    GHOST: Murder—most foul, as in the best it is;
        But this most foul, strange, and unnatural.
    HAMLET: Haste me to know't, that I, with wings as swift
30   As meditation or the thoughts of love,
        May sweep to my revenge.
    GHOST: I find thee apt;
        And duller shouldst thou be than the fat weed
        That rots itself in ease on Lethe[3] wharf,
        Wouldst thou not stir in this. Now, Hamlet,
35   'Tis given out that, sleeping in mine orchard,
        A serpent stung me; so the whole ear of Denmark
        Is by a forged process of my death
        Rankly abus'd: but know, thou noble youth,
        The serpent that did sting thy father's life
40   Now wears his crown.
    HAMLET: O my prophetic soul! mine uncle!
    GHOST: Ay, that incestuous, that adulterate beast,
        With witchcraft of his wit, with traitorous gifts,—
        O wicked wit and gifts that have the power
        So to seduce!—won to his shameful lust
45   The will of my most seeming virtuous queen:
        O Hamlet, what a falling-off was there!
        From me, whose love was of that dignity
        That it went hand in hand even with the vow
        I made to her in marriage: and to decline
50   Upon a wretch whose natural gifts were poor
        To those of mine!
        But virtue, as it never will be mov'd,
        Though lewdness court it in a shape of heaven;
        So lust, though to a radiant angel link'd,
55   Will sate itself in a celestial bed
        And prey on garbage.
        But, soft! methinks I scent the morning air;
        Brief let me be.—Sleeping within mine orchard,
        My custom always in the afternoon,
60   Upon my sécure hour thy uncle stole,
        With juice of cursed hebenon[4] in a vial,
        And in the porches of mine ears did pour
        The leperous distilment; whose effect
        Holds such an enmity with blood of man

---

[3]The river of forgetfulness of the past, out of which the dead drink.   [4]Ebony.

65   That, swift as quicksilver, it courses through
      The natural gates and alleys of the body;
      And with a sudden vigor it doth posset[5]
      And curd, like eager[6] droppings into milk,
      The thin and wholesome blood: so did it mine;
70   And a most instant tetter bark'd about,
      Most lazar-like,[7] with vile and loathsome crust,
      All my smooth body.
      Thus was I, sleeping, by a brother's hand,
      Of life, of crown, of queen, at once despatch'd:
75   Cut off even in the blossoms of my sin,
      Unhousel'd, unanointed, unanel'd;
      No reckoning made, but sent to my account
      With all my imperfections on my head:
      O, horrible! O, horrible! most horrible!
80   If thou hast nature in thee, bear it not;
      Let not the royal bed of Denmark be
      A couch for luxury[8] and damned incest.
      But, howsoever thou pursu'st this act,
      Taint not thy mind, nor let thy soul contrive
85   Against thy mother aught: leave her to heaven,
      And to those thorns that in her bosom lodge,
      To prick and sting her. Fare thee well at once!
      The glowworm shows the matin to be near,
      And 'gins to pale his uneffectual fire:
90   Adieu, adieu! Hamlet, remember me. *(Exit.)*
   HAMLET: O all you host of heaven! O earth! what else?
      And shall I couple hell?—O, fie!—Hold, my heart;
      And you, my sinews, grow not instant old,
      But bear me stiffly up.—Remember thee!
95   Ay, thou poor ghost, while memory holds a seat
      In this distracted globe. Remember thee!
      Yea, from the table of my memory
      I'll wipe away all trivial fond[9] recórds,
      All saws of books, all forms, all pressures past,
100   That youth and observation copied there;
      And thy commandment all alone shall live
      Within the book and volume of my brain,
      Unmix'd with baser matter: yes, by heaven.—
      O most pernicious woman!
105   O villain, villain, smiling, damned villain!
      My tables,—meet it is I set it down,

---

[5]Coagulate.   [6]Acid.   [7]Like a leper, whose skin is rough.   [8]Lechery.   [9]Foolish.

That one may smile, and smile, and be a villain;
At least, I am sure, it may be so in Denmark:

(Writing)

So, uncle, there you are. Now to my word;
110   It is, *Adieu, adieu! remember me:*
I have sworn't.
HORATIO: *(Within)* My lord, my lord,—
MARCELLUS: *(Within)*   Lord Hamlet,—
HORATIO: *(Within)*   Heaven secure
him!
MARCELLUS: *(Within)* So be it!
HORATIO: *(Within)* Illo, ho, ho, my lord!
115 **HAMLET:**   Hillo, ho, ho, boy! come, bird, come.[10]

(Enter Horatio and Marcellus.)

MARCELLUS: How is't, my noble lord?
HORATIO: What news, my lord?
HAMLET: O, wonderful!
HORATIO: Good my lord, tell it.
HAMLET: No; you'll reveal it.
HORATIO: Not I, my lord, by heaven.
MARCELLUS: Nor I, my lord.
120 **HAMLET:**   How say you, then; would heart of man once think it?—
But you'll be secret?
HORATIO and **MARCELLUS:**   Ay, by heaven, my lord.
HAMLET: There's ne'er a villain dwelling in all Denmark
But he's an arrant knave.
125 **HORATIO:**   There needs no ghost, my lord, come from the grave
To tell us this.
HAMLET: Why, right; you are i' the right;
And so, without more circumstance at all,
I hold it fit that we shake hands and part:
130   You, as your business and desire shall point you,—
For every man has business and desire,
Such as it is;—and for mine own poor part,
Look you, I'll go pray.
HORATIO: These are but wild and whirling words, my lord.
135 **HAMLET:**   I'm sorry they offend you, heartily;
Yes, faith, heartily.
HORATIO: There's no offence, my lord.

---

[10]Hamlet used the word "bird" because this is a falconer's call.

HAMLET: Yes, by Saint Patrick, but there is, Horatio,
  And much offence too. Touching this vision here,—
  It is an honest ghost, that let me tell you:
140 For you desire to know what is between us,
  O'ermaster't as you may. And now, good friends,
  As you are friends, scholars, and soldiers,
  Give me one poor request.
HORATIO: What is't, my lord? we will.
145 **HAMLET:**   Never make known what you have seen to-night.
HORATIO and **MARCELLUS:**   My lord, we will not.
HAMLET: Nay, but swear't.
HORATIO: In faith,
  My lord, not I.
MARCELLUS: Nor I, my lord, in faith.
HAMLET: Upon my sword.
MARCELLUS: We have sworn, my lord, already.
HAMLET: Indeed, upon my sword, indeed.
150 **GHOST:**   *(Beneath)* Swear.
HAMLET: Ha, ha, boy! say'st thou so? art thou there, truepenny?—
  Come on,—you hear this fellow in the cellarage,—
  Consent to swear.
HORATIO: Propose the oath, my lord.
HAMLET: Never to speak of this that you have seen,
155 Swear by my sword.
GHOST: *(Beneath)* Swear.
HAMLET: *Hic et ubique?*[11] then we'll shift our ground.—
  Come hither, gentlemen,
  And lay your hands again upon my sword:
160 Never to speak of this that you have heard,
  Swear by my sword.
GHOST: *(Beneath)* Swear.
HAMLET: Well said! old mole! canst work i' the earth so fast?
  A worthy pioneer![12]—Once more remove, good friends.
165 **HORATIO:**   O day and night, but this is wondrous strange!
HAMLET: And therefore as a stranger give it welcome.
  There are more things in heaven and earth, Horatio,
  Than are dreamt of in your philosophy.
  But come;—
170 Here, as before, never, so help you mercy,
  How strange or odd soe'er I bear myself,—
  As I, perchance, hereafter shall think meet
  To put an antic disposition on,—

[11]Here and everywhere?   [12]A soldier who digs trenches and undermines fortresses.

That you, at such times seeing me, never shall,
175 With arms encumber'd[13] thus, or this headshake,
Or by pronouncing of some doubtful phrase,
As, *Well, well, we know;*—or, *We could, an if we would;*—
Or, *If we list to speak;*—or, *There be, an if they might;*—
Or such ambiguous giving out, to note
180 That you know aught of me:—this not to do,
So grace and mercy at your most need help you,
Swear.

GHOST: *(Beneath)* Swear.

HAMLET: Rest, rest, perturbed spirit!—So, gentlemen,
185 With all my love I do commend to you:
And what so poor a man as Hamlet is
May do, to express his love and friending to you,
God willing, shall not lack. Let us go in together;
And still your fingers on your lips, I pray.
190 The time is out of joint:—O cursed spite,
That ever I was born to set it right!—
Nay, come, let's go together.

(Exeunt.)

Act II

SCENE I

A room in Polonius' house.

(Enter Polonius and Reynaldo.)

POLONIUS: Give him this money and these notes, Reynaldo.
REYNALDO: I will, my lord.
POLONIUS: You shall do marvelous wisely, good Reynaldo,
Before you visit him, to make inquiry
5 On his behavior.
REYNALDO: My lord, I did intend it.
POLONIUS: Marry, well said; very well said. Look you, sir,
Inquire me first what Danskers[1] are in Paris;
And how, and who, what means, and where they keep,
What company, at what expense; and finding,
10 By this encompassment and drift of question,
That they do know my son, come you more nearer
Than your particular demands will touch it:
Take you, as 'twere, some distant knowledge of him;

---

[13]Folded.   [1]Danes.

As thus, *I know his father and his friends,*
15   *And in part him;*—do you mark this, Reynaldo?
REYNALDO: Ay, very well, my lord.
POLONIUS: *And in part him;*—*but,* you may say, *not well:*
    But if't be he I mean, he's very wild;
    Addicted so and so; and there put on him
20   What forgeries you please; marry, none so rank
    As may dishonor him; take heed of that;
    But, sir, such wanton, wild, and usual slips
    As are companions noted and most known
    To youth and liberty.
REYNALDO: As gaming, my lord.
25 **POLONIUS:**   Ay, or drinking, fencing, swearing, quarreling,
    Drabbing:[2]—you may go so far.
REYNALDO: My lord, that would dishonor him.
POLONIUS: Faith, no; as you may season it in the charge.
    You must not put another scandal on him,
30   That he is open to incontinency;
    That's not my meaning: but breathe his faults so quaintly
    That they may seem the taints of liberty;
    The flash and outbreak of a fiery mind;
    A savageness in unreclaimed blood,
35   Of general assault.
REYNALDO: But, my good lord,—
POLONIUS: Wherefore should you do this?
REYNALDO: Ay, my lord,
    I would know that.
POLONIUS: Marry, sir, here's my drift;
    And I believe it is a fetch of warrant:[3]
    You laying these slight sullies on my son.
40   As 'twere a thing a little soil'd i' the working,
    Mark you,
    Your party in converse, him you would sound,
    Having ever seen in the prenominate crimes
    The youth you breathe of guilty, be assur'd
45   He closes with you in this consequence;
    Good sir, or so; or *friend,* or *gentleman,*—
    According to the phrase or the addition[4]
    Of man and country.
REYNALDO: Very good, my lord.

---

[2]Going about with loose women.   [3]A good device.   [4]Form of address.

POLONIUS: And then, sir, does he this,—he does,—
50   What was I about to say?—By the mass, I was
About to say something:—where did I leave?
REYNALDO: At *closes in the consequence,*
At *friend or so,* and *gentleman.*
POLONIUS: At—closes in the consequence,—ay, marry;
55   He closes with you thus:—*I know the gentleman;*
I saw him yesterday, or t'other day,
Or then, or then; with such, or such; and, as you say,
There was he gaming; there o'ertook in's rouse;
There falling out at tennis: or perchance,
60   *I saw him enter such a house of sale,—*
Videlicet, a brothel,—or so forth.—
See you now;
Your bait of falsehood takes this carp of truth:
And thus do we of wisdom and of reach,
65   With windlasses, and with assays of bias,
By indirections find directions out:
So, by my former lecture and advice,
Shall you my son. You have me, have you not?
REYNALDO: My lord, I have.
POLONIUS: God b' wi' you; fare you well.
70 **REYNALDO:**   Good my lord!
POLONIUS: Observe his inclination in yourself.
REYNALDO: I shall, my lord.
POLONIUS: And let him ply his music.
REYNALDO: Well, my lord.
POLONIUS: Farewell!

(Exit Reynaldo.)

(Enter Ophelia.)

75   How now, Ophelia! what's the matter?
OPHELIA: Alas, my lord, I have been so affrighted.
POLONIUS: With what, i' the name of God?
OPHELIA: My lord, as I was sewing in my chamber,
Lord Hamlet,—with his doublet all unbrac'd;
80   No hat upon his head; his stockings foul'd,
Ungarter'd, and down-gyved[5] to his ankle;
Pale as his shirt; his knees knocking each other;
And with a look so piteous in purport

---

[5]Dangling like chains.

As if he had been loosed out of hell
85   To speak of horrors,—he comes before me.
POLONIUS: Mad for thy love?
OPHELIA: My lord, I do not know;
But truly I do fear it.
POLONIUS: What said he?
OPHELIA: He took me by the wrist, and held me hard;
Then goes he to the length of all his arm;
90   And with his other hand thus o'er his brow,
He falls to such perusal of my face
As he would draw it. Long stay'd he so;
At last,—a little shaking of mine arm,
And thrice his head thus waving up and down,—
95   He rais'd a sigh so piteous and profound
That it did seem to shatter all his bulk
And end his being; that done, he lets me go:
And, with his head over his shoulder turn'd,
He seem'd to find his way without his eyes;
100   For out o' doors he went without their help,
And to the last bended their light on me.
POLONIUS: Come, go with me: I will go seek the king.
This is the very ecstasy[6] of love;
Whose violent property fordoes itself,[7]
105 And leads the will to desperate undertakings,
As oft as any passion under heaven
That does afflict our nature. I am sorry,—
What, have you given him any hard words of late?
OPHELIA: No, my good lord; but, as you did command,
110 I did repel his letters, and denied
His access to me.
POLONIUS: That hath made him mad.
I am sorry that with better heed and judgment
I had not quoted him: I fear'd he did but trifle,
And meant to wreck thee; but, beshrew my jealousy!
115 It seems it is as proper to our age
To cast beyond ourselves in our opinions
As it is common for the younger sort
To lack discretion. Come, go we to the king:
This must be known; which, being kept close, might move
120 More grief to hide than hate to utter love.

(Exeunt.)

[6]Madness.   [7]Destroys itself.

SCENE II

A room in the castle.

(Enter King, Queen, Rosencrantz, Guildenstern, and Attendants.)

KING: Welcome, dear Rosencrantz and Guildenstern!
    Moreover that we much did long to see you,
    The need we have to use you did provoke
    Our hasty sending. Something have you heard
5   Of Hamlet's transformation; so I call it,
    Since nor the exterior nor the inward man
    Resembles that it was. What it should be,
    More than his father's death, that thus hath put him
    So much from the understanding of himself,
10   I cannot dream of: I entreat you both,
    That being of so young days brought up with him,
    And since so neighbor'd to his youth and humor,
    That you vouchsafe your rest here in our court
    Some little time: so by your companies
15   To draw him on to pleasures, and to gather,
    So much as from occasion you may glean,
    Whether aught, to us unknown, afflicts him thus,
    That, open'd, lies within our remedy.
  QUEEN: Good gentlemen, he hath much talk'd of you;
20   And sure I am two men there are not living
    To whom he more adheres. If it will please you
    To show us so much gentry and good-will
    As to expend your time with us awhile,
    For the supply and profit of our hope,
25   Your visitation shall receive such thanks
    As fits a king's remembrance.
  ROSENCRANTZ: Both your majesties
    Might, by the sovereign power you have of us,
    Put your dread pleasures more into command
    Than to entreaty.
  GUILDENSTERN: We both obey,
30   And here give up ourselves, in the full bent,
    To lay our service freely at your feet,
    To be commanded.
  KING: Thanks, Rosencrantz and gentle Guildenstern.
  QUEEN: Thanks, Guildenstern and gentle Rosencrantz:
35   And I beseech you instantly to visit
    My too-much-changed son.—Go, some of you,
    And bring these gentlemen where Hamlet is.

GUILDENSTERN: Heavens make our presence and our practices
　　Pleasant and helpful to him!
QUEEN:　　　　　　　　　　Ay, amen!

(Exeunt Rosencrantz, Guildenstern, and some Attendants.)

(Enter Polonius.)

40 **POLONIUS:** The ambassadors from Norway, my good lord,
　　Are joyfully return'd.
KING: Thou still has been the father of good news.
POLONIUS: Have I, my lord? Assure you, my good liege,
　　I hold my duty, as I hold my soul,
45　　Both to my God and to my gracious king:
　　And I do think,—or else this brain of mine
　　Hunts not the trail of policy[1] so sure
　　As it hath us'd to do,—that I have found
　　The very cause of Hamlet's lunacy.
50 **KING:** O, speak of that; that do I long to hear.
POLONIUS: Give first admittance to the ambassadors;
　　My news shall be the fruit to that great feast.
KING: Thyself do grace to them, and bring them in.

(Exit Polonius.)

　　He tells me, my sweet queen, that he hath found
55　　The head and source of all your son's distemper.
QUEEN: I doubt it is no other but the main,—
　　His father's death and our o'erhasty marriage.
KING: Well, we shall sift him.

(Re-enter Polonius, with Voltimand and Cornelius.)

　　　　　　　　　　Welcome, my good friends!
　　Say, Voltimand, what from our brother Norway?
60 **VOLTIMAND:** Most fair return of greetings and desires.
　　Upon our first, he sent out to suppress
　　His nephew's levies; which to him appear'd
　　To be a preparation 'gainst the Polack;
　　But, better look'd into, he truly found
65　　It was against your highness: whereat griev'd,—
　　That so his sickness, age, and impotence
　　Was falsely borne in hand,—sends out arrests
　　On Fortinbras; which he, in brief, obeys;
　　Receives rebuke from Norway; and, in fine,
70　　Makes vows before his uncle never more

---

[1]Statecraft.

To give the assay of arms against your majesty.
Whereon old Norway, overcome with joy,
Gives him three thousand crowns in annual fee;
And his commission to employ those soldiers,
75 So levied as before, against the Polack:
With an entreaty, herein further shown *(gives a paper)*
That it might please you to give quiet pass
Through your dominions for this enterprise,
On such regards of safety and allowance
80 As therein are set down.
   KING: It likes us well;
And at our more consider'd time we'll read,
Answer, and think upon this business.
Meantime we thank you for your well-took labor:
Go to your rest; at night we'll feast together:
85 Most welcome home!

(Exeunt Voltimand and Cornelius.)

   POLONIUS: This business is well ended.—
My liege, and madam,—to expostulate
What majesty should be, what duty is,
Why day is day, night night, and time is time,
Were nothing but to waste night, day, and time.
90 Therefore, since brevity is the soul of wit,
And tediousness the limbs and outward flourishes,
I will be brief:—your noble son is mad:
Mad call I it; for to define true madness,
What is't but to be nothing else but mad?
95 But let that go.
   QUEEN: More matter with less art.
   POLONIUS: Madam, I swear I use no art at all.
That he is mad, 'tis true 'tis pity;
And pity 'tis 'tis true: a foolish figure;
But farewell it, for I will use no art.
100 Mad let us grant him, then: and now remains
That we find out the cause of this effect;
Or rather say, the cause of this defect,
For this effect defective comes by cause:
Thus it remains, and the remainder thus.
105 Perpend.
I have a daughter,—have whilst she is mine,—
Who, in her duty and obedience, mark,
Hath given me this: now gather, and surmise

(Reads)

To the celestial, and my soul's idol, the most beautified Ophelia,—

110 That's an ill phrase, a vile phrase,—*beautified* is a vile phrase: but
you shall hear. Thus:

(Reads)

In her excellent white bosom, these, &c.
QUEEN: Came this from Hamlet to her?
POLONIUS: Good madam, stay a while; I will be faithful.

(Reads)

115   *Doubt thou the stars are fire;*
         Doubt that the sun doth move;
         Doubt truth to be a liar;
         But never doubt I love.
         O dear Ophelia, I am ill at these numbers,
120   *I have not art to reckon my groans: but that I love thee best, O most*
         best, believe it. Adieu.
         Thine evermore, most dear lady, whilst this machine is to him, Hamlet
         This, in obedience, hath my daughter show'd me:
         And more above, hath his solicitings,
125   As they fell out by time, by means, and place,
         All given to mine ear.
KING: But how hath she
         Receiv'd his love?
POLONIUS: What do you think of me?
KING: As of a man faithful and honorable.
POLONIUS: I would fain prove so. But what might you think,
130   When I had seen this hot love on the wing,—
         As I perceiv'd it, I must tell you that,
         Before my daughter told me,—what might you,
         Or my dear majesty your queen here, think,
         If I had play'd the desk or table-book;[2]
135   Or given my heart a winking, mute and dumb;
         Or look'd upon this love with idle sight;—
         What might you think? No, I went round to work,
         And my young mistress thus I did bespeak:
         Lord Hamlet is a prince out of thy sphere;
140   *This must not be:* and then I precepts gave her,
         That she should lock herself from his resort,
         Admit no messengers, receive no tokens.
         Which done, she took the fruits of my advice;
         And he, repulsed,—a short tale to make,—

[2]Memorandum pad.

145 Fell into a sadness; then into a fast;
Thence to a watch; thence into a weakness;
Thence to a lightness; and, by this declension,
Into the madness wherein now he raves
And all we wail for.

KING: Do you think 'tis this?

150 **QUEEN:** It may be, very likely.

POLONIUS: Hath there been such a time,—I'd fain know that,—
That I have positively said, *'Tis so,*
When it prov'd otherwise?

KING: Not that I know.

POLONIUS: Take this from this, if this be otherwise: *(Pointing to his head and shoulder)*

155 If circumstances lead me, I will find
Where truth is hid, though it were hid indeed
Within the center.

KING: How may we try it further?

POLONIUS: You know, sometimes he walks for hours together
Here in the lobby.

QUEEN: So he does, indeed.

160 **POLONIUS:** At such a time I'll loose my daughter to him:
Be you and I behind an arras[3] then;
Mark the encounter: if he love her not,
And be not from his reason fall'n thereon,
Let me be no assistant for a state,

165 But keep a farm and carters.

KING: We will try it.

QUEEN: But look, where sadly the poor wretch comes reading.

POLONIUS: Away, I do beseech you, both away:
I'll board[4] him presently:—O, give me leave.

(Exeunt King, Queen, and Attendants.)

(Enter Hamlet, reading.)

How does my good Lord Hamlet?

170 **HAMLET:** Well, God-a-mercy.

POLONIUS: Do you know me, my lord?

HAMLET: Excellent, excellent well; you're a fishmonger.

POLONIUS: Not I, my lord.

HAMLET: Then I would you were so honest a man.

175 **POLONIUS:** Honest, my lord!

HAMLET: Ay, sir; to be honest, as this world goes, is to be one man picked
out of ten thousand.

---

[3]Tapestry, hung some distance away from a wall. [4]Address.

POLONIUS: That's very true, my lord.

HAMLET: For if the sun breed maggots in a dead dog, being a god kissing
180 carrion,—Have you a daughter?

POLONIUS: I have, my lord.

HAMLET: Let her not walk i' the sun: conception is a blessing; but not as
your daughter may conceive:—friend, look to't.

POLONIUS: How say you by that?—*(Aside)* Still harping on my daughter:—
185 yet he knew me not at first; he said I was a fishmonger: he is far gone, far
gone: and truly in my youth I suffered much extremity for love; very near
this. I'll speak to him again.—What do you read, my lord?

HAMLET: Words, words, words.

POLONIUS: What is the matter, my lord?

190 **HAMLET:** Between who?

POLONIUS: I mean, the matter that you read, my lord.

HAMLET: Slanders, sir: for the satirical slave says here that old men have
gray beards; that their faces are wrinkled; their eyes purging thick amber
and plum-tree gum; and that they have a plentiful lack of wit, together
195 with most weak hams: all which, sir, though I most powerfully and po-
tently believe, yet I hold it not honesty to have it thus set down; for you
yourself, sir, should be old as I am, if, like a crab, you could go backward.

POLONIUS: *(Aside)* Though this be madness, yet there is method in't.—Will
you walk out of the air, my lord?

200 **HAMLET:** Into my grave?

POLONIUS: Indeed, that is out o' the air.—*(Aside)* How pregnant[5] sometimes
his replies are! a happiness that often madness hits on, which reason and
sanity could not so prosperously be delivered of. I will leave him, and suddenly contrive the means of meeting between him and my daughter.—
205 More honorable lord, I will most humbly take my leave of you.

HAMLET: You cannot, sir, take from me anything that I will more willingly
part withal,—except my life, except my life, except my life.

POLONIUS: Fare you well, my lord.

HAMLET: These tedious old fools!

(Enter Rosencrantz and Guildenstern.)

210 **POLONIUS:** You go to seek the Lord Hamlet; there he is.

ROSENCRANTZ: *(To Polonius)* God save you, sir!

(Exit Polonius.)

GUILDENSTERN: Mine honored lord!

ROSENCRANTZ: My most dear lord!

HAMLET: My excellent good friends! How dost thou, Guildenstern? Ah,
215 Rosencrantz? Good lads, how do ye both?

ROSENCRANTZ: As the indifferent children of the earth.

[5]Ready, and clever.

GUILDENSTERN: Happy in that we are not overhappy; on fortune's cap we are not the very button.

HAMLET: Nor the soles of her shoe?

220 **ROSENCRANTZ:** Neither, my lord.

HAMLET: Then you live about her waist, or in the middle of her favors?

GUILDENSTERN: Faith, her privates we.

HAMLET: In the secret parts of fortune? O, most true; she is a strumpet. What's the news?

225 **ROSENCRANTZ:** None, my lord, but that the world's grown honest.

HAMLET: Then is doomsday near: but your news is not true. Let me question more in particular: what have you, my good friends, deserved at the hands of fortune, that she sends you to prison hither?

GUILDENSTERN: Prison, my lord!

230 **HAMLET:** Denmark's a prison.

ROSENCRANTZ: Then is the world one.

HAMLET: A goodly one; in which there are many confines, wards, and dungeons, Denmark being one o' the worst.

ROSENCRANTZ: We think not so, my lord.

235 **HAMLET:** Why, then, 'tis none to you; for there is nothing either good or bad, but thinking makes it so: to me it is a prison.

ROSENCRANTZ: Why, then, your ambition makes it one; 'tis too narrow for your mind.

HAMLET: O God, I could be bounded in a nutshell, and count myself a king
240   of infinite space, were it not that I have bad dreams.

GUILDENSTERN: Which dreams, indeed, are ambition; for the very substance of the ambitious is merely the shadow of a dream.

HAMLET: A dream itself is but a shadow.

ROSENCRANTZ: Truly, and I hold ambition of so airy and light a quality that
245   it is but a shadow's shadow.

HAMLET: Then are our beggars bodies, and our monarchs and outstretched heroes the beggars' shadows. Shall we to the court? for, by my fay, I cannot reason.

ROSENCRANTZ and **GUILDENSTERN:** We'll wait upon you.

250 **HAMLET:** No such matter: I will not sort you with the rest of my servants; for, to speak to you like an honest man, I am most dreadfully attended. But, in the beaten way of friendship, what make you at Elsinore?

ROSENCRANTZ: To visit you, my lord; no other occasion.

HAMLET: Beggar that I am, I am even poor in thanks; but I thank you: and
255   sure, dear friends, my thanks are too dear a halfpenny. Were you not sent for? Is it your own inclining? Is it a free visitation? Come, deal justly with me: come, come; nay, speak.

GUILDENSTERN: What should we say, my lord?

HAMLET: Why, anything—but to the purpose. You were sent for; and there
260   is a kind of confession in your looks, which your modesties have not craft enough to color: I know the good king and queen have sent for you.

ROSENCRANTZ: To what end, my lord?

HAMLET: That you must teach me. But let me conjure you, by the rights of our fellowship, by the consonancy of our youth, by the obligation of our
265 ever-preserved love, and by what more dear a better proposer could charge you withal, be even and direct with me, whether you were sent for or no?

ROSENCRANTZ: What say you? *(To Guildenstern)*

HAMLET: *(Aside)* Nay, then, I have an eye of you.—If you love me, hold not
270 off.

GUILDENSTERN: My lord, we were sent for.

HAMLET: I will tell you why; so shall my anticipation prevent your discovery, and your secrecy to the king and queen moult no feather. I have of late,—but wherefore I know not,—lost all my mirth, forgone all custom of
275 exercises; and, indeed, it goes so heavily with my disposition that this goodly frame, the earth, seems to me a sterile promontory; this most excellent canopy, the air, look you, this brave o'erhanging firmament, this majestical roof fretted[6] with golden fire,—why, it appears no other thing to me than a foul and pestilent congregation of vapors. What a piece of
280 work is man! How noble in reason! how infinite in faculties! in form and moving, how express and admirable! in action, how like an angel! in apprehension, how like a god! the beauty of the world! the paragon of animals! And yet, to me, what is this quintessence of dust? man delights not me; no, nor woman neither, though by your smiling you seem to say so.

285 **ROSENCRANTZ:** My lord, there was no such stuff in my thoughts.

HAMLET: Why did you laugh, then, when I said, *Man delights not me?*

ROSENCRANTZ: To think, my lord, if you delight not in man, what lenten entertainment[7] the players shall receive from you: we coted[8] them on the way; and hither are they coming, to offer you service.

290 **HAMLET:** He that plays the king shall be welcome,—his majesty shall have tribute of me; the adventurous knight shall use his foil and target; the lover shall not sigh gratis; the humorous[9] man shall end his part in peace; the clown shall make those laugh whose lungs are tickled o' the sere;[10] and the lady shall say her mind freely, or the blank verse shall halt[11]
295 for't.—What players are they?

ROSENCRANTZ: Even those you were wont to take delight in,—the tragedians of the city.

HAMLET: How chances it they travel? their residence, both in reputation and profit, was better both ways.

300 **ROSENCRANTZ:** I think their inhibition[12] comes by the means of the late innovation.

---

[6]A roof with fretwork.   [7]Poor reception.   [8]Passed.   [9]Eccentric.   [10]Whose lungs, for laughter, are easily tickled.   [11]Limp.   [12]Difficulty, preventing them from remaining in the capital.

HAMLET: Do they hold the same estimation they did when I was in the city? Are they so followed?

ROSENCRANTZ: No, indeed, they are not.

305 **HAMLET:** How comes it? do they grow rusty?

ROSENCRANTZ: Nay, their endeavor keeps in the wonted pace; but there is, sir, an aery[13] of children, little eyases,[14] that cry out on the top of question, and are most tyrannically clapped for't: these are now the fashion; and so berattle the common stages,—so they call them,—that many wear-

310 ing rapiers are afraid of goose-quills, and dare scarce come thither.

HAMLET: What, are they children? who maintains 'em? how are they escoted?[15] Will they pursue the quality[16] no longer than they can sing? will they not say afterwards, if they should grow themselves to common players,—as it is most like, if their means are no better,—their writers do

315 them wrong, to make them exclaim against their own succession?

ROSENCRANTZ: Faith, there has been much to do on both sides; and the nation holds it no sin to tarre[17] them to controversy: there was for awhile no money bid for argument, unless the poet and the player went to cuffs in the question.

320 **HAMLET:** Is't possible?

GUILDENSTERN: O, there has been much throwing about of brains.

HAMLET: Do the boys carry it away?

ROSENCRANTZ: Ay, that they do, my lord; Hercules and his load[18] too.

HAMLET: It is not strange; for mine uncle is king of Denmark, and those

325 that would make mouths at him while my father lived, give twenty, forty, fifty, an hundred ducats a-piece for his picture in little. 'Sblood, there is something in this more than natural, if philosophy could find it out.

(Flourish of trumpets within.)

GUILDENSTERN: There are the players.

HAMLET: Gentlemen, you are welcome to Elsinore. Your hands, come: the

330 appurtenance of welcome is fashion and ceremony: let me comply with you in this garb; lest my extent[19] to the players, which, I tell you, must show fairly outward, should more appear like entertainment[20] than yours. You are welcome: but my uncle-father and aunt-mother are deceived.

GUILDENSTERN: In what, my dear lord?

335 **HAMLET:** I am but mad north-north-west: when the wind is southerly I know a hawk from a handsaw.

(Enter Polonius.)

---

[13]Aery: brood of birds of prey.   [14]Young hawks; a reference to the boys' companies that became popular rivals of Shakespeare's company of players.   [15]Financially supported.
[16]Profession.   [17]Egg them on.   [18]The globe, or the world.   [19]Show of friendliness.
[20]Welcome.

POLONIUS: Well be with you, gentlemen!

HAMLET: Hark you, Guildenstern;—and you too;—at each ear a hearer: that great baby you see there is not yet out of his swathing-clouts.

340 **ROSENCRANTZ:** Happily he's the second time come to them; for they say an old man is twice a child.

HAMLET: I will prophesy he comes to tell me of the players; mark it.—You say right, sir: o' Monday morning; 'twas so indeed.

POLONIUS: My lord, I have news to tell you.

345 **HAMLET:** My lord, I have news to tell you. When Roscius was an actor in Rome,—

POLONIUS: The actors are come hither, my lord.

HAMLET: Buzz, buzz!

POLONIUS: Upon mine honor,—

350 **HAMLET:** Then came each actor on his ass,—

POLONIUS: The best actors in the world, either for tragedy, comedy, history, pastoral, pastoral-comical, historical-pastoral, tragical-historical, tragical-comical-historical-pastoral, scene individable,[21] or poem unlimited:[22] Seneca cannot be too heavy nor Plautus too light. For the law of
355 writ and the liberty,[23] these are the only men.

HAMLET: O Jephthah, judge of Israel, what a treasure hadst thou!

POLONIUS: What a treasure had he, my lord?

HAMLET: Why—

> One fair daughter, and no more,
360 > The which he loved passing well.

POLONIUS: *(Aside)* Still on my daughter.

HAMLET: Am I not i' the right, old Jephthah?

POLONIUS: If you call me Jephthah, my lord, I have a daughter that I love passing well.

365 **HAMLET:** Nay, that follows not.

POLONIUS: What follows, then, my lord?

HAMLET: Why—

> As by lot, God wot,

and then, you know,

370 > It came to pass, as most like it was,—

the first row of the pious chanson will show you more; for look where my abridgement comes.

(Enter four or five Players.)

---

[21]A play that observes the unities of time and place.   [22]A typical multiscened Elizabethan type of drama, not restricted by the unities. Examples are *Hamlet, Macbeth, King Lear,* and virtually any other play by Shakespeare.   [23]For the laws of the unities and for playwriting that is not so restricted.

You are welcome, masters; welcome, all:—I am glad to see thee well:—
welcome, good friends.—O, my old friend! Thy face is valanced since I
375   saw thee last; comest thou to beard me in Denmark?—What, my young
lady and mistress! By'r lady, your ladyship is nearer heaven than when I
saw you last, by the altitude of a chopine.[24] Pray God, your voice, like a
piece of uncurrent gold, be not cracked within the ring.—Masters, you
are all welcome. We'll e'en to't like French falconers, fly at anything we
380   see: we'll have a speech straight: come, give us a taste of your quality;
come, a passionate speech.

1ST PLAYER: What speech, my lord?

HAMLET: I heard thee speak me a speech once,—but it was never acted; or,
if it was, not above once; for the play, I remember, pleased not the million;
385   'twas caviare to the general: but it was,—as I received it, and others whose
judgments in such matters cried in the top of mine,—an excellent play,
well digested in the scenes, set down with as much modesty as cunning.
I remember, one said there were no sallets in the lines to make the matter
savory, nor no matter in the phrase that might indite the author of affect-
390   tion; but called it an honest method, as wholesome as sweet, and by very
much more handsome than fine. One speech in it I chiefly loved: 'twas Ae-
neas' tale to Dido; and thereabout of it especially where he speaks of
Priam's slaughter: if it live in your memory, begin at this line;—let me see,
let me see:—

395   The rugged Pyrrhus, like the Hyrcanian beast,[25]

—it is not so:—it begins with Pyrrhus:—

The rugged Pyrrhus,—he whose sable arms,
Black as his purpose, did the night resemble
When he lay couched in the ominous horse,—
400   Hath now this dread and black complexion smear'd
With heraldry more dismal; head to foot
Now is he total gules; horridly trick'd
With blood of fathers, mothers, daughters, sons,
Bak'd and impasted with the parching streets,
405   That lend a tyrannous and damned light
To their vile murders: roasted in wrath and fire,
And thus o'er-sized with coagulate gore,
With eyes like carbuncles, the hellish Pyrrhus
Old grandsire Priam seeks.—
410   So proceed you.

---

[24]A wooden stilt more than a foot high used under a woman's shoe; a Venetian fashion introduced into England.   [25]This speech is an example of the declamatory style of drama,
which Shakespeare surely must have considered outmoded.

POLONIUS: 'Fore God, my lord, well spoken, with good accent and good discretion.

1ST PLAYER: Anon he finds him
  Striking too short at Greeks; his antique sword,
415   Rebellious to his arm, lies where it falls,
  Repugnant to command: unequal match'd,
  Pyrrhus at Priam drives; in rage strikes wide;
  But with the whiff and wind of his fell sword
  The unnerved father falls. Then senseless Ilium,
420   Seeming to feel this blow, with flaming top
  Stoops to his base; and with a hideous crash
  Takes prisoner Pyrrhus' ear: for, lo! his sword,
  Which was declining on the milky head
  Of reverend Priam, seem'd i' the air to stick:
425   So, as a painted tyrant, Pyrrhus stood;
  And, like a neutral to his will and matter,
  Did nothing.
  But as we often see, against some storm,
  A silence in the heavens, the rack stand still,
430   The blood winds speechless, and the orb below
  As hush as death, anon the dreadful thunder
  Doth rend the region; so, after Pyrrhus' pause,
  A roused vengeance sets him new a-work;
  And never did the Cyclops' hammers fall
435   On Mars his armor, forg'd for proof eterne,
  With less remorse than Pyrrhus' bleeding sword
  Now falls on Priam.—
  Out, out, thou strumpet, Fortune! All you gods,
  In general synod, take away her power;
440   Break all the spokes and fellies from her wheel,
  And bowl the round knave down the hill of heaven,
  As low as to the fiends!

POLONIUS: This is too long.

HAMLET: It shall to the barber's, with your beard.—Pr'ythee, say on.—He's
445   for a jig, or a tale of bawdry, or he sleeps:—say on; come to Hecuba.

1ST PLAYER: But who, O, who had seen the mobled queen,—

HAMLET: *The mobled queen?*

POLONIUS: That's good; *mobled queen* is good.

1ST PLAYER: Run barefoot up and down, threatening the flames
450   With bissom rheum; a clout upon that head
  Where late the diadem stood; and, for a robe,
  About her lank and all o'er-teemed loins,
  A blanket, in the alarm of fear caught up;—
  Who this had seen, with tongue in venom steep'd,
455   'Gainst Fortune's state would treason have pronounc'd:
  But if the gods themselves did see her then,

When she saw Pyrrhus make malicious sport
In mincing with his sword her husband's limbs,
The instant burst of clamor that she made,—
460 Unless things mortal move them not at all,—
Would have made milch the burning eyes of heaven,
And passion in the gods.

POLONIUS: Look, whether he has not turn'd his color, and has tears in's eyes.—Pray you, no more.

465 **HAMLET:** 'Tis well; I'll have thee speak out the rest soon.—Good my lord, will you see the players well bestowed? Do you hear, let them be well used; for they are the abstracts and brief chronicles of the time; after your death you were better have a bad epitaph than their ill report while you live.

470 **POLONIUS:** My lord, I will use them according to their desert.

HAMLET: Odd's bodikin, man, better: use every man after his desert, and who should scape whipping? Use them after your own honor and dignity: the less they deserve the more merit is in your bounty. Take them in.

POLONIUS: Come, sirs.

475 **HAMLET:** Follow him, friends: we'll hear a play to-morrow.

(Exit Polonius with all the Players but the First.)

Dost thou hear me, old friend; can you play the Murder of Gonzago?

1ST PLAYER: Ay, my lord.

HAMLET: We'll ha't to-morrow night. You could, for a need, study a speech of some dozen or sixteen lines which I would set down and insert in't?
480 could you not?

1ST PLAYER: Ay, my lord.

HAMLET: Very well.—Follow that lord; and look you mock him not.

(Exit First Player.)

—My good friends, *(to Rosencrantz and Guildenstern)* I'll leave you till night: you are welcome to Elsinore.

485 **ROSENCRANTZ:** Good my lord!

(Exeunt Rosencrantz and Guildenstern.)

HAMLET: Ay, so God b' wi' ye!—Now I am alone.
O, what a rogue[26] and pleasant slave am I!
Is it not monstrous that this player here,
But in a fiction, in a dream of passion,
490 Could force his soul so to his own conceit[27]
That from her working all his visage wan'd;
Tears in his eyes, distraction in's aspéct,
A broken voice, and his whole function suiting

---

[26]Wretched creature.   [27]Conception.

With forms to his conceit? And all for nothing!
495 For Hecuba?
What's Hecuba to him or he to Hecuba,
That he should weep for her? What would he do,
Had he the motive and the cue for passion
That I have? He would drown the stage with tears,
500 And cleave the general ear with horrid speech;
Make mad the guilty, and appal the free;
Confound the ignorant, and amaze, indeed,
The very faculties of eyes and ears.
Yet I,
505 A dull and muddy-mettled rascal, peak,
Like John-a-dreams, unpregnant of my cause,
And can say nothing; no, not for a king
Upon whose property and most dear life
A damn'd defeat was made. Am I a coward?
510 Who calls me villain? breaks my pate across?
Plucks off my beard and blows it in my face?
Tweaks me by the nose? gives me the lie i' the throat,
As deep as to the lungs? who does me this, ha?
'Swounds, I should take it: for it cannot be
515 But I am pigeon-liver'd, and lack gall
To make oppression bitter; or ere this
I should have fatted all the region kites
With this slave's offal:—bloody, bawdy villain!
Remorseless, treacherous, lecherous, kindless villain!
520 O, vengeance!
Why, what an ass am I! This is most brave,
That I, the son of a dear father murder'd,
Prompted to my revenge by heaven and hell,
Must, like a whore, unpack my heart with words,
525 And fall a-cursing like a very drab,
A scullion!
Fie upon't! foh!—About, my brain! I have heard
That guilty creatures, sitting at a play,
Have by the very cunning of the scene
530 Been struck so to the soul that presently
They have proclaim'd their malefactions;
For murder, though it have no tongue, will speak
With most miraculous organ. I'll have these players
Play something like the murder of my father
535 Before mine uncle: I'll observe his looks;
I'll tent[28] him to the quick: if he but blench,

---

[28]Probe.

I know my course. The spirit that I have seen
May be the devil: and the devil hath power
To assume a pleasing shape; yea, and perhaps
540   Out of my weakness and my melancholy,—
As he is very potent with such spirits,—
Abuses me to damn me: I'll have grounds
More relative than this:—the play's the thing
Wherein I'll catch the conscience of the king. *(Exit.)*

Act III

SCENE I

A room in the castle.

(Enter King, Queen, Polonius, Ophelia, Rosencrantz, and Guildenstern.)

KING: And can you, by no drift of circumstance,
Get from him why he puts on this confusion,
Grating so harshly all his days of quiet
With turbulent and dangerous lunacy?
5   ROSENCRANTZ: He does confess he feels himself distracted;
But from what cause he will by no means speak.
GUILDENSTERN: Nor do we find him forward to be sounded;
But, with a crafty madness, keeps aloof
When we would bring him on to some confession
10   Of his true state.
QUEEN: Did he receive you well?
ROSENCRANTZ: Most like a gentleman.
GUILDENSTERN: But with much forcing of his disposition.
ROSENCRANTZ: Niggard of question; but, of our demands,
Most free in his reply.
QUEEN: Did you assay him
15   To any pastime?
ROSENCRANTZ: Madam, it so fell out that certain players
We o'er-raught on the way: of these we told him;
And there did seem in him a kind of joy
To hear of it: they are about the court;
20   And, as I think, they have already order
This night to play before him.
POLONIUS: 'Tis most true:
And he beseech'd me to entreat your majesties
To hear and see the matter.
KING: With all my heart; and it doth much content me
25   To hear him so inclin'd.

Good gentlemen, give him a further edge,
And drive his purpose on to these delights.
ROSENCRANTZ: We shall, my lord.

(Exeunt Rosencrantz and Guildenstern.)

KING: Sweet Gertrude, leave us too;
For we have closely sent for Hamlet hither
30   That he, as 'twere by accident, may here
Affront Ophelia:
Her father and myself,—lawful espials,[1]—
Will so bestow ourselves that, seeing, unseen,
We may of their encounter frankly judge;
35   And gather by him, as he is behav'd,
If 't be the affliction of his love or no
That thus he suffers for.
QUEEN: I shall obey you:—
And for your part, Ophelia, I do wish
That your good beauties be the happy cause
40   Of Hamlet's wildness: so shall I hope your virtues
Will bring him to his wonted way again,
To both your honors.
OPHELIA: Madam, I wish it may.

(Exit Queen.)

POLONIUS: Ophelia, walk you here.—Gracious, so please you,
We will bestow ourselves.—*(To Ophelia)* Read on this book;
45   That show of such an exercise may color
Your loneliness.—We are oft to blame in this,—
'Tis too much prov'd,—that with devotion's visage
And pious action we do sugar o'er
The devil himself.
KING: *(Aside)*   O, 'tis too true!
50   How smart a lash that speech doth give my conscience!
The harlot's cheek, beautied with plastering art,
Is not more ugly to the thing that helps it
Than is my deed to my most painted word:
O heavy burden!
55 **POLONIUS:**   I hear him coming: let's withdraw, my lord.

(Exeunt King and Polonius.)

(Enter Hamlet.)

---

[1]Spies.

HAMLET: To be, or not to be,—that is the question:
Whether 'tis nobler in the mind to suffer
The slings and arrows of outrageous fortune,
Or to take arms against a sea of troubles,
60   And by opposing end them?—To die,—to sleep,—
No more; and by a sleep to say we end
The heart-ache and the thousand natural shocks
That flesh is heir to,—'tis a consummation
Devoutly to be wish'd. To die,—to sleep;—
65   To sleep! perchance to dream:—ay, there's the rub;
For in that sleep of death what dreams may come,
When we have shuffled off this mortal coil,
Must give us pause: there's the respect
That makes a calamity of so long life;
70   For who would bear the whips and scorns of time,
The oppressor's wrong, the proud man's contumely,
The pangs of déspis'd love, the law's delay,
The insolence of office, and the spurns
That patient merit of the unworthy takes,
75   When he himself might his quietus make
With a bare bodkin?[2] who would fardels[3] bear,
To grunt[4] and sweat under a weary life,
But that the dread of something after death,—
The undiscover'd country, from whose bourn[5]
80   No traveler returns,—puzzles the will,
And makes us rather bear those ills we have
Than to fly to others that we know not of?
Thus conscience does make cowards of us all;
And thus the native hue of resolution
85   Is sicklied o'er with the pale cast of thought;
And enterprises of great pith and moment,
With this regard, their currents turn awry,
And lose the name of action.—Soft you now!
The fair Ophelia.—Nymph, in thy orisons[6]
90   Be all my sins remember'd.
OPHELIA: Good my lord,
How does your honor for this many a day?
HAMLET: I humbly thank you; well, well, well.
OPHELIA: My lord, I have remembrances of yours,
That I have longed long to re-deliver;
95   I pray you, now receive them.
HAMLET: No, not I;
I never gave you aught.

---

[2]Stiletto.   [3]Burdens.   [4]Groan.   [5]Boundary.   [6]Prayers.

OPHELIA: My honor'd lord, you know right well you did;
And with them, words of so sweet breath compos'd
As made the things more rich: their perfume lost,
100   Take these again; for to the noble mind
Rich gifts wax poor when givers prove unkind.
There, my lord.

HAMLET: Ha, ha! are you honest?

OPHELIA: My lord?

105 **HAMLET:** Are you fair?

OPHELIA: What means your lordship?

HAMLET: That if you be honest and fair, your honesty should admit no discourse to your beauty.

OPHELIA: Could beauty, my lord, have better commerce than with honesty?

110 **HAMLET:** Ay, truly; for the power of beauty will sooner transform honesty from what it is to a bawd than the force of honesty can translate beauty into his likeness: this was sometime a paradox, but now the time gives it proof. I did love you once.

OPHELIA: Indeed, my lord, you made me believe so.

115 **HAMLET:** You should not have believed me; for virtue cannot so inoculate our old stock but we shall relish of it: I loved you not.

OPHELIA: I was the more deceived.

HAMLET: Get thee to a nunnery: why wouldst thou be a breeder of sinners? I am myself indifferent[7] honest; but yet I could accuse me of such things
120   that it were better my mother had not borne me: I am very proud, revengeful, ambitious; with more offences at my beck than I have thoughts to put them in, imagination to give them shape, or time to act them in. What should such fellows as I do crawling between heaven and earth? We are arrant knaves, all; believe none of us. Go thy ways to a nunnery.
125   Where's your father?

OPHELIA: At home, my lord.

HAMLET: Let the doors be shut upon him, that he may play the fool nowhere but in's own house. Farewell.

OPHELIA: O, help him, you sweet heavens!

130 **HAMLET:** If thou dost marry, I'll give thee this plague for thy dowry,—be thou as chaste as ice, as pure as snow, thou shalt not escape calumny. Get thee to a nunnery, go: farewell. Or, if thou wilt needs marry, marry a fool; for wise men know well enough what monsters you make of them. To a nunnery, go; and quickly too. Farewell.

135 **OPHELIA:** O heavenly powers, restore him!

HAMLET: I have heard of your paintings too, well enough; God has given you one face and you make yourselves another: you jig, you amble, and you lisp, and nickname God's creatures, and make your wantonness your ignorance. Go to, I'll no more on't; it hath made me mad. I say, we will

[7]Tolerably.

140 have no more marriages: those that are married already, all but one, shall
live; the rest shall keep as they are. To a nunnery, go. *(Exit.)*

OPHELIA: O, what a noble mind is here o'erthrown!
The courtier's, soldier's, scholar's eye, tongue, sword:
The expectancy and rose of the fair state,
145 The glass of fashion and the mould of form,
The observ'd of all observers,—quite, quite down!
And I, of ladies most deject and wretched
That suck'd the honey of his music vows,
Now see that noble and most sovereign reason,
150 Like sweet bells jangled, out of tune and harsh;
That unmatch'd form and feature of blown[8] youth
Blasted with ecstasy: O, woe is me,
To have seen what I have seen, see what I see!

(Re-enter King and Polonius.)

KING: Love! his affections do not that way tend;
155 Nor what he spake, though it lack'd form a little,
Was not like madness. There's something in his soul
O'er which his melancholy sits on brood;
And I do doubt[9] the hatch and the disclose
Will be some danger: which for to prevent,
160 I have in quick determination
Thus set it down:—he shall with speed to England
For the demand of our neglected tribute:
Haply, the seas and countries different,
With variable objects, shall expel
165 This something-settled matter in his heart;
Whereon his brains still beating puts him thus
From fashion of himself. What think you on't?

POLONIUS: It shall do well: but yet do I believe
The origin and commencement of his grief
170 Sprung from neglected love.—How now, Ophelia!
You need not tell us what Lord Hamlet said;
We heard it all.—My lord, do as you please;
But if you hold it fit, after the play,
Let his queen mother all alone entreat him
175 To show his grief: let her be round with him;
And I'll be plac'd, so please you, in the ear
Of all their conference. If she finds him not,[10]
To England send him; or confine him where
Your wisdom best shall think.

---

[8]Full-blown. [9]Fear. [10]Does not find him out.

KING: It shall be so:
180   Madness in great ones must not unwatch'd go.

(Exeunt.)

SCENE II

A hall in the castle.

(Enter Hamlet and certain Players.)

HAMLET: Speak the speech, I pray you, as I pronounced it to you, trippingly
on the tongue: but if you mouth it, as many of your players do, I had as lief
the town-crier spoke my lines. Nor do not saw the air too much with your
hand, thus; but use all gently: for in the very torrent, tempest, and, as I may
5   say, the whirlwind of passion, you must acquire and beget a temperance
that may give it smoothness. O, it offends me to the soul, to hear a robustious periwigpated fellow tear a passion to tatters, to very rags, to split the
ears of the groundlings, who, for the most part, are capable of nothing but
inexplicable dumb shows and noise: I could have such a fellow whipped
10   for o'erdoing Termagant;[1] it out-herods Herod:[2] pray you, avoid it.
1ST PLAYER: I warrant your honor.
HAMLET: Be not too tame neither, but let your own discretion be your
tutor; suit the action to the word, the word to the action; with this special
observance, that you o'erstep not the modesty of nature: for anything so
15   overdone is from the purpose of playing, whose end, both at the first and
now, was and is, to hold, as 'twere, the mirror up to nature; to show
virtue her own feature, scorn her own image, and the very age and body
of the time his form and pressure. Now, this overdone or come tardy off,
though it make the unskilful laugh, cannot but make the judicious grieve;
20   the censure of the which one must, in your allowance, o'erweigh a whole
theater of others. O, there be players that I have seen play,—and heard
others praise, and that highly,—not to speak it profanely, that, neither
having the accent of Christians, nor the gait of Christian, pagan, nor man,
have so strutted and bellowed that I have thought some of nature's
25   journeymen had made men, and not made them well, they imitated humanity so abominably.
1ST PLAYER: I hope we have reformed that indifferently with us, sir.
HAMLET: O, reform it altogether. And let those that play your clowns speak
no more than is set down for them: for there be of them that will them-
30   selves laugh, to set on some quantity of barren spectators to laugh too;
though, in the meantime, some necessary question of the play be then to

---

[1]A violent pagan deity, supposedly Mohammedan.   [2]Outrants the ranting Herod, who figures in medieval drama.

be considered: that's villainous, and shows a most pitiful ambition in the
fool that uses it. Go, make you ready.

(Exeunt Players.)

(Enter Polonius, Rosencrantz, and Guildenstern.)

How now, my lord! will the king hear this piece of work?
35 **POLONIUS:**   And the queen, too, and that presently.
HAMLET: Bid the players make haste.

(Exit Polonius.)

Will you two help to hasten them?
ROSENCRANTZ and **GUILDENSTERN:**   We will, my lord. *(Exeunt.)*
HAMLET: What, ho, Horatio!

(Enter Horatio.)

40 **HORATIO:**   Here, sweet lord, at your service.
HAMLET: Horatio, thou art e'en as just a man
    As e'er my conversation cop'd withal.
HORATIO: O, my dear lord,—
HAMLET: Nay, do not think I flatter;
    For what advancement may I hope from thee,
45   That no revénue hast, but thy good spirits,
    To feed and clothe thee? Why should the poor be flatter'd?
    No, let the candied tongue lick ábsurd pomp;
    And crook the pregnant hinges of the knee
    Where thrift may follow fawning. Dost thou hear?
50   Since my dear soul was mistress of her choice,
    And could of men distinguish, her election
    Hath seal'd thee for herself: for thou hast been
    As one, in suffering all, that suffers nothing;
    A man that Fortune's buffets and rewards
55   Hast ta'en with equal thanks: and bless'd are those
    Whose blood and judgment are so well commingled
    That they are not a pipe for Fortune's finger
    To sound what stop she please. Give me that man
    That is not passion's slave, and I will wear him
60   In my heart's core, ay, in my heart of heart,
    As I do thee.—Something too much of this.—
    There is a play to-night before the king;
    One scene of it comes near the circumstance
    Which I have told thee of my father's death:
65   I pr'ythee, when thou see'st that act a-foot,
    Even with the very comment of thy soul
    Observe mine uncle: if this his occulted guilt

Do not itself unkennel in one speech,
It is a damned ghost that we have seen;
70 And my imaginations are as foul
As Vulcan's stithy.[3] Give him heedful note:
For I mine eyes will rivet to his face;
And, after, we will both our judgments join
In censure of his seeming.
HORATIO: Well, my lord:
75 If he steal aught the whilst this play is playing,
And scape detecting, I will pay the theft.
HAMLET: They are coming to the play; I must be idle:[4]
Get you a place.

(Danish march. A flourish. Enter King, Queen, Polonius, Ophelia, Rosen-crantz, Guildenstern, and others.)

KING: How fares our cousin Hamlet?
80 **HAMLET:**   Excellent, i'faith; of the chameleon's dish:[5] I eat the air, promise-crammed: you cannot feed capons so.
KING: I have nothing with this answer, Hamlet; these words are not mine.
HAMLET: No, nor mine now. *(To Polonius)* My lord, you played once i' the university, you say?
85 **POLONIUS:**   That did I, my lord, and was accounted a good actor.
HAMLET: And what did you enact?
POLONIUS: I did enact Julius Caesar: I was killed i' the Capitol; Brutus killed me.
HAMLET: It was a brute part of him to kill so capital a calf there.—Be the
90 players ready.
ROSENCRANTZ: Ay, my lord; they stay upon your patience.
QUEEN: Come hither, my good Hamlet, sit by me.
HAMLET: No, good mother, here's metal more attractive.
POLONIUS: O, ho! do you mark that? *(To the King)*
95 **HAMLET:**   Lady, shall I lie in your lap? *(Lying down at Ophelia's feet)*
OPHELIA: No, my lord.
HAMLET: I mean, my head upon your lap?
OPHELIA: Ay, my lord.
HAMLET: Do you think I meant country matters?
100 **OPHELIA:**   I think nothing, my lord.
HAMLET: That's a fair thought to lie between maids' legs.
OPHELIA: What is, my lord?
HAMLET: Nothing.
OPHELIA: You are merry, my lord.
105 **HAMLET:**   Who, I?

---

[3]Smithy.   [4]Foolish.   [5]Chameleons were supposed to live on air.

OPHELIA: Ay, my lord.

HAMLET: O, your only jig-maker. What should a man do but be merry? for, look you, how cheerfully my mother looks, and my father died within's two hours.

110 **OPHELIA:**   Nay, 'tis twice two months, my lord.

HAMLET: So long? Nay, then, let the devil wear black, for I'll have a suit of sables. O heavens! die two months ago, and not forgotten yet? Then there's hope a great man's memory may outlive his life half a year: but, by'r lady, he must build churches, then; or else shall he suffer not thinking on, with

115   the hobby-horse, whose epitaph is, *For, O, for, O, the hobby-horse is forgot.*

(Trumpets sound. The dumb show enters.)

(Enter a King and a Queen, very lovingly; the Queen embracing him and he her. She kneels, and makes show of protestation unto him. He takes her up, and declines his head upon her neck: lays him down upon a bank of flowers: she, seeing him asleep, leaves him. Anon comes in a fellow, takes off his crown, kisses it, and pours poison in the King's ears, and exit. The Queen returns; finds the King dead, and makes passionate action. The Poisoner, with some two or three Mutes, comes in again, seeming to lament with her. The dead body is carried away. The Poisoner woos the Queen with gifts: she seems loth and unwilling awhile, but in the end accepts his love.)

(Exeunt.)

OPHELIA: What means this, my lord?

HAMLET: Marry, this is miching mallecho;[6] it means mischief.

OPHELIA: Belike this show imports the argument of the play.

(Enter Prologue.)

HAMLET: We shall know by this fellow: the players cannot keep counsel;

120   they'll tell all.

OPHELIA: Will he tell us what this show meant?

HAMLET: Ay, or any show that you'll show him: be not you ashamed to show, he'll not shame to tell you what it means.

OPHELIA: You are naught, you are naught: I'll mark the play.

125 **PROLOGUE:**   *For us, and for our tragedy,*
                                Here stooping to your clemency,
                                We beg your hearing patiently.

HAMLET: Is this a prologue, or the posy[7] of a ring?

OPHELIA: 'Tis brief, my lord.

130 **HAMLET:**   As woman's love.

(Enter a King and a Queen.)

---

[6]A sneaking misdeed.   [7]Motto or inscription.

PROLOGUE KING: Full thirty times hath Phoebus' cart gone round
Neptune's salt wash and Tellus' orbed ground,[8]
And thirty dozen moons with borrow'd sheen
About the world have times twelve thirties been,
135   Since love our hearts, and Hymen did our hands
Unite commutual in most sacred bands.
PROLOGUE QUEEN: So many journeys may the sun and moon
Make us again count o'er ere love be done!
But, woe is me, you are so sick of late,
140   So far from cheer and from your former state
That I distrust you.[9] Yet, though I distrust,
Discomfort you, my lord, it nothing must:
For women's fear and love holds quantity,[10]
In neither aught, or in extremity.
145   Now, what my love is, proof hath made you know;
And as my love is siz'd, my fear is so:
Where love is great, the littlest doubts are fear;
Where little fears grow great, great love grows there.
PROLOGUE KING: Faith, I must leave thee, love, and shortly too;
150   My operant powers their functions leave[11] to do:
And thou shalt live in this fair world behind,
Honor'd, belov'd; and haply one as kind
For husband shalt thou,—
PROLOGUE QUEEN: O, confound the rest!
Such love must needs be treason in my breast:
155   In second husband let me be accurst!
None wed the second but who kill'd the first.
HAMLET: *(Aside)* Wormwood, wormwood.
PROLOGUE QUEEN: The instances that second marriage move
Are base respects of thrift, but none of love:
160   A second time I kill my husband, dead,
When second husband kisses me in bed.
PROLOGUE KING: I do believe you think what now you speak;
But what we do determine oft we break.
Purpose is but the slave to memory;
165   Of violent birth, but poor validity:
Which now, like fruit unripe, sticks on the tree;
But fall unshaken when they mellow be.
Most necessary 'tis that we forget
To pay ourselves what to ourselves is debt:
170   What to ourselves in passion we propose,
The passion ending, doth the purpose lose.

---

[8]The globe.   [9]Worry about you.   [10]Correspond in degree.   [11]Cease.

The violence of either grief or joy
Their own enactures with themselves destroy:
Where joy most revels grief doth most lament;
175 Grief joys, joy grieves, on slender accident.
This world is not for aye; nor 'tis not strange
That even our loves should with our fortunes change;
For 'tis a question left us yet to prove
Whether love lead fortune or else fortune love.
180 The great man down, you mark his favorite flies;
The poor advanc'd makes friends of enemies.
And hitherto doth love on fortune tend:
For who not needs shall never lack a friend;
And who in want a hollow friend doth try,
185 Directly seasons him his enemy.
But, orderly to end where I begun,—
Our wills and fates do so contráry run
That our devices still are overthrown;
Our thoughts are ours, their ends none of our own:
190 So think thou wilt no second husband wed;
But die thy thoughts when thy first lord is dead.
PROLOGUE QUEEN: Nor earth to me give food, nor heaven light!
Sport and repose lock from me day and night!
To desperation turn my trust and hope!
195 An anchor's[12] cheer in prison be my scope!
Each opposite, that blanks the face of joy,
Meet what I would have well, and it destroy!
Both here and hence, pursue me lasting strife,
If, once a widow, ever I be wife!
200 **HAMLET:**   If she should break it now! *(To Ophelia)*
PROLOGUE KING: 'Tis deeply sworn. Sweet, leave me here awhile;
My spirits grow dull, and fain I would beguile
The tedious day with sleep. *(Sleeps)*
PROLOGUE QUEEN: Sleep rock thy brain,
And never come mischance between us twain! *(Exit.)*
205 **HAMLET:**   Madam, how like you this play?
QUEEN: The lady doth protest too much, methinks.
HAMLET: O, but she'll keep her word.
KING: Have you heard the argument? Is there no offence in't?
HAMLET: No, no, they do but jest, poison in jest; no offence i' the world.
210 **KING:**   What do you call the play?
HAMLET: The Mouse-trap. Marry, how? Tropically.[13] This play is the image of
a murder done in Vienna: Gonzago is the duke's name: his wife, Baptista:

---

[12]Anchorite's, or hermit's.   [13]Figuratively, or metaphorically; by means of a "trope."

you shall see anon; 'tis a knavish piece of work: but what o' that? your
majesty, and we that have free souls, it touches us not: let the galled
215   jade wince, our withers are unwrung.

(Enter Lucianus.)

This is one Lucianus, nephew to the king.

OPHELIA: You are a good chorus, my lord.

HAMLET: I could interpret between you and your love, if I could see the
puppets dallying.

220 **OPHELIA:**   You are keen, my lord, you are keen.

HAMLET: It would cost you a groaning to take off my edge.

OPHELIA: Still better, and worse.

HAMLET: So you must take your husbands.—Begin, murderer; pox, leave
thy damnable faces and begin. Come:—*The croaking raven doth bellow*
225   *for revenge.*

LUCIANUS: Thoughts black, hands apt, drugs fit, and time agreeing;
Confederate season, else no creature seeing;
Thou mixture rank, of midnight weeds collected,
With Hecate's ban[14] thrice blasted, thrice infected,
230   Thy natural magic and dire property
On wholesome life usurp immediately.

(Pours the poison into the sleeper's ears.)

HAMLET: He poisons him i' the garden for's estate. His name's Gonzago:
the story is extant, and writ in choice Italian: you shall see anon how the
murderer gets the love of Gonzago's wife.

235 **OPHELIA:**   The king rises.

HAMLET: What, frighted with false fire!

QUEEN: How fares my lord?

POLONIUS: Give o'er the play.

KING: Give me some light:—away!

240 **ALL:**   Lights, lights, lights!

(Exeunt all but Hamlet and Horatio.)

HAMLET: Why, let the stricken deer go weep,
The hart ungalled play;
For some must watch, while some must sleep:
So runs the world away.—
245   Would not this, sir, and a forest of feathers,
If the rest of my fortunes turn Turk with me,
With two Provencial roses on my razed shoes,
Get me a fellowship in a cry[15] of players, sir?

---

[14]The spell of the goddess of witchcraft.   [15]Company.

HORATIO: Half a share.

250 **HAMLET:** A whole one, I.

> For thou dost know, O Damon dear,
> This realm dismantled was
> Of Jove himself; and now reigns here
> A very, very—pajock.[16]

255 **HORATIO:** You might have rhymed.

HAMLET: O good Horatio, I'll take the ghost's word for a thousand pound. Didst perceive?

HORATIO: Very well, my lord.

HAMLET: Upon the talk of the poisoning,—

260 **HORATIO:** I did very well note him.

HAMLET: Ah, ha!—Come, some music! come, the recorders!—
For if the king like not the comedy,
Why, then, belike,—he likes it not, perdy. Come, some music!

(Re-enter Rosencrantz and Guildenstern.)

GUILDENSTERN: Good my lord, vouchsafe me a word with you.

265 **HAMLET:** Sir, a whole history.

GUILDENSTERN: The king, sir,—

HAMLET: Ay, sir, what of him?

GUILDENSTERN: Is, in his retirement, marvelous distempered.

HAMLET: With drink, sir?

270 **GUILDENSTERN:** No, my lord, rather with choler.

HAMLET: Your wisdom should show itself more richer to signify this to his doctor; for, for me to put him to his purgation would perhaps plunge him into far more choler.

GUILDENSTERN: Good my lord, put your discourse into some frame, and
275 start not so wildly from my affair.

HAMLET: I am tame, sir:—pronounce.

GUILDENSTERN: The queen, your mother, in most great affliction of spirit, hath sent me to you.

HAMLET: You are welcome.

280 **GUILDENSTERN:** Nay, good my lord, this courtesy is not of the right breed. If it shall please you to make me a wholesome answer, I will do you mother's commandment: if not, your pardon and my return shall be the end of my business.

HAMLET: Sir, I cannot.

285 **GUILDENSTERN:** What, my lord?

HAMLET: Make you a wholesome answer; my wit's diseas'd: but, sir, such answer as I can make, you shall command; or, rather, as you say, my mother: therefore no more, but to the matter: my mother, you say,—

[16]Peacock.

ROSENCRANTZ: Then thus she says: your behavior hath struck her into
290 amazement and admiration.
HAMLET: O wonderful son, that can so astonish a mother!—But is there no
sequel at the heels of this mother's admiration?
ROSENCRANTZ: She desires to speak with you in her closet[17] ere you go
to bed.
295 HAMLET: We shall obey, were she ten times our mother. Have you any further trade with us?
ROSENCRANTZ: My lord, you once did love me.
HAMLET: So I do still, by these pickers and stealers.[18]
ROSENCRANTZ: Good, my lord, what is your cause of distemper? you do,
300 surely, bar the door upon your own liberty if you deny your griefs to your
friend.
HAMLET: Sir, I lack advancement.
ROSENCRANTZ: How can that be, when you have the voice of the king himself for your succession in Denmark?
305 HAMLET: Ay, but *While the grass grows,*—the proverb is something musty.

(Re-enter the Players, with recorders.)

O, the recorders:—let me see one.—To withdraw with you:—why do you
go about to recover the wind of me, as if you would drive me into a toil?
GUILDENSTERN: O, my lord, if my duty be too bold, my love is too un-
mannerly.
310 HAMLET: I do not well understand that. Will you play upon this pipe?
GUILDENSTERN: My lord, I cannot.
HAMLET: I pray you.
GUILDENSTERN: Believe me, I cannot.
HAMLET: I do beseech you.
315 GUILDENSTERN: I know no touch of it, my lord.
HAMLET: 'Tis as easy as lying: govern these ventages[19] with your finger and
thumb, give it breath with your mouth, and it will discourse most eloquent music. Look you, these are the stops.
GUILDENSTERN: But these cannot I command to any utterance of harmony; I
320 have not the skill.
HAMLET: Why, look you now, how unworthy a thing you make of me! You
would play upon me; you would seem to know my stops; you would pluck
out the heart of my mystery; you would sound me from my lowest note to
the top of my compass: and there is much music, excellent voice, in this
325 little organ; yet cannot you make it speak. 'Sblood, do you think that I am
easier to be played on than a pipe? Call me what instrument you will,
though you can fret me you cannot play upon me.

(Enter Polonius.)

---

[17]Boudoir.   [18]Fingers.   [19]Holes.

God bless you, sir!

POLONIUS: My lord, the queen would speak with you, and presently.

330 **HAMLET:**   Do you see yonder cloud that's almost in shape of a camel?

POLONIUS: By the mass, and 'tis like a camel indeed.

HAMLET: Methinks it is like a weasel.

POLONIUS: It is backed like a weasel.

HAMLET: Or like a whale?

335 **POLONIUS:**   Very like a whale.

HAMLET: Then will I come to my mother by and by.—They fool me to the top of my bent.—I will come by and by.

POLONIUS: I will say so.

HAMLET: By and by is easily said.

(Exit Polonius.)

340   Leave me, friends.

(Exeunt Rosencrantz, Guildenstern, Horatio, and Players.)

'Tis now the very witching time of night,
When churchyards yawn, and hell itself breathes out
Contagion to this world: now could I drink hot blood,
And do such bitter business as the day
345   Would quake to look on. Soft! now to my mother.—
O heart, lose not thy nature; let not ever
The soul of Nero[20] enter this firm bosom:
Let me be cruel, not unnatural:
I will speak daggers to her, but use none;
350   My tongue and soul in this be hypocrites,—
How in my words soever she be shent,
To give them seals never, my soul, consent! *(Exit.)*

SCENE III

A room in the castle.

(Enter King, Rosencrantz, and Guildenstern.)

KING: I like him not; nor stands it safe with us
To let his madness range. Therefore prepare you;
I your commission with forthwith despatch,
And he to England shall along with you:
5   The terms of our estate may not endure
Hazard so dangerous as doth hourly grow
Out of his lunacies.

---

[20]Nero killed his mother, a crime of which Hamlet does not want to be guilty.

GUILDENSTERN: We will ourselves provide:
    Most holy and religious fear it is
    To keep those many many bodies safe
10   That live and feed upon your majesty.
ROSENCRANTZ: The single and peculiar life is bound,
    With all the strength and armor of the mind,
    To keep itself from 'noyance; but much more
    That spirit upon whose weal depend and rest
15   The lives of many. The cease of majesty
    Dies not alone; but like a gulf doth draw
    What's near it with it: it is a massy wheel,
    Fix'd on the summit of the highest mount,
    To whose huge spokes ten thousand lesser things
20   Are mortis'd and adjoin'd; which, when it falls,
    Each small annexment, petty consequence,
    Attends the boisterous ruin. Never alone
    Did the king sigh, but with a general groan.
KING: Arm you, I pray you, to this speedy voyage;
25   For we will fetters put upon this fear,
    Which now goes too free-footed.
ROSENCRANTZ and **GUILDENSTERN:**   We will haste us.

(Exeunt Rosencrantz and Guildenstern.)

(Enter Polonius.)

POLONIUS: My lord, he's going to his mother's closet:
    Behind the arras I'll convey myself
    To hear the process; I'll warrant she'll tax him home:[1]
30   And, as you said, and wisely was it said,
    'Tis meet that some more audience than a mother,
    Since nature makes them partial, should o'erhear
    The speech, of vantage. Fare you well, my liege:
    I'll call upon you ere you go to bed,
35   And tell you what I know.
KING: Thanks, dear my lord.

(Exit Polonius.)

    O, my offence is rank, it smells to heaven;
    It hath the primal eldest curse upon't,—
    A brother's murder!—Pray can I not,
    Though inclination be as sharp as will:
40   My stronger guilt defeats my strong intent;
    And, like a man to double business bound,

---

[1]Reprove him properly.

I stand in pause where I shall first begin,
And both neglect. What if this cursed hand
Were thicker than itself with brother's blood,—
45 Is there not rain enough in the sweet heavens
To wash it white as snow? Whereto serves mercy
But to confront the visage of offence?
And what's in prayer but this twofold force,—
To be forestalled ere we come to fall,
50 Or pardon'd being down? Then I'll look up;
My fault is past. But, O, what form of prayer
Can serve my turn? Forgive me my foul murder?—
That cannot be; since I am still possess'd
Of those effects for which I did the murder,—
55 My crown, mine own ambition, and my queen.
May one be pardon'd and retain the offence?[2]
In the corrupted currents of this world
Offence's gilded hand may shove by justice;
And oft 'tis seen the wicked prize itself
60 Buys out the law: but 'tis not so above;
There is no shuffling,—there the action lies
In his true nature; and we ourselves compell'd,
Even to the teeth and forehead of our faults,
To give in evidence. What then? what rests?[3]
65 Try what repentance can: what can it not?
Yet what can it when one can not repent?
O wretched state! O bosom black as death!
O limed[4] soul, that, struggling to be free,
Art more engag'd! Help, angels! make assay:
70 Bow, stubborn knees; and, heart, with strings of steel,
Be soft as sinews of the new-born babe!
All may be well. *(Retires and kneels)*

(Enter Hamlet.)

HAMLET: Now might I do it pat, now he is praying;
And now I'll do't—and so he goes to heaven;
75 And so am I reveng'd:—that would be scann'd:
A villain kills my father; and for that,
I, his sole son, do this same villain send
To heaven.
O, this is hire and salary, not revenge.
80 He took my father grossly, full of bread;
With all his crimes broad blown, as flush as May;

---

[2]That is, the gains won by the offense.   [3]Remains.   [4]Snared.

And how his audit stands who knows save heaven?
But in our circumstance and course of thought
'Tis heavy with him: and am I, then, reveng'd,
85 To take him in the purging of his soul,
When he is fit and season'd for his passage?
No.
Up, sword; and know thou a more horrid hent:[5]
When he is drunk, asleep, or in his rage;
90 Or in the incestuous pleasure of his bed;
At gaming, swearing; or about some act
That has no relish of salvation in't;—
Then trip him, that his heels may kick at heaven;
And that his soul may be as damn'd and black
95 As hell, whereto it goes. My mother stays:
This physic but prolongs thy sickly days. *(Exit.)*

(The King rises and advances.)

KING: My words fly up, my thoughts remain below:
Words without thoughts never to heaven go. *(Exit.)*

SCENE IV

Another room in the castle.

(Enter Queen and Polonius.)

POLONIUS: He will come straight. Look you lay home to him:
Tell him his pranks have been too broad to bear with,
And that your grace hath screen'd and stood between
Much heat and him. I'll silence me e'en here.
5 Pray you, be round with him.
HAMLET: *(Within)* Mother, mother, mother!
QUEEN: I'll warrant you:
Fear me not:—withdraw, I hear him coming.

(Polonius goes behind the arras.)

(Enter Hamlet.)

HAMLET: Now, mother, what's the matter?
QUEEN: Hamlet, thou hast thy father much offended.
10 **HAMLET:**   Mother, you have my father much offended.
QUEEN: Come, come, you answer with an idle tongue.

[5]Opportunity.

HAMLET: Go, go, you question with a wicked tongue.

QUEEN: Why, how now, Hamlet!

HAMLET: What's the matter now?

QUEEN: Have you forgot me?

HAMLET: No, by the rood, not so:

15   You are the queen, your husband's brother's wife;

And,—would it were not so!—you are my mother.

QUEEN: Nay, then, I'll set those to you that can speak.

HAMLET: Come, come, and sit you down; you shall not budge;

You go not till I set you up a glass

20   Where you may see the inmost part of you.

QUEEN: What wilt thou do? thou wilt not murder me?—

Help, help, ho!

POLONIUS: *(Behind)* What, ho! help, help, help!

HAMLET: How now! a rat?

(Draws.)

Dead, for a ducat, dead! *(Makes a pass through the arras)*

25 **POLONIUS:**   *(Behind)* O, I am slain! *(Falls and dies.)*

QUEEN: O me, what hast thou done?

HAMLET: Nay, I know not:

Is it the king? *(Draws forth Polonius)*

QUEEN: O, what a rash and bloody deed is this!

HAMLET: A bloody deed!—almost as bad, good mother,

30   As kill a king and marry with his brother.

QUEEN: As kill a king!

HAMLET: Ay, lady, 'twas my word.—

Thou wretched, rash, intruding fool, farewell! *(To Polonius)*

I took thee for thy better: take thy fortune;

Thou find'st to be too busy is some danger.—

35   Leave wringing of your hands: peace; sit you down,

And let me wring your heart: for so I shall,

If it be made of penetrable stuff;

If damned custom have not braz'd it so

That it is proof and bulwark against sense.

40 **QUEEN:**   What have I done, that thou dar'st wag thy tongue

In noise so rude against me?

HAMLET: Such an act

That blurs the grace and blush of modesty;

Calls virtue hypocrite; takes off the rose

From the fair forehead of an innocent love,

45   And sets a blister there; makes marriage-vows

As false as dicers' oaths: O, such a deed

As from the body of contraction plucks

The very soul, and sweet religion makes

A rhapsody of words: heaven's face doth glow;

50   Yea, this solidity and compound mass,
       With tristful[1] visage, as against the doom,
       Is thought-sick at the act.
    QUEEN: Ah me, what act,
       That roars so loud, and thunders in the index?
    HAMLET: Look here upon this picture and on this,—
55   The counterfeit presentment of two brothers.
       See what grace was seated on this brow;
       Hyperion's curls; the front of Jove himself;
       An eye like Mars, to threaten and command;
       A station like the herald Mercury
60   New-lighted on a heaven-kissing hill;
       A combination and a form, indeed,
       Where every god did seem to set his seal,
       To give the world assurance of a man:
       This was your husband.—Look you now, what follows:
65   Here is your husband, like a mildew'd ear
       Blasting his wholesome brother. Have you eyes?
       Could you on this fair mountain leave to feed,
       And batten on this moor? Ha! have you eyes?
       You cannot call it love; for at your age
70   The hey-day in the blood is tame, it's humble,
       And waits upon the judgment: and what judgment
       Would step from this to this? Sense, sure, you have,
       Else could you not have motion: but sure that sense
       Is apoplex'd: for madness would not err;
75   Nor sense to ecstasy was ne'er so thrill'd
       But it reserv'd some quantity of choice
       To serve in such a difference. What devil was't
       That thus hath cozen'd you at hoodman-blind?[2]
       Eyes without feeling, feeling without sight,
80   Ears without hand or eyes, smelling sans all,
       Or but a sickly part of one true sense
       Could not so mope.
       O shame! where is thy blush! Rebellious hell,
       If thou canst mutine in a matron's bones,
85   To flaming youth let virtue be as wax,
       And melt in her own fire: proclaim no shame
       When the compulsive ardor gives the charge,
       Since frost itself as actively doth burn,
       And reason panders[3] will.

---

[1]Gloomy.   [2]Tricked you at blindman's buff.   [3]Becomes subservient to.

QUEEN: O Hamlet, speak no more:
90   Thou turn'st mine eyes into my very soul;
      And there I see such black and grained spots
      As will not leave their tinct.[4]
HAMLET: Nay, but to live
      In the rank sweat of an enseamed bed,
      Stew'd in corruption, honeying and making love
95   Over the nasty sty,—
QUEEN: O, speak to me no more;
      These words like daggers enter in mine ears;
      No more, sweet Hamlet.
HAMLET: A murderer and a villain;
      A slave that is not twentieth part the tithe
      Of your precedent lord; a voice of kings;[5]
100   A cutpurse of the empire and the rule,
      That from a shelf the precious diadem stole,
      And put it in his pocket!
QUEEN: No more.
HAMLET: A king of shreds and patches,—

(Enter Ghost.)

      Save me, and hover o'er me with your wings,
105   You heavenly guards!—What would your gracious figure?
QUEEN: Alas, he's mad!
HAMLET: Do you not come your tardy son to chide,
      That, laps'd in time and passion, lets go by
      The important acting of your dread command?
110   O, say!
GHOST: Do not forget: this visitation
      Is but to whet thy almost blunted purpose.
      But, look, amazement on thy mother sits:
      O, step between her and her fighting soul,—
115   Conceit in weakest bodies strongest works,—
      Speak to her, Hamlet.
HAMLET: How is it with you, lady?
QUEEN: Alas, how is't with you,
      That you do bend your eye on vacancy,
      And with the incorporal air do hold discourse?
120   Forth at your eyes your spirits wildly peep;
      And, as the sleeping soldiers in the alarm,
      Your bedded hair, like life in excrements,[6]

---

[4]As will not yield up their color.   [5]A buffoon among kings. The "Vice" in morality plays.
[6]In outgrowths or extremities.

Starts up and stands on end. O gentle son,
Upon the heat and flame of thy distemper
125　Sprinkle cool patience. Whereon do you look?
HAMLET:　On him, on him! Look you, how pale he glares!
His form and cause conjoin'd, preaching to stones,
Would make them capable.—Do not look upon me;
Lest with this piteous action you convert
130　My stern effects: then what I have to do
Will want true color; tears perchance for blood.
QUEEN:　To whom do you speak this?
HAMLET:　　　　　　　　　　　　　　Do you see nothing there?
QUEEN:　Nothing at all; yet all that is I see.
HAMLET:　Nor did you nothing hear?
135　QUEEN:　No, nothing but ourselves.
HAMLET:　Why, look you there! look, how it steals away!
My father, in his habit as he liv'd!
Look, where he goes, even now, out at the portal!

(Exit Ghost.)

QUEEN:　This is the very coinage of your brain:
140　This bodiless creation ecstasy
Is very cunning in.
HAMLET:　　　　　　　　Ecstasy!
My pulse, as yours, doth temperately keep time.
And makes as healthful music: it is not madness
That I have utter'd: bring me to the test,
145　And I the matter will re-word; which madness
Would gambol from. Mother, for love of grace,
Lay not that flattering unction to your soul,
That not your trespass, but my madness speaks:
It will but skin and film the ulcerous place,
150　Whilst rank corruption, mining all within,
Infects unseen. Confess yourself to Heaven;
Repent what's past; avoid what is to come;
And do not spread the compost on the weeds,
To make them ranker. Forgive me this my virtue;
155　For in the fatness[7] of these pursy times
Virtue itself of vice must pardon beg,
Yea, curb and woo for leave to do him good.
QUEEN:　O Hamlet, thou hast cleft my heart in twain.
HAMLET:　O, throw away the worser part of it,
160　And live the purer with the other half.

---

[7]Corruption.

Good-night: but go not to mine uncle's bed;
Assume a virtue, if you have it not.
That monster custom, who all sense doth eat,
Of habits devil, is angel yet in this,—
165   That to the use of actions fair and good
He likewise gives a frock or livery
That aptly is put on. Refrain to-night;
And that shall lend a kind of easiness
To the next abstinence: the next more easy;
170   For use almost can change the stamp of nature,
And either curb the devil, or throw him out
With wondrous potency. Once more, good-night:
And when you are desirous to be bless'd,
I'll blessing beg of you.—For this same lord *(pointing to Polonius)*
175   I do repent: but Heaven hath pleas'd it so,
To punish me with this, and this with me,
That I must be their[8] scourge and minister.
I will bestow him, and will answer well
The death I gave him. So, again, good-night.—
180   I must be cruel only to be kind:
Thus bad begins and worse remains behind.—
One word more, good lady.
    QUEEN: What shall I do?
    HAMLET: Not this, by no means, that I bid you do:
Let the bloat king tempt you again to bed;
185   Pinch wanton on your cheek; call you his mouse;
And let him, for a pair of reechy kisses,
Or paddling in your neck with his damn'd fingers,
Make you to ravel all this matter out,
That I essentially am not in madness,
190   But mad in craft. 'Twere good you let him know;
For who that's but a queen, fair, sober, wise,
Would from a paddock,[9] from a bat, a gib,
Such dear concernings hide? who would do so?
No, in despite of sense and secrecy,
195   Unpeg the basket on the house's top,
Let the birds fly, and, like the famous ape,
To try conclusions, in the basket creep,
And break your own neck down.
    QUEEN: Be thou assur'd, if words be made of breath
200   And breath of life, I have not life to breathe
What thou hast said to me.

---

[8]Heaven's, or the heavens'.   [9]Paddock: toad; gib: tomcat.

HAMLET: I must to England; you know that?
QUEEN: Alack,
    I had forgot: 'tis so concluded on.
HAMLET: There's letters seal'd: and my two school-fellows,—
205   Whom I will trust as I will adders fang'd,
    They bear the mandate; they must sweep my way,
    And marshal me to knavery. Let it work;
    For 'tis the sport to have the éngineer
    Hoist with his own petard: and't shall go hard
210   But I will delve one yard below their mines,
    And blow them at the moon: O, 'tis most sweet,
    When in one line two crafts directly meet.—
    This man shall set me packing:
    I'll lug the guts into the neighbor room.—
215   Mother, good-night.—Indeed, this counsellor
    Is now most still, most secret, and most grave,
    Who was in life a foolish prating knave.
    Come, sir, to draw toward an end with you:—
    Good-night, mother.

(Exeunt severally; Hamlet dragging out Polonius.)

Act IV

SCENE I

A room in the castle.

(Enter King, Queen, Rosencrantz, and Guildenstern.)

KING: There's matter in these sighs, these prófound heaves:
    You must translate: 'tis fit we understand them.
    Where is your son?
QUEEN: Bestow this place on us a little while. *(To Rosencrantz and*
5   *Guildenstern, who go out)* Ah, my good lord, what have I seen to-night!
KING: What, Gertrude? How does Hamlet?
QUEEN: Mad as the sea and wind, when both contend
    Which is the mightier: in his lawless fit,
    Behind the arras hearing something stir,
10   He whips his rapier out, and cries, *A rat, a rat!*
    And, in this brainish apprehension,[1] kills
    The unseen good old man.
KING: O heavy deed!
    It had been so with us had we been there:

---

[1]Mad notion.

His liberty is full of threats to all;
15 To you yourself, to us, to every one.
Alas, how shall this bloody deed be answer'd?
It will be laid to us, whose providence
Should have kept short, restrain'd, and out of haunt
This mad young man: but so much was our love,
20 We would not understand what was most fit;
But, like the owner of a foul disease,
To keep if from divulging, let it feed
Even on the pith of life. Where is he gone?
QUEEN: To draw apart the body he hath kill'd:
25 O'er whom his very madness, like some ore
Among a mineral of metals base,
Shows itself pure; he weeps for what is done.
KING: O Gertrude, come away!
The sun no sooner shall the mountains touch
30 But we will ship him hence: and this vile deed
We must, with all our majesty and skill,
Both countenance and excuse.—Ho, Guildenstern!

(Enter Rosencrantz and Guildenstern.)

Friends both, go join you with some further aid:
Hamlet in madness hath Polonius slain,
35 And from his mother's closet hath he dragg'd him:
Go seek him out; speak fair, and bring the body
Into the chapel. I pray you, haste in this.

(Exeunt Rosencrantz and Guildenstern.)

Come, Gertrude, we'll call up our wisest friends;
And let them know both what we mean to do
40 And what's untimely done: so haply slander,—
Whose whisper o'er the world's diameter,
As level as the cannon to his blank,
Transports his poison'd shot,—may amiss our name,
And hit the woundless air.—O, come away!
45 My soul is full of discord and dismay.

(Exeunt.)

SCENE II

Another room in the castle.

(Enter Hamlet.)

HAMLET: Safely stowed.
ROSENCRANTZ and **GUILDENSTERN:** *(Within)* Hamlet! Lord Hamlet!

HAMLET: What noise? who calls on Hamlet?
O, here they come.

(Enter Rosencrantz and Guildenstern.)

5 **ROSENCRANTZ:** What have you done, my lord, with the dead body?
HAMLET: Compounded it with dust, whereto 'tis kin.
ROSENCRANTZ: Tell us where 'tis, that we may take it thence,
And bear it to the chapel.
HAMLET: Do not believe it.
10 **ROSENCRANTZ:** Believe what?
HAMLET: That I can keep your counsel, and not mine own. Besides, to be demanded of a sponge!—what replication should be made by the son of a king?
ROSENCRANTZ: Take you me for a sponge, my lord?
15 **HAMLET:** Ay, sir; that soaks up the king's countenance, his rewards, his authorities. But such officers do the king best service in the end: he keeps them, like an ape, in the corner of his jaw; first mouthed, to be last swallowed: when he needs what you have gleaned, it is but squeezing you, and, sponge, you shall be dry again.
20 **ROSENCRANTZ:** I understand you not, my lord.
HAMLET: I am glad of it: a knavish speech sleeps in a foolish ear.
ROSENCRANTZ: My lord, you must tell us where the body is, and go with us to the king.
HAMLET: The body is with the king, but the king is not with the body. The
25 king is a thing,—
GUILDENSTERN: A thing, my lord!
HAMLET: Of nothing: bring me to him.
Hide fox, and all after.

(Exeunt.)

SCENE III

Another room in the castle.

(Enter King, attended.)

KING: I have sent to seek him, and to find the body.
How dangerous is it that this man goes loose!
Yet must not we put the strong law on him:
He's lov'd of the distracted multitude,
5 Who like not in their judgment, but their eyes;
And where 'tis so, the offender's scourge is weigh'd,
But never the offence. To bear all smooth and even,
This sudden sending him away must seem
Deliberate pause: diseases desperate grown

10   By desperate appliance are reliev'd,
      Or not at all.

(Enter Rosencrantz.)

    How now! what hath befallen!
ROSENCRANTZ: Where the dead body is bestow'd, my lord,
    We cannot get from him.
KING: But where is he?
15 **ROSENCRANTZ:**   Without, my lord; guarded, to know your pleasure.
KING: Bring him before us.
ROSENCRANTZ: Ho, Guildenstern! bring in my lord.

(Enter Hamlet and Guildenstern.)

KING: Now, Hamlet, where's Polonius?
HAMLET: At supper.
20 **KING:**   At supper! where?
HAMLET: Not where he eats, but where he is eaten: a certain convocation of politic worms are e'en at him. Your worm is your only emperor for diet: we fat all creatures else to fat us, and we fat ourselves for maggots: your fat king and your lean beggar is but variable service,—two dishes,
25   but to one table: that's the end.
KING: Alas, alas!
HAMLET: A man may fish with the worm that hath eat of a king, and eat of the fish that hath fed of that worm.
KING: What does thou mean by this?
30 **HAMLET:**   Nothing but to show you how a king may go a progress through the guts of a beggar.
KING: Where is Polonius?
HAMLET: In heaven; send thither to see: if your messenger find him not there, seek him i' the other place yourself. But, indeed, if you find him not
35   within this month, you shall nose him as you go up the stairs into the lobby.
KING: Go seek him there. *(To some Attendants)*
HAMLET: He will stay till ye come.

(Exeunt Attendants.)

KING: Hamlet, this deed, for thine especial safety,—
40   Which we do tender, as we dearly grieve
    For that which thou hast done,—must send thee hence
    With fiery quickness: therefore prepare thyself;
    The bark is ready, and the wind at help,
    The associates tend, and everything is bent
45   For England.
HAMLET: For England!
KING: Ay, Hamlet.

HAMLET: Good.

KING: So is it, if thou knew'st our purposes.

HAMLET: I see a cherub that sees them.—But, come; for England!—Farewell, dear mother.

KING: Thy loving father, Hamlet.

50 **HAMLET:** My mother: father and mother is man and wife; man and wife is one flesh; and so, my mother.—Come, for England! *(Exit.)*

KING: Follow him at foot; tempt him with speed aboard;

  Delay it not; I'll have him hence to-night:

  Away! for everything is seal'd and done

55 That else leans on the affair, pray you, make haste.

(Exeunt Rosencrantz and Guildenstern.)

  And, England, if my love thou hold'st at aught,—

  As my great power thereof may give thee sense,

  Since yet thy cicatrice looks raw and red

  After the Danish sword, and thy free awe

60 Pays homage to us,—thou mayst not coldly set

  Our sovereign process; which imports at full,

  By letters conjuring to that effect,

  The present death of Hamlet. Do it, England;

  For like the hectic in my blood he rages,

65 And thou must cure me: till I know 'tis done,

  Howe'er my haps, my joys will ne'er begin. *(Exit)*

SCENE IV

A plain in Denmark.

(Enter Fortinbras, and Forces marching.)

FORTINBRAS: Go, from me greet the Danish king:

  Tell him that, by his license, Fortinbras

  Craves the conveyance of a promis'd march

  Over his kingdom. You know the rendezvous,

5 If that his majesty would aught with us,

  We shall express our duty in his eye,

  And let him know so.

CAPTAIN: I will do't, my lord.

FORTINBRAS: Go softly on.

(Exeunt Fortinbras and Forces.)

(Enter Hamlet, Rosencrantz, Guildenstern, &c.)

HAMLET: Good sir, whose powers are these?

10 **CAPTAIN:** They are of Norway, sir.

HAMLET: How purpos'd, sir, I pray you?

CAPTAIN: Against some part of Poland.

HAMLET: Who commands them, sir?

CAPTAIN: The nephew to old Norway, Fortinbras.

15 **HAMLET:**   Goes it against the main of Poland, sir,
Or for some frontier?

CAPTAIN: Truly to speak, and with no addition,
We go to gain a little patch of ground
That hath in it no profit but the name.

20   To pay five ducats, five, I would not farm it;
Nor will it yield to Norway or the Pole
A ranker[1] rate should it be sold in fee.

HAMLET: Why, then the Polack never will defend it.

CAPTAIN: Yes, it is already garrison'd.

25 **HAMLET:**   Two thousand souls and twenty thousand ducats
Will not debate the question of this straw:
This is the imposthume[2] of much wealth and peace,
That inward breaks, and shows no cause without
Why the man dies.—I humbly thank you, sir.

30 **CAPTAIN:**   God b' wi' you, sir. *(Exit.)*

ROSENCRANTZ: Will't please you go, my lord?

HAMLET: I'll be with you straight. Go a little before.

(Exeunt all but Hamlet.)

How all occasions do inform against me,
And spur my dull revenge! What is a man,
35   If his chief good and market of his time
Be but to sleep and feed? a beast, no more.
Sure he that made us with such large discourse,[3]
Looking before and after, gave us not
That capability and godlike reason
40   To fust[4] in us unus'd. Now, whether it be
Bestial oblivion or some craven scruple
Of thinking too precisely on the event,—
A thought which, quarter'd, hath but one part wisdom
And ever three parts coward,—I do not know
45   Why yet I live to say, *This thing's to do;*
Sith[5] I have cause, and will, and strength, and means
To do't. Examples, gross as earth, exhort me:
Witness this army, of such mass and charge,
Led by a delicate and tender prince;
50   Whose spirit, with divine ambition puff'd,

---

[1]Dearer.   [2]Ulcer.   [3]Reasoning faculty.   [4]Grow musty.   [5]Since.

Makes mouths at the invisible event;
Exposing what is mortal and unsure
To all that fortune, death, and danger dare,
Even for an egg-shell. Rightly to be great
55   Is not to stir without great argument,
But greatly to find quarrel in a straw
When honor's at the stake. How stand I, then,
That have a father kill'd, a mother stain'd,
Excitements of my reason and my blood,
60   And let all sleep? while, to my shame, I see
The imminent death of twenty thousand men,
That, for a fantasy and trick of fame,
Go to their graves like beds; fight for a plot
Whereon the numbers cannot try the cause,
65   Which is not tomb enough and continent[6]
To hide the slain?—O, from this time forth,
My thoughts be bloody, or be nothing worth! *(Exit.)*

Scene V

Elsinore. A room in the castle.

(Enter Queen and Horatio.)

Queen: I will not speak with her.
Horatio: She is importunate; indeed, distract:
  Her mood will needs be pitied.
Queen: What would she have?
Horatio: She speaks much of her father; says she hears
5   There's tricks i' the world; and hems, and beats her heart;
Spurns enviously at straws; speaks things in doubt,
That carry but half sense: her speech is nothing,
Yet the unshapéd use of it doth move
The hearers to collection; they aim at it,
10   And botch the words up fit to their own thoughts;
Which, as her winks, and nods, and gestures yield them,
Indeed would make one think there might be thought,
Though nothing sure, yet much unhappily.
'Twere good she were spoken with; for she may strew
15   Dangerous conjectures in ill-breeding minds.
Queen: Let her come in.

(Exit Horatio.)

[6]Container.

To my sick soul, as sin's true nature is,
Each toy seems prologue to some great amiss:
So full of artless jealousy is guilt,
20   It spills itself in fearing to be spilt.

(Re-enter Horatio and Ophelia.)

OPHELIA: Where is the beauteous majesty of Denmark?
QUEEN: How now, Ophelia!
OPHELIA: *(Sings)*

> How should I your true love know
> From another one?
25   By his cockle hat and staff,
> And his sandal shoon.

QUEEN: Alas, sweet lady, what imports this song?
OPHELIA: Say you? nay, pray you, mark.

(Sings)

> He is dead and gone, lady,
30   He is dead and gone;
> At his head a grass green turf,
> At his heels a stone.

QUEEN: Nay, but, Ophelia,—
OPHELIA: Pray you, mark.

(Sings)

White his shroud as the mountain snow,

(Enter King.)

35 **QUEEN:**   Alas, look here, my lord.
OPHELIA: *(Sings)*

> Larded with sweet flowers;
> Which bewept to the grave did go
> With true-love showers.

KING: How do you, pretty lady?
40 **OPHELIA:**   Well, God 'ild[1] you! They say the owl was a baker's daughter. Lord, we know what we are, but know not what we may be. God be at your table!
KING: Conceit upon her father.

---

[1]Yield you—that is, reward you.

OPHELIA: Pray you, let's have no words of this; but when they ask you what
45   it means, say you this:

(Sings.)

> To-morrow is Saint Valentine's day
>   All in the morning betime,
> And I a maid at your window,
>   To be your Valentine.

50
> Then up he rose, and donn'd his clothes,
>   And dupp'd the chamber-door;
> Let in the maid, that out a maid
>   Never departed more.

KING: Pretty Ophelia!
55 **OPHELIA:**   Indeed, la, without an oath, I'll make an end on't;

(Sings)

> By Gis[2] and by Saint Charity,
>   Alack, and fie for shame!
> Young men will do't, if they come to't;
>   By cock, they are to blame.

60
> Quoth she, before you tumbled me,
>   You promis'd me to wed.
> So would I ha' done, by yonder sun,
>   An thou hadst not come to my bed.

KING: How long hath she been thus?
65 **OPHELIA:**   I hope all will be well. We must be patient: but I cannot choose
but weep, to think they should lay him i' the cold ground. My brother
shall know of it: and so I thank you; for your good counsel.—Come, my
coach!—Good-night, ladies; good-night, sweet ladies; good-night, good-
night. *(Exit.)*
70 **KING:**   Follow her close; give her good watch, I pray you.

(Exit Horatio.)

> O, this is the poison of deep grief; it springs
> All from her father's death. O Gertrude, Gertrude,
> When sorrows come, they come not single spies,
> But in battalions! First, her father slain:
75 > Next, your son gone; and he most violent author
> Of his own just remove: the people muddied,
> Thick and unwholesome in their thoughts and whispers

---

[2]A contraction for "by Jesus."

For good Polonius' death; and we have done but greenly
In hugger-mugger[3] to inter him: poor Ophelia
80   Divided from herself and her fair judgment,
Without the which we are pictures, or mere beasts:
Last, and as much containing as all these,
Her brother is in secret come from France;
Feeds on his wonder, keeps himself in clouds,
85   And wants not buzzers to infect his ear
With pestilent speeches of his father's death;
Wherein necessity, of matter beggar'd,
Will nothing stick our person to arraign
In ear and ear. O my dear Gertrude, this,
90   Like to a murdering piece,[4] in many places
Gives me superfluous death.

(A noise within.)

QUEEN: Alack, what noise is this?
KING: Where are my Switzers?[5] let them guard the door.

(Enter a Gentleman.)

What is the matter?
GENTLEMAN: Save yourself, my lord:
The ocean, overpeering of his list,
95   Eats not the flats with more impetuous haste
Than young Laertes, in a riotous head,
O'erbears your officers. The rabble call him lord;
And, as the world were now but to begin,
Antiquity forgot, custom not known,
100   The ratifiers and props of every word,
They cry, *Choose we, Laertes shall be king!*
Caps, hands, and tongues applaud it to the clouds,
Laertes shall be king, Laertes king!
QUEEN: How cheerfully on the false trail they cry!
105   O, this is counter, you false Danish dogs!
KING: The doors are broke.

(Noise within)

(Enter Laertes armed; Danes following.)

LAERTES: Where is this king?—Sirs, stand you all without.
DANES: No, let's come in.
LAERTES: I pray you, give me leave.

---

[3]In great secrecy and haste.   [4]A cannon.   [5]Bodyguard of Swiss mercenaries.

DANES: We will, we will. (*They retire without the door.*)
110 **LAERTES:**   I thank you:—keep the door.—O thou vile king,
Give me my father!
QUEEN: Calmly, good Laertes.
LAERTES: That drop of blood that's calm proclaims me bastard;
Cries cuckold to my father; brands the harlot
Even here, between the chaste unsmirched brow
115   Of my true mother.
KING: What is the cause, Laertes,
That thy rebellion looks so giant-like?—
Let him go, Gertrude; do not fear our person:
There's such divinity doth hedge a king,
That treason can but peep to what it would,
120   Acts little of his will.—Tell me, Laertes,
Why thou art thus incens'd.—Let him go, Gertrude:—
Speak, man.
LAERTES: Where is my father?
KING: Dead.
QUEEN: But not by him.
KING: Let him demand his fill.
125 **LAERTES:**   How came he dead? I'll not be juggled with:
To hell, allegiance! vows, to the blackest devil!
Conscience and grace, to the profoundest pit!
I dare damnation:—to this point I stand,—
That both the worlds I give to negligence,
130   Let come what comes; only I'll be reveng'd
Most thoroughly for my father.
KING: Who shall stay you?
LAERTES: My will, not all the world:
And for my means, I'll husband them so well,
They shall go far with little.
KING: Good Laertes,
135   If you desire to know the certainty
Of your dear father's death, is't writ in your revenge
That, sweepstake, you will draw both friend and foe,
Winner or loser?
LAERTES: None but his enemies.
KING: Will you know them, then?
140 **LAERTES:**   To his good friends thus wide I'll ope my arms;
And, like the kind life-rendering pelican,[6]
Repast them with my blood.

---

[6]The pelican mother was believed to draw blood from itself to feed its young.

KING: Why, now you speak
  Like a good child and a true gentleman.
  That I am guiltless of your father's death,
145 And am most sensible in grief for it,
  It shall as level to your judgment pierce
  As day does to your eye.
DANES: *(Within)*   Let her come in.
LAERTES: How now! what noise is that?

(Re-enter Ophelia, fantastically dressed with straws and flowers.)

  O heat, dry up my brains! tears seven times salt
150 Burn out the sense and virtue of mine eyes!—
  By heaven, thy madness shall be paid by weight
  Till our scale turn the beam. O rose of May!
  Dear maid, kind sister, sweet Ophelia!—
  O heavens! is't possible a young maid's wits
155 Should be as mortal as an old man's life!
  Nature is fine in love; and where 'tis fine
  It sends some precious instance of itself
  After the thing it loves.
OPHELIA: *(Sings)*

              They bore him barefac'd on the bier;
160   Hey no nonny, nonny, hey nonny;
              And on his grave rain'd many a tear,—
                 Fare you well, my dove!

LAERTES: Hadst thou thy wits, and didst persuade revenge,
  It could not move thus.
165 **OPHELIA:**   You must sing, *Down-a-down, an you call him a-down-a.* O,
  how the wheel becomes it! It is the false steward, that stole his master's
  daughter.
LAERTES: This nothing's more than matter.
OPHELIA: There's rosemary, that's for remembrance; pray, love, remember:
170 and there is pansies that's for thoughts.
LAERTES: A document in madness,—thoughts and remembrance fitted.
OPHELIA: There's fennel for you, and columbines:—there's rue for you; and
  here's some for me:—we may call it herb-grace o' Sundays:—O, you must
  wear your rue with a difference.—There's a daisy:—I would give you
175 some violets, but they withered all when my father died:—they say, he
  made a good end,—

(Sings)
              For bonny sweet Robin is all my joy,—

LAERTES: Thoughts and affliction, passion, hell itself,
  She turns to favor and to prettiness.

OPHELIA: *(Sings)*

180
      And will he not come again?
      And will he not come again?
        No, no, he is dead,
        Go to thy death-bed,
      He never will come again.

185
      His beard was as white as snow
      All flaxen was his poll:
        He is gone, he is gone,
        And we cast away moan:
      God ha' mercy on his soul!

190
And of all Christian souls, I pray God.—God b' wi' ye. *(Exit.)*
LAERTES: Do you see this, O God?
KING: Laertes, I must commune with your grief,
Or you deny me right. Go but apart,
Make choice of whom your wisest friends you will,
195 And they shall hear and judge 'twixt you and me:
If by direct or by collateral hand
They find us touch'd, we will our kingdom give,
Our crown, our life, and all that we call ours,
To you in satisfaction; but if not,
200 Be you content to lend your patience to us,
And we shall jointly labor with your soul
To give it due content.
LAERTES: Let this be so;
His means of death, his óbscure burial,—
No trophy, sword, nor hatchment[7] o'er his bones
205 No noble rite nor formal ostentation,—
Cry to be heard, as 'twere from heaven to earth,
That I must call't in question.
KING: So you shall;
And where the offence is, let the great axe fall.
I pray you, go with me.

(Exeunt.)

SCENE VI

Another room in the castle.

(Enter Horatio and a Servant.)

---

[7]A tablet with coat of arms.

HORATIO: What are they that would speak with me?
SERVANT: Sailors, sir: they say they have letters for you.
HORATIO: Let them come in.—

(Exit Servant.)

I do not know from what part of the world
5   I should be greeted, if not from Lord Hamlet.

(Enter Sailors.)

1ST SAILOR: God bless you, sir.
HORATIO: Let him bless thee too.
1ST SAILOR: He shall, sir, an't please him. There's a letter for you, sir; it
      comes from the ambassador that was bound for England; if your name be
10   Horatio, as I am let to know it is.
HORATIO: *(Reads) Horatio, when thou shalt have overlooked this, give*
      these fellows some means to the king: they have letters for him. Ere we
      were two days old at sea, a pirate of very warlike appointment gave us
      chase. Finding ourselves too slow of sail, we put on a compelled valor;
15   *and in the grapple I boarded them; on the instant they got clear of our*
      ship; so I alone became their prisoner. They have dealt with me like
      thieves of mercy: but they knew what they did; I am to do a good turn
      for them. Let the king have the letters I have sent; and repair thou to me
      with as much haste as thou wouldst fly death. I have words to speak in
20   *thine ear will make thee dumb; yet are they much too light for the bore*
      of the matter. These good fellows will bring thee where I am. Rosen-
      crantz and Guildenstern hold their course for England: of them I have
      much to tell thee. Farewell. He that thou knowest thine.   Hamlet
      Come, I will give you way for these your letters;
25   And do't the speedier, that you may direct me
      To him from whom you brought them.

(Exeunt.)

SCENE VII

Another room in the castle.

(Enter King and Laertes.)

KING: Now must your conscience my acquittance seal,
      And you must put me in your heart for friend,
      Sith you have heard, and with a knowing ear,
      That he which hath your noble father slain
5   Pursu'd my life.
LAERTES: It well appears:—but tell me
      Why you proceeded not against these feats,

So crimeful and so capital in nature.
As by your safety, wisdom, all things else,
You mainly were stirr'd up.

KING: O, for two special reasons;

10   Which may to you, perhaps, seem much unsinew'd,
But yet to me they are strong. The queen his mother
Lives almost by his looks; and for myself,—
My virtue or my plague, be it either which,—
She's so conjunctive to my life and soul,

15   That, as the star moves not but in his sphere,
I could not but by her. The other motive,
Why to a public count I might not go,
Is the great love the general gender bear him;
Who, dipping all his faults in their affection,

20   Would, like the spring that turneth wood to stone,
Convert his gyves to graces; so that my arrows,
Too slightly timber'd for so loud a wind,
Would have reverted to my bow again,
And not where I had aim'd them.

25 **LAERTES:**   And so have I a noble father lost;
A sister driven into desperate terms,—
Whose worth, if praises may go back again,
Stood challenger on mount of all the age
For her perfections:—but my revenge will come.

30 **KING:**   Break not your sleeps for that: you must not think
That we are made of stuff so flat and dull
That we can let our beard be shook with danger,
And think it pastime. You shortly shall hear more:
I lov'd your father, and we love ourself;

35   And that, I hope, will teach you to imagine,—

(Enter a Messenger.)

How now! what news?

MESSENGER: Letters, my lord, from Hamlet:
This to your majesty; this to the queen.

KING: From Hamlet! Who brought them?

MESSENGER: Sailors, my lord, they say; I saw them not:

40   They were given me by Claudio,—he receiv'd them
Of him that brought them.

KING: Laertes, you shall hear them.—Leave us.

(Exit Messenger.)

*(Reads) High and mighty,—You shall know I am set naked on your
kingdom. To-morrow shall I beg leave to see your kingly eyes: when I*

45   *shall, first asking your pardon thereunto, recount the occasions of my*
      sudden and more strange return.   Hamlet
      What should this mean? Are all the rest come back?
      Or is it some abuse,[1] and no such thing?
      LAERTES: Know you the hand?
50   **KING:**   'Tis Hamlet's character:[2]—*Naked,*—
      And in a postscript here, he says, *alone.*
      Can you advise me?
      LAERTES: I am lost in it, my lord. But let him come;
      It warms the very sickness in my heart,
55   That I shall live, and tell him to his teeth,
      Thus diddest thou.
      KING: If it be so, Laertes,—
      As how should it be so? how otherwise?—
      Will you be rul'd by me?
      LAERTES: Ay, my lord:
      So you will not o'errule me to a peace.
60   **KING:**   To thine own peace. If he be now return'd,—
      As checking at his voyage, and that he means
      No more to undertake it,—I will work him
      To an exploit, now ripe in my device,
      Under the which he shall not choose but fall:
65   And for his death no wind of blame shall breathe;
      But even his mother shall uncharge the practice
      And call it accident.
      LAERTES: My lord, I will be rul'd;
      The rather if you could devise it so
      That I might be the organ.
      KING: It falls right.
70   You have been talk'd of since your travel much,
      And that in Hamlet's hearing, for a quality
      Wherein they say you shine: your sum of parts
      Did not together pluck such envy from him
      As did that one; and that, in my regard,
75   Of the unworthiest siege.
      LAERTES: What part is that, my lord?
      KING: A very riband in the cap of youth,
      Yet needful too; for youth no less becomes
      The light and careless livery that it wears
      Than settled age his sables and his weeds,
80   Importing health and graveness.—Two months since,
      Here was a gentleman of Normandy,—

---

[1]Ruse.   [2]Handwriting.

I've seen myself, and serv'd against, the French,
And they can well on horseback: but this gallant
Had witchcraft in't; he grew unto his seat;
85 And to such wondrous doing brought his horse,
As he had been incorps'd and demi-natur'd[3]
With the brave beast: so far he topp'd my thought,
That I, in forgery of shapes and tricks,[4]
Come short of what he did.
LAERTES: A Norman was't?
90 **KING:** A Norman.
LAERTES: Upon my life, Lamond.
KING: The very same.
LAERTES: I know him well: he is the brooch, indeed,
And gem of all the nation.
KING: He made confession of you;
95 And gave you such a masterly report
For art and exercise in your defence,
And for your rapier most especially,
That he cried out, 'twould be a sight indeed
If one could match you: the scrimers[5] of their nation,
100 He swore, had neither motion, guard, nor eye,
If you oppos'd them. Sir, this report of his
Did Hamlet so envenom with his envy,
That he could nothing do but wish and beg
Your sudden coming o'er, to play with him.
105 Now, out of this,—
LAERTES: What out of this, my lord?
KING: Laertes, was your father dear to you?
Or are you like the painting of a sorrow,
A face without a heart?
LAERTES: Why ask you this?
KING: Not that I think you did not love your father;
110 But that I know love is begun by time;
And that I see, in passages of proof,[6]
Time qualifies the spark and fire of it.
There lives within the very flame of love
A kind of wick or snuff that will abate it;
115 And nothing is at a like goodness still;
For goodness, growing to a pleurisy,[7]
Dies in his own too much: that we would do

---

[3]Made as one body and formed into half man, half horse—or centaur. [4]In imagining tricks of horsemanship. [5]Fencers. [6]The evidence of experience. [7]Plethora, an excess of blood.

We should do when we would; for this *would* changes,
And hath abatements and delays as many
120 As there are tongues, or hands, or accidents;
And then this *should* is like a spendthrift sigh
That hurts by easing. But to the quick o' the ulcer:—
Hamlet comes back: what would you undertake
To show yourself your father's son in deed
125 More than in words?

LAERTES: To cut his throat i' the church.

KING: No place, indeed, should murder sanctuarize;
Revenge should have no bounds. But, good Laertes,
Will you do this, keep close within your chamber.
Hamlet return'd shall know you are come home:
130 We'll put on those shall praise your excellence,
And set a double varnish on the fame
The Frenchman gave you; bring you, in fine, together,
And wager on yours heads: he, being remiss,[8]
Most generous, and free from all contriving,
135 Will not peruse the foils; so that, with ease,
Or with a little shuffling, you may choose
A sword unbated, and, in a pass of practice,
Requite him for your father.

LAERTES: I will do't it:
And, for that purpose, I'll anoint my sword.
140 I bought an unction of a mountebank,
So mortal that but dip a knife in it,
Where it draws blood no cataplasm so rare,[9]
Collected from all simples that have virtue
Under the moon, can save the thing from death
145 That is but scratch'd withal: I'll touch my point
With this contagion, that, if I gall him slightly,
It may be death.

KING: Let's further think of this;
Weigh what convenience both of time and means
May fit us to our shape: if this should fail,
150 And that our drift look through our bad performance,
'Twere better not assay'd: therefore this project
Should have a back or second, that might hold
If this should blast in proof. Soft! let me see:—
We'll make a solemn wager on your cunnings,—
155 I ha't:
When in your motion you are hot and dry,—

---

[8]Unguarded and free from suspicion.   [9]No poultice, however remarkably efficacious.

As make your bouts more violent to that end,—
And that he calls for drink, I'll have prepar'd him
A chalice for the nonce;[10] whereon but sipping,
160 If he by chance escape your venom'd stuck
Our purpose may hold there.

(Enter Queen.)

How now, sweet queen!
QUEEN: One woe doth tread upon another's heel,
So fast they follow:—your sister's drown'd, Laertes.
LAERTES: Drown'd! O, where?
165 QUEEN: There is a willow grows aslant a brook,
That shows his hoar leaves in the glassy stream;
There with fantastic garlands did she come
Of crowflowers, nettles, daisies, and long purples,
That liberal shepherds give a grosser name,
170 But our cold maids do dead men's fingers call them.
There, on the pendant boughs her coronet weeds
Clambering to hang, an envious[11] sliver broke;
When down her weedy trophies and herself
Fell in the weeping brook. Her clothes spread wide;
175 And, mermaid-like, awhile they bore her up:
Which time she chanted snatches of old tunes;
As one incapable of her own distress,
Or like a creature native and indu'd
Unto that element: but long it could not be
180 Till that her garments, heavy with their drink,
Pull'd the poor wretch from her melodious lay
To muddy death.
LAERTES: Alas, then, she is drown'd?
QUEEN: Drown'd, drown'd.
LAERTES: Too much of water hast thou, poor Ophelia,
185 And therefore I forbid my tears: but yet
It is our trick; nature her custom holds,
Let shame say what it will: when these are gone,
The woman will be out.[12]—Adieu, my lord:
I have a speech of fire, that fain would blaze,
190 But that this folly douts it.[13] *(Exit.)*
KING: Let's follow, Gertrude;
How much I had to do to calm his rage!
Now fear I this will give it start again;
Therefore let's follow.

(Exeunt.)

[10]Purpose.   [11]Malicious.   [12]That is, "I shall be ruthless."   [13]Drowns it.

Act V

SCENE I

A churchyard.

(Enter two Clowns[1] with spades, &c.)

1ST CLOWN: Is she to be buried in Christian burial that wilfully seeks her own salvation?

2ND CLOWN: I tell thee she is; and therefore make her grave straight: the crowner[2] hath sat on her, and finds it Christian burial.

5 **1ST CLOWN:** How can that be, unless she drowned herself in her own defence?

2ND CLOWN: Why, 'tis found so.

1ST CLOWN: It must be *se offendendo,*[3] it cannot be else. For here lies the point: if I drown myself wittingly, it argues an act: and an act hath three

10 branches; it is to act, to do, and to perform: argal,[4] she drowned herself wittingly.

2ND CLOWN: Nay, but hear you, goodman delver,—

1ST CLOWN: Give me leave. Here lies the water; good: here stands the man; good: if the man go to this water and drown himself, it is, will he, nill he,

15 he goes,—mark you that: but if the water come to him and drown him, he drowns not himself: argal, he that is not guilty of his own death shortens not his own life.

2ND CLOWN: But is this law?

1ST CLOWN: Ay, marry, is't; crowner's quest law.

20 **2ND CLOWN:** Will you ha' the truth on't? If this had not been a gentlewoman she should have been buried out of Christian burial.

1ST CLOWN: Why, there thou say'st: and the more pity that great folks should have countenance in this world to drown or hang themselves more than their even-Christian.[5]—Come, my spade. There is no ancient gentle-

25 men but gardeners, ditchers, and grave-makers; they hold up Adam's profession.

2ND CLOWN: Was he a gentleman?

1ST CLOWN: He was the first that ever bore arms.

2ND CLOWN: Why, he had none.

30 **1ST CLOWN:** What, art a heathen? How dost thou understand the Scripture? The Scripture says, Adam digged: could he dig without arms? I'll put another question to thee: if thou answerest me not to the purpose, confess thyself,[6]—

2ND CLOWN: Go to.

35 **1ST CLOWN:** What is he that builds stronger than either the mason, the shipwright, or the carpenter?

---

[1]Rustic fellows. [2]Coroner. [3]In self-offense; he means *se defendendo,* in self-defense.
[4]He means *ergo,* therefore. [5]Fellow Christian. [6]"Confess thyself an ass," perhaps.

2ND CLOWN: The gallows-maker; for that frame outlives a thousand tenants.

1ST CLOWN: I like thy wit well, in good faith: the gallows does well; but
how does it well? it does well to those that do ill: now thou dost ill to say
40   the gallows is built stronger than the church: argal, the gallows may do
well to thee. To't again, come.

2ND CLOWN: Who builds stronger than a mason, a shipwright, or a
carpenter?

1ST CLOWN: Ay, tell me that, and unyoke.

45 **2ND CLOWN:**   Marry, now I can tell.

1ST CLOWN: To't.

2ND CLOWN: Mass, I cannot tell.

(Enter Hamlet and Horatio, at a distance.)

1ST CLOWN: Cudgel thy brains no more about it, for your dull ass will not
mend his pace with beating; and when you are asked this question next,
50   say a grave-maker; the houses that he makes last till doomsday. Go, get
thee to Yaughan: fetch me a stoup of liquor.

(Exit Second Clown.)

(Digs and sings)

In youth, when I did love, did love,
   Methought it was very sweet,
To contract, O, the time, for, ah, my behove,[7]
55   O, methought there was nothing meet.

HAMLET: Has this fellow no feeling of his business, that he sings at grave-
making?

HORATIO: Custom hath made it in him a property of easiness.

HAMLET: 'Tis e'en so: the hand of little employment hath the daintier
60   sense.

1ST CLOWN: *(Sings)*

But age, with his stealing steps,
   Hath claw'd me in his clutch,
And hath shipp'd me intil the land,
   As if I had never been such.

(Throws up a skull)

65 **HAMLET:**   That skull had a tongue in it, and could sing once: how the knave
joels[8] it to the ground, as if it were Cain's jawbone, that did the first murder! This might be the pate of a politician, which this ass now o'er-
reaches; one that would circumvent God, might it not?

---

[7]Behoof, or advantage.   [8]Throws.

HORATIO: It might, my lord.

70 **HAMLET:**   Or of a courtier; which could say, *Good-morrow, sweet lord! How dost thou, good lord?* This might be my lord such-a-one, that praised my lord such-a-one's horse, when he meant to beg it,—might it not?

HORATIO: Ay, my lord.

HAMLET: Why, e'en so: and now my Lady Worm's; chapless,[9] and knocked
75   about the mazard[10] with a sexton's spade: here's fine revolution, an we had the trick to see't. Did these bones cost no more the breeding but to play at loggats[11] with 'em? Mine ache to think on't.

1ST CLOWN: *(Sings)*

> A pick-axe and a spade, a spade,
>   For and a shrouding sheet:
80 > O, a pit of clay for to be made
>   For such a guest is meet.

(Throws up another)

HAMLET: There's another: why may not that be the skull of a lawyer? Where be his quiddits[12] now, his quillets,[13] his cases, his tenures, and his tricks? why does he suffer this rude knave now to knock him about the
85   sconce with a dirty shovel, and will not tell him of his action of battery? Hum! This fellow might be in's time a great buyer of land, with his statutes, his recognizances, his fines, his double vouchers, his recoveries: is this the fine of his fines, and the recovery of his recoveries, to have his fine pate full of fine dirt? will his vouchers vouch him no more of his
90   purchases, and double ones too, than the length and breadth of a pair of indentures? The very conveyances of his lands will hardly lie in this box; and must the inheritor himself have no more, ha?

HORATIO: Not a jot more, my lord.

HAMLET: Is not parchment made of sheep-skins?

95 **HORATIO:**   Ay, my lord, and of calf-skins too.

HAMLET: They are sheep and calves which seek out assurance in that. I will speak to this fellow.—Whose grave's this, sir?

1ST CLOWN: Mine, sir.—*(Sings)*
> O, a pit of clay for to be made
100 > For such a guest is meet.

HAMLET: I think it be thine indeed; for thou liest in't.

1ST CLOWN: You lie out on't, sir, and therefore it is not yours: for my part, I do not lie in't, and yet it is mine.

HAMLET: Thou dost lie in't, to be in't, and say it is thine: 'tis for the dead,
105   not for the quick; therefore thou liest.

---

[9]Without a lower jaw.   [10]Head.   [11]A game in which small pieces of wood are hurled at a stake.   [12]"Whatnesses"—that is, hair-splittings.   [13]Quibbling distinctions.

1st Clown: 'Tis a quick lie, sir: 'twill away again from me to you.

Hamlet: What man dost thou dig it for?

1st Clown: For no man, sir.

Hamlet: What woman, then?

110 **1st Clown:** For none, neither.

Hamlet: Who is to be buried in't?

1st Clown: One that was a woman, sir; but, rest her soul, she's dead.

Hamlet: How absolute the knave is! we must speak by the card, or equivocation will undo us. By the Lord, Horatio, these three years I have taken

115   note of it; the age is grown so picked[14] that the toe of the peasant comes so near the heel of the courtier, he galls his kibe.[15]—How long hast thou been a grave-maker?

1st Clown: Of all the days i' the year, I came to't that day that our last King Hamlet o'ercame Fortinbras.

120 **Hamlet:** How long is that since?

1st Clown: Cannot you tell that? every fool can tell that: it was the very day that young Hamlet was born,—he that is mad, and sent into England.

Hamlet: Ay, marry, why was he sent into England?

1st Clown: Why, because he was mad: he shall recover his wits there; or,

125   if he do not, it's no great matter there.

Hamlet: Why?

1st Clown: 'Twill not be seen in him there; there the men are as mad as he.

Hamlet: How came he mad?

1st Clown: Very strangely, they say.

130 **Hamlet:** How strangely?

1st Clown: Faith, e'en with losing his wits.

Hamlet: Upon what ground?

1st Clown: Why, here in Denmark: I have been sexton here, man and boy, thirty years.

135 **Hamlet:** How long will a man lie i' the earth ere he rot?

1st Clown: Faith, if he be not rotten before he die,—as we have many pocky corses now-a-days, that will scarce hold the laying in,—he will last you some eight year or nine year: a tanner will last you nine year.

Hamlet: Why he more than another?

140 **1st Clown:** Why, sir, his hide is so tanned with his trade that he will keep out water a great while; and your water is a sore decayer of your whoreson dead body. Here's a skull now; this skull has lain in the earth three-and-twenty years.

Hamlet: Whose was it?

145 **1st Clown:** A whoreson mad fellow's it was: whose do you think it was?

Hamlet: Nay, I know not.

---

[14]Refined or educated.   [15]Rubs and irritates the chilblain sore on the courtier's heel.

1st Clown: A pestilence on him for a mad rogue! 'a poured a flagon of Rhenish on my head once. This same skull, sir, was Yorick's skull, the king's jester.

150 **Hamlet:**   This?

1st Clown: E'en that.

Hamlet: Let me see. *(Takes the skull)*—Alas, poor Yorick!—I knew him, Horatio; a fellow of infinite jest, of most excellent fancy: he hath borne me on his back a thousand times; and now, how abhorred in my imagination it

155 is! my gorge rises at it. Here hung those lips that I have kissed I know not how oft. Where be your gibes now? your gambols? your songs? your flashes of merriment, that were wont to set the table on a roar? Not one now, to mock your own grinning? quite chap-fallen? Now get you to my lady's chamber, and tell her, let her paint an inch thick, to this favor[16] she

160 must come; make her laugh at that.—Pr'ythee, Horatio, tell me one thing.

Horatio: What's that, my lord?

Hamlet: Dost thou think Alexander looked o' this fashion i' the earth?

Horatio: E'en so.

Hamlet: And smelt so? pah! *(Throws down the skull)*

165 **Horatio:**   E'en so, my lord.

Hamlet: To what base uses we may return, Horatio! Why may not imagination trace the noble dust of Alexander till he find it stopping a bung-hole?

Horatio: 'Twere to consider too curiously to consider so.

Hamlet: No, faith, not a jot; but to follow him thither with modesty

170 enough, and likelihood to lead it: as thus; Alexander died, Alexander was buried, Alexander returneth into dust; the dust is earth; of earth we make loam; and why of that loam whereto he was converted might they not stop a beer-barrel?

> Imperious Caesar, dead and turn'd to clay,
175 > Might stop a hole to keep the wind away:
> O, that that earth which kept the world in awe
> Should patch a wall to expel the winter's flaw!—

But soft! but soft! aside.—Here comes the king.

(Enter Priests, &c., in procession; the corpse of Ophelia, Laertes and Mourners following; King, Queen, their Trains, &c.)

The queen, the courtiers: who is that they follow?
180 And with such maimed rites? This doth betoken
The corse they follow did with desperate hand
Fordo its own life: 'twas of some estate.
Couch we awhile and mark. *(Retiring with Horatio)*

[16]Face.

LAERTES: What ceremony else?

HAMLET: That is Laertes,

185 A very noble youth: mark.

LAERTES: What ceremony else?

1ST PRIEST: Her obsequies have been as far enlarg'd
As we have warrantise: her death was doubtful,
And, but that great command o'ersways the order,

190 She should in ground unsanctified have lodg'd
Till the last trumpet; for charitable prayers,
Shards, flints, and pebbles, should be thrown on her,
Yet here she is allowed her virgin rites,
Her maiden strewments, and the bringing home

195 Of bell and burial.

LAERTES: Must there no more be done?

1ST PRIEST: No more be done:
We should profane the service of the dead
To sing a *requiem,* and such rest to her
As to peace-parted souls.

LAERTES: Lay her i' the earth;—

200 And from her fair and unpolluted flesh
May violets spring!—I tell thee, churlish priest,
A ministering angel shall my sister be
When thou liest howling.

HAMLET: What, the fair Ophelia!

QUEEN: Sweets to the sweet: farewell! *(Scattering flowers)*

205 I hop'd thou shouldst have been my Hamlet's wife;
I thought thy bride-bed to have deck'd, sweet maid,
And not have strew'd thy grave.

LAERTES: O, treble woe
Fall ten times treble on that cursed head
Whose wicked deed thy most ingenious sense

210 Depriv'd thee of!—Hold off the earth awhile,
Till I have caught her once more in mine arms:

(Leaps into the grave)

Now pile your dust upon the quick and dead,
Till of this flat a mountain you have made,
To o'er-top old Pelion[17] or the skyish head

215 Of blue Olympus.

HAMLET: *(Advancing)* What is he whose grief
Bears such an emphasis? whose phrase of sorrow
Conjures the wandering stars, and makes them stand

---

[17] A mountain in Greece.

Like wonder-wounded hearers? this is I, Hamlet the
220   Dane. *(Leaps into the grave)*
    LAERTES: The devil take thy soul! *(Grappling with him)*
    HAMLET: Thou pray'st not well.
        I pr'ythee, take thy fingers from my throat;
        For, though I am not splenetive and rash,
225   Yet have I in me something dangerous,
        Which let thy wiseness fear: away thy hand.
    KING: Pluck them asunder.
    QUEEN: Hamlet! Hamlet!
    ALL: Gentlemen,—
    HORATIO: Good my lord, be quiet.

(The Attendants part them, and they come out of the grave.)

    HAMLET: Why, I will fight with him upon this theme
230   Until my eyelids will no longer wag.
    QUEEN: O my son, what theme?
    HAMLET: I lov'd Ophelia; forty thousand brothers
        Could not, with all their quantity of love,
        Make up my sum.—What wilt thou do for her?
235 KING: O, he is mad, Laertes.
    QUEEN: For love of God, forbear him.
    HAMLET: 'Swounds, show me what thou'lt do:
        Woul't weep? woul't fight? woul't fast? woul't tear thyself?
        Woul't drink up eisel?[18] eat a crocodile?
240   I'll do't.—Dost thou come here to whine?
        To outface me with leaping in her grave?
        Be buried quick[19] with her, and so will I:
        And, if thou prate of mountains, let them throw
        Millions of acres on us, till our ground,
245   Singeing his pate against the burning zone,[20]
        Make Ossa[21] like a wart! Nay, an thou'lt mouth,
        I'll rant as well as thou.
    QUEEN: This is mere madness:
        And thus awhile the fit will work on him;
        Anon, as patient as the female dove,
250   When that her golden couplets are disclos'd,[22]
        His silence will sit drooping.
    HAMLET: Hear you, sir;
        What is the reason that you use me thus?
        I lov'd you ever: but it is no matter;

[18]Vinegar.   [19]Alive.   [20]The fiery zone of the celestial sphere.   [21]A high mountain in Greece.   [22]When the golden twins are hatched.

Let Hercules himself do what he may,
255   The cat will mew, and dog will have his day. *(Exit.)*
KING: I pray thee, good Horatio, wait upon him.—

(Exit Horatio.)

(To Laertes) Strengthen your patience in our last night's speech;
We'll put the matter to the present push.—
Good Gertrude, set some watch over your son.—
260   This grave shall have a living monument:
An hour of quiet shortly shall we see;
Till then, in patience our proceeding be.

(Exeunt.)

SCENE II

A hall in the castle.

(Enter Hamlet and Horatio.)

HAMLET: So much for this, sir: now let me see the other;
You do remember all the circumstance?
HORATIO: Remember it, my lord!
HAMLET: Sir, in my heart there was a kind of fighting
5   That would not let me sleep: methought I lay
Worse than the mutines in the bilboes.[1] Rashly,
And prais'd be rashness for it,—let us know,
Our indiscretion sometimes serves us well,
When our deep plots do fail: and that should teach us
10   There's a divinity that shapes our ends,
Rough-hew them how we will.
HORATIO: This is most certain.
HAMLET: Up from my cabin,
My sea-gown scarf'd about me, in the dark
Grop'd I to find out them: had my desire;
15   Finger'd their packet; and, in fine, withdrew
To mine own room again: making so bold,
My fears forgetting manners, to unseal
Their grand commission; where I found, Horatio,
O royal knavery! an exact command,—
20   Larded with many several sorts of reasons,
Importing Denmark's health and England's too,
With, ho! such bugs[2] and goblins in my life,—

---

[1]Mutineers in the iron stocks on board ship.   [2]Bugbears.

That, on the supervise, no leisure bated,
No, not to stay the grinding of the axe,
25   My head should be struck off.
HORATIO: Is't possible?
HAMLET: Here's the commission: read it at more leisure.
  But wilt thou hear me how I did proceed?
HORATIO: I beseech you.
HAMLET: Being thus benetted round with villainies,—
30   Ere I could make a prologue to my brains,
They had begun the play,—I sat me down;
Devis'd a new commission; wrote it fair:
I once did hold it, as our statists do,
A baseness to write fair, and labor'd much
35   How to forget that learning; but, sir, now
It did me yeoman's service. Wilt thou know
The effect of what I wrote?
HORATIO: Ay, good my lord.
HAMLET: An earnest conjuration from the king,—
As England was his faithful tributary;
40   As love between them like the palm might flourish;
As peace should still her wheaten garland wear
And stand a comma[3] 'tween their amities;
And many such like as's of great charge,—
That, on the view and know of these contents,
45   Without debatement further, more or less,
He should the bearers put to sudden death,
Not shriving-time allow'd.
HORATIO: How was this seal'd?
HAMLET: Why, even in that was heaven ordinant.
I had my father's signet in my purse,
50   Which was the model of that Danish seal:
Folded the writ up in form of the other;
Subscrib'd it; gav't the impression; plac'd it safely,
The changeling never known. Now, the next day
Was our sea-fight; and what to this was sequent
55   Thou know'st already.
HORATIO: So Guildenstern and Rosencrantz go to't.
HAMLET: Why, man, they did make love to this employment;
They are not near my conscience; their defeat
Does by their own insinuation[4] grow:
60   'Tis dangerous when the baser nature[5] comes

---

[3]Link.   [4]By their own "sticking their noses" into the business.   [5]Men of lower rank.

Between the pass and fell[6] incensed points
Of mighty opposites.

HORATIO: Why, what a king is this!

HAMLET: Does it not, think'st thee, stand me now upon,[7]
He that hath kill'd my king and whor'd my mother;
65 Popp'd in between the election and my hopes;
Thrown out his angle for my proper life,
And with such cozenage,[8]—is't not perfect conscience
To quit him with this arm? and is't not to be damn'd,
To let this canker of our nature come
70 In further evil?

HORATIO: It must be shortly known to him from England
What is the issue of the business there.

HAMLET: It will be short: the interim is mine;
And a man's life's no more than to say One.
75 But I am very sorry, good Horatio,
That to Laertes I forgot myself;
For by the image of my cause I see
The portraiture of his: I'll court his favors:
But, sure, the bravery[9] of his grief did put me
80 Into a towering passion.

HORATIO: Peace; who comes here?

(Enter Osric.)

OSRIC: Your lordship is right welcome back to Denmark.

HAMLET: I humbly thank you, sir.—Dost know this water-fly?

HORATIO: No, my good lord.

HAMLET: Thy state is the more gracious; for 'tis a vice to know him. He
85 hath much land, and fertile: let a beast be lord of beasts, and his crib shall
stand at the king's mess: 'tis a chough;[10] but, as I say, spacious in the possession of dirt.

OSRIC: Sweet lord, if your lordship were at leisure, I should impart a thing
to you from his majesty.

90 **HAMLET:** I will receive it with all diligence of spirit. Put your bonnet to his
right use; 'tis for the head.

OSRIC: I thank your lordship, 'tis very hot.

HAMLET: No, believe me, 'tis very cold; the wind is northerly.

OSRIC: It is indifferent cold, my lord, indeed.

95 **HAMLET:** Methinks it is very sultry and hot for my complexion.

---

[6]Fierce. [7]That is, "Don't you think it is my duty?" [8]Deceit. [9]Ostentation. [10]He
shall have his trough at the king's table: he is a chattering fool.

OSRIC: Exceedingly, my lord; it is very sultry,—as't were,—I cannot tell how.—But, my lord, his majesty bade me signify to you that he has laid a great wager on your head. Sir, this is the matter,—

HAMLET: I beseech you, remember,—

(Hamlet moves him to put on his hat.)

100   **OSRIC:**   Nay, in good faith; for mine ease, in good faith. Sir, here is newly come to court Laertes; believe me, an absolute gentleman, full of most excellent differences, of very soft society and great showing: indeed, to speak feelingly of him, he is the card or calendar of gentry, for you shall find in him the continent of what part a gentleman would see.

105   **HAMLET:**   Sir, his definement suffers no perdition in you;—though, I know, to divide him inventorially would dizzy the arithmetic of memory, and yet but yaw neither, in respect of his quick sail. But, in the verity of extolment, I take him to be a soul of great article; and his infusion of such dearth[11] and rareness as, to make true diction of him, his semblable is his
110   mirror; and who else would trace him, his umbrage,[12] nothing more.

OSRIC: Your lordship speaks most infallibly of him.

HAMLET: The concernancy, sir? why do we wrap the gentleman in our more rawer breath?

OSRIC: Sir?

115   **HORATIO:**   Is't not possible to understand in another tongue? You will do't sir, really.

HAMLET: What imports the nomination[13] of this gentleman?

OSRIC: Of Laertes?

HORATIO: His purse is empty already; all's golden words are spent.

120   **HAMLET:**   Of him, sir.

OSRIC: I know, you are not ignorant,—

HAMLET: I would you did, sir; yet, in faith, if you did, it would not much approve me.[14]—Well, sir.

OSRIC: You are not ignorant of what excellence Laertes is,—

125   **HAMLET:**   I dare not confess that, lest I should compare with him in excellence; but to know a man well were to know himself.

OSRIC: I mean, sir, for his weapon; but in the imputation laid on him by them, in his meed he's unfellowed.[15]

HAMLET: What's his weapon?

130   **OSRIC:**   Rapier and dagger.

HAMLET: That's two of his weapons: but, well.

---

[11]Rareness, or excellence.   [12]Shadow.   [13]Naming.   [14]If you, who are a fool, thought me not ignorant, that would not be particularly to my credit.   [15]In his worth he has no equal.

Osric: The king, sir, hath wagered with him six Barbary horses: against the
   which he has imponed,[16] as I take it, six French rapiers and poniards, with
   their assigns, as girdle, hangers, and so: three of the carriages, in faith, are
135   very dear to fancy, very responsive to the hilts, most delicate carriages,
   and of very liberal conceit.

Hamlet: What call you the carriages?

Horatio: I knew you must be edified by the margent ere you had done.[17]

Osric: The carriages, sir, are the hangers.

140 **Hamlet:**   The phrase would be more german to the matter if we could
   carry cannon by our sides: I would it might be hangers till then. But, on:
   six Barbary horses against six French swords, their assigns, and three liberal conceited carriages; that's the French bet against the Danish: why is
   this imponed, as you call it?

145 **Osric:**   The king, sir, hath laid, that in a dozen passes between you and him
   he shall not exceed you three hits: he hath laid on twelve for nine; and it
   would come to immediate trial if your lordship would vouchsafe the
   answer.

Hamlet: How if I answer no?

150 **Osric:**   I mean, my lord, the opposition of your person in trial.[18]

Hamlet: Sir, I will walk here in the hall: if it please his majesty, it is the
   breathing time of day with me: let the foils be brought, the gentleman
   willing, and the king hold his purpose, I will win for him if I can; if not, I
   will gain nothing but my shame and the odd hits.

155 **Osric:**   Shall I re-deliver you[19] e'en so?

Hamlet: To this effect, sir; after what flourish your nature will.

Osric: I commend my duty to your lordship.

Hamlet: Yours, yours.

(Exit Osric.)

   He does well to commend it himself; there are no tongues else for's turn.

160 **Horatio:**   This lapwing runs away with the shell on his head.[20]

Hamlet: He did comply with his dug before he sucked it.[21] Thus has he,—
   and many more of the same bevy, that I know the drossy age dotes on,—
   only got the tune of the time, and outward habit of encounter; a kind of
   yesty collection,[22] which carries them through and through the most
165   fanned and winnowed opinions; and do but blow them to their trial, the
   bubbles are out.

(Enter a Lord.)

---

[16]Staked.   [17]Informed by a note in the margin of your instructions.   [18]That is, the presence of your person as Laertes' opponent in the fencing contest.   [19]Carry back your answer.   [20]This precocious fellow is like a lapwing that starts running when it is barely out
of the shell.   [21]He paid compliments to his mother's breast before he sucked it.
[22]Yeasty or frothy affair.

LORD: My lord, his majesty commended him to you by young Osric, who brings back to him that you attend him in the hall: he sends to know if your pleasure hold to play with Laertes, or that you will take longer time.

170 **HAMLET:** I am constant to my purposes; they follow the king's pleasure: if his fitness speaks, mine is ready; now or whensoever, provided I be so able as now.

LORD: The king and queen and all are coming down.

HAMLET: In happy time.

175 **LORD:** The queen desires you to use some gentle entertainment to Laertes before you fall to play.

HAMLET: She well instructs me.

(Exit Lord.)

HORATIO: You will lose this wager, my lord.

HAMLET: I do not think so; since he went into France I have been in
180   continual practice: I shall win at the odds. But thou wouldst not think how ill all's here about my heart: but it is no matter.

HORATIO: Nay, good my lord,—

HAMLET: It is but foolery; but it is such a kind of gain-giving[23] as would perhaps trouble a woman.

185 **HORATIO:** If your mind dislike anything, obey it: I will forestall their repair hither, and say you are not fit.

HAMLET: Not a whit, we defy augury: there's a special providence in the fall of a sparrow. If it be now, 'tis not to come; if it be not to come, it will be now; if it be not now, yet it will come: the readiness is all. Since no
190   man has aught of what he leaves, what is't to leave betimes?[24]

(Enter King, Queen, Laertes, Lords, Osric, and Attendants with foils, &c.)

KING: Come, Hamlet, come, and take this hand from me.

(The King puts Laertes' hand into Hamlet's.)

HAMLET: Give me your pardon, sir: I have done you wrong:
         But pardon't, as you are a gentleman.
         This presence knows, and you must needs have heard,
195   How I am punish'd with sore distraction.
         What I have done,
         That might your nature, honor, and exception
         Roughly awake, I here proclaim was madness.
         Was't Hamlet wrong'd Laertes? Never Hamlet:
200   If Hamlet from himself be ta'en away,
         And when he's not himself does wrong Laertes,
         Then Hamlet does it not, Hamlet denies it.

---

[23]Misgiving.   [24]What does an early death matter?

Who does it, then? His madness: if't be so,
Hamlet is of the faction that is wrong'd;
205 His madness is poor Hamlet's enemy.
Sir, in this audience,
Let my disclaiming from a purpos'd evil
Free me so far in your most generous thoughts
That I have shot mine arrow o'er the house
210 And hurt my brother.
LAERTES: I am satisfied in nature,
Whose motive, in this case, should stir me most
To my revenge: but in my terms of honor
I stand aloof; and will no reconcilement
Till by some elder masters of known honor
215 I have a voice and precedent of peace
To keep my name ungor'd. But till that time
I do receive your offer'd love like love,
And will not wrong it.
HAMLET: I embrace it freely;
And will this brother's wager frankly play.[25]—
220 Give us the foils; come on.
LAERTES: Come, one for me.
HAMLET: I'll be your foil, Laertes; in mine ignorance
Your skill shall, like a star in the darkest night,
Stick fiery off indeed.
LAERTES: You mock me, sir.
HAMLET: No, by this hand.
225 **KING:** Give them the foils, young Osric.
Cousin Hamlet,
You know the wager?
HAMLET: Very well, my lord;
Your grace hath laid the odds o' the weaker side.
KING: I do not fear it; I have seen you both;
230 But since he's better'd, we have therefore odds.
LAERTES: This is too heavy, let me see another.
HAMLET: This likes we well. These foils have all a length?

(They prepare to play.)

OSRIC: Ay, my good lord.
KING: Set me the stoups of wine upon that table,—
235 If Hamlet give the first or second hit,
Or quit in answer of the third exchange,
Let all the battlements their ordnance fire;

---

[25]Fence with a heart free from resentment.

The king shall drink to Hamlet's better breath;
And in the cup an union[26] shall he throw,
240   Richer than that which four successive kings
In Denmark's crown have worn. Give me the cups;
And let the kettle[27] to the trumpet speak,
The trumpet to the cannoneer without,
The cannons to the heavens, the heavens to earth,
245   *Now the king drinks to Hamlet.*—Come, begin;—
And you, the judges, bear a wary eye.

HAMLET: Come on, sir.
LAERTES: Come, my lord.

(They play.)

HAMLET: One.
LAERTES: No.
HAMLET: Judgment.
OSRIC: A hit, a very palpable hit.
LAERTES: Well;—again.
KING: Stay, give me a drink.—Hamlet, this pearl is thine;
250   Here's to thy health.—

(Trumpets sound, and cannon shot off within.)

Give him the cup.
HAMLET: I'll play this bout first; set it by awhile.—
Come.—Another hit; what say you?

(They play.)

LAERTES: A touch, a touch, I do confess.
255 **KING:** Our son shall win.
QUEEN: He's fat, and scant of breath.—
Here, Hamlet, take my napkin, rub thy brows:
The queen carouses to thy fortune, Hamlet.
HAMLET: Good madam!
KING: Gertrude, do not drink.
QUEEN: I will, my lord; I pray you, pardon me.
260 **KING:** *(Aside)* It is the poison'd cup; it is too late.
HAMLET: I dare not drink yet, madam; by and by.
QUEEN: Come, let me wipe thy face.
LAERTES: My lord, I'll hit him now.
KING: I do not think't.
LAERTES: *(Aside)* And yet 'tis almost 'gainst my conscience.

---

[26]A pearl.   [27]Kettledrum.

265 **HAMLET:**   Come, for the third, Laertes: you but dally;
     I pray you, pass with your best violence:
     I am afeard you make a wanton of me.
LAERTES: Say you so? come on.

(They play.)

OSRIC: Nothing, neither way.
270 **LAERTES:**   Have at you now!

(Laertes wounds Hamlet; then, in scuffling, they change rapiers, and Hamlet wounds Laertes.)

KING: Part them; they are incens'd.
HAMLET: Nay, come, again.

(The Queen falls.)

OSRIC: Look to the queen there, ho!
HORATIO: They bleed on both sides.—How is it, my lord?
OSRIC: How is't, Laertes?
LAERTES: Why, as a woodcock to my own springe, Osric;
275   I am justly kill'd with mine own treachery.
HAMLET: How does the queen?
KING: She swoons to see them bleed.
QUEEN: No, no, the drink, the drink,—O my dear Hamlet,—
     The drink, the drink!—I am poison'd. *(Dies.)*
HAMLET: O villainy!—Ho! let the door be lock'd:
280   Treachery! seek it out.

(Laertes falls.)

LAERTES: It is here, Hamlet: Hamlet, thou art slain;
     No medicine in the world can do thee good;
     In thee there is not half an hour of life;
     The treacherous instrument is in thy hand,
285   Unbated and envenom'd: the foul practice
     Hath turn'd itself on me; lo, here I lie,
     Never to rise again: thy mother's poison'd:
     I can no more:—the king, the king's to blame.
HAMLET: The point envenom'd too!—
290   Then venom to thy work. *(Stabs the King.)*
OSRIC and LORDS: Treason! treason!
KING: O, yet defend me, friends; I am but hurt.
HAMLET: Here, thou incestuous, murderous, damned Dane,
     Drink off this potion.—Is thy union here?
295   Follow my mother.

(King dies.)

LAERTES: He is justly serv'd;
It is a poison temper'd by himself.—
Exchange forgiveness with me, noble Hamlet:
Mine and my father's death come not upon thee,
300 Nor thine on me! *(Dies.)*
HAMLET: Heaven make thee free of it! I follow thee.—
I am dead, Horatio.—Wretched queen, adieu!—
You that look pale and tremble at this chance,
That art but mutes or audience to this act,
305 Had I but time,—as this fell sergeant, death,
Is strict in his arrest,—O, I could tell you,—
But let it be.—Horatio, I am dead;
Thou liv'st; report me and my cause aright
To the unsatisfied.[28]
HORATIO: Never believe it:
310 I am more an antique Roman than a Dane,—
Here's yet some liquor left.
HAMLET: As thou'rt a man,
Give me the cup; let go; by heaven, I'll have't.—
O good Horatio, what a wounded name,
Things standing thus unknown, shall live behind me!
315 If thou didst ever hold me in thy heart,
Absent thee from felicity awhile,
And in this harsh world draw thy breath in pain,
To tell my story.—

(March afar off, and shot within.)

What warlike noise is this?
OSRIC: Young Fortinbras, with conquest come from Poland,
320 To the ambassadors of England gives
This warlike volley.
HAMLET: O, I die, Horatio;
The potent poison quite o'er-crows my spirit:
I cannot live to hear the news from England;
But I do prophesy the election lights
325 On Fortinbras: he has my dying voice;
So tell him, with the occurrents, more and less,
Which have solicited.[29]—The rest is silence. *(Dies.)*
HORATIO: Now cracks a noble heart.—Good-night, sweet prince,
And flights of angels sing thee to thy rest!
330 Why does the drum come hither?

---

[28]The uninformed. [29]So tell him, together with the events, more or less, that have brought on this tragic affair.

(March within. Enter Fortinbras, the English Ambassadors, and others.)

FORTINBRAS: Where is this sight?

HORATIO: What is it you would see?

If aught of woe or wonder, cease your search.

FORTINBRAS: This quarry cries on havoc.[30]—O proud death,

What feast is toward in thine eternal cell,

335   That thou so many princes at a shot

So bloodily hast struck?

1ST AMBASSADOR: The sight is dismal;

And our affairs from England come too late:

The ears are senseless that should give us hearing,

To tell him his commandment is fulfill'd,

340   That Rosencrantz and Guildenstern are dead:

Where should we have our thanks?

HORATIO: Not from his mouth,

Had it the ability of life to thank you:

He never gave commandment for their death.

But since, so jump[31] upon this bloody question,

345   You from the Polack wars, and you from England,

Are here arriv'd, give order that these bodies

High on a stage be placed to the view;

And let me speak to the yet unknowing world

How these things came about: so shall you hear

350   Of carnal, bloody, and unnatural acts;

Of accidental judgments, casual slaughters;

Of deaths put on by cunning and forc'd cause;

And, in this upshot, purposes mistook

Fall'n on the inventors' heads: all this can I

355   Truly deliver.

FORTINBRAS: Let us haste to hear it,

And call the noblest to the audience.

For me, with sorrow I embrace my fortune:

I have some rights of memory in this kingdom,[32]

Which now to claim my vantage doth invite me.

360 **HORATIO:**   Of that I shall have also cause to speak,

And from his mouth whose voice will draw on more:

But let this same be presently perform'd,

Even while men's minds are wild: lest more mischance

On plots and errors happen.

[30]This collection of dead bodies cries out havoc.   [31]Opportunely.   [32]I have some un-
forgotten rights to this kingdom.

FORTINBRAS: Let four captains
365 Bear Hamlet like a soldier to the stage;
For he was likely, had he been put on,[33]
To have prov'd most royally: and, for his passage,
The soldier's music and the rites of war
Speak loudly for him.—
370 Take up the bodies.—Such a sight as this
Becomes the field, but here shows much amiss.
Go, bid the soldiers shoot.

(A dead march)

(Exeunt, bearing off the dead bodies: after which a peal of ordnance is shot off.)

Reviews of Three Major Productions of *Hamlet*

John Corbin (11/17/22)

SHAKESPEARE'S HAMLET . . . . At the Sam H. Harris Theatre.
Francisco . . . . John Clark
Bernardo . . . . Lark Taylor
Horatio . . . . Frederick Lewis
Marcellus . . . . E. J. Ballantine
Ghost of Hamlet's Father . . . . . Reginald Pole
Hamlet . . . . John Barrymore
Claudius . . . . Tyrone Power
Gertrude . . . . Blanche Yurka
Polonius . . . . John S. O'Brien
Laertes . . . . Sidney Mather
Ophelia . . . . Rosalind Fuller
Rosencrantz . . . . Paul Huber
Guildenstern . . . . Lawrence Cecil
First Player . . . . Lark Taylor
Player King . . . . Burnel Lundee
Second Player . . . . Norman Hearn
Player Queen . . . . Richard Skinner
Lucianus . . . . Vadini Uraneff
A Gentlewoman . . . . Stephanie D'Este
King's Messenger . . . . Frank Boyd
First Grave Digger . . . . Whitford Kane
Second Grave Digger . . . . Cecil Clovelly

[33]Tested by succession to the throne.

A Priest .... Reginald Pole
Osric .... Edgar Stehli
Fortinbras .... Lowden Adams

The atmosphere of historic happening surrounded John Barrymore's appearance last night as the Prince of Denmark; it was unmistakable as it was indefinable. It sprang from the quality and intensity of the applause, from the hushed murmurs that swept the audience at the most unexpected moments, from the silent crowds that all evening long swarmed about the theatre entrance. It was nowhere—and everywhere. In all likelihood we have a new and a lasting Hamlet.

It was an achievement against obstacles. The setting provided by Robert Edmund Jones, though beautiful as his setting for Lionel Barrymore's "Macbeth" was trivial and grotesque, encroached upon the playing space and introduced incongruities of locale quite unnecessary. Scenically, there was really no atmosphere. Many fine dramatic values went by the board and the incomparably stirring and dramatic narrative limped. But the all important spark of genius was there.

Mr. Barrymore disclosed a new personality and a fitting one. The luminous, decadent profile of his recent Italian and Russian impersonations had vanished, and with it the exotic beauty that etched itself so unforgettably upon the memory, bringing a thrill of admiration that was half pain. This youth was wan and haggard, but right manly and forthright—dark and true and tender as befits the North. The slender figure, with its clean limbs, broad shoulders and massive head "made statues all over the stage," as was once said of Edwin Booth.

Vocally, the performance was keyed low. Deep tones prevailed, tones of a brooding, half-conscious melancholy. The "reading" of the lines was flawless—an art that is said to have been lost. The manner, for the most part, was that of conversation, almost colloquial, but the beauty of rhythm was never lost, the varied, flexible harmonies of Shakespeare's crowning period in metric mastery. Very rarely did speech quicken or the voice rise to the pitch of drama, but when this happened the effect was electric, thrilling.

It is the bad custom to look for "originality" in every successive Hamlet. In a brief and felicitous curtain speech Mr. Barrymore remarked that every one knows just how the part should be acted and he expressed pleasure that, as it seemed, he agreed with them all. The originality of his conception is that of all great Hamlets. Abandoning fine-spun theories and tortured "interpretations" he played the part for its prima facie dramatic values—sympathetically and intelligently always, but always simply. When thus rendered, no doubt has ever arisen as to the character, which is as popularly intelligible in the theatre as it has proved mysterious on the critical dissecting table.

Here is a youth of the finest intelligence, the tenderest susceptibility, with a natural vein of gayety and shrewd native wit, who is caught in the toils of moral horror and barbaric crime. Even as his will struggles impotently to master his external environment, perform the duty enjoined on him by supernatural authority, so his spirit struggles against the overbrooding cloud of melancholy.

If the performance had any major fault it was monotony, and the effect was abetted by the incubus of the scenic investiture. There was simply no room to play in. It may be noted as characteristic that the Ghost was not visible: the majesty of buried Denmark spoke off-stage while a vague light wavered fitfully in the centre of the backdrop. In one way or another the play within the play, the scene of the King at prayer and that of Ophelia's burial all more or less failed to register dramatically.

The production came precious near to qualifying as a platform recitation. But even at that Mr. Barrymore might have vitalized more fully many moments. With repetition he will doubtless do so. The important point is that he revealed last night all the requisite potentialities of personality, of intelligence and of histrionic art.

The supporting company was adequate, but nothing more. The outstanding figures were the King of Tyrone Power and the Queen of Blanche Yurka. Neither Polonius nor the Grave Diggers registered the comedy values of their parts, a fact which contributed largely to the effect of monotony. But, strange to relate, the speaking of lines was uniformly good.

Brooks Atkinson (10/9/36)

> HAMLET in two acts and nineteen scenes. Settings and costumes by Jo Mielziner; staged and revived by Guthrie McClintic. At the Empire Theatre.

Francisco	Murvyn Vye
Bernardo	Reed Herring
Horatio	Harry Andrews
Marcellus	Barry Kelly
Ghost, Claudius	Malcolm Keen
Cornelius	Whitner Bissell
Voltimand	James Dinan
Laertes	John Emery
Polonius	Arthur Byron
Hamlet	John Gielgud
Gertrude	Judith Anderson
Ophelia	Lillian Gish
Reynaldo	Murvyn Vye
Rosencrantz	John Cromwell
Guildenstern	William Roehrick
The Player King	Harry Mestayer
Prologue	Ivan Triesault
The Player Queen	Ruth March

```
Lucianus . . . . . . . . . . . . . . . . . . . . . . Whitner Bissell
Fortinbras  . . . . . . . . . . . . . . . . . . . . Reed Herring
A Captain . . . . . . . . . . . . . . . . . . . . . George Vincent
A Sailor . . . . . . . . . . . . . . . . . . . . . . . William Stanley
First Grave-Digger  . . . . . . . . . . . . . . George Nash
Second Grave-Digger  . . . . . . . . . . . . Barry Kelly
Priest  . . . . . . . . . . . . . . . . . . . . . . . . Ivan Triesault
Osric  . . . . . . . . . . . . . . . . . . . . . . . . Morgan Farley
```

They have seen "Hamlet" well bestowed at the Empire, where he was produced last evening. They have brought to America John Gielgud, whose Hamlet has a prodigious reputation in London, and surrounded him with a cast that includes Judith Anderson, Lillian Gish, Arthur Byron, Malcolm Keen and John Emery. Under Guthrie McClintic's direction, Jo Mielziner has been poking ominous battlements into the night air and stretching royal brocades across the king's apartments. And so the magnificoes of the modern theater, who latterly were creating a masterly "Romeo and Juliet," have come to a greater panel in the Shakespearean screen and performed honorably before it.

Although Mr. Gielgud once acted here in "The Patriot," he comes now on the clouds of glory that in the last few years have been rising around him in London. He is young, slender and handsome, with a sensitive, mobile face and blond hair, and he plays his part with extraordinary grace and winged intelligence. For this is no roaring, robustious Hamlet, lost in melancholy, but an appealing young man brimming over with grief. His suffering is that of a cultivated youth whose affections are warm and whose honor is bright. Far from being a traditional Hamlet, beating the bass notes of some mighty lines, Mr. Gielgud speaks the lines with the quick spontaneity of a modern man. His emotions are keen. He looks on tragedy with the clarity of the mind's eye.

As the results prove in the theatre, this is one mettlesome way of playing the English stage's most familiar classic—one way of modernizing the character. But it is accomplished somewhat at the expense of the full-blooded verse of Shakespeare. What Mr. Gielgud's Hamlet lacks is a solid body of overpowering emotion, the command, power and storm of Elizabethan tragedy. For it is a paradox of Hamlet that vigorous actors who know a good deal less about the character than Mr. Gielgud does can make the horror more harrowing and the tragedy more deeply felt.

Like Mr. Gielgud, Mr. McClintic and his actors have studied the play with fresh eyes. Arthur Byron's Polonius, for example, is no doddering fool but a credible old man with the grooved mind of a trained statesman. Malcolm Keen's King is physically and mentally alive. As the Queen, Judith Anderson has abandoned the matronly stuffiness that usually plagues that part and given us a woman of strong and bewildered feeling. What any actress can do for Ophelia Lillian Gish has done with innocence of perception, but that disordered part contains some of the sorriest interludes that ever blotted paper. Inscribe on the credit side the Laertes of John Emery, the first grave-digger of George Nash and the honest Horatio of Harry Andrews.

Mr. McClintic and Mr. Mielziner have done better, especially in "Romeo and Juliet." There is a studied balance to some of Mr. Mielziner's designs that gives them an unpleasant rigidity, although his costumes are vivid with beauty. And the performance of "Hamlet" does not proceed with the single impetuosity of a perfectly orchestrated work of art, as most of Mr. McClintic's do. This is an admirable "Hamlet" that requires comparison with the best. For intellectual beauty, in fact, it ranks with the best. But there is a coarser ferocity to Shakespeare's tragedy that is sound theatre and that is wanting in Mr. Gielgud's art.

◆ ◆ ◆

Keanu Reeves as *Hamlet*

Shelley Levitt and *Natasha Stoynoff (1/19/95)*

Something is . . . Well, not rotten but, you know, *weird* in Winnipeg. In that Manitoba, Canada, city of 652,000, the *Collected Works of William Shakespeare* has become a hot seller. The fashion rage is $20 black T-shirts emblazoned with the famous admonition of Polonius, "To thine own self be true." The 24-day run of *Hamlet* in the 789-seat Manitoba Theatre Centre, scheduled to end on Feb. 4, has been sold out for weeks; scalpers are offering $36 tickets for upward of $750—and finding grateful buyers. Elke Schnell, a 38-year-old flight attendant, came all the way from Düsseldorf, Germany, to see the show *without* a ticket. She scored one at the last minute. "I was," she says, "desperate." So are the hundreds of teenage girls who stand outside the stage door, even though the temperature can drop to 20° below. Inside, meanwhile, it's downright cozy as sighs and gasps rise nightly from the audience.

The frenzy has very little to do with a melancholy Dane and everything to do with a muscular dude named Keanu Reeves. As a Shakespearean actor, Reeves has, as one 15-year-old fan points out, "a great butt." Yet more serious critics have also been kind. Roger Lewis of London's *Sunday Times* flew in from Europe and lauded Reeves as "wonderful. He quite embodied the . . . splendid fury, the animal grace . . . that form the Prince of Denmark."

"And," adds H. J. Kirchhoff of Toronto's *Globe and Mail,* "he does look great in tights."

Though he is better known for such movies as *Speed* and *Bill and Ted's Excellent Adventure,* this is not Reeves's first brush with the Bard. He is, in fact, a veritable Slacker-on-Avon, having played Trinculo in a Lenox, Mass., production of *The Tempest* in 1989, and a sullen Don John in Kenneth Branagh's 1993 screen version of *Much Ado About Nothing.*

Last spring, when Reeves was shooting the futuristic thriller *Johnny Mnemonic,* he got a call from Lewis Baumander, who had directed him in *Romeo and Juliet* (Keanu played Mercutio) in the actor's hometown of Toronto 10 years ago. When Baumander offered the chance to play Hamlet, Reeves, who gets $7 million per picture, agreed to take the role for $2,000 a week. Doing Hamlet also meant turning down a chance to work with Al Pacino and Robert De Niro in a movie called *Heat,* which is about to begin shooting in L.A. "It was painful," Reeves said of passing up that part. And yet the play really was the thing. "This seemed a good opportunity for him to get back to the basics," says Baumander, "and out of the spotlight—or so we thought."

Instead, the spotlight has come to Winnipeg, a city seized by what a local bar owner calls Keanu fever. Since the production was announced last summer, the box office has been fielding frantic calls from would-be buyers as far away as Finland and Japan. A woman from Australia bought tickets for eight shows and has moved here for the month. Says ticket seller Michaela Porter: "It's been madness."

Things only got crazier when Reeves arrived in early December to begin rehearsals. "Fans had the place surrounded," says Porter. But Reeves, clad in an oversize blue parka, black cap and scarf, looked pretty much like everyone else in town and slipped in unnoticed. The *Winnipeg Free Press* launched a Keanu Hotline to record sightings, then abandoned the enterprise. "As it turned out," says entertainment editor Morley Walker, "all he was doing was going to work, going back to his hotel room and occasionally eating in a restaurant."

Though reclusive, Reeves has been good for the local economy. The Pocket Bar and Grill has seen a sharp rise in female patrons since Keanu paid a few visits. And the *Free Press* reported that a riot nearly ensued at a local shopping mall after Reeves left his charge card at a clothing store and the manager had him paged so he could retrieve it. (Reeves sent a friend in his stead.)

If you can find him, though, the star is friendly. After the Jan. 12 opening, he stayed for two hours signing autographs. And though Reeves has said he wants to do "a Hamlet of passion and reason," he is not taking himself too seriously. When he nearly missed an entrance cue one night, he flew to the stage, then mugged to a fellow actor, "So, where were *you?*"

That kind of attitude has earned him fans among the cast. "Everyone was nervous except Keanu," says Wayne Nicklas, who plays Marcellus. "He was the bravest of the cast, always leading the way." Kenneth Clark, head of the English department at Winnipeg's River East Collegiate high school, offers Reeves another kind of praise. "He has kindled an interest," Clark says. "To a new generation, Keanu has made Shakespeare come alive."

Henrik Ibsen, 1828–1906

A Doll's House (1879)

translated by Rolf Fjelde

CHARACTERS

Torvald Helmer, *a lawyer*
Nora, *his wife*
Dr. Rank
Mrs. Linde
Nils Krogstad, *a bank clerk*
The Helmers' three small children
Anne-Marie, *their nurse*
Helene, *a maid*
A Delivery Boy

The action takes place in Helmer's residence.

Act I

A comfortable room, tastefully but not expensively furnished. A door to the right in the back wall leads to the entryway; another to the left leads to Helmer's study. Between these doors, a piano. Midway in the left-hand wall a door, and further back a window. Near the window a round table with an armchair and a small sofa. In the right-hand wall, toward the rear, a door, and nearer the foreground a porcelain stove with two armchairs and a rocking chair beside it. Between the stove and the side door, a small table. Engravings on the walls. An étagère with china figures and other small art objects; a small bookcase with richly bound books; the floor carpeted; a fire burning in the stove. It is a winter day.

A bell rings in the entryway; shortly after we hear the door being unlocked. Nora comes into the room, humming happily to herself; she is wearing street clothes and carries an armload of packages, which she puts down on the table to the right. She has left the hall door open; and through it a Delivery Boy is seen, holding a Christmas tree and a basket, which he gives to the Maid who let them in.

NORA: Hide the tree well, Helene. The children mustn't get a glimpse of it till this evening, after it's trimmed. *(To the Delivery Boy, taking out her purse.)* How much?

DELIVERY BOY: Fifty, ma'am.

NORA: There's a crown. No, keep the change. *(The Boy thanks her and leaves. Nora shuts the door. She laughs softly to herself while taking off her street things. Drawing a bag of macaroons from her pocket, she eats a couple, then steals over and listens at her husband's study door.)* Yes, he's home. *(Hums again as she moves to the table right.)*

HELMER: *(from the study)* Is that my little lark twittering out there?

5 **NORA:** *(busy opening some packages)* Yes, it is.

HELMER: Is that my squirrel rummaging around?

NORA: Yes!

HELMER: When did my squirrel get in?

NORA: Just now. *(Putting the macaroon bag in her pocket and wiping her mouth.)* Do come in, Torvald, and see what I've bought.

10 **HELMER:** Can't be disturbed. *(After a moment he opens the door and peers in, pen in hand.)* Bought, you say? All that there? Has the little spendthrift been out throwing money around again?

NORA: Oh, but Torvald, this year we really should let ourselves go a bit. It's the first Christmas we haven't had to economize.

HELMER: But you know we can't go squandering.

NORA: Oh yes, Torvald, we can squander a little now. Can't we? Just a tiny, wee bit. Now that you've got a big salary and are going to make piles and piles of money.

HELMER: Yes—starting New Year's. But then it's a full three months till the raise comes through.

15 **NORA:** Pooh! We can borrow that long.

HELMER: Nora! *(Goes over and playfully takes her by the ear.)* Are your scatterbrains off again? What if today I borrowed a thousand crowns, and you squandered them over Christmas week, and then on New Year's Eve a roof tile fell on my head, and I lay there—

NORA: *(putting her hand on his mouth)* Oh! Don't say such things!

HELMER: Yes, but what if it happened—then what?

NORA: If anything so awful happened, then it just wouldn't matter if I had debts or not.

20 **HELMER:** Well, but the people I'd borrowed from?

NORA: Them? Who cares about them! They're strangers.

HELMER: Nora, Nora, how like a woman! No, but seriously, Nora, you know what I think about that. No debts! Never borrow! Something of freedom's lost—and something of beauty, too—from a home that's founded on borrowing and debt. We've made a brave stand up to now, the two of us; and we'll go right on like that the little while we have to.

NORA: *(going toward the stove)* Yes, whatever you say, Torvald.

HELMER: *(following her)* Now, now, the little lark's wings mustn't droop. Come on, don't be a sulky squirrel. *(Taking out his wallet.)* Nora, guess what I have here.

25 **NORA:** *(turning quickly)* Money!

HELMER: There, see. *(Hands her some notes.)* Good grief, I know how costs go up in a house at Christmastime.

NORA: Ten—twenty—thirty—forty. Oh, thank you, Torvald; I can manage no end on this.

HELMER: You really will have to.

NORA: Oh yes, I promise I will! But come here so I can show you everything I bought. And so cheap! Look, new clothes for Ivar here—and a sword. Here a horse and a trumpet for Bob. And a doll and a doll's bed here for Emmy; they're nothing much, but she'll tear them to bits in no time anyway. And here I have dress material and handkerchiefs for the maids. Old Anne-Marie really deserves something more.

30 **HELMER:** And what's in that package there?

NORA: *(with a cry)* Torvald, no! You can't see that till tonight!

HELMER: I see. But tell me now, you little prodigal, what have you thought of for yourself?

NORA: For myself? Oh, I don't want anything at all.

HELMER: Of course you do. Tell me just what—within reason—you'd most like to have.

35 **NORA:** I honestly don't know. Oh, listen, Torvald—

HELMER: Well?

NORA: *(fumbling at his coat buttons, without looking at him)* If you want to give me something, then maybe you could—you could—

HELMER: Come on, out with it.

NORA: *(hurriedly)* You could give me money, Torvald. No more than you think you can spare; then one of these days I'll buy something with it.

40 **HELMER:** But Nora—

NORA: Oh, please, Torvald darling, do that! I beg you, please. Then I could hang the bills in pretty gilt paper on the Christmas tree. Wouldn't that be fun?

HELMER: What are those little birds called that always fly through their fortunes?

NORA: Oh yes, spendthrifts; I know all that. But let's do as I say, Torvald; then I'll have time to decide what I really need most. That's very sensible, isn't it?

HELMER: *(smiling)* Yes, very—that is, if you actually hung onto the money I give you, and you actually used it to buy yourself something. But it goes for the house and for all sorts of foolish things, and then I only have to lay out some more.

45 **NORA:** Oh, but Torvald—

HELMER: Don't deny it, my dear little Nora. *(Putting his arm around her waist.)* Spendthrifts are sweet, but they use up a frightful amount of money. It's incredible what it costs a man to feed such birds.

NORA: Oh, how can you say that! Really, I save everything I can.

HELMER: *(laughing)* Yes, that's the truth. Everything you can. But that's nothing at all.

NORA: *(humming, with a smile of quiet satisfaction)* Hm, if you only knew what expenses we larks and squirrels have, Torvald.

50 **HELMER:** You're an odd little one. Exactly the way your father was. You're never at a loss for scaring up money; but the moment you have it, it runs right out through your fingers; you never know what you've done with it. Well, one takes you as you are. It's deep in your blood. Yes, these things are hereditary, Nora.

NORA: Ah, I could wish I'd inherited many of Papa's qualities.

HELMER: And I couldn't wish you anything but just what you are, my sweet little lark. But wait; it seems to me you have a very—what should I call it?—a very suspicious look today—

NORA: I do?

HELMER: You certainly do. Look me straight in the eye.

55 **NORA:** *(looking at him)* Well?

HELMER: *(shaking an admonitory finger)* Surely my sweet tooth hasn't been running riot in town today, has she?

NORA: No. Why do you imagine that?

HELMER: My sweet tooth really didn't make a little detour through the confectioner's?

NORA: No, I assure you, Torvald—

60 **HELMER:** Hasn't nibbled some pastry?

NORA: No, not at all.

HELMER: Nor even munched a macaroon or two?

NORA: No, Torvald, I assure you, really—

HELMER: There, there now. Of course I'm only joking.

65 **NORA:** *(going to the table, right)* You know I could never think of going against you.

HELMER: No, I understand that; and you *have* given me your word. *(Going over to her.)* Well, you keep your little Christmas secrets to yourself, Nora darling. I expect they'll come to light this evening, when the tree is lit.

NORA: Did you remember to ask Dr. Rank?

HELMER: No. But there's no need for that; it's assumed he'll be dining with us. All the same, I'll ask him when he stops by here this morning. I've ordered some fine wine. Nora, you can't imagine how I'm looking forward to this evening.

NORA: So am I. And what fun for the children, Torvald!

70 **HELMER:** Ah, it's so gratifying to know that one's gotten a safe, secure job, and with a comfortable salary. It's a great satisfaction, isn't it?

NORA: Oh, it's wonderful!

HELMER: Remember last Christmas? Three whole weeks before, you shut yourself in every evening till long after midnight, making flowers for the Christmas tree, and all the other decorations to surprise us. Ugh, that was the dullest time I've ever lived through.

NORA: It wasn't at all dull for me.

HELMER: *(smiling)* But the outcome *was* pretty sorry, Nora.

75 **NORA:** Oh, don't tease me with that again. How could I help it that the cat came in and tore everything to shreds.

HELMER: No, poor thing, you certainly couldn't. You wanted so much to please us all, and that's what counts. But it's just as well that the hard times are past.

NORA: Yes, it's really wonderful.

HELMER: Now I don't have to sit here alone, boring myself, and you don't have to tire your precious eyes and your fair little delicate hands—

NORA: *(clapping her hands)* No, is it really true, Torvald, I don't have to? Oh, how wonderfully lovely to hear! *(Taking his arm.)* Now I'll tell you just how I've thought we should plan things. Right after Christmas—*(The doorbell rings.)* Oh, the bell. *(Straightening the room up a bit.)* Somebody would have to come. What a bore!

80 **HELMER:** I'm not at home to visitors, don't forget.

MAID: *(from the hall doorway)* Ma'am, a lady to see you—

NORA: All right, let her come in.

MAID: *(to Helmer)* And the doctor's just come too.

HELMER: Did he go right to my study?

85 **MAID:** Yes, he did.

Helmer goes into his room. The Maid shows in Mrs. Linde, dressed in traveling clothes, and shuts the door after her.

MRS. LINDE: *(in a dispirited and somewhat hesitant voice)* Hello, Nora.

NORA: *(uncertain)* Hello—

MRS. LINDE: You don't recognize me.

NORA: No, I don't know—but wait, I think—*(Exclaiming.)* What! Kristine! Is it really you?

90 **MRS. LINDE:** Yes, it's me.

NORA: Kristine! To think I didn't recognize you. But then, how could I? *(More quietly.)* How you've changed, Kristine!

MRS. LINDE: Yes, no doubt I have. In nine—ten long years.

NORA: Is it so long since we met! Yes, it's all of that. Oh, these last eight years have been a happy time, believe me. And so now you've come in to town, too. Made the long trip in the winter. That took courage.

MRS. LINDE: I just got here by ship this morning.

95 **NORA:**   To enjoy yourself over Christmas, of course. Oh, how lovely! Yes, enjoy ourselves, we'll do that. But take your coat off. You're not still cold? *(Helping her.)* There now, let's get cozy here by the stove. No, the easy chair there! I'll take the rocker here. *(Seizing her hands.)* Yes, now you have your old look again; it was only in that first moment. You're a bit more pale, Kristine—and maybe a bit thinner.

MRS. LINDE: And much, much older, Nora.

NORA: Yes, perhaps a bit older; a tiny, tiny bit; not much at all. *(Stopping short; suddenly serious.)* Oh, but thoughtless me, to sit here, chattering away. Sweet, good Kristine, can you forgive me?

MRS. LINDE: What do you mean, Nora?

NORA: *(softly)* Poor Kristine, you've become a widow.

100 **MRS. LINDE:**   Yes, three years ago.

NORA: Oh, I knew it, of course: I read it in the papers. Oh, Kristine, you must believe me; I often thought of writing you then, but I kept postponing it, and something always interfered.

MRS. LINDE: Nora dear, I understand completely.

NORA: No, it was awful of me, Kristine. You poor thing, how much you must have gone through. And he left you nothing?

MRS. LINDE: No.

105 **NORA:**   And no children?

MRS. LINDE: No.

NORA: Nothing at all, then?

MRS. LINDE: Not even a sense of loss to feed on.

NORA: *(looking incredulously at her)* But Kristine, how could that be?

110 **MRS. LINDE:**   *(smiling wearily and smoothing her hair)* Oh, sometimes it happens, Nora.

NORA: So completely alone. How terribly hard that must be for you. I have three lovely children. You can't see them now; they're out with the maid. But now you must tell me everything—

MRS. LINDE: No, no, no, tell me about yourself.

NORA: No, you begin. Today I don't want to be selfish. I want to think only of you today. But there *is* something I must tell you. Did you hear of the wonderful luck we had recently?

MRS. LINDE: No, what's that?

115 **NORA:**   My husband's been made manager in the bank, just think!

MRS. LINDE: Your husband? How marvelous!

NORA: Isn't it? Being a lawyer is such an uncertain living, you know, especially if one won't touch any cases that aren't clean and decent. And of course Torvald would never do that, and I'm with him completely there. Oh, we're simply delighted, believe me! He'll join the bank right after New Year's and start getting a huge salary and lots of commissions. From now on we can live quite differently—just as we want. Oh, Kristine, I feel

so light and happy! Won't it be lovely to have stacks of money and not a
care in the world?

MRS. LINDE: Well, anyway, it would be lovely to have enough for necessities.

NORA: No, not just for necessities, but stacks and stacks of money!

120 MRS. LINDE: *(smiling)* Nora, Nora, aren't you sensible yet? Back in school
you were such a free spender.

NORA: *(with a quiet laugh)* Yes, that's what Torvald still says. *(Shaking her
finger.)* But "Nora, Nora" isn't as silly as you all think. Really, we've been
in no position for me to go squandering. We've had to work, both of us.

MRS. LINDE: You too?

NORA: Yes, at odd jobs—needlework, crocheting, embroidery, and such—
(casually) and other things too. You remember that Torvald left the department when we were married? There was no chance of promotion in
his office, and of course he needed to earn more money. But that first
year he drove himself terribly. He took on all kinds of extra work that
kept him going morning and night. It wore him down, and then he fell
deathly ill. The doctors said it was essential for him to travel south.

MRS. LINDE: Yes, didn't you spend a whole year in Italy?

125 NORA: That's right. It wasn't easy to get away, you know. Ivar had just been
born. But of course we had to go. Oh, that was a beautiful trip, and it
saved Torvald's life. But it cost a frightful sum, Kristine.

MRS. LINDE: I can well imagine.

NORA: Four thousand, eight hundred crowns it cost. That's really a lot of
money.

MRS. LINDE: But it's lucky you had it when you needed it.

NORA: Well, as it was, we got it from Papa.

130 MRS. LINDE: I see. It was just about the time your father died.

NORA: Yes, just about then. And, you know, I couldn't make that trip out
to nurse him. I had to stay here, expecting Ivar any moment, and with
my poor sick Torvald to care for. Dearest Papa, I never saw him again,
Kristine. Oh, that was the worst time I've known in all my marriage.

MRS. LINDE: I know how you loved him. And then you went off to Italy?

NORA: Yes. We had the means now, and the doctors urged us. So we left a
month after.

MRS. LINDE: And your husband came back completely cured?

135 NORA: Sound as a drum!

MRS. LINDE: But—the doctor?

NORA: Who?

MRS. LINDE: I thought the maid said he was a doctor, the man who came in
with me.

NORA: Yes, that was Dr. Rank—but he's not making a sick call. He's our
closest friend, and he stops by at least once a day. No, Torvald hasn't had a
sick moment since, and the children are fit and strong, and I am, too.
(Jumping up and clapping her hands.) Oh, dear God, Kristine, what a
lovely thing to live and be happy! But how disgusting of me—I'm talking

of nothing but my own affairs. *(Sits on a stool close by Kristine, arms resting across her knees.)* Oh, don't be angry with me! Tell me, is it really true that you weren't in love with your husband? Why did you marry him, then?

140   **MRS. LINDE:** My mother was still alive, but bedridden and helpless—and I had my two younger brothers to look after. In all conscience, I didn't think I could turn him down.

NORA: No, you were right there. But was he rich at the time?

MRS. LINDE: He was very well off, I'd say. But the business was shaky, Nora. When he died, it all fell apart, and nothing was left.

NORA: And then—?

MRS. LINDE: Yes, so I had to scrape up a living with a little shop and a little teaching and whatever else I could find. The last three years have been like one endless workday without a rest for me. Now it's over, Nora. My poor mother doesn't need me, for she's passed on. Nor the boys, either; they're working now and can take care of themselves.

145   **NORA:** How free you must feel—

MRS. LINDE: No—only unspeakably empty. Nothing to live for now. *(Standing up anxiously.)* That's why I couldn't take it any longer out in that desolate hole. Maybe here it'll be easier to find something to do and keep my mind occupied. If I could only be lucky enough to get a steady job, some office work—

NORA: Oh, but Kristine, that's so dreadfully tiring, and you already look so tired. It would be much better for you if you could go off to a bathing resort.

MRS. LINDE: *(going toward the window)* I have no father to give me travel money, Nora.

NORA: *(rising)* Oh, don't be angry with me.

150   **MRS. LINDE:** *(going to her)* Nora dear, don't you be angry with me. The worst of my kind of situation is all the bitterness that's stored away. No one to work for, and yet you're always having to snap up your opportunities. You have to live; and so you grow selfish. When you told me the happy change in your lot, do you know I was delighted less for your sakes than for mine?

NORA: How so? Oh, I see. You think Torvald could do something for you.

MRS. LINDE: Yes, that's what I thought.

NORA: And he will, Kristine! Just leave it to me; I'll bring it up so delicately—find something attractive to humor him with. Oh, I'm so eager to help you.

MRS. LINDE: How very kind of you, Nora, to be so concerned over me—doubly kind, considering you really know so little of life's burdens yourself.

155   **NORA:** I—? I know so little—?

MRS. LINDE: *(smiling)* Well my heavens—a little needlework and such— Nora, you're just a child.

NORA: *(tossing her head and pacing the floor)* You don't have to act so superior.

MRS. LINDE: Oh?

NORA: You're just like the others. You all think I'm incapable of anything serious—

160 **MRS. LINDE:**   Come now—

NORA: That I've never had to face the raw world.

MRS. LINDE: Nora dear, you've just been telling me all your troubles.

NORA: Hm! Trivial! *(Quietly.)* I haven't told you the big thing.

MRS. LINDE: Big thing? What do you mean?

165 **NORA:**   You look down on me so, Kristine, but you shouldn't. You're proud that you worked so long and hard for your mother.

MRS. LINDE: I don't look down on a soul. But it *is* true: I'm proud—and happy, too—to think it was given to me to make my mother's last days almost free of care.

NORA: And you're also proud thinking of what you've done for your brothers.

MRS. LINDE: I feel I've a right to be.

NORA: I agree. But listen to this, Kristine—I've also got something to be proud and happy for.

170 **MRS. LINDE:**   I don't doubt it. But whatever do you mean?

NORA: Not so loud. What if Torvald heard! He mustn't, not for anything in the world. Nobody must know, Kristine. No one but you.

MRS. LINDE: But what is it, then?

NORA: Come here. *(Drawing her down beside her on the sofa.)* It's true— I've also got something to be proud and happy for. I'm the one who saved Torvald's life.

MRS. LINDE: Saved—? Saved how?

175 **NORA:**   I told you about the trip to Italy. Torvald never would have lived if he hadn't gone south—

MRS. LINDE: Of course; your father gave you the means—

NORA: *(smiling)* That's what Torvald and all the rest think, but—

MRS. LINDE: But—?

NORA: Papa didn't give us a pin. I was the one who raised the money.

180 **MRS. LINDE:**   You? That whole amount?

NORA: Four thousand, eight hundred crowns. What do you say to that?

MRS. LINDE: But Nora, how was it possible? Did you win the lottery?

NORA: *(disdainfully)* The lottery? Pooh! No art to that.

MRS. LINDE: But where did you get it from then?

185 **NORA:**   *(humming, with a mysterious smile)* Hmm, tra-la-la-la.

MRS. LINDE: Because you couldn't have borrowed it.

NORA: No? Why not?

MRS. LINDE: A wife can't borrow without her husband's consent.

NORA: *(tossing her head)* Oh, but a wife with a little business sense, a wife who knows how to manage—

190 **MRS. LINDE:**   Nora, I simply don't understand—

NORA: You don't have to. Whoever said I *borrowed* the money? I could have gotten it other ways. *(Throwing herself back on the sofa.)* I could

have gotten it from some admirer or other. After all, a girl with my rav-
ishing appeal—

MRS. LINDE: You lunatic.

NORA: I'll bet you're eaten up with curiosity, Kristine.

MRS. LINDE: Now listen here, Nora—you haven't done something indiscreet?

195 **NORA:**   *(sitting up again)* Is it indiscreet to save your husband's life?

MRS. LINDE: I think it's indiscreet that without his knowledge you—

NORA: But that's the point: he mustn't know! My Lord, can't you understand? He mustn't ever know the close call he had. It was to *me* the doctors came to say his life was in danger—that nothing could save him but a
stay in the south. Didn't I try strategy then! I began talking about how
lovely it would be for me to travel abroad like other young wives; I begged
and I cried; I told him please to remember my condition, to be kind and indulge me; and then I dropped a hint that he could easily take out a loan.
But at that, Kristine, he nearly exploded. He said I was frivolous, and it
was his duty as man of the house not to indulge me in whims and fan-
cies—as I think he called them. Aha, I thought, now you'll just have to be
saved—and that's when I saw my chance.

MRS. LINDE: And your father never told Torvald the money wasn't from
him?

NORA: No, never. Papa died right about then. I'd considered bringing him
into my secret and begging him never to tell. But he was too sick at the
time—and then, sadly, it didn't matter.

200 **MRS. LINDE:**   And you've never confided in your husband since?

NORA: For heaven's sake, no! Are you serious? He's so strict on that subject.
Besides—Torvald, with all his masculine pride—how painfully humiliat-
ing for him if he ever found out he was in debt to me. That would just ruin
our relationship. Our beautiful, happy home would never be the same.

MRS. LINDE: Won't you ever tell him?

NORA: *(thoughtfully, half smiling)* Yes—maybe sometime, years from
now, when I'm no longer so attractive. Don't laugh! I only mean when
Torvald loves me less than now, when he stops enjoying my dancing and
dressing up and reciting for him. Then it might be wise to have something
in reserve—*(Breaking off.)* How ridiculous! That'll never happen—Well,
Kristine, what do you think of my big secret? I'm capable of something
too, hm? You can imagine, of course, how this thing hangs over me. It really hasn't been easy meeting the payments on time. In the business
world there's what they call quarterly interest and what they call amorti-
zation, and these are always so terribly hard to manage. I've had to skimp
a little here and there, wherever I could, you know. I could hardly spare
anything from my house allowance, because Torvald has to live well. I
couldn't let the children go poorly dressed; whatever I got for them, I felt
I had to use up completely—the darlings!

MRS. LINDE: Poor Nora, so it had to come out of your own budget, then?

205 **NORA:**   Yes, of course. But I was the one most responsible, too. Every time
Torvald gave me money for new clothes and such, I never used more than

half; always bought the simplest, cheapest outfits. It was a godsend that everything looks so well on me that Torvald never noticed. But it did weigh me down at times, Kristine. It *is* such a joy to wear fine things. You understand.

MRS. LINDE: Oh, of course.

NORA: And then I found other ways of making money. Last winter I was lucky enough to get a lot of copying to do. I locked myself in and sat writing every evening till late in the night. Ah, I was tired so often, dead tired. But still it was wonderful fun, sitting and working like that, earning money. It was almost like being a man.

MRS. LINDE: But how much have you paid off this way so far?

NORA: That's hard to say, exactly. These accounts, you know, aren't easy to figure. I only know that I've paid out all I could scrape together. Time and again I haven't known where to turn. *(Smiling.)* Then I'd sit here dreaming of a rich old gentleman who had fallen in love with me—

210 MRS. LINDE: What! Who is he?

NORA: Oh, really! And that he'd died, and when his will was opened, there in big letters it said, "All my fortune shall be paid over in cash, immediately, to that enchanting Mrs. Nora Helmer."

MRS. LINDE: But Nora dear—who *was* this gentleman?

NORA: Good grief, can't you understand? The old man never existed; that was only something I'd dream up time and again whenever I was at my wits' end for money. But it makes no difference now; the old fossil can go where he pleases for all I care; I don't need him or his will—because now I'm free. *(Jumping up.)* Oh, how lovely to think of that, Kristine! Carefree! To know you're carefree, utterly carefree; to be able to romp and play with the children, and to keep up a beautiful, charming home—everything just the way Torvald likes it! And think, spring is coming, with big blue skies. Maybe we can travel a little then. Maybe I'll see the ocean again. Oh yes, it *is* so marvelous to live and be happy!

(The front doorbell rings.)

MRS. LINDE: *(rising)* There's the bell. It's probably best that I go.

215 NORA: No, stay. No one's expected. It must be for Torvald.

MAID: *(from the hall doorway)* Excuse me, ma'am—there's a gentleman here to see Mr. Helmer, but I didn't know—since the doctor's with him—

NORA: Who is the gentleman?

KROGSTAD: *(from the doorway)* It's me, Mrs. Helmer.

Mrs. Linde starts and turns away toward the window.

NORA: *(stepping toward him, tense, her voice a whisper)* You? What is it? Why do you want to speak to my husband?

220 KROGSTAD: Bank business—after a fashion. I have a small job in the investment bank, and I hear now your husband is going to be our chief—

NORA: In other words, it's—

KROGSTAD: Just dry business, Mrs. Helmer. Nothing but that.

NORA: Yes, then please be good enough to step into the study. *(She nods indifferently as she sees him out by the hall door, then returns and begins stirring up the stove.)*

MRS. LINDE: Nora—who was that man?

225 **NORA:** That was a Mr. Krogstad—a lawyer.

MRS. LINDE: Then it really was him.

NORA: Do you know that person?

MRS. LINDE: I did once—many years ago. For a time he was a law clerk in our town.

NORA: Yes, he's been that.

230 **MRS. LINDE:** How he's changed.

NORA: I understand he had a very unhappy marriage.

MRS. LINDE: He's a widower now.

NORA: With a number of children. There now, it's burning. *(She closes the stove door and moves the rocker a bit to one side.)*

MRS. LINDE: They say he has a hand in all kinds of business.

235 **NORA:** Oh? That may be true: I wouldn't know. But let's not think about business. It's so dull.

Dr. Rank enters from Helmer's study.

RANK: *(still in the doorway)* No, no, really—I don't want to intrude, I'd just as soon talk a little while with your wife. *(Shuts the door, then notices Mrs. Linde.)* Oh, beg pardon. I'm intruding here too.

NORA: No, not at all. *(Introducing him.)* Dr. Rank, Mrs. Linde.

RANK: Well now, that's a name much heard in this house. I believe I passed the lady on the stairs as I came.

MRS. LINDE: Yes, I take the stairs very slowly. They're rather hard on me.

240 **RANK:** Uh-hm, some touch of internal weakness?

MRS. LINDE: More overexertion, I'd say.

RANK: Nothing else? Then you're probably here in town to rest up in a round of parties?

MRS. LINDE: I'm here to look for work.

RANK: Is that the best cure for overexertion?

245 **MRS. LINDE:** One has to live, Doctor.

RANK: Yes, there's a common prejudice to that effect.

NORA: Oh, come on, Dr. Rank—you really do want to live yourself.

RANK: Yes, I really do. Wretched as I am, I'll gladly prolong my torment indefinitely. All my patients feel like that. And it's quite the same, too, with the morally sick. Right at this moment there's one of those moral invalids in there with Helmer—

MRS. LINDE: *(softly)* Ah!

250 **NORA:** Who do you mean?

RANK: Oh, it's a lawyer, Krogstad, a type you wouldn't know. His character is rotten to the root—but even he began chattering all-importantly about how he had to *live.*

NORA: Oh? What did he want to talk to Torvald about?

RANK: I really don't know. I only heard something about the bank.

NORA: I didn't know that Krog—that this man Krogstad had anything to do with the bank.

255 **RANK:** Yes, he's gotten some kind of berth down there. *(To Mrs. Linde.)* I don't know if you also have, in your neck of the woods, a type of person who scuttles about breathlessly, sniffing out hints of moral corruption, and then maneuvers his victim into some sort of key position where he can keep an eye on him. It's the healthy these days that are out in the cold.

MRS. LINDE: All the same, it's the sick who most need to be taken in.

RANK: *(with a shrug)* Yes, there we have it. That's the concept that's turning society into a sanatorium.

Nora, lost in her thoughts, breaks out into quiet laughter and claps her hands.

RANK: Why do you laugh at that? Do you have any real idea of what society is?

NORA: What do I care about dreary old society? I was laughing at something quite different—something terribly funny. Tell me, Doctor—is everyone who works in the bank dependent now on Torvald?

260 **RANK:** Is that what you find so terribly funny?

NORA: *(smiling and humming)* Never mind, never mind! *(Pacing the floor.)* Yes, that's really immensely amusing: that we—that Torvald has so much power now over all those people. *(Taking the bag out of her pocket.)* Dr. Rank, a little macaroon on that?

RANK: See here, macaroons! I thought they were contraband here.

NORA: Yes, but these are some that Kristine gave me.

MRS. LINDE: What? I—?

265 **NORA:** Now, now, don't be afraid. You couldn't possibly know that Torvald had forbidden them. You see, he's worried they'll ruin my teeth. But hmp! Just this once! Isn't that so, Dr. Rank? Help yourself! *(Puts a macaroon in his mouth.)* And you too, Kristine. And I'll also have one, only a little one—or two, at the most. *(Walking about again.)* Now I'm really tremendously happy. Now there's just one last thing in the world that I have an enormous desire to do.

RANK: Well! And what's that?

NORA: It's something I have such a consuming desire to say so Torvald could hear.

RANK: And why can't you say it?

NORA: I don't dare. It's quite shocking.

270 **MRS. LINDE:** Shocking?

RANK: Well, then it isn't advisable. But in front of us you certainly can. What do you have such a desire to say so Torvald could hear?

NORA: I have such a huge desire to say—to hell and be damned!

RANK: Are you crazy?

MRS. LINDE: My goodness, Nora!

275 **RANK:** Go on, say it. Here he is.

NORA: *(hiding the macaroon bag)* Shh, shh, shh!

Helmer comes in from his study, hat in hand, overcoat over his arm.

NORA: *(going toward him)* Well, Torvald dear, are you through with him?

HELMER: Yes, he just left.

NORA: Let me introduce you—this is Kristine, who's arrived here in town.

280 **HELMER:** Kristine—? I'm sorry, but I don't know—

NORA: Mrs. Linde, Torvald dear. Mrs. Kristine Linde.

HELMER: Of course. A childhood friend of my wife's, no doubt?

MRS. LINDE: Yes, we knew each other in those days.

NORA: And just think, she made the long trip down here in order to talk with you.

285 **HELMER:** What's this?

MRS. LINDE: Well, not exactly—

NORA: You see, Kristine is remarkably clever in office work, and so she's terribly eager to come under a capable man's supervision and add more to what she already knows—

HELMER: Very wise, Mrs. Linde.

NORA: And then when she heard that you'd become a bank manager—the story was wired out to the papers—then she came in as fast as she could and—Really, Torvald, for my sake you can do a little something for Kristine, can't you?

290 **HELMER:** Yes, it's not at all impossible. Mrs. Linde, I suppose you're a widow?

MRS. LINDE: Yes.

HELMER: Any experience in office work?

MRS. LINDE: Yes, a good deal.

HELMER: Well, it's quite likely that I can make an opening for you—

295 **NORA:** *(clapping her hands)* You see, you see!

HELMER: You've come at a lucky moment, Mrs. Linde.

MRS. LINDE: Oh, how can I thank you?

HELMER: Not necessary. *(Putting his overcoat on.)* But today you'll have to excuse me—

RANK: Wait, I'll go with you. *(He fetches his coat from the hall and warms it at the stove.)*

300 **NORA:** Don't stay out long, dear.

HELMER: An hour; no more.

NORA: Are you going too, Kristine?

MRS. LINDE: *(putting on her winter garments)* Yes, I have to see about a room now.

HELMER: Then perhaps we can all walk together.

305 **NORA:** *(helping her)* What a shame we're so cramped here, but it's quite impossible for us to—

MRS. LINDE: Oh, don't even think of it! Good-bye, Nora dear, and thanks for everything.

NORA: Good-bye for now. Of course you'll be back this evening. And you too, Dr. Rank. What? If you're well enough? Oh, you've got to be! Wrap up tight now.

In a ripple of small talk the company moves out into the hall; children's voices are heard outside on the steps.

NORA: There they are! There they are! *(She runs to open the door. The children come in with their nurse, Anne-Marie.)* Come in, come in! *(Bends down and kisses them.)* Oh, you darlings—! Look at them, Kristine. Aren't they lovely!

RANK: No loitering in the draft here.

310 **HELMER:** Come, Mrs. Linde—this place is unbearable now for anyone but mothers.

Dr. Rank, Helmer, and Mrs. Linde go down the stairs. Anne-Marie goes into the living room with the children. Nora follows, after closing the hall door.

NORA: How fresh and strong you look. Oh, such red cheeks you have! Like apples and roses. *(The children interrupt her throughout the following.)* And it was so much fun? That's wonderful. Really? You pulled both Emmy and Bob on the sled? Imagine, all together! Yes, you're a clever boy, Ivar. Oh, let me hold her a bit, Anne-Marie. My sweet little doll baby! *(Takes the smallest from the nurse and dances with her.)* Yes, yes, Mama will dance with Bob as well. What? Did you throw snowballs? Oh, if I'd only been there! No, don't bother, Anne-Marie—I'll undress them myself. Oh yes, let me. It's such fun. Go in and rest; you look half frozen. There's hot coffee waiting for you on the stove. *(The nurse goes into the room to the left. Nora takes the children's winter things off, throwing them about, while the children talk to her all at once.)* Is that so? A big dog chased you? But it didn't bite? No, dogs never bite little, lovely doll babies. Don't peek in the packages, Ivar! What is it? Yes, wouldn't you like to know. No, no, it's an ugly something. Well? Shall we play? What shall we play? Hide-and-seek? Yes, let's play hide-and-seek. Bob must hide first. I must? Yes, let me hide first. *(Laughing and shouting, she and the children play in and out of the living room and the adjoining room to the right. At last Nora hides under the table. The children come storming in, search, but cannot find her, then hear her muffled laughter, dash over to the table, lift the cloth up and find her. Wild shouting. She creeps forward as if to scare them. More shouts. Meanwhile, a knock at the hall door; no one has* *noticed it. Now the door half opens, and Krogstad appears. He waits a moment; the game goes on.)*

KROGSTAD: Beg pardon, Mrs. Helmer—

NORA: *(with a strangled cry, turning and scrambling to her knees)* Oh! What do you want?

KROGSTAD: Excuse me. The outer door was ajar; it must be someone forgot to shut it—

315   **NORA:**   *(rising)* My husband isn't home, Mr. Krogstad.

KROGSTAD: I know that.

NORA: Yes—then what do you want here?

KROGSTAD: A word with you.

NORA: With—? *(To the children, quietly.)* Go in to Anne-Marie. What? No, the strange man won't hurt Mama. When he's gone, we'll play some more. *(She leads the children into the room to the left and shuts the door after them. Then, tense and nervous)* You want to speak to me?

320   **KROGSTAD:**   Yes, I want to.

NORA: Today? But it's not yet the first of the month—

KROGSTAD: No, it's Christmas Eve. It's going to be up to you how merry a Christmas you have.

NORA: What is it you want? Today I absolutely can't—

KROGSTAD: We won't talk about that till later. This is something else. You do have a moment to spare, I suppose?

325   **NORA:**   Oh yes, of course—I do, except—

KROGSTAD: Good. I was sitting over at Olsen's Restaurant when I saw your husband go down the street—

NORA: Yes?

KROGSTAD: With a lady.

NORA: Yes. So?

330   **KROGSTAD:**   If you'll pardon my asking: wasn't that lady a Mrs. Linde?

NORA: Yes.

KROGSTAD: Just now come into town?

NORA: Yes, today.

KROGSTAD: She's a good friend of yours?

335   **NORA:**   Yes, she is. But I don't see—

KROGSTAD: I also knew her once.

NORA: I'm aware of that.

KROGSTAD: Oh? You know all about it. I thought so. Well, then let me ask you short and sweet: is Mrs. Linde getting a job in the bank?

NORA: What makes you think you can cross-examine me, Mr. Krogstad— you, one of my husband's employees? But since you ask, you might as well know—yes, Mrs. Linde's going to be taken on at the bank. And I'm the one who spoke for her, Mr. Krogstad. Now you know.

340   **KROGSTAD:**   So I guessed right.

NORA: *(pacing up and down)* Oh, one does have a tiny bit of influence, I should hope. Just because I am a woman, don't think it means that—

When one has a subordinate position, Mr. Krogstad, one really ought to be careful about pushing somebody who—hm—

KROGSTAD: Who has influence?

NORA: That's right.

KROGSTAD: *(in a different tone)* Mrs. Helmer, would you be good enough to use your influence on my behalf?

345 **NORA:** What? What do you mean?

KROGSTAD: Would you please make sure that I keep my subordinate position in the bank?

NORA: What does that mean? Who's thinking of taking away your position?

KROGSTAD: Oh, don't play the innocent with me. I'm quite aware that your friend would hardly relish the chance of running into me again; and I'm also aware now whom I can thank for being turned out.

NORA: But I promise you—

350 **KROGSTAD:** Yes, yes, yes, to the point: there's still time, and I'm advising you to use your influence to prevent it.

NORA: But Mr. Krogstad, I have absolutely no influence.

KROGSTAD: You haven't? I thought you were just saying—

NORA: You shouldn't take me so literally. I! How can you believe that I have any such influence over my husband?

KROGSTAD: Oh, I've known your husband from our student days. I don't think the great bank manager's more steadfast than any other married man.

355 **NORA:** You speak insolently about my husband, and I'll show you the door.

KROGSTAD: The lady has spirit.

NORA: I'm not afraid of you any longer. After New Year's, I'll soon be done with the whole business.

KROGSTAD: *(restraining himself)* Now listen to me, Mrs. Helmer. If necessary, I'll fight for my little job in the bank as if it were life itself.

NORA: Yes, so it seems.

360 **KROGSTAD:** It's not just a matter of income; that's the least of it. It's something else—All right, out with it! Look, this is the thing. You know, just like all the others, of course, that once, a good many years ago, I did something rather rash.

NORA: I've heard rumors to that effect.

KROGSTAD: The case never got into court; but all the same, every door was closed in my face from then on. So I took up those various activities you know about. I had to grab hold somewhere; and I dare say I haven't been among the worst. But now I want to drop all that. My boys are growing up. For their sakes, I'll have to win back as much respect as possible here in town. That job in the bank was like the first rung in my ladder. And now your husband wants to kick me right back down in the mud again.

NORA: But for heaven's sake, Mr. Krogstad, it's simply not in my power to help you.

KROGSTAD: That's because you haven't the will to—but I have the means to make you.

365 **NORA:** You certainly won't tell my husband that I owe you money?

KROGSTAD: Hm—what if I told him that?

NORA: That would be shameful of you. *(Nearly in tears.)* This secret—my joy and my pride—that he should learn it in such a crude and disgusting way—learn it from you. You'd expose me to the most horrible unpleasantness—

KROGSTAD: Only unpleasantness?

NORA: *(vehemently)* But go on and try. It'll turn out the worse for you, because then my husband will really see what a crook you are, and then you'll *never* be able to hold your job.

370 **KROGSTAD:** I asked if it was just domestic unpleasantness you were afraid of.

NORA: If my husband finds out, then of course he'll pay what I owe at once, and then we'd be through with you for good.

KROGSTAD: *(a step closer)* Listen, Mrs. Helmer—you've either got a very bad memory, or else no head at all for business. I'd better put you a little more in touch with the facts.

NORA: What do you mean?

KROGSTAD: When your husband was sick, you came to me for a loan of four thousand, eight hundred crowns.

375 **NORA:** Where else could I go?

KROGSTAD: I promised to get you that sum—

NORA: And you got it.

KROGSTAD: I promised to get you that sum, on certain conditions. You were so involved in your husband's illness, and so eager to finance your trip, that I guess you didn't think out all the details. It might just be a good idea to remind you. I promised you the money on the strength of a note I drew up.

NORA: Yes, and that I signed.

380 **KROGSTAD:** Right. But at the bottom I added some lines for your father to guarantee the loan. He was supposed to sign down there.

NORA: Supposed to? He did sign.

KROGSTAD: I left the date blank. In other words, your father would have dated his signature himself. Do you remember that?

NORA: Yes, I think—

KROGSTAD: Then I gave you the note for you to mail to your father. Isn't that so?

385 **NORA:** Yes.

KROGSTAD: And naturally you sent it at once—because only some five, six days later you brought me the note, properly signed. And with that, the money was yours.

NORA: Well, then; I've made my payments regularly, haven't I?

KROGSTAD: More or less. But—getting back to the point—those were hard times for you then, Mrs. Helmer.

NORA: Yes, they were.

390 **KROGSTAD:** Your father was very ill, I believe.

NORA: He was near the end.

KROGSTAD: He died soon after?

Nora: Yes.

Krogstad: Tell me, Mrs. Helmer, do you happen to recall the date of your father's death? The day of the month, I mean.

395 **Nora:** Papa died the twenty-ninth of September.

Krogstad: That's quite correct; I've already looked into that. And now we come to a curious thing—*(taking out a paper)* which I simply cannot comprehend.

Nora: Curious thing? I don't know—

Krogstad: This is the curious thing: that your father co-signed the note for your loan three days after his death.

Nora: How—? I don't understand.

400 **Krogstad:** Your father died the twenty-ninth of September. But look. Here your father dated his signature October second. Isn't that curious, Mrs. Helmer? *(Nora is silent.)* Can you explain it to me? *(Nora remains silent.)* It's also remarkable that the words "October second" and the year aren't written in your father's hand, but rather in one that I think I know. Well, it's easy to understand. Your father forgot perhaps to date his signature, and then someone or other added it, a bit sloppily, before anyone knew of his death. There's nothing wrong in that. It all comes down to the signature. And there's no question about *that,* Mrs. Helmer. It really *was* your father who signed his own name here, wasn't it?

Nora: *(after a short silence, throwing her head back and looking squarely at him)* No, it wasn't. *I* signed Papa's name.

Krogstad: Wait, now—are you fully aware that this is a dangerous confession?

Nora: Why? You'll soon get your money.

Krogstad: Let me ask you a question—why didn't you send the paper to your father?

405 **Nora:** That was impossible. Papa was so sick. If I'd asked him for his signature, I also would have had to tell him what the money was for. But I couldn't tell him, sick as he was, that my husband's life was in danger. That was just impossible.

Krogstad: Then it would have been better if you'd given up the trip abroad.

Nora: I couldn't possibly. The trip was to save my husband's life. I couldn't give that up.

Krogstad: But didn't you ever consider that this was a fraud against me?

Nora: I couldn't let myself be bothered by that. You weren't any concern of mine. I couldn't stand you, with all those cold complications you made, even though you knew how badly off my husband was.

410 **Krogstad:** Mrs. Helmer, obviously you haven't the vaguest idea of what you've involved yourself in. But I can tell you this: it was nothing more and nothing worse than I once did—and it wrecked my whole reputation.

Nora: You? Do you expect me to believe that you ever acted bravely to save your wife's life?

KROGSTAD: Laws don't inquire into motives.

NORA: Then they must be very poor laws.

KROGSTAD: Poor or not—if I introduce this paper in court, you'll be judged according to law.

415 **NORA:** This I refuse to believe. A daughter hasn't a right to protect her dying father from anxiety and care? A wife hasn't a right to save her husband's life? I don't know much about laws, but I'm sure that somewhere in the books these things are allowed. And you don't know anything about it—you who practice the law? You must be an awful lawyer, Mr. Krogstad.

KROGSTAD: Could be. But business—the kind of business we two mixed up in—don't you think I know about that? All right. Do what you want now. But I'm telling you *this:* if I get shoved down a second time, you're going to keep me company. *(He bows and goes out through the hall.)*

NORA: *(pensive for a moment, then tossing her head)* Oh, really! Trying to frighten me! I'm not so silly as all that. *(Begins gathering up the children's clothes, but soon stops.)* But—? No, but that's impossible! I did it out of love.

THE CHILDREN: *(in the doorway, left)* Mama, that strange man's gone out the door.

NORA: Yes, yes, I know it. But don't tell anyone about the strange man. Do you hear? Not even Papa!

420 **THE CHILDREN:** No, Mama. But now will you play again?

NORA: No, not now.

THE CHILDREN: Oh, but Mama, you promised.

NORA: Yes, but I can't now. Go inside; I have too much to do. Go in, go in, my sweet darlings. *(She herds them gently back in the room and shuts the door after them. Settling on the sofa, she takes up a piece of embroidery and makes some stitches, but soon stops abruptly.)* No! *(Throws the work aside, rises, goes to the hall door and calls out.)* Helene! Let me have the tree in here. *(Goes to the table, left, opens the table drawer, and stops again.)* No, but that's utterly impossible!

MAID: *(with the Christmas tree)* Where should I put it, ma'am?

425 **NORA:** There. The middle of the floor.

MAID: Should I bring anything else?

NORA: No, thanks. I have what I need.

The Maid, who has set the tree down, goes out.

NORA: *(absorbed in trimming the tree)* Candles here—and flowers here. That terrible creature! Talk, talk, talk! There's nothing to it at all. The tree's going to be lovely. I'll do anything to please you, Torvald. I'll sing for you, dance for you—

Helmer comes in from the hall, with a sheaf of papers under his arm.

NORA: Oh! You're back so soon?

430 **HELMER:**   Yes. Has anyone been here?

NORA: Here? No.

HELMER: That's odd. I saw Krogstad leaving the front door.

NORA: So? Oh yes, that's true. Krogstad was here a moment.

HELMER: Nora, I can see by your face that he's been here, begging you to put in a good word for him.

435 **NORA:**   Yes.

HELMER: And it was supposed to seem like your own idea? You were to hide it from me that he'd been here. He asked you that, too, didn't he?

NORA: Yes, Torvald, but—

HELMER: Nora, Nora, and you could fall for that? Talk with that sort of person and promise him anything? And then in the bargain, tell me an untruth.

NORA: An untruth—?

440 **HELMER:**   Didn't you say that no one had been here? *(Wagging his finger.)* My little songbird must never do that again. A songbird needs a clean beak to warble with. No false notes. *(Putting his arm about her waist.)* That's the way it should be, isn't it? Yes, I'm sure of it. *(Releasing her.)* And so, enough of that. *(Sitting by the stove.)* Ah, how snug and cozy it is here. *(Leafing among his papers.)*

NORA: *(busy with the tree, after a short pause)* Torvald!

HELMER: Yes.

NORA: I'm so much looking forward to the Stenborgs' costume party, day after tomorrow.

HELMER: And I can't wait to see what you'll surprise me with.

445 **NORA:**   Oh, that stupid business!

HELMER: What?

NORA: I can't find anything that's right. Everything seems so ridiculous, so inane.

HELMER: So my little Nora's come to *that* recognition?

NORA: *(going behind his chair, her arms resting on its back)* Are you very busy, Torvald?

450 **HELMER:**   Oh—

NORA: What papers are those?

HELMER: Bank matters.

NORA: Already?

HELMER: I've gotten full authority from the retiring management to make all necessary changes in personnel and procedure. I'll need Christmas week for that. I want to have everything in order by New Year's.

455 **NORA:**   So that was the reason this poor Krogstad—

HELMER: Hm.

NORA: *(still leaning on the chair and slowly stroking the nape of his neck)* If you weren't so very busy, I would have asked you an enormous favor, Torvald.

HELMER: Let's hear. What is it?

Nora: You know, there isn't anyone who has your good taste—and I want so much to look well at the costume party. Torvald, couldn't you take over and decide what I should be and plan my costume?

460 **Helmer:**   Ah, is my stubborn little creature calling for a lifeguard?

Nora: Yes, Torvald, I can't get anywhere without your help.

Helmer: All right—I'll think it over. We'll hit on something.

Nora: Oh, how sweet of you. *(Goes to the tree again. Pause.)* Aren't the red flowers pretty—? But tell me, was it really such a crime that this Krogstad committed?

Helmer: Forgery. Do you have any idea what that means?

465 **Nora:**   Couldn't he have done it out of need?

Helmer: Yes, or thoughtlessness, like so many others. I'm not so heartless that I'd condemn a man categorically for just one mistake.

Nora: No, of course not, Torvald!

Helmer: Plenty of men have redeemed themselves by openly confessing their crimes and taking their punishment.

Nora: Punishment—?

470 **Helmer:**   But now Krogstad didn't go that way. He got himself out by sharp practices, and that's the real cause of his moral breakdown.

Nora: Do you really think that would—?

Helmer: Just imagine how a man with that sort of guilt in him has to lie and cheat and deceive on all sides, has to wear a mask even with the nearest and dearest he has, even with his own wife and children. And with the children, Nora—that's where it's most horrible.

Nora: Why?

Helmer: Because that kind of atmosphere of lies infects the whole life of a home. Every breath the children take in is filled with the germs of something degenerate.

475 **Nora:**   *(coming closer behind him)* Are you sure of that?

Helmer: Oh, I've seen it often enough as a lawyer. Almost everyone who goes bad early in life has a mother who's a chronic liar.

Nora: Why just—the mother?

Helmer: It's usually the mother's influence that's dominant, but the father's works in the same way, of course. Every lawyer is quite familiar with it. And still this Krogstad's been going home year in, year out, poisoning his own children with lies and pretense; that's why I call him morally lost. *(Reaching his hands out toward her.)* So my sweet little Nora must promise me never to plead his cause. Your hand on it. Come, come, what's this? Give me your hand. There, now. All settled. I can tell you it'd be impossible for me to work alongside of him. I literally feel physically revolted when I'm anywhere near such a person.

Nora: *(withdraws her hand and goes to the other side of the Christmas tree)* How hot it is here! And I've got so much to do.

480 **Helmer:**   *(getting up and gathering his papers)* Yes, and I have to think about getting some of these read through before dinner. I'll think about

your costume, too. And something to hang on the tree in gilt paper, I may even see about that. *(Putting his hand on her head.)* Oh you, my darling little songbird. *(He goes into his study and closes the door after him.)*

NORA: *(softly, after a silence)* Oh, really! It isn't so. It's impossible. It must be impossible.

ANNE-MARIE: *(in the doorway, left)* The children are begging so hard to come in to Mama.

NORA: No, no, no, don't let them in to me! You stay with them, Anne-Marie.

ANNE-MARIE: Of course, ma'am. *(Closes the door.)*

485 NORA: *(pale with terror)* Hurt my children—! Poison my home? *(A moment's pause; then she tosses her head.)* That's not true. Never. Never in all the world.

Act II

Same room. Beside the piano the Christmas tree now stands stripped of ornaments, burned-down candle stubs on its ragged branches. Nora's street clothes lie on the sofa. Nora, alone in the room, moves restlessly about; at last she stops at the sofa and picks up her coat.

NORA: *(dropping the coat again)* Someone's coming! *(Goes toward the door, listens.)* No—there's no one. Of course—nobody's coming today, Christmas Day—or tomorrow, either. But maybe—*(Opens the door and looks out.)* No, nothing in the mailbox. Quite empty. *(Coming forward.)* What nonsense! He won't do anything serious. Nothing terrible could happen. It's impossible. Why, I have three small children.

Anne-Marie, with a large carton, comes in from the room to the left.

ANNE-MARIE: Well, at last I found the box with the masquerade clothes.

NORA: Thanks. Put it on the table.

ANNE-MARIE: *(does so)* But they're all pretty much of a mess.

5 NORA: Ahh! I'd love to rip them in a million pieces!

ANNE-MARIE: Oh, mercy, they can be fixed right up. Just a little patience.

NORA: Yes, I'll go get Mrs. Linde to help me.

ANNE-MARIE: Out again now? In this nasty weather? Miss Nora will catch cold—get sick.

NORA: Oh, worse things could happen—How are the children?

10 ANNE-MARIE: The poor mites are playing with their Christmas presents, but—

NORA: Do they ask for me much?

ANNE-MARIE: They're so used to having Mama around, you know.

NORA: Yes. But Anne-Marie, I *can't* be together with them as much as I was.

ANNE-MARIE: Well, small children get used to anything.

15 **NORA:**   You think so? Do you think they'd forget their mother if she was gone for good?

ANNE-MARIE: Oh, mercy—gone for good!

NORA: Wait, tell me, Anne-Marie—I've wondered so often—how could you ever have the heart to give your child over to strangers?

ANNE-MARIE: But I had to, you know, to become little Nora's nurse.

NORA: Yes, but how could you *do* it?

20 **ANNE-MARIE:**   When I could get such a good place? A girl who's poor and who's gotten in trouble is glad enough for that. Because that slippery fish, he didn't do a thing for me, you know.

NORA: But your daughter's surely forgotten you.

ANNE-MARIE: Oh, she certainly has not. She's written to me, both when she was confirmed and when she was married.

NORA: *(clasping her about the neck)* You old Anne-Marie, you were a good mother for me when I was little.

ANNE-MARIE: Poor little Nora, with no other mother but me.

25 **NORA:**   And if the babies didn't have one, then I know that you'd—What silly talk! *(Opening the carton.)* Go in to them. Now I'll have to—Tomorrow you can see how lovely I'll look.

ANNE-MARIE: Oh, there won't be anyone at the party as lovely as Miss Nora. *(She goes off into the room, left.)*

NORA: *(begins unpacking the box, but soon throws it aside)* Oh, if I dared to go out. If only nobody would come. If only nothing would happen here while I'm out. What craziness—nobody's coming. Just don't think. This muff—needs a brushing. Beautiful gloves, beautiful gloves. Let it go. Let it go! One, two, three, four, five, six—*(With a cry.)* Oh, there they are! *(Poises to move toward the door, but remains irresolutely standing. Mrs. Linde enters from the hall, where she has removed her street clothes.)*

NORA: Oh, it's you, Kristine. There's no one else out there? How good that you've come.

MRS. LINDE: I hear you were up asking for me.

30 **NORA:**   Yes, I just stopped by. There's something you really can help me with. Let's get settled on the sofa. Look, there's going to be a costume party tomorrow evening at the Stenborgs' right above us, and now Torvald wants me to go as a Neapolitan peasant girl and dance the tarantella that I learned in Capri.

MRS. LINDE: Really, are you giving a whole performance?

NORA: Torvald says yes, I should. See, here's the dress. Torvald had it made for me down there; but now it's all so tattered that I just don't know—

MRS. LINDE: Oh, we'll fix that up in no time. It's nothing more than the trimmings—they're a bit loose here and there. Needle and thread? Good, now we have what we need.

NORA: Oh, how sweet of you!

35 **MRS. LINDE:**   *(sewing)* So you'll be in disguise tomorrow, Nora. You know what? I'll stop by then for a moment and have a look at you all dressed up.

But listen, I've absolutely forgotten to thank you for that pleasant evening yesterday.

NORA: *(getting up and walking about)* I don't think it was as pleasant as usual yesterday. You should have come to town a bit sooner, Kristine— Yes, Torvald really knows how to give a home elegance and charm.

MRS. LINDE: And you do, too, if you ask me. You're not your father's daughter for nothing. But tell me, is Dr. Rank always so down in the mouth as yesterday?

NORA: No, that was quite an exception. But he goes around critically ill all the time—tuberculosis of the spine, poor man. You know, his father was a disgusting thing who kept mistresses and so on—and that's why the son's been sickly from birth.

MRS. LINDE: *(lets her sewing fall to her lap)* But my dearest Nora, how do you know about such things?

40 NORA: *(walking more jauntily)* Hmp! When you've had three children, then you've had a few visits from—from women who know something of medicine, and they tell you this and that.

MRS. LINDE: *(resumes sewing; a short pause)* Does Dr. Rank come here every day?

NORA: Every blessed day. He's Torvald's best friend from childhood, and *my* good friend, too. Dr. Rank almost belongs to this house.

MRS. LINDE: But tell me—is he quite sincere? I mean, doesn't he rather enjoy flattering people?

NORA: Just the opposite. Why do you think that?

45 MRS. LINDE: When you introduced us yesterday, he was proclaiming that he'd often heard my name in this house; but later I noticed that your husband hadn't the slightest idea who I really was. So how could Dr. Rank—?

NORA: But it's all true, Kristine. You see, Torvald loves me beyond words, and, as he puts it, he'd like to keep me all to himself. For a long time he'd almost be jealous if I even mentioned any of my old friends back home. So of course I dropped that. But with Dr. Rank I talk a lot about such things, because he likes hearing about them.

MRS. LINDE: Now listen, Nora; in many ways you're still like a child. I'm a good deal older than you, with a little more experience. I'll tell you something: you ought to put an end to all this with Dr. Rank.

NORA: What should I put an end to?

MRS. LINDE: Both parts of it, I think. Yesterday you said something about a rich admirer who'd provide you with money—

50 NORA: Yes, one who doesn't exist—worse luck. So?

MRS. LINDE: Is Dr. Rank well off?

NORA: Yes, he is.

MRS. LINDE: With no dependents?

NORA: No, no one. But—

55 MRS. LINDE: And he's over here every day?

NORA: Yes, I told you that.

MRS. LINDE: How can a man of such refinement be so grasping?

NORA: I don't follow you at all.

MRS. LINDE: Now don't try to hide it, Nora. You think I can't guess who loaned you the forty-eight hundred crowns?

60 **NORA:**   Are you out of your mind? How could you think such a thing! A friend of ours, who comes here every single day. What an intolerable situation that would have been!

MRS. LINDE: Then it really wasn't him.

NORA: No, absolutely not. It never even crossed my mind for a moment— And he had nothing to lend in those days; his inheritance came later.

MRS. LINDE: Well, I think that was a stroke of luck for you, Nora dear.

NORA: No, it never would have occurred to me to ask Dr. Rank—Still, I'm quite sure that if I had asked him—

65 **MRS. LINDE:**   Which you won't, of course.

NORA: No, of course not. I can't see that I'd ever need to. But I'm quite positive that if I talked to Dr. Rank—

MRS. LINDE: Behind your husband's back?

NORA: I've got to clear up this other thing; *that's* also behind his back. I've *got* to clear it all up.

MRS. LINDE: Yes, I was saying that yesterday, but—

70 **NORA:**   *(pacing up and down)* A man handles these problems so much better than a woman—

MRS. LINDE: One's husband does, yes.

NORA: Nonsense. *(Stopping.)* When you pay everything you owe, then you get your note back, right?

MRS. LINDE: Yes, naturally.

NORA: And can rip it into a million pieces and burn it up—that filthy scrap of paper!

75 **MRS. LINDE:**   *(looking hard at her, laying her sewing aside, and rising slowly)* Nora, you're hiding something from me.

NORA: You can see it in my face?

MRS. LINDE: Something's happened to you since yesterday morning. Nora, what is it?

NORA: *(hurrying toward her)* Kristine! *(Listening.)* Shh! Torvald's home. Look, go in with the children a while. Torvald can't bear all this snipping and stitching. Let Anne-Marie help you.

MRS. LINDE: *(gathering up some of the things)* All right, but I'm not leaving here until we've talked this out. *(She disappears into the room, left, as Torvald enters from the hall.)*

80 **NORA:**   Oh, how I've been waiting for you, Torvald dear.

HELMER: Was that the dressmaker?

NORA: No, that was Kristine. She's helping me fix up my costume. You know, it's going to be quite attractive.

HELMER: Yes, wasn't that a bright idea I had?

NORA: Brilliant! But then wasn't I good as well to give in to you?

85 **HELMER:** Good—because you give in to your husband's judgment? All right, you little goose, I know you didn't mean it like that. But I won't disturb you. You'll want to have a fitting, I suppose.

NORA: And you'll be working?

HELMER: Yes. *(Indicating a bundle of papers.)* See. I've been down to the bank. *(Starts toward his study.)*

NORA: Torvald.

HELMER: *(stops)* Yes.

90 **NORA:** If your little squirrel begged you, with all her heart and soul, for something—?

HELMER: What's that?

NORA: Then would you do it?

HELMER: First, naturally, I'd have to know what it was.

NORA: Your squirrel would scamper about and do tricks, if you'd only be sweet and give in.

95 **HELMER:** Out with it.

NORA: Your lark would be singing high and low in every room—

HELMER: Come on, she does that anyway.

NORA: I'd be a wood nymph and dance for you in the moonlight.

HELMER: Nora—don't tell me it's that same business from this morning?

100 **NORA:** *(coming closer)* Yes, Torvald, I beg you, please!

HELMER: And you actually have the nerve to drag that up again?

NORA: Yes, yes, you've got to give in to me; you *have* to let Krogstad keep his job in the bank.

HELMER: My dear Nora, I've slated his job for Mrs. Linde.

NORA: That's awfully kind of you. But you could just fire another clerk instead of Krogstad.

105 **HELMER:** This is the most incredible stubbornness! Because you go and give an impulsive promise to speak up for him, I'm expected to—

NORA: That's not the reason, Torvald. It's for your own sake. That man does writing for the worst papers; you said it yourself. He could do you any amount of harm. I'm scared to death of him—

HELMER: Ah, I understand. It's the old memories haunting you.

NORA: What do you mean by that?

HELMER: Of course, you're thinking about your father.

110 **NORA:** Yes, all right. Just remember how those nasty gossips wrote in the papers about Papa and slandered him so cruelly. I think they'd have had him dismissed if the department hadn't sent you up to investigate, and if you hadn't been so kind and open-minded toward him.

HELMER: My dear Nora, there's a notable difference between your father and me. Your father's official career was hardly above reproach. But mine is; and I hope it'll stay that way as long as I hold my position.

NORA: Oh, who can ever tell what vicious minds can invent? We could be so snug and happy now in our quiet, carefree home—you and I and the children, Torvald! That's why I'm pleading with you so—

HELMER: And just by pleading for him you make it impossible for me to keep him on. It's already known at the bank that I'm firing Krogstad. What if it's rumored around now that the new bank manager was vetoed by his wife—

NORA: Yes, what then—?

115 **HELMER:** Oh yes—as long as our little bundle of stubbornness gets her way—! I should go and make myself ridiculous in front of the whole office—give people the idea I can be swayed by all kinds of outside pressure. Oh, you can bet I'd feel the effects of that soon enough! Besides—there's something that rules Krogstad right out at the bank as long as I'm the manager.

NORA: What's that?

HELMER: His moral failings I could maybe overlook if I had to—

NORA: Yes, Torvald, why not?

HELMER: And I hear he's quite efficient on the job. But he was a crony of mine back in my teens—one of those rash friendships that crop up again and again to embarrass you later in life. Well, I might as well say it straight out: we're on a first-name basis. And that tactless fool makes no effort at all to hide it in front of others. Quite the contrary—he thinks that entitles him to take a familiar air around me, and so every other second he comes booming out with his "Yes, Torvald!" and "Sure thing, Torvald!" I tell you, it's been excruciating for me. He's out to make my place in the bank unbearable.

120 **NORA:** Torvald, you can't be serious about all this.

HELMER: Oh no? Why not?

NORA: Because these are such petty considerations.

HELMER: What are you saying? Petty? You think I'm petty!

NORA: No, just the opposite, Torvald dear. That's exactly why—

125 **HELMER:** Never mind. You call my motives petty; then I might as well be just that. Petty! All right! We'll put a stop to this for good. *(Goes to the hall door and calls.)* Helene!

NORA: What do you want?

HELMER: *(searching among his papers)* A decision. *(The Maid comes in.)* Look here; take this letter; go out with it at once. Get hold of a messenger and have him deliver it. Quick now. It's already addressed. Wait, here's some money.

MAID: Yes, sir. *(She leaves with the letter.)*

HELMER: *(straightening his papers)* There, now, little Miss Willful.

130 **NORA:** *(breathlessly)* Torvald, what was that letter?

HELMER: Krogstad's notice.

NORA: Call it back, Torvald! There's still time. Oh, Torvald, call it back! Do it for my sake—for your sake, for the children's sake! Do you hear, Torvald; do it! You don't know how this can harm us.

HELMER: Too late.

NORA: Yes, too late.

135 **HELMER:**   Nora dear, I can forgive you this panic, even though basically
you're insulting me. Yes, you are! Or isn't it an insult to think that *I*
should be afraid of a courtroom hack's revenge? But I forgive you anyway,
because this shows so beautifully how much you love me. *(Takes her in
his arms.)* This is the way it should be, my darling Nora. Whatever comes,
you'll see: when it really counts, I have strength and courage enough as a
man to take on the whole weight myself.

NORA: *(terrified)* What do you mean by that?

HELMER: The whole weight, I said.

NORA: *(resolutely)* No, never in all the world.

HELMER: Good. So we'll share it, Nora, as man and wife. That's as it should
be. *(Fondling her.)* Are you happy now? There, there, there—not these
frightened dove's eyes. It's nothing at all but empty fantasies—Now you
should run through your tarantella and practice your tambourine. I'll go
to the inner office and shut both doors, so I won't hear a thing; you can
make all the noise you like. *(Turning in the doorway.)* And when Rank
comes, just tell him where he can find me. *(He nods to her and goes with
his papers into the study, closing the door.)*

140 **NORA:**   *(standing as though rooted, dazed with fright, in a whisper)* He really could do it. He will do it. He'll do it in spite of everything. No, not
that, never, never! Anything but that! Escape! A way out—*(The doorbell
rings.)* Dr. Rank! Anything but that! *Anything,* whatever it is! *(Her hands
pass over her face, smoothing it; she pulls herself together, goes over and
opens the hall door. Dr. Rank stands outside, hanging his fur coat up.
During the following scene, it begins getting dark.)*

NORA: Hello, Dr. Rank. I recognized your ring. But you mustn't go in to
Torvald yet; I believe he's working.

RANK: And you?

NORA: For you, I always have an hour to spare—you know that. *(He has entered, and she shuts the door after him.)*

RANK: Many thanks. I'll make use of these hours while I can.

145 **NORA:**   What do you mean by that? While you can?

RANK: Does that disturb you?

NORA: Well, it's such an odd phrase. Is anything going to happen?

RANK: What's going to happen is what I've been expecting so long—but I
honestly didn't think it would come so soon.

NORA: *(gripping his arm)* What is it you've found out? Dr. Rank, you have
to tell me!

150 **RANK:**   *(sitting by the stove)* It's all over with me. There's nothing to be
done about it.

NORA: *(breathing easier)* Is it you—then—?

RANK: Who else? There's no point in lying to one's self. I'm the most mis-
erable of all my patients, Mrs. Helmer. These past few days I've been au-
diting my internal accounts. Bankrupt! Within a month I'll probably be
laid out and rotting in the churchyard.

NORA: Oh, what a horrible thing to say.

RANK: The thing itself is horrible. But the worst of it is all the other horror before it's over. There's only one final examination left; when I'm finished with that, I'll know about when my disintegration will begin. There's something I want to say. Helmer with his sensitivity has such a sharp distaste for anything ugly. I don't want him near my sickroom.

155 **NORA:** Oh, but Dr. Rank—

RANK: I won't have him in there. Under no condition. I'll lock my door to him—As soon as I'm completely sure of the worst, I'll send you my calling card marked with a black cross, and you'll know then the wreck has started to come apart.

NORA: No, today you're completely unreasonable. And I wanted you so much to be in a really good humor.

RANK: With death up my sleeve? And then to suffer this way for somebody else's sins. Is there any justice in that? And in every single family, in some way or another, this inevitable retribution of nature goes on—

NORA: *(her hands pressed over her ears)* Oh, stuff! Cheer up! Please—be gay!

160 **RANK:** Yes, I'd just as soon laugh at it all. My poor, innocent spine, serving time for my father's gay army days.

NORA: *(by the table, left)* He was so infatuated with asparagus tips and *pâté de foie gras,* wasn't that it?

RANK: Yes—and with truffles.

NORA: Truffles, yes. And then with oysters, I suppose?

RANK: Yes, tons of oysters, naturally.

165 **NORA:** And then the port and champagne to go with it. It's so sad that all these delectable things have to strike at our bones.

RANK: Especially when they strike at the unhappy bones that never shared in the fun.

NORA: Ah, that's the saddest of all.

RANK: *(looks searchingly at her)* Hm.

NORA: *(after a moment)* Why did you smile?

170 **RANK:** No, it was you who laughed.

NORA: No, it was you who smiled, Dr. Rank!

RANK: *(getting up)* You're even a bigger tease than I'd thought.

NORA: I'm full of wild ideas today.

RANK: That's obvious.

175 **NORA:** *(putting both hands on his shoulders)* Dear, dear Dr. Rank, you'll never die for Torvald and me.

RANK: Oh, that loss you'll easily get over. Those who go away are soon forgotten.

NORA: *(looks fearfully at him)* You believe that?

RANK: One makes new connections, and then—

NORA: Who makes new connections?

180 **RANK:** Both you and Torvald will when I'm gone. I'd say you're well under way already. What was that Mrs. Linde doing here last evening?

NORA: Oh, come—you can't be jealous of poor Kristine?

RANK: Oh yes, I am. She'll be my successor here in the house. When I'm down under, that woman will probably—

NORA: Shh! Not so loud. She's right in there.

RANK: Today as well. So you see.

185 NORA: Only to sew on my dress. Good gracious, how unreasonable you are. *(Sitting on the sofa.)* Be nice now, Dr. Rank. Tomorrow you'll see how beautifully I'll dance; and you can imagine then that I'm dancing only for you—yes, and of course for Torvald, too—that's understood. *(Takes various items out of the carton.)* Dr. Rank, sit over here and I'll show you something.

RANK: *(sitting)* What's that?

NORA: Look here. Look.

RANK: Silk stockings.

NORA: Flesh-colored. Aren't they lovely? Now it's so dark here, but tomorrow—No, no, no, just look at the feet. Oh well, you might as well look at the rest.

190 RANK: Hm—

NORA: Why do you look so critical? Don't you believe they'll fit?

RANK: I've never had any chance to form an opinion on that.

NORA: *(glancing at him a moment)* Shame on you. *(Hits him lightly on the ear with the stockings.)* That's for you. *(Puts them away again.)*

RANK: And what other splendors am I going to see now?

195 NORA: Not the least bit more, because you've been naughty. *(She hums a little and rummages among her things.)*

RANK: *(after a short silence)* When I sit here together with you like this, completely easy and open, then I don't know—I simply can't imagine— whatever would have become of me if I'd never come into this house.

NORA: *(smiling)* Yes, I really think you feel completely at ease with us.

RANK: *(more quietly, staring straight ahead)* And then to have to go away from it all—

NORA: Nonsense, you're not going away.

200 RANK: *(his voice unchanged)*—and not even be able to leave some poor show of gratitude behind, scarcely a fleeting regret—no more than a vacant place that anyone can fill.

NORA: And if I asked you now for—? No—

RANK: For what?

NORA: For a great proof of your friendship—

RANK: Yes, yes?

205 NORA: No, I mean—for an exceptionally big favor—

RANK: Would you really, for once, make me so happy?

NORA: Oh, you haven't the vaguest idea what it is.

RANK: All right, then tell me.

NORA: No, but I can't, Dr. Rank—it's all out of reason. It's advice and help, too—and a favor—

210 RANK: So much the better. I can't fathom what you're hinting at. Just speak out. Don't you trust me?

NORA: Of course. More than anyone else. You're my best and truest friend, I'm sure. That's why I want to talk to you. All right, then, Dr. Rank: there's something you can help me prevent. You know how deeply, how inexpressibly dearly Torvald loves me; he'd never hesitate a second to give up his life for me.

RANK: *(leaning close to her)* Nora—do you think he's the only one—

NORA: *(with a slight start)* Who—?

RANK: Who'd gladly give up his life for you.

215 NORA: *(heavily)* I see.

RANK: I swore to myself you should know this before I'm gone. I'll never find a better chance. Yes, Nora, now you know. And also you know now that you can trust me beyond anyone else.

NORA: *(rising, natural and calm)* Let me by.

RANK: *(making room for her, but still sitting)* Nora—

NORA: *(in the hall doorway)* Helene, bring the lamp in. *(Goes over to the stove.)* Ah, dear Dr. Rank, that was really mean of you.

220 RANK: *(getting up)* That I've loved you just as deeply as somebody else? Was *that* mean?

NORA: No, but that you came out and told me. That was quite unnecessary—

RANK: What do you mean? Have you known—?

The Maid comes in with the lamp, sets it on the table, and goes out again.

RANK: Nora—Mrs. Helmer—I'm asking you: have you known about it?

NORA: Oh, how can I tell what I know or don't know? Really, I don't know what to say—Why did you have to be so clumsy, Dr. Rank! Everything was so good.

225 RANK: Well, in any case, you now have the knowledge that my body and soul are at your command. So won't you speak out?

NORA: *(looking at him)* After that?

RANK: Please, just let me know what it is.

NORA: You can't know anything now.

RANK: I have to. You mustn't punish me like this. Give me the chance to do whatever is humanly possible for you.

230 NORA: Now there's nothing you can do for me. Besides, actually, I don't need any help. You'll see—it's only my fantasies. That's what it is. Of course! *(Sits in the rocker, looks at him, and smiles.)* What a nice one you are, Dr. Rank. Aren't you a little bit ashamed, now that the lamp is here?

RANK: No, not exactly. But perhaps I'd better go—for good?

NORA: No, you certainly can't do that. You must come here just as you always have. You know Torvald can't do without you.

RANK: Yes, but *you?*

NORA: You know how much I enjoy it when you're here.

235 RANK: That's precisely what threw me off. You're a mystery to me. So many times I've felt you'd almost rather be with me than with Helmer.

NORA: Yes—you see, there are some people that one loves most and other people that one would almost prefer being with.

RANK: Yes, there's something to that.

NORA: When I was back home, of course I loved Papa most. But I always thought it was so much fun when I could sneak down to the maids' quarters, because they never tried to improve me, and it was always so amusing, the way they talked to each other.

RANK: Aha, so it's *their* place that I've filled.

240 **NORA:** *(jumping up and going to him)* Oh, dear, sweet Dr. Rank, that's not what I mean at all. But you can understand that with Torvald it's just the same as with Papa—

The Maid enters from the hall.

MAID: Ma'am—please! *(She whispers to Nora and hands her a calling card.)*

NORA: *(glancing at the card)* Ah! *(Slips it into her pocket.)*

RANK: Anything wrong?

NORA: No, no, not at all. It's only some—it's my new dress—

245 **RANK:** Really? But—there's your dress.

NORA: Oh, that. But this is another one—I ordered it—Torvald mustn't know—

RANK: Ah, now we have the big secret.

NORA: That's right. Just go in with him—he's back in the inner study. Keep him there as long as—

RANK: Don't worry. He won't get away. *(Goes into the study.)*

250 **NORA:** *(to the Maid)* And he's standing waiting in the kitchen?

MAID: Yes, he came up by the back stairs.

NORA: But didn't you tell him somebody was here?

MAID: Yes, but that didn't do any good.

NORA: He won't leave?

255 **MAID:** No, he won't go till he's talked with you, ma'am.

NORA: Let him come in, then—but quietly. Helene, don't breathe a word about this. It's a surprise for my husband.

MAID: Yes, yes, I understand—*(Goes out.)*

NORA: This horror—it's going to happen. No, no, no, it can't happen, it mustn't. *(She goes and bolts Helmer's door. The Maid opens the hall door for Krogstad and shuts it behind him. He is dressed for travel in a fur coat, boots, and a fur cap.)*

NORA: *(going toward him)* Talk softly. My husband's home.

260 **KROGSTAD:** Well, good for him.

NORA: What do you want?

KROGSTAD: Some information.

NORA: Hurry up, then. What is it?

KROGSTAD: You know, of course, that I got my notice.

265 **NORA:** I couldn't prevent it, Mr. Krogstad. I fought for you to the bitter end, but nothing worked.

KROGSTAD: Does your husband's love for you run so thin? He knows everything I can expose you to, and all the same he dares to—

NORA: How can you imagine he knows anything about this?

KROGSTAD: Ah, no—I can't imagine it either, now. It's not at all like my
fine Torvald Helmer to have so much guts—

NORA: Mr. Krogstad, I demand respect for my husband!

270 **KROGSTAD:**   Why, of course—all due respect. But since the lady's keeping it
so carefully hidden, may I presume to ask if you're also a bit better informed than yesterday about what you've actually done?

NORA: More than you ever could teach me.

KROGSTAD: Yes, I *am* such an awful lawyer.

NORA: What is it you want from me?

KROGSTAD: Just a glimpse of how you are, Mrs. Helmer. I've been thinking
about you all day long. A cashier, a night-court scribbler, a—well, a type
like me also has a little of what they call a heart, you know.

275 **NORA:**   Then show it. Think of my children.

KROGSTAD: Did you or your husband ever think of mine? But never mind. I
simply wanted to tell you that you don't need to take this thing too seriously. For the present, I'm not proceeding with any action.

NORA: Oh no, really! Well—I knew that.

KROGSTAD: Everything can be settled in a friendly spirit. It doesn't have to
get around town at all; it can stay just among us three.

NORA: My husband must never know anything of this.

280 **KROGSTAD:**   How can you manage that? Perhaps you can pay me the balance?

NORA: No, not right now.

KROGSTAD: Or you know some way of raising the money in a day or two?

NORA: No way that I'm willing to use.

KROGSTAD: Well, it wouldn't have done you any good, anyway. If you stood
in front of me with a fistful of bills, you still couldn't buy your signature
back.

285 **NORA:**   Then tell me what you're going to do with it.

KROGSTAD: I'll just hold onto it—keep it on file. There's no outsider who'll
even get wind of it. So if you've been thinking of taking some desperate
step—

NORA: I have.

KROGSTAD: Been thinking of running away from home—

NORA: I have!

290 **KROGSTAD:**   Or even of something worse—

NORA: How could you guess that?

KROGSTAD: You can drop those thoughts.

NORA: How could you guess I was thinking of *that?*

KROGSTAD: Most of us think about *that* at first. I thought about it too, but I
discovered I hadn't the courage—

295 **NORA:**   *(lifelessly)* I don't either.

KROGSTAD: *(relieved)* That's true, you haven't the courage? You too?

NORA: I don't have it—I don't have it.

KROGSTAD: It would be terribly stupid, anyway. After that first storm at home blows out, why, then—I have here in my pocket a letter for your husband—

NORA: Telling everything?

300 **KROGSTAD:** As charitably as possible.

NORA: *(quickly)* He mustn't ever get that letter. Tear it up. I'll find some way to get money.

KROGSTAD: Beg pardon, Mrs. Helmer, but I think I just told you—

NORA: Oh, I don't mean the money I owe you. Let me know how much you want from my husband, and I'll manage it.

KROGSTAD: I don't want any money from your husband.

305 **NORA:** What do you want, then?

KROGSTAD: I'll tell you what. I want to recoup, Mrs. Helmer; I want to get on in the world—and there's where your husband can help me. For a year and a half I've kept myself clean of anything disreputable—all that time struggling with the worst conditions; but I was satisfied, working my way up step by step. Now I've been written right off, and I'm just not in the mood to come crawling back. I tell you, I want to move on. I want to get back in the bank—in a better position. Your husband can set up a job for me—

NORA: He'll never do that!

KROGSTAD: He'll do it. I know him. He won't dare breathe a word of protest. And once I'm in there together with him, you just wait and see! Inside of a year, I'll be the manager's right-hand man. It'll be Nils Krogstad, not Torvald Helmer, who runs the bank.

NORA: You'll never see the day!

310 **KROGSTAD:** Maybe you think you can—

NORA: I have the courage now—for *that*.

KROGSTAD: Oh, you don't scare me. A smart, spoiled lady like you—

NORA: You'll see; you'll see!

KROGSTAD: Under the ice, maybe? Down in the freezing, coal-black water? There, till you float up in the spring, ugly, unrecognizable, with your hair falling out—

315 **NORA:** You don't frighten me.

KROGSTAD: Nor do you frighten me. One doesn't do these things, Mrs. Helmer. Besides, what good would it be? I'd still have him safe in my pocket.

NORA: Afterwards? When I'm no longer—?

KROGSTAD: Are you forgetting that *I'll* be in control then over your final reputation? *(Nora stands speechless, staring at him.)* Good; now I've warned you. Don't do anything stupid. When Helmer's read my letter, I'll be waiting for his reply. And bear in mind that it's your husband himself who's forced me back to my old ways. I'll never forgive him for that. Good-bye, Mrs. Helmer. *(He goes out through the hall.)*

NORA: *(goes to the hall door, opens it a crack, and listens)* He's gone. Didn't leave the letter. Oh no, no, that's impossible too! *(Opening the door more and more.)* What's that? He's standing outside—not going downstairs. He's thinking it over? Maybe he'll—? *(A letter falls in the mailbox; then Krogstad's footsteps are heard, dying away down a flight of stairs. Nora gives a muffled cry and runs over toward the sofa table. A short pause.)* In the mailbox. *(Slips warily over to the hall door.)* It's lying there. Torvald, Torvald—now we're lost!

320 MRS. LINDE: *(entering with the costume from the room, left)* There now, I can't see anything else to mend. Perhaps you'd like to try—

NORA: *(in a hoarse whisper)* Kristine, come here.

MRS. LINDE: *(tossing the dress on the sofa)* What's wrong? You look upset.

NORA: Come here. See that letter? *There!* Look—through the glass in the mailbox.

MRS. LINDE: Yes, yes, I see it.

325 NORA: That letter's from Krogstad—

MRS. LINDE: Nora—it's Krogstad who loaned you the money!

NORA: Yes, and now Torvald will find out everything.

MRS. LINDE: Believe me, Nora, it's best for both of you.

NORA: There's more you don't know. I forged a name.

330 MRS. LINDE: But for heaven's sake—?

NORA: I only want to tell you that, Kristine, so that you can be my witness.

MRS. LINDE: Witness? Why should I—?

NORA: If I should go out of my mind—it could easily happen—

MRS. LINDE: Nora!

335 NORA: Or anything else occurred—so I couldn't be present here—

MRS. LINDE: Nora, Nora, you aren't yourself at all!

NORA: And someone should try to take on the whole weight, all of the guilt, you follow me—

MRS. LINDE: Yes, of course, but why do you think—?

NORA: Then you're the witness that it isn't true, Kristine. I'm very much myself; my mind right now is perfectly clear; and I'm telling you: nobody else has known about this; I alone did everything. Remember that.

340 MRS. LINDE: I will. But I don't understand all this.

NORA: Oh, how could you ever understand it? It's the miracle now that's going to take place.

MRS. LINDE: The miracle?

NORA: Yes, the miracle. But it's so awful, Kristine. It mustn't take place, not for anything in the world.

MRS. LINDE: I'm going right over and talk with Krogstad.

345 NORA: Don't go near him; he'll do you some terrible harm!

MRS. LINDE: There was a time once when he'd gladly have done anything for me.

NORA: He?

MRS. LINDE: Where does he live?

NORA: Oh, how do I know? Yes. *(Searches in her pocket.)* Here's his card. But the letter, the letter—!

350 **HELMER:** *(from the study, knocking on the door)* Nora!

NORA: *(with a cry of fear)* Oh! What is it? What do you want?

HELMER: Now, now, don't be so frightened. We're not coming in. You locked the door—are you trying on the dress?

NORA: Yes, I'm trying it. I'll look just beautiful, Torvald.

MRS. LINDE: *(who has read the card)* He's living right around the corner.

355 **NORA:** Yes, but what's the use? We're lost. The letter's in the box.

MRS. LINDE: And your husband has the key?

NORA: Yes, always.

MRS. LINDE: Krogstad can ask for his letter back unread; he can find some excuse—

NORA: But it's just this time that Torvald usually—

360 **MRS. LINDE:** Stall him. Keep him in there. I'll be back as quick as I can. *(She hurries out through the hall entrance.)*

NORA: *(goes to Helmer's door, opens it, and peers in)* Torvald!

HELMER: *(from the inner study)* Well—does one dare set foot in one's own living room at last? Come on, Rank, now we'll get a look—*(In the doorway.)* But what's this?

NORA: What, Torvald dear?

HELMER: Rank had me expecting some grand masquerade.

365 **RANK:** *(in the doorway)* That was my impression, but I must have been wrong.

NORA: No one can admire me in my splendor—not till tomorrow.

HELMER: But Nora dear, you look so exhausted. Have you practiced too hard?

NORA: No, I haven't practiced at all yet.

HELMER: You know, it's necessary—

370 **NORA:** Oh, it's absolutely necessary, Torvald. But I can't get anywhere without your help. I've forgotten the whole thing completely.

HELMER: Ah, we'll soon take care of that.

NORA: Yes, take care of me, Torvald, please! Promise me that? Oh, I'm so nervous. That big party—You must give up everything this evening for me. No business—don't even touch your pen. Yes? Dear Torvald, promise?

HELMER: It's a promise. Tonight I'm totally at your service—you little helpless thing. Hm—but first there's one thing I want to—*(Goes toward the hall door.)*

NORA: What are you looking for?

375 **HELMER:** Just to see if there's any mail.

NORA: No, no, don't do that, Torvald!

HELMER: Now what?

NORA: Torvald, please. There isn't any.

HELMER: Let me look, though. *(Starts out. Nora, at the piano, strikes the first notes of the tarantella. Helmer, at the door, stops.)* Aha!

380 **NORA:** I can't dance tomorrow if I don't practice with you.

HELMER: *(going over to her)* Nora dear, are you really so frightened?

NORA: Yes, so terribly frightened. Let me practice right now; there's still time before dinner. Oh, sit down and play for me, Torvald. Direct me. Teach me, the way you always have.

HELMER: Gladly, if it's what you want. *(Sits at the piano.)*

NORA: *(snatches the tambourine up from the box, then a long, varicolored shawl, which she throws around herself, whereupon she springs forward and cries out)* Play for me now! Now I'll dance!

Helmer plays and Nora dances. Rank stands behind Helmer at the piano and looks on.

385 **HELMER:** *(as he plays)* Slower. Slow down.

NORA: Can't change it.

HELMER: Not so violent, Nora!

NORA: Has to be just like this.

HELMER: *(stopping)* No, no, that won't do at all.

390 **NORA:** *(laughing and swinging her tambourine)* Isn't that what I told you?

RANK: Let me play for her.

HELMER: *(getting up)* Yes, go on. I can teach her more easily then.

Rank sits at the piano and plays; Nora dances more and more wildly. Helmer has stationed himself by the stove and repeatedly gives her directions; she seems not to hear them; her hair loosens and falls over her shoulders; she does not notice, but goes on dancing. Mrs. Linde enters.

MRS. LINDE: *(standing dumbfounded at the door)* Ah—!

NORA: *(still dancing)* See what fun, Kristine!

395 **HELMER:** But Nora darling, you dance as if your life were at stake.

NORA: And it is.

HELMER: Rank, stop! This is pure madness. Stop it, I say!

Rank breaks off playing, and Nora halts abruptly.

HELMER: *(going over to her)* I never would have believed it. You've forgotten everything I taught you.

NORA: *(throwing away the tambourine)* You see for yourself.

400 **HELMER:** Well, there's certainly room for instruction here.

NORA: Yes, you see how important it is. You've got to teach me to the very last minute. Promise me that, Torvald?

HELMER: You can bet on it.

NORA: You mustn't, either today or tomorrow, think about anything else but me; you mustn't open any letters—or the mailbox—

HELMER: Ah, it's still the fear of that man—

405 **NORA:** Oh yes, yes, that too.

HELMER: Nora, it's written all over you—there's already a letter from him out there.

NORA: I don't know. I guess so. But you mustn't read such things now; there mustn't be anything ugly between us before it's all over.

RANK: *(quietly to Helmer)* You shouldn't deny her.

HELMER: *(putting his arm around her)* The child can have her way. But tomorrow night, after you've danced—

410 **NORA:** Then you'll be free.

MAID: *(in the doorway, right)* Ma'am, dinner is served.

NORA: We'll be wanting champagne, Helene.

MAID: Very good, ma'am. *(Goes out.)*

HELMER: So—a regular banquet, hm?

415 **NORA:** Yes, a banquet—champagne till daybreak! *(Calling out.)* And some macaroons, Helene. Heaps of them—just this once.

HELMER: *(taking her hands)* Now, now, now—no hysterics. Be my own little lark again.

NORA: Oh, I will soon enough. But go on in—and you, Dr. Rank. Kristine, help me put up my hair.

RANK: *(whispering, as they go)* There's nothing wrong—really wrong, is there?

HELMER: Oh, of course not. It's nothing more than this childish anxiety I was telling you about. *(They go out, right.)*

420 **NORA:** Well?

MRS. LINDE: Left town.

NORA: I could see by your face.

MRS. LINDE: He'll be home tomorrow evening. I wrote him a note.

NORA: You shouldn't have. Don't try to stop anything now. After all, it's a wonderful joy, this waiting here for the miracle.

425 **MRS. LINDE:** What is it you're waiting for?

NORA: Oh, you can't understand that. Go in to them: I'll be along in a moment.

Mrs. Linde goes into the dining room. Nora stands a short while as if composing herself; then she looks at her watch.

NORA: Five. Seven hours to midnight. Twenty-four hours to the midnight after, and then the tarantella's done. Seven and twenty-four? Thirty-one hours to live.

HELMER: *(in the doorway, right)* What's become of the little lark?

NORA: *(going toward him with open arms)* Here's your lark!

Act III

Same scene. The table, with chairs around it, has been moved to the center of the room. A lamp on the table is lit. The hall door stands open. Dance music drifts down from the floor above. Mrs. Linde sits at the table, absently paging through a book, trying to read, but apparently unable to focus her thoughts. Once or twice she pauses, tensely listening for a sound at the outer entrance.

MRS. LINDE: *(glancing at her watch)* Not yet—and there's hardly any time left. If only he's not—*(Listening again.)* Ah, there he is. *(She goes out in the hall and cautiously opens the outer door. Quiet footsteps are heard on the stairs. She whispers:)* Come in. Nobody's here.

KROGSTAD: *(in the doorway)* I found a note from you at home. What's back of all this?

MRS. LINDE: I just *had* to talk to you.

KROGSTAD: Oh? And it just *had* to be here in this house?

5 **MRS. LINDE:** At my place it was impossible; my room hasn't a private entrance. Come in; we're all alone. The maid's asleep, and the Helmers are at the dance upstairs.

KROGSTAD: *(entering the room)* Well, well, the Helmers are dancing tonight? Really?

MRS. LINDE: Yes, why not?

KROGSTAD: How true—why not?

MRS. LINDE: All right, Krogstad, let's talk.

10 **KROGSTAD:** Do we two have anything more to talk about?

MRS. LINDE: We have a great deal to talk about.

KROGSTAD: I wouldn't have thought so.

MRS. LINDE: No, because you've never understood me, really.

KROGSTAD: Was there anything more to understand—except what's all too common in life? A calculating woman throws over a man the moment a better catch comes by.

15 **MRS. LINDE:** You think I'm so thoroughly calculating? You think I broke it off lightly?

KROGSTAD: Didn't you?

MRS. LINDE: Nils—is that what you really thought?

KROGSTAD: If you cared, then why did you write me the way you did?

MRS. LINDE: What else could I do? If I had to break off with you, then it was my job as well to root out everything you felt for me.

20 **KROGSTAD:** *(wringing his hands)* So that was it. And this—all this, simply for money!

MRS. LINDE: Don't forget I had a helpless mother and two small brothers. We couldn't wait for you, Nils; you had such a long road ahead of you then.

KROGSTAD: That may be; but you still hadn't the right to abandon me for somebody else's sake.

MRS. LINDE: Yes—I don't know. So many, many times I've asked myself if I did have that right.

KROGSTAD: *(more softly)* When I lost you, it was as if all the solid ground dissolved from under my feet. Look at me; I'm a half-drowned man now, hanging onto a wreck.

25 **MRS. LINDE:**   Help may be near.

KROGSTAD: It was near—but then you came and blocked it off.

MRS. LINDE: Without my knowing it, Nils. Today for the first time I learned that it's you I'm replacing at the bank.

KROGSTAD: All right—I believe you. But now that you know, will you step aside?

MRS. LINDE: No, because that wouldn't benefit you in the slightest.

30 **KROGSTAD:**   Not "benefit" me, hm! I'd step aside anyway.

MRS. LINDE: I've learned to be realistic. Life and hard, bitter necessity have taught me that.

KROGSTAD: And life's taught me never to trust fine phrases.

MRS. LINDE: Then life's taught you a very sound thing. But you do have to trust in actions, don't you?

KROGSTAD: What does that mean?

35 **MRS. LINDE:**   You said you were hanging on like a half-drowned man to a wreck.

KROGSTAD: I've good reason to say that.

MRS. LINDE: I'm also like a half-drowned woman on a wreck. No one to suffer with; no one to care for.

KROGSTAD: You made your choice.

MRS. LINDE: There wasn't any choice then.

40 **KROGSTAD:**   So—what of it?

MRS. LINDE: Nils, if only we two shipwrecked people could reach across to each other.

KROGSTAD: What are you saying?

MRS. LINDE: Two on one wreck are at least better off than each on his own.

KROGSTAD: Kristine!

45 **MRS. LINDE:**   Why do you think I came into town?

KROGSTAD: Did you really have some thought of me?

MRS. LINDE: I have to work to go on living. All my born days, as long as I can remember, I've worked, and it's been my best and my only joy. But now I'm completely alone in the world; it frightens me to be so empty and lost. To work for yourself—there's no joy in that. Nils, give me something—someone to work for.

KROGSTAD: I don't believe all this. It's just some hysterical feminine urge to go out and make a noble sacrifice.

MRS. LINDE: Have you ever found me to be hysterical?

50 **KROGSTAD:**   Can you honestly mean this? Tell me—do you know everything about my past?

MRS. LINDE: Yes.

KROGSTAD: And you know what they think I'm worth around here.

MRS. LINDE: From what you were saying before, it would seem that with me you could have been another person.

KROGSTAD: I'm positive of that.

55 **MRS. LINDE:**   Couldn't it happen still?

Krogstad: Kristine—you're saying this in all seriousness? Yes, you are! I can see it in you. And do you really have the courage, then—?

Mrs. Linde: I need to have someone to care for; and your children need a mother. We both need each other. Nils, I have faith that you're good at heart—I'll risk everything together with you.

Krogstad: *(gripping her hands)* Kristine, thank you, thank you—Now I know I can win back a place in their eyes. Yes—but I forgot—

Mrs. Linde: *(listening)* Shh! The tarantella. Go now! Go on!

60 **Krogstad:**   Why? What is it?

Mrs. Linde: Hear the dance up there? When that's over, they'll be coming down.

Krogstad: Oh, then I'll go. But—it's all pointless. Of course, you don't know the move I made against the Helmers.

Mrs. Linde: Yes, Nils, I know.

Krogstad: And all the same, you have the courage to—?

65 **Mrs. Linde:**   I know how far despair can drive a man like you.

Krogstad: Oh, if I only could take it all back.

Mrs. Linde: You easily could—your letter's still lying in the mailbox.

Krogstad: Are you sure of that?

Mrs. Linde: Positive. But—

70 **Krogstad:**   *(looks at her searchingly)* Is that the meaning of it, then? You'll save your friend at any price. Tell me straight out. Is that it?

Mrs. Linde: Nils—anyone who's sold herself for somebody else once isn't going to do it again.

Krogstad: I'll demand my letter back.

Mrs. Linde: No, no.

Krogstad: Yes, of course. I'll stay here till Helmer comes down; I'll tell him to give me my letter again—that it only involves my dismissal—that he shouldn't read it—

75 **Mrs. Linde:**   No, Nils, don't call the letter back.

Krogstad: But wasn't that exactly why you wrote me to come here?

Mrs. Linde: Yes, in that first panic. But it's been a whole day and night since then, and in that time I've seen such incredible things in this house. Helmer's got to learn everything; this dreadful secret has to be aired; those two have to come to a full understanding; all these lies and evasions can't go on.

Krogstad: Well, then, if you want to chance it. But at least there's one thing I can do, and do right away—

Mrs. Linde: *(listening)* Go now, go, quick! The dance is over. We're not safe another second.

80 **Krogstad:**   I'll wait for you downstairs.

Mrs. Linde: Yes, please do; take me home.

Krogstad: I can't believe it; I've never been so happy. *(He leaves by way of the outer door; the door between the room and the hall stays open.)*

MRS. LINDE: *(straightening up a bit and getting together her street clothes)* How different now! How different! Someone to work for, to live for—a home to build. Well, it is worth the try! Oh, if they'd only come! *(Listening.)* Ah, there they are. Bundle up. *(She picks up her hat and coat. Nora's and Helmer's voices can be heard outside; a key turns in the lock, and Helmer brings Nora into the hall almost by force. She is wearing the Italian costume with a large black shawl about her; he has on evening dress, with a black domino open over it.)*

NORA: *(struggling in the doorway)* No, no, no, not inside! I'm going up again. I don't want to leave so soon.

85 **HELMER:** But Nora dear—

NORA: Oh, I beg you, please, Torvald. From the bottom of my heart, *please*—only an hour more!

HELMER: Not a single minute, Nora darling. You know our agreement. Come on, in we go; you'll catch cold out here. *(In spite of her resistance, he gently draws her into the room.)*

MRS. LINDE: Good evening.

NORA: Kristine!

90 **HELMER:** Why, Mrs. Linde—are you here so late?

MRS. LINDE: Yes, I'm sorry, but I did want to see Nora in costume.

NORA: Have you been sitting here, waiting for me?

MRS. LINDE: Yes. I didn't come early enough; you were all upstairs; and then I thought I really couldn't leave without seeing you.

HELMER: *(removing Nora's shawl)* Yes, take a good look. She's worth looking at, I can tell you that, Mrs. Linde. Isn't she lovely?

95 **MRS. LINDE:** Yes, I should say—

HELMER: A dream of loveliness, isn't she? That's what everyone thought at the party, too. But she's horribly stubborn—this sweet little thing. What's to be done with her? Can you imagine, I almost had to use force to pry her away.

NORA: Oh, Torvald, you're going to regret you didn't indulge me, even for just a half hour more.

HELMER: There, you see. She danced her tarantella and got a tumultuous hand—which was well earned, although the performance may have been a bit too naturalistic—I mean it rather overstepped the proprieties of art. But never mind—what's important is, she made a success, an overwhelming success. You think I could let her stay on after that and spoil the effect? Oh no; I took my lovely little Capri girl—my capricious little Capri girl, I should say—took her under my arm; one quick tour of the ballroom, a curtsy to every side, and then—as they say in novels—the beautiful vision disappeared. An exit should always be effective, Mrs. Linde, but that's what I can't get Nora to grasp. Phew, it's hot in here. *(Flings the domino on a chair and opens the door to his room.)* Why's it dark in here? Oh yes, of course. Excuse me. *(He goes in and lights a couple of candles.)*

NORA: *(in a sharp, breathless whisper)* So?

100 **MRS. LINDE:** *(quietly)* I talked with him.

NORA: And—?

MRS. LINDE: Nora—you must tell your husband everything.

NORA: *(dully)* I knew it.

MRS. LINDE: You've got nothing to fear from Krogstad, but you have to speak out.

105 **NORA:** I won't tell.

MRS. LINDE: Then the letter will.

NORA: Thanks, Kristine. I know now what's to be done. Shh!

HELMER: *(reentering)* Well, then, Mrs. Linde—have you admired her?

MRS. LINDE: Yes, and now I'll say good night.

110 **HELMER:** Oh, come, so soon? Is this yours, this knitting?

MRS. LINDE: Yes, thanks. I nearly forgot it.

HELMER: Do you knit, then?

MRS. LINDE: Oh yes.

HELMER: You know what? You should embroider instead.

115 **MRS. LINDE:** Really? Why?

HELMER: Yes, because it's a lot prettier. See here, one holds the embroidery so, in the left hand, and then one guides the needle with the right—so— in an easy, sweeping curve—right?

MRS. LINDE: Yes, I guess that's—

HELMER: But, on the other hand, knitting—it can never be anything but ugly. Look, see here, the arms tucked in, the knitting needles going up and down—there's something Chinese about it. Ah, that was really a glorious champagne they served.

MRS. LINDE: Yes, good night, Nora, and don't be stubborn any more.

120 **HELMER:** Well put, Mrs. Linde!

MRS. LINDE: Good night, Mr. Helmer.

HELMER: *(accompanying her to the door)* Good night, good night. I hope you get home all right. I'd be very happy to—but you don't have far to go. Good night, good night. *(She leaves. He shuts the door after her and returns.)* There, now, at last we got her out the door. She's a deadly bore, that creature.

NORA: Aren't you pretty tired, Torvald?

HELMER: No, not a bit.

125 **NORA:** You're not sleepy?

HELMER: Not at all. On the contrary, I'm feeling quite exhilarated. But you? Yes, you really look tired and sleepy.

NORA: Yes, I'm very tired. Soon now I'll sleep.

HELMER: See! You see! I was right all along that we shouldn't stay longer.

NORA: Whatever you do is always right.

130 **HELMER:** *(kissing her brow)* Now my little lark talks sense. Say, did you notice what a time Rank was having tonight?

NORA: Oh, was he? I didn't get to speak with him.

HELMER: I scarcely did either, but it's a long time since I've seen him in such high spirits. *(Gazes at her a moment, then comes nearer her.)* Hm—it's marvelous, though, to be back home again—to be completely alone with you. Oh, you bewitchingly lovely young woman!

NORA: Torvald, don't look at me like that!

HELMER: Can't I look at my richest treasure? At all that beauty that's mine, mine alone—completely and utterly.

135 **NORA:** *(moving around to the other side of the table)* You mustn't talk to me that way tonight.

HELMER: *(following her)* The tarantella is still in your blood, I can see—and it makes you even more enticing. Listen. The guests are beginning to go. *(Dropping his voice.)* Nora—it'll soon be quiet through this whole house.

NORA: Yes, I hope so.

HELMER: You do, don't you, my love? Do you realize—when I'm out at a party like this with you—do you know why I talk to you so little, and keep such a distance away; just send you a stolen look now and then—you know why I do it? It's because I'm imagining then that you're my secret darling, my secret young bride-to-be, and that no one suspects there's anything between us.

NORA: Yes, yes; oh, yes, I know you're always thinking of me.

140 **HELMER:** And then when we leave and I place the shawl over those fine young rounded shoulders—over that wonderful curving neck—then I pretend that you're my young bride, that we're just coming from the wedding, that for the first time I'm bringing you into my house—that for the first time I'm alone with you—completely alone with you, your trembling young beauty! All this evening I've longed for nothing but you. When I saw you turn and sway in the tarantella—my blood was pounding till I couldn't stand it—that's why I brought you down here so early—

NORA: Go away, Torvald! Leave me alone. I don't want all this.

HELMER: What do you mean? Nora, you're teasing me. You will, won't you? Aren't I your husband—?

A knock at the outside door.

NORA: *(startled)* What's that?

HELMER: *(going toward the hall)* Who is it?

145 **RANK:** *(outside)* It's me. May I come in a moment?

HELMER: *(with quiet irritation)* Oh, what does he want now? *(Aloud.)* Hold on. *(Goes and opens the door.)* Oh, how nice that you didn't just pass us by!

RANK: I thought I heard your voice, and then I wanted so badly to have a look in. *(Lightly glancing about.)* Ah, me, these old familiar haunts. You have it snug and cozy in here, you two.

HELMER: You seemed to be having it pretty cozy upstairs, too.

RANK: Absolutely. Why shouldn't I? Why not take in everything in life? As much as you can, anyway, and as long as you can. The wine was superb—

150 HELMER: The champagne especially.

RANK: You noticed that too? It's amazing how much I could guzzle down.

NORA: Torvald also drank a lot of champagne this evening.

RANK: Oh?

NORA: Yes, and that always makes him so entertaining.

155 RANK: Well, why shouldn't one have a pleasant evening after a well-spent day?

HELMER: Well spent? I'm afraid I can't claim that.

RANK: *(slapping him on the back)* But I can, you see!

NORA: Dr. Rank, you must have done some scientific research today.

RANK: Quite so.

160 HELMER: Come now—little Nora talking about scientific research!

NORA: And can I congratulate you on the results?

RANK: Indeed you may.

NORA: Then they were good?

RANK: The best possible for both doctor and patient—certainty.

165 NORA: *(quickly and searchingly)* Certainty?

RANK: Complete certainty. So don't I owe myself a gay evening afterwards?

NORA: Yes, you're right, Dr. Rank.

HELMER: I'm with you—just so long as you don't have to suffer for it in the morning.

RANK: Well, one never gets something for nothing in life.

170 NORA: Dr. Rank—are you very fond of masquerade parties?

RANK: Yes, if there's a good array of odd disguises—

NORA: Tell me, what should we two go as at the next masquerade?

HELMER: You little featherhead—already thinking of the next!

RANK: We two? I'll tell you what: you must go as Charmed Life—

175 HELMER: Yes, but find a costume for *that!*

RANK: Your wife can appear just as she looks every day.

HELMER: That was nicely put. But don't you know what you're going to be?

RANK: Yes, Helmer, I've made up my mind.

HELMER: Well?

180 RANK: At the next masquerade I'm going to be invisible.

HELMER: That's a funny idea.

RANK: They say there's a hat—black, huge—have you never heard of the hat that makes you invisible? You put it on, and then no one on earth can see you.

HELMER: *(suppressing a smile)* Ah, of course.

RANK: But I'm quite forgetting what I came for. Helmer, give me a cigar, one of the dark Havanas.

185 HELMER: With the greatest of pleasure. *(Holds out his case.)*

RANK: Thanks. *(Takes one and cuts off the tip.)*

NORA: *(striking a match)* Let me give you a light.

RANK: Thank you. *(She holds the match for him; he lights the cigar.)* And now good-bye.

HELMER: Good-bye, good-bye, old friend.

190 **NORA:** Sleep well, Doctor.

RANK: Thanks for that wish.

NORA: Wish me the same.

RANK: You? All right, if you like—Sleep well. And thanks for the light. *(He nods to them both and leaves.)*

HELMER: *(his voice subdued)* He's been drinking heavily.

195 **NORA:** *(absently)* Could be. *(Helmer takes his keys from his pocket and goes out in the hall.)* Torvald—what are you after?

HELMER: Got to empty the mailbox; it's nearly full. There won't be room for the morning papers.

NORA: Are you working tonight?

HELMER: You know I'm not. Why—what's this? Someone's been at the lock.

NORA: At the lock—?

200 **HELMER:** Yes, I'm positive. What do you suppose—? I can't imagine one of the maids—? Here's a broken hairpin. Nora, it's yours—

NORA: *(quickly)* Then it must be the children—

HELMER: You'd better break them of that. Hm, hm—well, opened it after all. *(Takes the contents out and calls into the kitchen.)* Helene! Helene, would you put out the lamp in the hall. *(He returns to the room, shutting the hall door, then displays the handful of mail.)* Look how it's piled up. *(Sorting through them.)* Now what's this?

NORA: *(at the window)* The letter! Oh, Torvald, no!

HELMER: Two calling cards—from Rank.

205 **NORA:** From Dr. Rank?

HELMER: *(examining them)* "Dr. Rank, Consulting Physician." They were on top. He must have dropped them in as he left.

NORA: Is there anything on them?

HELMER: There's a black cross over the name. See? That's a gruesome notion. He could almost be announcing his own death.

NORA: That's just what he's doing.

210 **HELMER:** What! You've heard something? Something he's told you?

NORA: Yes. That when those cards came, he'd be taking his leave of us. He'll shut himself in now and die.

HELMER: Ah, my poor friend! Of course I knew he wouldn't be here much longer. But so soon—And then to hide himself away like a wounded animal.

NORA: If it has to happen, then it's best it happens in silence—don't you think so, Torvald?

HELMER: *(pacing up and down)* He'd grown right into our lives. I simply can't imagine him gone. He with his suffering and loneliness—like a dark cloud setting off our sunlit happiness. Well, maybe it's best this way. For him, at least. *(Standing still.)* And maybe for us too, Nora. Now we're thrown back on each other, completely. *(Embracing her.)* Oh you, my darling wife, how can I hold you close enough? You know what, Nora— time and again I've wished you were in some terrible danger, just so I could stake my life and soul and everything, for your sake.

215 **NORA:** *(tearing herself away, her voice firm and decisive)* Now you must read your mail, Torvald.

HELMER: No, no, not tonight. I want to stay with you, dearest.

NORA: With a dying friend on your mind?

HELMER: You're right. We've both had a shock. There's ugliness between us—these thoughts of death and corruption. We'll have to get free of them first. Until then—we'll stay apart.

NORA: *(clinging about his neck)* Torvald—good night! Good night!

220 **HELMER:** *(kissing her on the cheek)* Good night, little songbird. Sleep well, Nora. I'll be reading my mail now. *(He takes the letters into his room and shuts the door after him.)*

NORA: *(with bewildered glances, groping about, seizing Helmer's domino, throwing it around her, and speaking in short, hoarse, broken whispers)* Never see him again. Never, never. *(Putting her shawl over her head.)* Never see the children either—them, too. Never, never. Oh, the freezing black water! The depths—down—Oh, I wish it were over—He has it now; he's reading it—now. Oh no, no, not yet. Torvald, good-bye, you and the children—*(She starts for the hall; as she does, Helmer throws open his door and stands with an open letter in his hand.)*

HELMER: Nora!

NORA: *(screams)* Oh—!

HELMER: What is this? You know what's in this letter?

225 **NORA:** Yes, I know. Let me go! Let me out!

HELMER: *(holding her back)* Where are you going?

NORA: *(struggling to break loose)* You can't save me, Torvald!

HELMER: *(slumping back)* True! Then it's true what he writes? How horrible! No, no, it's impossible—it can't be true.

NORA: It *is* true. I've loved you more than all this world.

230 **HELMER:** Ah, none of your slippery tricks.

NORA: *(taking one step toward him)* Torvald—!

HELMER: What *is* this you've blundered into!

NORA: Just let me loose. You're not going to suffer for my sake. You're not going to take on my guilt.

HELMER: No more playacting. *(Locks the hall door.)* You stay right here and give me a reckoning. You understand what you've done? Answer! You understand?

235 **NORA:** *(looking squarely at him, her face hardening)* Yes. I'm beginning to understand everything now.

HELMER: *(striding about)* Oh, what an awful awakening! In all these eight years—she who was my pride and joy—a hypocrite, a liar—worse, worse—a criminal! How infinitely disgusting it all is! The shame! *(Nora* *says nothing and goes on looking straight at him. He stops in front of her.)* I should have suspected something of the kind. I should have known. All your father's flimsy values—Be still! All your father's flimsy values have come out in you. No religion, no morals, no sense of duty— Oh, how I'm punished for letting him off! I did it for your sake, and you repay me like this.

NORA: Yes, like this.

HELMER: Now you've wrecked all my happiness—ruined my whole future. Oh, it's awful to think of. I'm in a cheap little grafter's hands; he can do anything he wants with me, ask for anything, play with me like a puppet—and I can't breathe a word. I'll be swept down miserably into the depths on account of a featherbrained woman.

NORA: When I'm gone from this world, you'll be free.

240 HELMER: Oh, quit posing. Your father had a mess of those speeches too. What good would that ever do me if you were gone from this world, as you say? Not the slightest. He can still make the whole thing known; and if he does, I could be falsely suspected as your accomplice. They might even think that I was behind it—that I put you up to it. And all that I can thank you for—you that I've coddled the whole of our marriage. Can you see now what you've done to me?

NORA: *(icily calm)* Yes.

HELMER: It's so incredible, I just can't grasp it. But we'll have to patch up whatever we can. Take off the shawl. I said, take if off! I've got to appease him somehow or other. The thing has to be hushed up at any cost. And as for you and me, it's got to seem like everything between us is just as it was—to the outside world, that is. You'll go right on living in this house, of course. But you can't be allowed to bring up the children; I don't dare trust you with them—Oh, to have to say this to someone I've loved so much! Well, that's done with. From now on happiness doesn't matter; all that matters is saving the bits and pieces, the appearance—*(The doorbell rings. Helmer starts.)* What's that? And so late. Maybe the worst—? You think he'd—? Hide, Nora! Say you're sick. *(Nora remains standing motionless. Helmer goes and opens the door.)*

MAID: *(half dressed, in the hall)* A letter for Mrs. Helmer.

HELMER: I'll take it. *(Snatches the letter and shuts the door.)* Yes, it's from him. You don't get it; I'm reading it myself.

245 NORA: Then read it.

HELMER: *(by the lamp)* I hardly dare. We may be ruined, you and I. But— I've got to know. *(Rips open the letter, skims through a few lines, glances at an enclosure, then cries out joyfully.)* Nora! *(Nora looks inquiringly at him.)* Nora! Wait—better check it again—Yes, yes, it's true. I'm saved. Nora, I'm saved!

NORA: And I?

HELMER: You too, of course. We're both saved, both of us. Look. He's sent back your note. He says he's sorry and ashamed—that a happy development in his life—oh, who cares what he says! Nora, we're saved! No one can hurt you. Oh, Nora, Nora—but first, this ugliness all has to go. Let me see— *(Takes a look at the note.)* No, I don't want to see it; I want the whole thing to fade like a dream. *(Tears the note and both letters to pieces, throws them into the stove and watches them burn.)* There—now there's nothing left—He wrote that since Christmas Eve you—Oh, they must have been three terrible days for you, Nora.

NORA: I fought a hard fight.

250 **HELMER:**   And suffered pain and saw no escape but—No, we're not going to dwell on anything unpleasant. We'll just be grateful and keep on repeating: it's over now, it's over! You hear me, Nora? You don't seem to realize—it's over. What's it mean—that frozen look? Oh, poor little Nora, I understand. You can't believe I've forgiven you. But I have, Nora; I swear I have. I know that what you did, you did out of love for me.

NORA: That's true.

HELMER: You loved me the way a wife ought to love her husband. It's simply the means that you couldn't judge. But you think I love you any the less for not knowing how to handle your affairs? No, no—just lean on me; I'll guide you and teach you. I wouldn't be a man if this feminine helplessness didn't make you twice as attractive to me. You mustn't mind those sharp words I said—that was all in the first confusion of thinking my world had collapsed. I've forgiven you, Nora; I swear I've forgiven you.

NORA: My thanks for your forgiveness. *(She goes out through the door, right.)*

HELMER: No, wait—*(Peers in.)* What are you doing in there?

255 **NORA:**   *(inside)* Getting out of my costume.

HELMER: *(by the open door)* Yes, do that. Try to calm yourself and collect your thoughts again, my frightened little songbird. You can rest easy now; I've got wide wings to shelter you with. *(Walking about close by the door.)* How snug and nice our home is, Nora. You're safe here; I'll keep you like a hunted dove I've rescued out of a hawk's claws. I'll bring peace to your poor, shuddering heart. Gradually it'll happen, Nora; you'll see. Tomorrow all this will look different to you; then everything will be as it was. I won't have to go on repeating I forgive you; you'll feel it for yourself. How can you imagine I'd ever conceivably want to disown you—or even blame you in any way? Ah, you don't know a man's heart, Nora. For a man there's something indescribably sweet and satisfying in knowing he's forgiven his wife—and forgiven her out of a full and open heart. It's as if she belongs to him in two ways now: in a sense he's given her fresh into the world again, and she's become his wife and his child as well. From now on that's what you'll be to me—you little, bewildered, helpless thing. Don't be afraid of anything, Nora; just open your heart to me, and I'll be conscience and will to you both—*(Nora enters in her regular clothes.)* What's this? Not in bed? You've changed your dress?

NORA: Yes, Torvald, I've changed my dress.

HELMER: But why now, so late?

NORA: Tonight I'm not sleeping.

260 **HELMER:** But Nora dear—

NORA: *(looking at her watch)* It's still not so very late. Sit down, Torvald; we have a lot to talk over. *(She sits at one side of the table.)*

HELMER: Nora—what is this? That hard expression—

NORA: Sit down. This'll take some time. I have a lot to say.

HELMER: *(sitting at the table directly opposite her)* You worry me, Nora. And I don't understand you.

265 **NORA:** No, that's exactly it. You don't understand me. And I've never understood you either—until tonight. No, don't interrupt. You can just listen to what I say. We're closing out accounts, Torvald.

HELMER: How do you mean that?

NORA: *(after a short pause)* Doesn't anything strike you about our sitting here like this?

HELMER: What's that?

NORA: We've been married now eight years. Doesn't it occur to you that this is the first time we two, you and I, man and wife, have ever talked seriously together?

270 **HELMER:** What do you mean—seriously?

NORA: In eight whole years—longer even—right from our first acquaintance, we've never exchanged a serious word on any serious thing.

HELMER: You mean I should constantly go and involve you in problems you couldn't possibly help me with?

NORA: I'm not talking of problems. I'm saying that we've never sat down seriously together and tried to get to the bottom of anything.

HELMER: But dearest, what good would that ever do you?

275 **NORA:** That's the point right there: you've never understood me. I've been wronged greatly, Torvald—first by Papa, and then by you.

HELMER: What! By us—the two people who've loved you more than anyone else?

NORA: *(shaking her head)* You never loved me. You've thought it fun to be in love with me, that's all.

HELMER: Nora, what a thing to say!

NORA: Yes, it's true now, Torvald. When I lived at home with Papa, he told me all his opinions, so I had the same ones too; or if they were different I hid them, since he wouldn't have cared for that. He used to call me his doll-child, and he played with me the way I played with my dolls. Then I came into your house—

280 **HELMER:** How can you speak of our marriage like that?

NORA: *(unperturbed)* I mean, then I went from Papa's hands into yours. You arranged everything to your own taste, and so I got the same taste as you—or I pretended to; I can't remember. I guess a little of both, first one, then the other. Now when I look back, it seems as if I'd lived here like a beggar—just from hand to mouth. I've lived by doing tricks for you,

Torvald. But that's the way you wanted it. It's a great sin what you and Papa did to me. You're to blame that nothing's become of me.

HELMER: Nora, how unfair and ungrateful you are! Haven't you been happy here?

NORA: No, never. I thought so—but I never have.

HELMER: Not—not happy!

285 **NORA:** No, only lighthearted. And you've always been so kind to me. But our home's been nothing but a playpen. I've been your doll-wife here, just as at home I was Papa's doll-child. And in turn the children have been my dolls. I thought it was fun when you played with me, just as they thought it fun when I played with them. That's been our marriage, Torvald.

HELMER: There's some truth in what you're saying—under all the raving exaggeration. But it'll all be different after this. Playtime's over; now for the schooling.

NORA: Whose schooling—mine or the children's?

HELMER: Both yours and the children's, dearest.

NORA: Oh, Torvald, you're not the man to teach me to be a good wife to you.

290 **HELMER:** And you can say that?

NORA: And I—how am I equipped to bring up children?

HELMER: Nora!

NORA: Didn't you say a moment ago that that was no job to trust me with?

HELMER: In a flare of temper! Why fasten on that?

295 **NORA:** Yes, but you were so very right. I'm not up to the job. There's another job I have to do first. I have to try to educate myself. You can't help me with that. I've got to do it alone. And that's why I'm leaving you now.

HELMER: *(jumping up)* What's that?

NORA: I have to stand completely alone, if I'm ever going to discover myself and the world out there. So I can't go on living with you.

HELMER: Nora, Nora!

NORA: I want to leave right away. Kristine should put me up for the night—

300 **HELMER:** You're insane! You've no right! I forbid you!

NORA: From here on, there's no use forbidding me anything. I'll take with me whatever is mine. I don't want a thing from you, either now or later.

HELMER: What kind of madness is this!

NORA: Tomorrow I'm going home—I mean, home where I came from. It'll be easier up there to find something to do.

HELMER: Oh, you blind, incompetent child!

305 **NORA:** I must learn to be competent, Torvald.

HELMER: Abandon your home, your husband, your children! And you're not even thinking what people will say.

NORA: I can't be concerned about that. I only know how essential this is.

HELMER: Oh, it's outrageous. So you'll run out like this on your most sacred vows.

NORA: What do you think are my most sacred vows?

310 **HELMER:** And I have to tell you that! Aren't they your duties to your husband and children?

NORA: I have other duties equally sacred.

HELMER: That isn't true. What duties are they?

NORA: Duties to myself.

HELMER: Before all else, you're a wife and a mother.

315 **NORA:** I don't believe in that any more. I believe that, before all else, I'm a human being, no less than you—or anyway, I ought to try to become one. I know the majority thinks you're right, Torvald, and plenty of books agree with you, too. But I can't go on believing what the majority says, or what's written in books. I have to think over these things myself and try to understand them.

HELMER: Why can't you understand your place in your own home? On a point like that, isn't there one everlasting guide you can turn to? Where's your religion?

NORA: Oh, Torvald, I'm really not sure what religion is.

HELMER: What—?

NORA: I only know what the minister said when I was confirmed. He told me religion was this thing and that. When I get clear and away by myself, I'll go into that problem too. I'll see if what the minister said was right, or, in any case, if it's right for me.

320 **HELMER:** A young woman your age shouldn't talk like that. If religion can't move you, I can try to rouse your conscience. You do have some moral feeling? Or, tell me—has that gone too?

NORA: It's not easy to answer that, Torvald. I simply don't know. I'm all confused about these things. I just know I see them so differently from you. I find out, for one thing, that the law's not at all what I'd thought—but I can't get it through my head that the law is fair. A woman hasn't a right to protect her dying father or save her husband's life! I can't believe that.

HELMER: You talk like a child. You don't know anything of the world you live in.

NORA: No, I don't. But now I'll begin to learn for myself. I'll try to discover who's right, the world or I.

HELMER: Nora, you're sick; you've got a fever. I almost think you're out of your head.

325 **NORA:** I've never felt more clearheaded and sure in my life.

HELMER: And—clearheaded and sure—you're leaving your husband and children?

NORA: Yes.

HELMER: Then there's only one possible reason.

NORA: What?

330 **HELMER:** You no longer love me.

NORA: No. That's exactly it.

HELMER: Nora! You can't be serious!

NORA: Oh, this is so hard, Torvald—you've been so kind to me always. But I can't help it. I don't love you any more.

HELMER: *(struggling for composure)* Are you also clearheaded and sure about that?

335 **NORA:** Yes, completely. That's why I can't go on staying here.

HELMER: Can you tell me what I did to lose your love?

NORA: Yes, I can tell you. It was this evening when the miraculous thing didn't come—then I knew you weren't the man I'd imagined.

HELMER: Be more explicit; I don't follow you.

NORA: I've waited now so patiently eight long years—for, my Lord, I know miracles don't come every day. Then this crisis broke over me, and such a certainty filled me: *now* the miraculous event would occur. While Krogstad's letter was lying out there, I never for an instant dreamed that you could give in to his terms. I was so utterly sure you'd say to him: go on, tell your tale to the whole wide world. And when he'd done that—

340 **HELMER:** Yes, what then? When I'd delivered my own wife into shame and disgrace—!

NORA: When he'd done that, I was so utterly sure that you'd step forward, take the blame on yourself and say: I am the guilty one.

HELMER: Nora—!

NORA: You're thinking I'd never accept such a sacrifice from you? No, of course not. But what good would my protests be against you? That was the miracle I was waiting for, in terror and hope. And to stave that off, I would have taken my life.

HELMER: I'd gladly work for you day and night, Nora—and take on pain and deprivation. But there's no one who gives up honor for love.

345 **NORA:** Millions of women have done just that.

HELMER: Oh, you think and talk like a silly child.

NORA: Perhaps. But you neither think nor talk like the man I could join my-self to. When your big fright was over—and it wasn't from any threat against me, only for what might damage you—when all the danger was past, for you it was just as if nothing had happened. I was exactly the same, your little lark, your doll, that you'd have to handle with double care now that I'd turned out so brittle and frail. *(Gets up.)* Torvald—in that instant it dawned on me that for eight years I've been living here with a stranger, and that I'd even conceived three children—oh, I can't stand the thought of it! I could tear myself to bits.

HELMER: *(heavily)* I see. There's a gulf that's opened between us—that's clear. Oh, but Nora, can't we bridge it somehow?

NORA: The way I am now, I'm no wife for you.

350 **HELMER:** I have the strength to make myself over.

NORA: Maybe—if your doll gets taken away.

HELMER: But to part! To part from you! No, Nora, no—I can't imagine it.

NORA: *(going out, right)* All the more reason why it has to be. *(She reenters with her coat and a small overnight bag, which she puts on a chair by the table.)*

HELMER: Nora, Nora, not now! Wait till tomorrow.

355   **NORA:**   I can't spend the night in a strange man's room.

HELMER: But couldn't we live here like brother and sister—

NORA: You know very well how long that would last. *(Throws her shawl about her.)* Good-bye, Torvald. I won't look in on the children. I know they're in better hands than mine. The way I am now, I'm no use to them.

HELMER: But someday, Nora—someday—?

NORA: How can I tell? I haven't the least idea what'll become of me.

360   **HELMER:**   But you're my wife, now and wherever you go.

NORA: Listen, Torvald—I've heard that when a wife deserts her husband's house just as I'm doing, then the law frees him from all responsibility. In any case, I'm freeing you from being responsible. Don't feel yourself bound, any more than I will. There has to be absolute freedom for us both. Here, take your ring back. Give me mine.

HELMER: That too?

NORA: That too.

HELMER: There it is.

365   **NORA:**   Good. Well, now it's all over. I'm putting the keys here. The maids know all about keeping up the house—better than I do. Tomorrow, after I've left town, Kristine will stop by to pack up everything that's mine from home. I'd like those things shipped up to me.

HELMER: Over! All over! Nora, won't you ever think about me?

NORA: I'm sure I'll think of you often, and about the children and the house here.

HELMER: May I write you?

NORA: No—never. You're not to do that.

370   **HELMER:**   Oh, but let me send you—

NORA: Nothing. Nothing.

HELMER: Or help you if you need it.

NORA: No. I accept nothing from strangers.

HELMER: Nora—can I never be more than a stranger to you?

375   **NORA:**   *(picking up the overnight bag)* Ah, Torvald—it would take the greatest miracle of all—

HELMER: Tell me the greatest miracle!

NORA: You and I both would have to transform ourselves to the point that—Oh, Torvald, I've stopped believing in miracles.

HELMER: But I'll believe. Tell me! Transform ourselves to the point that—?

NORA: That our living together could be a true marriage. *(She goes out down the hall.)*

380   **HELMER:**   *(sinks down on a chair by the door, face buried in his hands)* Nora! Nora! *(Looking about and rising.)* Empty. She's gone. *(A sudden hope leaps in him.)* The greatest miracle—?

(From below, the sound of a door slamming shut.)

CURTAIN

—— A Feminist Perspective on *A Doll's House,* (1982) ——

M. C. Bradbrook

> [Bradbrook is an English critic who has written primarily on the Elizabethan theater. In the following excerpt, she examines the theme of personal growth and development, which she deems central to *A Doll's House.*]

At Christmas 1879—though not quite immediately—the appearance of *A Doll's House* brought the fame of Henrik Ibsen to England. The social emancipation of women, especially through literary women, had been established a generation earlier; in 1846 Elizabeth Barrett Browning had eloped to Italy, and George Eliot, who had gone abroad in 1854 to live with G. H. Lewes, was, by the end of the 1870s, a venerated figure. In this year, 1879, Sarah Bernhardt came to London, having walked out of the Comédie Française and slammed the door.

But in the preliminary notes for his play Ibsen had set forward a position so radical that it might well be used today as a feminist manifesto:

> There are two kinds of moral law, two kinds of conscience, one in man, and a completely different one in woman. They do not understand each other; but in matters of practical living the woman is judged by a man's law, as if she were not a woman but a man. . . . A woman cannot be herself in contemporary society; it is an exclusively male society, with laws drafted by men, and with counsel and judges who judge feminine conduct from the masculine point of view. . . . She has committed a crime and is proud of it because she did it for love of her husband and to save his life. . . . Now and then like a woman, she shrugs off her thoughts. Sudden return of dread and terror. Everything must be borne alone.

However, at the end of the "Ibsen decade" (the 1880s) when the play had appeared in London, Milan, Paris and Budapest Ibsen told the Society for Extended Female Education in Vienna, in 1891, that it was not about women's rights but the rights of humanity in general; in 1898 he repeated this to the Norwegian Women's Rights League ("What courage!" observed Nigel Dennis), adding "I am not even quite sure what women's rights are."

In the terms of a later generation his interests were psychological rather than sociological; he said he did not believe in "external revolutions"; the revolution "must come from within."

Ibsen's work made its effect in translation into languages he did not always understand; it was read much more than performed. Today it survives because of its power in performance. Modern rediscovery of Ibsen followed the stage and broadcast revivals of the 1950s. The full impact of this play survives across language barriers because Ibsen has employed all the arts of the theatre. Perhaps because the theatre in which he was trained had relied on translations for most of its performances and had little of its own, Ibsen succeeded in developing (at the age of fifty-one and in his fifteenth play) a reticulation or meshing of human relationships which elastically adapts itself in live action; the space between the characters, the links that divide and unite them, the space between actors and audience, and the flow of empathy that sustains performance, each derives from Ibsen's employment of all the kinds of communication possible in drama. Words and subtext, the setting and the invisible, eliminated or superseded drafts upon which Ibsen worked forward to his final form supply a "complex variable" capable of all the modulations recently chronicled in Daniel Haakonsen's *Henrik Ibsen, mennesket og kunstneren* (1981).

The original Nora, Betty Hennings, had begun her career as a ballerina; one of Ibsen's final inspirations, Nora's tarantella, embodies the heroine's terror and despair, while concentrating her power as Eve, the prime delight and temptress of men. Like the dance of Anitra in *Peer Gynt,* the dance of the Capri fishergirl belongs to an untamed Southern scene, but it has now been transported from Egypt to the cosy little home with its stove, draped table and upright piano, from which the dancer will depart into a Norwegian night.

The delicious life-giving power radiating from Nora must be controlled and kept jealously from her male circle: "You and papa have done me a grave wrong," she finally tells her husband. Nora's forging of her dying father's signature has outraged her husband equally as a lawyer and as President of the Bank; but to her the gold of his wedding ring has become a bigger fraud, since the President is found to be spiritually bankrupt, totally self-deceived.

Livsglaeden, that untranslateable word, the fountain of life, dances in the faded images of the little skylark, the little squirrel; an actress can still embody it. Nowhere else in Ibsen do the lineaments of animal desire show as plainly as in Torvald Helmer's "Don't want to? don't want to? aren't I your husband?" Payment on the nail is the protector's right; it is no "demand of the ideal."

Whatever harsh privation his new urban environment inflicted on man's primal energies, the child-wife and father-husband relation, that popular model for happy marriages in the mid-nineteenth century, immensely fortified the home as enclosure, cradle and prison. The skylark, the pet squirrel plays in a cage. At the end, Torvald's magnanimous act of forgiving his wife leaves her in exactly the position that he had seen as being his own under the blackmailer's power:

> Here I am, in the grip of a man without a conscience; he can do whatever he
> likes with me, demand anything he wants, order me about just as he
> chooses . . . and I daren't breathe a word.

The happy state of affairs to which Torvald later looks forward was a sort of spiritual cannibalism: "Open your whole heart to me, and I shall become both your will-power and your conscience." At the beginning, he had been forbidding his baby doll to eat macaroons or do mending in the drawing-room; he kept the key of the letter-box in his pocket, and when Nora inadvertently let slip a word of criticism, he straightway asserted his authority over her by dispatching Krogstad's letter of dismissal. For once he and Krogstad agree as lawyers in thinking that Nora's disappearance or suicide would not absolve him from possible accusations of having instigated her forgery. Nora's rejection of his sexual approach is dismissed with "What's this? You've played the fool with me long enough, little Nora." Finally, he opens her last letter from Krogstad, refusing to give it her. Her childish pet name (she was christened Eleanora, as Ibsen explained to his family, who gave that name to his grand-daughter) means that to translate "Nora," something like "Nolly-dolly" is needed.

The eternal child-wife must remain unconscious of the sexual implications of her own pretty games whilst she daydreams about legacies from elderly admirers. She is expert at undressing herself in imagination for Dr. Rank. She dresses up and plays parts for Torvald almost like Harold Pinter's girls. In Ibsen's first draft she reveals that her father liked her to write poetry and learn French, but Torvald preferred dramatic recitations, and disapproved of French literature; his own fantasies of secret mistresses and bridal nights, revealed in his cups, come out of cheap novelettes. Dr. Rank slips into calling her "Nora" but the truly familiar "du" is reserved for the men between each other, the two women together, and the husband and wife; three different linkings of the threads. Inside "Nolly-dolly" another self is growing up. She may enjoy playing at secrets, the secrets of the Christmas tree; but her copying work (in the first draft *not* a secret from Torvald) makes her feel "almost like a man"; and at the news of Torvald's power to dismiss such bank employees as Krogstad, she feels an impulse to swear.

The audience is never told of the emergent adult growing in the chrysalis of the doll's house; they are left to fill her in, or fill her out. Her unconscious growth towards maturity is accompanied by self-delusive dreams of Torvald, the chivalrous knight-errant; and by blank disregard for the concerns of others. When her instinct to love and cherish is in collision with brute facts, she cannot bear to hurt, and would rather lie. . . . Nora begs Krogstad to think of her children, and his reply "Did you or your husband think of mine?" is quite as devastating as Torvald's "I am saved, Nora, I am saved," when he finds the fatal IOU has been returned. (In the first draft he says "We are saved.")

◆ ◆ ◆

Rank and Krogstad are both old school friends of Torvald, Kristine of Nora; each presents a shadow side of the twin. The cross-relationships become a closed system. We do not know what Torvald's chief clerk is like, the details of Rank's practice were suppressed; we do not know whether Nora's childbirths were hard or easy, or what was the character of Krogstad's first wife. But we know that Kristine has been forced by necessity to develop her masculine qualities, to become a breadwinner (also, earlier, to sell herself in the marriage-market). The hard, cold insight which makes her tell Krogstad she won't resign the job at the bank in which she has displaced him "for that wouldn't help you at all" created what is eventually Nora's equally hard, cold insight into her own situation. Kristine deliberately stops Krogstad from claiming back his letter of disclosure; replacing Dr. Rank as ruthless experimenter, she detonates the explosion. Yet Kristine herself is hungry for a home, hungry to be needed, as Nora is hungry for freedom. She had long ago broken Krogstad as Nora breaks Torvald ("I felt as though the ground were cut from under my feet") but now the family for whom she sacrificed herself are no longer in need of her, she feels desolate and empty. In the first draft she was still supporting her brothers; this detracts from her egoistic energy, as she greets the future in words that anticipate Nora's. Tidying up a little, and putting ready her outdoor clothes, to meet Krogstad who is waiting below:

> What a change! O what a change! [literally a turning in the road]. People to work for—people to live for. A home that needs to *feel* like home! Well, now I'll set to, straight away. [In the first draft, "We'll set to"] . . . I wish they'd hurry! Ah, there they are! Get my things.

But the competent Kristine radiates from no fountain of life; "she's a bore, that woman," says Torvald. Malice would recall the epigram "She lives for others. You can tell the others by the hunted look in their eyes." When Nora comes in after putting off her fancy dress, Torvald cries "What's this? Not going to bed? You've changed?," and she replies "Yes, Torvald, I've changed." There is no verbal echo in the Norwegian, as there is in English, but to dress for a journey links the two scenes dramatically and in action. As Kristine finds a city home, Nora sets out for her birthplace, in search of herself.

In her last speech Nora brings together her whole life, the dead father and her eight years' marriage "with a stranger" so that the past looms into the present at several levels, not only at the one of her dangerous secret. Torvald reproaches her for her ingratitude, and blames himself for having turned advocate for the defence when sent by his ministry to investigate her father's affairs. Ibsen suppressed the passage from the first draft, where he says that he could find no trace of the 1200 dollars her father was supposed to have given her just before his death, for it would be tactless to enquire why Torvald, the lawyer, did not check fully the details of a transaction from which so unexpectedly he had benefited. An audience should not have its notice drawn to the inconsistency. It has rightly been allowed to feel, earlier, that Nora has some basis for her dreams of Torvald's chivalry in the kindness he had shown her "poor papa."

As we never hear about anyone outside the charmed circle of home, so the close detail and meshing of the foreground distinguish *A Doll's House* from its immediate predecessor, *Pillars of the Community* (1877). Here women's rights are shown in a feminine group ranging from the emancipated Lona to the patient Martha, who, like Solveig in *Peer Gynt,* sits at home spinning and waiting for her lover to return. Though Ibsen had begun the art of elimination and of carving in high relief, Bernick's relations with his whole community dominate. (The women do not supply the action of the play.) A large cast of nineteen are found flowing in and out of the garden-room at Bernick's. The irony is far more direct ("Just repaired! and in your own yard, Mr. Bernick! . . . now if she's been one of those floating coffins you hear about in the bigger countries!"), and is not so fully integrated with the language of stage movement.

By contrast, Torvald's address to Nora through the half-open door as, un-known to him, she is "changing," allows him in half-soliloquy to cast himself as a hero, till in his inflation he triumphantly reaches the cheap image of a dove rescued from a hawk—almost becoming something birdlike. The script must be his alone—to her earlier cry "You mustn't take it on yourself!" he had snapped "Stop play-acting!" Her language from this moment is naked, plain (in contrast to her horror when Dr. Rank spoke out to her of his love). But at the end, when Torvald in a mixture of threat and appeal says "Then only one explanation is possible . . . you don't love me any more," her simple "No; that's it. Exactly" brings back the angry cross-examining lawyer: "Then perhaps you can also explain to me?" In the first draft she had attacked Tor-vald; in the final version she defines and describes, gives orders to her hus-band, to which he responds with bewildered questions. The last difficult definition of the "miracle" that their "common life" (*samliv*) "might become a marriage" (*ekteskap*) annihilates Torvald as lawyer and as man.

The word's power is extended in its context. The silences of Dr. Rank, his "Thanks for the light," and the black cross above his name on the visiting card that, according to social ritual, has been dropped, anticipate the depth of Nora's own speech. Her inner death does not leave enough relationship to merit reproaches.

◆ ◆ ◆

In Ibsen's prose the tensions come partly from the relation between the characters, partly from that between his play and what was expected of such dramas (the model of Scribe). On stage the first audience, while enjoy-ing the charm of Nora, actually took Torvald's point of view and thought him a decent husband. In the theatre they followed the familiar code which Ibsen was breaking. It was reading that convinced them of his intention. By the time he had finished drafting and redrafting *A Doll's House* the original notes did not apply, and he was justified in saying it was not a question of women's rights. The tensions come from the marriage between the word and its context, and this works as rhythm works in poetry. But the verse rhythms of Ibsen were very simple; it was only in prose that he gained the classic freedom of his great predecessors.

As he said again and again, his resources were within; he created out of himself, yet he did not subsequently impose an interpretation. He would not tell actors how to play their roles, nor tell the audience how Mrs. Alving acted with the morphine: "That everyone must decide for himself." The plays grew into contexts he did not know. One translation was called

Breaking a Butterfly. Hauptmann wrote *Before Sunrise,* and Brieux *Damaged Goods* out of *Ghosts;* Shaw put back a lot of theory, and wrote *Candida.*

The play is not a dramatic monologue for Nora with supporting assistance. The great final scene impresses with its truth, but not as a transcript of anything that could actually happen; it is itself the "miracle" it postulated. Passions are disentangled from the criss-cross tangles of ordinary life; all the characters being at once so closely enmeshed with each other, yet so isolated from any other crowd or chorus figures, the detail is not realistic.

Ibsen said that as well as character, his people must have a fate. Nora's fate is to embrace an unknown future—to carry the bright flame of her vitality into the dark. "Out into the storm of life" is one of Borkman's most ironic fantasies; Nora seeks a deep solitude. "It is necessary that I stand alone."

◆ ◆ ◆

The characters of Ibsen's plays stem most clearly from his own innermost heart when he has sometimes to drive out minor, gesticulatory, symbolic figures who come irrelevantly. In the first draft of *A Doll's House,* Dr. Rank talks of a patient, a miner who blew his own right hand off when in drink. Rank may have his special reasons to be hard on this sort of case. (He thinks social care for social failures is turning Norway into a clinic!) The self-mutilated, the murderer in *Brand,* the conscript in *Peer Gynt,* are almost as innocent as the victims in *The Wild Duck* and old Foldal in *John Gabriel Borkman.* Brendel challenges Rebekka to chop off her finger or her ear, Hedda's demands on Løvborg have a squalid sequel. Consul Bernick puts the case of the engineer's need to send a workman to almost certain death. Ibsen killed part of himself. Here, more subtly, Torvald's cruelty is closely linked with squeamishness. The ruthless visionary, the expansive self-intoxicated orator, the down-and-out with visions of grandeur, the doomed child, the woman of narrow aims and iron will, the doctor who judges, are all part of Ibsen's inner society. (Yeats termed his own "the circus animals.") Some ghosts found local homes in people Ibsen met, others represent only facets of himself; none is simply repeated. The black comedy or satire from *Pillars of the Community* is concentrated in aspects of Torvald.

. . . In the title of *A Doll's House* both his separation from and his ingestion of the theatre where he had learnt his trade is faintly adumbrated; for to look into the peep-show of the nineteenth century's picture-stage is indeed to look into a doll's house (with furniture painted on the backcloth). Not as the result of planning, but of steady, patient work on experience that has been "lived through"—as he phrased it—the final form emerged; imperative, autonomous, a mimesis that generates new forms of mimesis, with their own life, within the audience and through the years.

Creative opportunities for this third mimesis by the audience are still open. (For example, in this age when racial inequalities have largely replaced sexual inequalities as ground for public concern, the effect of having a white Torvald and a black Nora might be worth some director's experiment.)

The integration of conscious and unconscious functions in the verbal and non-verbal languages of the play generates valid new performance in the live theatre. In a book much studied by Ibsen, it is said of wisdom that "remaining in herself, she maketh all things new."

M. C. Bradbrook, "'A Doll's House': The Unweaving of the Web," in her *Women and Literature, 1779-1982: The Collected Papers of Muriel Bradbrook, Vol. 2*, The Harvester Press, Sussex, 1982. pp. 81-92.

Tennessee Williams, 1911–1983

The Glass Menagerie (1945)

Nobody, not even the rain, has such small hands.   E. E. CUMMINGS

CHARACTERS

AMANDA WINGFIELD, *the mother. A little woman of great but confused vitality clinging frantically to another time and place. Her characterization must be carefully created, not copied from type. She is not paranoiac, but her life is paranoia. There is much to admire in Amanda, and as much to love and pity as there is to laugh at. Certainly she has endurance and a kind of heroism, and though her foolishness makes her unwittingly cruel at times, there is tenderness in her slight person.*

LAURA WINGFIELD, *her daughter. Amanda, having failed to establish contact with reality, continues to live vitally in her illusions, but Laura's situation is even graver. A childhood illness has left her crippled, one leg slightly shorter than the other, and held in a brace. This defect need not be more than suggested on the stage. Stemming from this, Laura's separation increases till she is like a piece of her own glass collection, too exquisitely fragile to move from the shelf.*

TOM WINGFIELD, *her son. And the narrator of the play. A poet with a job in a warehouse. His nature is not remorseless, but to escape from a trap he has to act without pity.*

JIM O'CONNOR, *the gentleman caller. A nice, ordinary, young man.*

SCENE.
An alley in St. Louis.

PART I.
Preparation for a Gentleman Caller.

PART II.
The Gentleman Calls.

TIME.
Now and the Past.

SCENE I

The Wingfield apartment is in the rear of the building, one of those vast hive-like conglomerations of cellular living-units that flower as warty growths in overcrowded urban centers of lower middle-class population and are symptomatic of the impulse of this largest and fundamentally enslaved section of American society to avoid fluidity and differentiation and to exist and function as one interfused mass of automatism.

The apartment faces an alley and is entered by a fire-escape, a structure whose name is a touch of accidental poetic truth, for all of these huge buildings are always burning with the slow and implacable fires of human desperation. The fire-escape is included in the set—that is, the landing of it and steps descending from it.

The scene is memory and is therefore nonrealistic. Memory takes a lot of poetic license. It omits some details; others are exaggerated, according to the emotional value of the articles it touches, for memory is seated predominantly in the heart. The interior is therefore rather dim and poetic.

At the rise of the curtain, the audience is faced with the dark, grim rear wall of the Wingfield tenement. This building, which runs parallel to the footlights, is flanked on both sides by dark, narrow alleys which run into murky canyons of tangled clotheslines, garbage cans and the sinister lattice-work of neighboring fire-escapes. It is up and down these side alleys that exterior entrances and exits are made, during the play. At the end of Tom's opening commentary, the dark tenement wall slowly reveals (by means of a transparency) the interior of the ground floor Wingfield apartment.

Downstage is the living room, which also serves as a sleeping room for Laura, the sofa unfolding to make her bed. Upstage, center, and divided by a wide arch or second proscenium with transparent faded portieres (or second curtain), is the dining room. In an old-fashioned what-not in the living room are seen scores of transparent glass animals. A blown-up photograph of the father hangs on the wall of the living room, facing the audience, to the left of the archway. It is the face of a very handsome young man in a doughboy's First World War cap. He is gallantly smiling, ineluctably smiling, as if to say, "I will be smiling forever."

The audience hears and sees the opening scene in the dining room through both the transparent fourth wall of the building and the transparent gauze portieres of the dining-room arch. It is during this revealing scene that the fourth wall slowly ascends, out of sight. This transparent exterior wall is not brought down again until the very end of the play, during Tom's final speech.

The narrator is an undisguised convention of the play. He takes whatever license with dramatic convention as is convenient to his purposes.

Tom enters dressed as a merchant sailor from the alley, stage left, and strolls across the front of the stage to the fire-escape. There he stops and lights a cigarette. He addresses the audience.

Tom: Yes, I have tricks in my pocket, I have things up my sleeve. But I am the opposite of a stage magician. He gives you illusion that has the appearance of truth. I give you truth in the pleasant disguise of illusion. To begin with, I turn back time. I reverse it to that quaint period, the thirties, when the huge middle class of America was matriculating in a school for the blind. Their eyes had failed them, or they had failed their eyes, and so they were having their fingers pressed forcibly down on the fiery Braille alphabet of a dissolving economy. In Spain there was revolution.[1] Here there was only shouting and confusion. In Spain there was Guernica.[2] Here there were disturbances of labor, sometimes pretty violent, in otherwise peaceful cities such as Chicago, Cleveland, Saint Louis. . . . This is the social background of the play.

(Music.)

The play is memory. Being a memory play, it is dimly lighted, it is sentimental, it is not realistic. In memory everything seems to happen to music. That explains the fiddle in the wings. I am the narrator of the play, and also a character in it. The other characters are my mother, Amanda, my sister, Laura, and a gentleman caller who appears in the final scenes. He is the most realistic character in the play, being an emissary from a world of reality that we were somehow set apart from. But since I have a poet's weakness for symbols, I am using this character also as a symbol; he is the long delayed but always expected something that we live for. There is a fifth character in the play who doesn't appear except in this larger-than-life photograph over the mantel. This is our father who left us a long time ago. He was a telephone man who fell in love with long distances; he gave up his job with the telephone company and skipped the light fantastic out of town . . . The last we heard of him was a picture post-card from Mazatlan, on the Pacific coast of Mexico, containing a message of two words—"Hello—Good-bye!" and an address. I think the rest of the play will explain itself. . . .

Amanda's voice becomes audible through the portieres.

(Legend On Screen: "Où Sont Les Neiges.")[3]

He divides the portieres and enters the upstage area.
  Amanda and Laura are seated at a drop-leaf table. Eating is indicated by gestures without food or utensils. Amanda faces the audience. Tom and Laura are seated in profile.

---

[1] The Spanish Civil War (1936–1939).
[2] A Basque town in northern Spain, bombed and virtually destroyed on April 27, 1937, by German planes aiding fascist General Francisco Franco's Nationalists. The destruction is depicted in one of Pablo Picasso's most famous paintings, *Guernica* (1937).
[3] "Where are the snows [of yesteryear]." A famous line by French poet François Villon (1431–1463?).

The interior has lit up softly and through the scrim we see Amanda and Laura seated at the table in the upstage area.

AMANDA: *(calling)* Tom?

TOM: Yes, Mother.

AMANDA: We can't say grace until you come to the table!

5 **TOM:** Coming, Mother. *(He bows slightly and withdraws, reappearing a few moments later in his place at the table.)*

AMANDA: *(to her son)* Honey, don't *push* with your *fingers.* If you have to push with something, the thing to push with is a crust of bread. And chew—chew! Animals have sections in their stomachs which enable them to digest food without mastication, but human beings are supposed to chew their food before they swallow it down. Eat food leisurely, son, and really enjoy it. A well-cooked meal has lots of delicate flavors that have to be held in the mouth for appreciation. So chew your food and give your salivary glands a chance to function!

Tom deliberately lays his imaginary fork down and pushes his chair back from the table.

TOM: I haven't enjoyed one bite of this dinner because of your constant directions on how to eat it. It's you that makes me rush through meals with your hawk-like attention to every bite I take. Sickening—spoils my appetite—all this discussion of animals' secretion—salivary glands—mastication!

AMANDA: *(lightly)* Temperament like a Metropolitan star! *(He rises and crosses downstage.)* You're not excused from the table.

TOM: I am getting a cigarette.

10 **AMANDA:** You smoke too much.

Laura rises.

LAURA: I'll bring in the blanc mange.

He remains standing with his cigarette by the portieres during the following.

AMANDA: *(rising)* No, sister, no, sister—you be the lady this time and I'll be the darky.

LAURA: I'm already up.

AMANDA: Resume your seat, little sister—I want you to stay fresh and pretty—for gentlemen callers!

15 **LAURA:** I'm not expecting any gentlemen callers.

AMANDA: *(crossing out to kitchenette. Airily)* Sometimes they come when they are least expected! Why, I remember one Sunday afternoon in Blue Mountain—*(Enters kitchenette.)*

TOM: I know what's coming!

LAURA: Yes. But let her tell it.

TOM: Again?

20 **LAURA:** She loves to tell it.

Amanda returns with bowl of dessert.

AMANDA: One Sunday afternoon in Blue Mountain—your mother received—*seventeen!*—gentlemen callers! Why, sometimes there weren't
chairs enough to accommodate them all. We had to send the nigger over
to bring in folding chairs from the parish house.

TOM: *(remaining at portieres)* How did you entertain those gentlemen
callers?

AMANDA: I understood the art of conversation!

TOM: I bet you could talk.

25 **AMANDA:** Girls in those days *knew* how to talk, I can tell you.

TOM: Yes?

(Image: Amanda As A Girl On A Porch Greeting Callers.)

AMANDA: They knew how to entertain their gentlemen callers. It wasn't
enough for a girl to be possessed of a pretty face and a graceful figure—
although I wasn't slighted in either respect. She also needed to have a
nimble wit and a tongue to meet all occasions.

TOM: What did you talk about?

AMANDA: Things of importance going on in the world! Never anything
coarse or common or vulgar. *(She addresses Tom as though he were
seated in the vacant chair at the table though he remains by portieres.
He plays this scene as though he held the book.)* My callers were gentlemen—all! Among my callers were some of the most prominent young
planters of the Mississippi Delta—planters and sons of planters!

*Tom motions for music and a spot of light on Amanda. Her eyes lift, her
face glows, her voice becomes rich and elegiac.*

(Screen Legend: "Où Sont Les Neiges.")

There was young Champ Laughlin who later became vice-president of the
Delta Planters Bank. Hadley Stevenson who was drowned in Moon Lake
and left his widow one hundred and fifty thousand in Government bonds.
There were the Cutrere brothers, Wesley and Bates. Bates was one of my
bright particular beaux! He got in a quarrel with that wild Wainright boy.
They shot it out on the floor of Moon Lake Casino. Bates was shot through
the stomach. Died in the ambulance on his way to Memphis. His widow
was also well-provided for, came into eight or ten thousand acres, that's
all. She married him on the rebound—never loved her—carried my picture on him the night he died! And there was that boy that every girl in
the Delta had set her cap for! That beautiful, brilliant young Fitzhugh boy
from Green County!

30 **TOM:** What did he leave his widow?

AMANDA: He never married! Gracious, you talk as though all of my old admirers had turned up their toes to the daisies!

Tom: Isn't this the first you mentioned that still survives?

Amanda: That Fitzhugh boy went North and made a fortune—came to be known as the Wolf of Wall Street! He had the Midas touch, whatever he touched turned to gold! And I could have been Mrs. Duncan J. Fitzhugh, mind you! But—I picked your *father!*

Laura: *(rising)* Mother, let me clear the table.

35 **Amanda:**   No dear, you go in front and study your typewriter chart. Or practice your shorthand a little. Stay fresh and pretty!—It's almost time for our gentlemen callers to start arriving. *(She flounces girlishly toward the kitchenette.)* How many do you suppose we're going to entertain this afternoon?

Tom throws down the paper and jumps up with a groan.

Laura: *(alone in the dining room)* I don't believe we're going to receive any, Mother.

Amanda: *(reappearing, airily)* What? No one—not one? You must be joking! *(Laura nervously echoes her laugh. She slips in a fugitive manner through the half-open portieres and draws them gently behind her. A shaft of very clear light is thrown on her face against the faded tapestry of the curtains.) (Music: "The Glass Menagerie" Under Faintly.) (Lightly.)* Not one gentleman caller? It can't be true! There must be a flood, there must have been a tornado!

Laura: It isn't a flood, it's not a tornado, Mother. I'm just not popular like you were in Blue Mountain. . . . *(Tom utters another groan. Laura glances at him with a faint, apologetic smile. Her voice catching a little.)* Mother's afraid I'm going to be an old maid.

(The Scene Dims Out With "Glass Menagerie" Music.)

Scene II

"Laura, Haven't You Ever Liked Some Boy?"
   On the dark stage the screen is lighted with the image of blue roses.
   Gradually Laura's figure becomes apparent and the screen goes out.
   The music subsides.
   Laura is seated in the delicate ivory chair at the small clawfoot table.
   She wears a dress of soft violet material for a kimono—her hair tied back from her forehead with a ribbon.
   She is washing and polishing her collection of glass.
   Amanda appears on the fire-escape steps. At the sound of her ascent, Laura catches her breath, thrusts the bowl of ornaments away and seats herself stiffly before the diagram of the typewriter keyboard as though it held her spellbound. Something has happened to Amanda. It is written in her face as she climbs to the landing: a look that is grim and hopeless and a little absurd.

She has on one of those cheap or imitation velvety-looking cloth coats with imitation fur collar. Her hat is five or six years old, one of those dreadful cloche hats that were worn in the late twenties, and she is clasping an enormous black patent-leather pocketbook with nickel clasp and initials. This is her fulldress outfit, the one she usually wears to the D.A.R.[4]

Before entering she looks through the door.

She purses her lips, opens her eyes wide, rolls them upward and shakes her head.

Then she slowly lets herself in the door. Seeing her mother's expression Laura touches her lips with a nervous gesture.

LAURA: Hello, Mother, I was—*(She makes a nervous gesture toward the chart on the wall. Amanda leans against the shut door and stares at Laura with a martyred look.)*

AMANDA: Deception? Deception? *(She slowly removes her hat and gloves, continuing the swift suffering stare. She lets the hat and gloves fall on the floor—a bit of acting.)*

LAURA: *(shakily)* How was the D.A.R. meeting? *(Amanda slowly opens her purse and removes a dainty white handkerchief which she shakes out delicately and delicately touches to her lips and nostrils.)* Didn't you go to the D.A.R. meeting, Mother?

AMANDA: *(faintly, almost inaudibly)*—No.—No. *(Then more forcibly.)* I did not have the strength—to go to the D.A.R. In fact, I did not have the courage! I wanted to find a hole in the ground and hide myself in it forever! *(She crosses slowly to the wall and removes the diagram of the typewriter keyboard. She holds it in front of her for a second, staring at it sweetly and sorrowfully—then bites her lips and tears it in two pieces.)*

5 **LAURA:**   *(faintly)* Why did you do that, Mother? *(Amanda repeats the same procedure with the chart of the Gregg Alphabet.)* Why are you—

AMANDA: Why? Why? How old are you, Laura?

LAURA: Mother, you know my age.

AMANDA: I thought that you were an adult; it seems that I was mistaken. *(She crosses slowly to the sofa and sinks down and stares at Laura.)*

LAURA: Please don't stare at me, Mother.

Amanda closes her eyes and lowers her head. Count ten.

10 **AMANDA:**   What are we going to do, what is going to become of us, what is the future?

Count ten.

---

[4] The Daughters of the American Revolution, an organization for female descendants of participants in the American Revolution, founded in 1890. That Amanda is a member says much about her concern with the past, as well as about her pride and affectations.

LAURA: Has something happened, Mother? *(Amanda draws a long breath and takes out the handkerchief again. Dabbing process.)* Mother, has—something happened?

AMANDA: I'll be all right in a minute. I'm just bewildered—*(count five)*—by life. . . .

LAURA: Mother, I wish that you would tell me what's happened.

AMANDA: As you know, I was supposed to be inducted into my office at the D.A.R. this afternoon. *(Image: A Swarm of Typewriters.)* But I stopped off at Rubicam's Business College to speak to your teachers about your having a cold and ask them what progress they thought you were making down there.

15 **LAURA:** Oh. . . .

AMANDA: I went to the typing instructor and introduced myself as your mother. She didn't know who you were. Wingfield, she said. We don't have any such student enrolled at the school! I assured her she did, that you had been going to classes since early in January. "I wonder," she said, "if you could be talking about that terribly shy little girl who dropped out of school after only a few days' attendance?" "No," I said, "Laura, my daughter, has been going to school every day for the past six weeks!" "Excuse me," she said. She took the attendance book out and there was your name, unmistakably printed, and all the dates you were absent until they decided that you had dropped out of school. I still said, "No, there must have been some mistake! There must have been some mix-up in the records!" And she said, "No—I remember her perfectly now. Her hand shook so that she couldn't hit the right keys! The first time we gave a speed-test, she broke down completely—was sick at the stomach and almost had to be carried into the wash-room! After that morning she never showed up any more. We phoned the house but never got any answer"—while I was working at Famous and Barr, I suppose, demonstrating those—Oh! I felt so weak I could barely keep on my feet. I had to sit down while they got me a glass of water! Fifty dollars' tuition, all of our plans—my hopes and ambitions for you—just gone up the spout, just gone up the spout like that. *(Laura draws a long breath and gets awkwardly to her feet. She crosses to the victrola and winds it up.)* What are you doing?

LAURA: Oh! *(She releases the handle and returns to her seat.)*

AMANDA: Laura, where have you been going when you've gone out pretending that you were going to business college?

LAURA: I've just been going out walking.

20 **AMANDA:** That's not true.

LAURA: It is. I just went walking.

AMANDA: Walking? Walking? In winter? Deliberately courting pneumonia in that light coat? Where did you walk to, Laura?

LAURA: It was the lesser of two evils, Mother. *(Image: Winter Scene In Park.)* I couldn't go back up. I—threw up—on the floor!

AMANDA: From half past seven till after five every day you mean to tell me you walked around in the park, because you wanted to make me think that you were still going to Rubicam's Business College?

25 **LAURA:**   It wasn't as bad as it sounds. I went inside places to get warmed up.

AMANDA: Inside where?

LAURA: I went in the art museum and the bird-houses at the Zoo. I visited the penguins every day! Sometimes I did without lunch and went to the movies. Lately I've been spending most of my afternoons in the Jewel-box, that big glass house where they raise the tropical flowers.

AMANDA: You did all this to deceive me, just for the deception? *(Laura looks down.)* Why?

LAURA: Mother, when you're disappointed, you get that awful suffering look on your face, like the picture of Jesus' mother in the museum!

30 **AMANDA:**   Hush!

LAURA: I couldn't face it.

Pause. A whisper of strings.

(Legend: "The Crust of Humility.")

AMANDA: *(hopelessly fingering the huge pocketbook)* So what are we going to do the rest of our lives? Stay home and watch the parades go by? Amuse ourselves with the glass menagerie, darling? Eternally play those worn-out phonograph records your father left as a painful reminder of him? We won't have a business career—we've given that up because it gave us nervous indigestion! *(Laughs wearily.)* What is there left but dependency all our lives? I know so well what becomes of unmarried women who aren't prepared to occupy a position. I've seen such pitiful cases in the South—barely tolerated spinsters living upon the grudging patronage of sister's husband or brother's wife!—stuck away in some little mouse-trap of a room—encouraged by one in-law to visit another—little birdlike women without any nest—eating the crust of humility all their life! Is that the future that we've mapped out for ourselves? I swear it's the only alternative I can think of! It isn't a very pleasant alternative, is it? Of course—some girls *do marry. (Laura twists her hands nervously.)* Haven't you ever liked some boy?

LAURA: Yes I liked one once. *(Rises.)* I came across his picture a while ago.

AMANDA: *(with some interest)* He gave you his picture?

35 **LAURA:**   No, it's in the year-book.

AMANDA: *(disappointed)* Oh—a high-school boy.

(Screen Image: Jim As A High-School Hero Bearing A Silver Cup.)

LAURA: Yes. His name was Jim. *(Laura lifts the heavy annual from the clawfoot table.)* Here he is in *The Pirates of Penzance.*[5]

---

[5] An operetta by Gilbert and Sullivan.

AMANDA: *(absently)* The what?

LAURA: The operetta the senior class put on. He had a wonderful voice and we sat across the aisle from each other Mondays, Wednesdays and Fridays in the Aud. Here he is with the silver cup for debating! See his grin?

40 AMANDA: *(absently)* He must have had a jolly disposition.

LAURA: He used to call me—Blue Roses.

(Image: Blue Roses.)

AMANDA: Why did he call you such a name as that?

LAURA: When I had that attack of pleurosis—he asked me what was the matter when I came back. I said pleurosis—he thought that I said Blue Roses! So that's what he always called me after that. Whenever he saw me, he'd holler, "Hello, Blue Roses!" I didn't care for the girl that he went out with. Emily Meisenbach. Emily was the best-dressed girl at Soldan. She never struck me, though, as being sincere . . . It says in the Personal Section— they're engaged. That's—six years ago! They must be married by now.

AMANDA: Girls that aren't cut out for business careers usually wind up married to some nice man. *(Gets up with a spark of revival.)* Sister, that's what you'll do!

Laura utters a startled, doubtful laugh. She reaches quickly for a piece of glass.

45 LAURA: But, Mother—

AMANDA: Yes? *(Crossing to photograph.)*

LAURA: *(in a tone of frightened apology)* I'm—crippled!

(Image: Screen.)

AMANDA: Nonsense! Laura, I've told you never, never to use that word. Why, you're not crippled, you just have a little defect—hardly noticeable, even! When people have some slight disadvantage like that, they cultivate other things to make up for it—develop charm—and vivacity—and— *charm!* That's all you have to do! *(She turns again to the photograph.)* One thing your father had *plenty of*—was *charm!*

Tom motions to the fiddle in the wings.

(The Scene Fades Out With Music.)

SCENE III

(Legend On The Screen: "After The Fiasco—")

Tom speaks from the fire-escape landing.

TOM: After the fiasco at Rubicam's Business College, the idea of getting a gentleman caller for Laura began to play a more important part in Mother's calculations. It became an obsession. Like some archetype of the universal unconscious, the image of the gentleman caller haunted our small apartment. . . . *(Image: Young Man At Door With Flowers.)* An evening at home rarely passed without some allusion to this image, this spectre, this hope. . . . Even when he wasn't mentioned, his presence hung in Mother's preoccupied look and in my sister's frightened, apologetic manner—hung like a sentence passed upon the Wingfields! Mother was a woman of action as well as words. She began to take logical steps in the planned direction. Late that winter and in the early spring—realizing that extra money would be needed to properly feather the nest and plume the bird—she conducted a vigorous campaign on the telephone, roping in subscribers to one of those magazines for matrons called *The Homemaker's Companion,* the type of journal that features the serialized sublimations of ladies of letters who think in terms of delicate cup-like breasts, slim, tapering waists, rich, creamy thighs, eyes like wood-smoke in autumn, fingers that soothe and caress like strains of music, bodies as powerful as Etruscan sculpture.

(Screen Image: a glamour magazine cover.)

Amanda enters with phone on long extension cord. She is spotted in the dim stage.

AMANDA: Ida Scott? This is Amanda Wingfield! We *missed* you at the D.A.R. last Monday! I said to myself: She's probably suffering with that sinus condition! How is that sinus condition? Horrors! Heaven have mercy!—You're a Christian martyr, yes, that's what you are, a Christian martyr! Well, I just now happened to notice that your subscription to the *Companion's* about to expire! Yes, it expires with the next issue, honey!—just when that wonderful new serial by Bessie Mae Hopper is getting off to such an exciting start. Oh, honey, it's something that you can't miss! You remember how *Gone With the Wind* took everybody by storm? You simply couldn't go out if you hadn't read it. All everybody *talked* about was Scarlett O'Hara. Well, this is a book that critics already compare to *Gone With the Wind.* It's the *Gone With the Wind* of the post-World War generation!—What?—Burning?—Oh, honey, don't let them burn, go take a look in the oven and I'll hold the wire! Heavens—I think she's hung up!

(Dim Out.)

(Legend On Screen: "You Think I'm In Love With Continental Shoemakers?")

Before the stage is lighted, the violent voices of Tom and Amanda are heard. They are quarreling behind the portieres. In front of them stands Laura with clenched hands and panicky expression.
   A clear pool of light on her figure throughout this scene.

TOM: What in Christ's name am I—
AMANDA: *(shrilly)* Don't you use that—
5 **TOM:**   Supposed to do!

AMANDA: Expression! Not in my—

TOM: Ohhh!

AMANDA: Presence! Have you gone out of your senses?

TOM: I have, that's true, *driven* out!

10 AMANDA: What is the matter with you, you—big—big—IDIOT!

TOM: Look—I've got *no thing,* no single thing—

AMANDA: Lower your voice!

TOM: In my life here that I can call my OWN! Everything is—

AMANDA: Stop that shouting!

15 TOM: Yesterday you confiscated my books! You had the nerve to—

AMANDA: I took that horrible novel back to the library—yes! That hideous book by that insane Mr. Lawrence. *(Tom laughs wildly.)* I cannot control the output of diseased minds or people who cater to them—*(Tom laughs still more wildly.)* BUT I WON'T ALLOW SUCH FILTH BROUGHT INTO MY HOUSE! No, no, no, no, no!

TOM: House, house! Who pays rent on it, who makes a slave of himself to—

AMANDA: *(fairly screeching)* Don't you DARE to—

TOM: No, no, *I* mustn't say things! *I've* got to just—

20 AMANDA: Let me tell you—

TOM: I don't want to hear any more! *(He tears the portieres open. The up-stage area is lit with a turgid smoky red glow.)*

Amanda's hair is in metal curlers and she wears a very old bathrobe, much too large for her slight figure, a relic of the faithless Mr. Wingfield.

An upright typewriter and a wild disarray of manuscripts are on the dropleaf table. The quarrel was probably precipitated by Amanda's interruption of his creative labor. A chair lying overthrown on the floor.

Their gesticulating shadows are cast on the ceiling by the fiery glow.

AMANDA: You *will* hear more, you—

TOM: No, I won't hear more, I'm going out!

AMANDA: You come right back in—

25 TOM: Out, out out! Because I'm—

AMANDA: Come back here, Tom Wingfield! I'm not through talking to you!

TOM: Oh, go—

LAURA: *(desperately)* Tom!

AMANDA: You're going to listen, and no more insolence from you! I'm at the end of my patience! *(He comes back toward her.)*

30 TOM: What do you think I'm at? Aren't I supposed to have any patience to reach the end of, Mother? I know, I know. It seems unimportant to you, what I'm *doing*—what I *want* to do—having a little *difference* between them! You don't think that—

AMANDA: I think you've been doing things that you're ashamed of. That's why you act like this. I don't believe that you go every night to the movies. Nobody goes to the movies night after night. Nobody in their right mind goes to the movies as often as you pretend to. People don't go to the movies at nearly midnight, and movies don't let out at two A.M. Come in stumbling. Muttering to yourself like a maniac! You get three hours' sleep and then go to work. Oh, I can picture the way you're doing down there. Moping, doping, because you're in no condition.

TOM: *(wildly)* No, I'm in no condition!

AMANDA: What right have you got to jeopardize your job? Jeopardize the security of us all? How do you think we'd manage if you were—

TOM: Listen! You think I'm crazy *about* the *warehouse? (He bends fiercely toward her slight figure.)* You think I'm in love with the Continental Shoemakers? You think I want to spend fifty-five *years* down there in that—*celotex interior!* with—*fluorescent—tubes!* Look! I'd rather somebody picked up a crowbar and battered out my brains—than go back mornings! I *go!* Every time you come in yelling that God damn *"Rise and Shine!" "Rise and Shine!"* I say to myself *"How lucky dead* people are!" But I get up. I *go!* For sixty-five dollars a month I give up all that I dream of doing and being *ever!* And you say self—*self's* all I ever think of. Why, listen, if self is what I thought of, Mother, I'd be where he is—GONE! *(Pointing to father's picture.)* As far as the system of transportation reaches! *(He starts past her. She grabs his arm.)* Don't grab at me, Mother!

35 **AMANDA:** Where are you going?

TOM: I'm going to the *movies!*

AMANDA: I don't believe that lie!

TOM: *(crouching toward her, overtowering her tiny figure. She backs away, gasping)* I'm going to opium dens! Yes, opium dens, dens of vice and criminals' hang-outs, Mother. I've joined the Hogan gang, I'm a hired assassin, I carry a tommy-gun in a violin case! I run a string of cat-houses in the Valley! They call me Killer, Killer Wingfield, I'm leading a double-life, a simple, honest warehouse worker by day, by night a dynamic *czar* of the *underworld, Mother.* I go to gambling casinos, I spin away fortunes on the roulette table! I wear a patch over one eye and a false mustache, sometimes I put on green whiskers. On those occasions they call me—*El Diablo!* Oh, I could tell you things to make you sleepless! My enemies plan to dynamite this place. They're going to blow us all sky-high some night! I'll be glad, very happy, and so will you! You'll go up, up on a broomstick, over Blue Mountain with seventeen gentlemen callers! You ugly—babbling old—*witch.* . . . *(He goes through a series of violent, clumsy movements, seizing his overcoat, lunging to the door, pulling it fiercely open. The women watch him, aghast. His arm catches in the sleeve of the coat as he struggles to pull it on. For a moment he is pinioned by the bulky garment. With an outraged groan he tears the coat off again, splitting the shoulders of it, and hurls it across the room. It strikes against the shelf of Laura's glass collection, there is a tinkle of shattering glass. Laura cries out as if wounded.)*

(Music Legend: "The Glass Menagerie.")

LAURA: *My glass!*—menagerie. . . . *(She covers her face and turns away.)*

But Amanda is still stunned and stupefied by the "ugly witch" so that she barely notices this occurrence. Now she recovers her speech.

40 AMANDA: *(in an awful voice)* I won't speak to you—until you apologize! *(She crosses through portieres and draws them together behind her. Tom is left with Laura. Laura clings weakly to the mantel with her face averted. Tom stares at her stupidly for a moment. Then he crosses to shelf. Drops awkwardly to his knees to collect the fallen glass, glancing at Laura as if he would speak but couldn't.)*

"The Glass Menagerie" steals in as

(The Scene Dims Out.)

SCENE IV

The interior is dark. Faint in the alley.

A deep-voiced bell in a church is tolling the hour of five as the scene commences.

Tom appears at the top of the alley. After each solemn boom of the bell in the tower, he shakes a little noise-maker or rattle as if to express the tiny spasm of man in contrast to the sustained power and dignity of the Almighty. This and the unsteadiness of his advance make it evident that he has been drinking.

As he climbs the few steps to the fire-escape landing light steals up inside. Laura appears in night-dress, observing Tom's empty bed in the front room.

Tom fishes in his pockets for the door-key, removing a motley assortment of articles in the search, including a perfect shower of movie-ticket stubs and an empty bottle. At last he finds the key, but just as he is about to insert it, it slips from his fingers. He strikes a match and crouches below the door.

TOM: *(bitterly)* One crack—and it falls through!

Laura opens the door.

LAURA: Tom! Tom, what are you doing?
TOM: Looking for a door-key.
LAURA: Where have you been all this time?
5 TOM: I have been to the movies.
LAURA: All this time at the movies?
TOM: There was a very long program. There was a Garbo picture and a Mickey Mouse and a travelogue and a newsreel and a preview of coming attractions. And there was an organ solo and a collection for the milk-fund—

simultaneously—which ended up in a terrible fight between a fat lady and an usher!

LAURA: *(innocently)* Did you have to stay through everything?

TOM: Of course! And, oh, I forgot! There was a big stage show! The head-liner on this stage show was Malvolio the Magician. He performed won-derful tricks, many of them, such as pouring water back and forth between pitchers. First it turned to wine and then it turned to beer and then it turned to whiskey. I know it was whiskey it finally turned into be-cause he needed somebody to come up out of the audience to help him, and I came up—both shows! It was Kentucky Straight Bourbon. A very generous fellow, he gave souvenirs. *(He pulls from his back pocket a shimmering rainbow-colored scarf.)* He gave me this. This is his magic scarf. You can have it, Laura. You wave it over a canary cage and you get a bowl of gold-fish. You wave it over the gold-fish bowl and they fly away canaries. . . . But the wonderfullest trick of all was the coffin trick. We nailed him into a coffin and he got out of the coffin without removing one nail. *(He has come inside.)* There is a trick that would come in handy for me—get me out of this 2 by 4 situation! *(Flops onto bed and starts re-moving shoes.)*

10 **LAURA:** Tom—Shhh!

TOM: What you shushing me for?

LAURA: You'll wake up Mother.

TOM: Goody, goody! Pay 'er back for all those "Rise an' Shines." *(Lies down, groaning.)* You know it don't take much intelligence to get your-self into a nailed-up coffin, Laura. But who in hell ever got himself out of one without removing one nail?

As if in answer, the father's grinning photograph lights up.

(Scene Dims Out.)

Immediately following: The church bell is heard striking six. At the sixth stroke the alarm clock goes off in Amanda's room, and after a few mo-ments we hear her calling: "Rise and Shine! Rise and Shine! Laura, go tell your brother to rise and shine!"

TOM: *(sitting up slowly)* I'll rise—but I won't shine.

The light increases.

15 **AMANDA:** Laura, tell your brother his coffee is ready.

Laura slips into front room.

LAURA: Tom! it's nearly seven. Don't make Mother nervous. *(He stares at her stupidly. Beseechingly.)* Tom, speak to Mother this morning. Make up with her, apologize, speak to her!

TOM: She won't to me. It's her that started not speaking.

LAURA: If you just say you're sorry she'll start speaking.

Tom: Her not speaking—is that such a tragedy?

20 **Laura:**   Please—please!

Amanda: *(calling from kitchenette)* Laura, are you going to do what I asked you to do, or do I have to get dressed and go out myself?

Laura: Going, going—soon as I get on my coat! *(She pulls on a shapeless felt hat with nervous, jerky movement, pleadingly glancing at Tom. Rushes awkwardly for coat. The coat is one of Amanda's inaccurately made-over, the sleeves too short for Laura.)* Butter and what else?

Amanda: *(entering upstage)* Just butter. Tell them to charge it.

Laura: Mother, they make such faces when I do that.

25 **Amanda:**   Sticks and stones may break my bones, but the expression on Mr. Garfinkel's face won't harm us! Tell your brother his coffee is getting cold.

Laura: *(at door)* Do what I asked you, will you, will you, Tom?

He looks sullenly away.

Amanda: Laura, go now or just don't go at all!

Laura: *(rushing out)* Going—going! *(A second later she cries out. Tom springs up and crosses to the door. Amanda rushes anxiously in. Tom opens the door.)*

Tom: Laura?

30 **Laura:**   I'm all right. I slipped, but I'm all right.

Amanda: *(peering anxiously after her)* If anyone breaks a leg on those fire-escape steps, the landlord ought to be sued for every cent he possesses! *(She shuts door. Remembers she isn't speaking and returns to other room.)*

As Tom enters listlessly for his coffee, she turns her back to him and stands rigidly facing the window on the gloomy gray vault of the areaway. Its light on her face with its aged but childish features is cruelly sharp, satirical as a Daumier print.

(Music Under: "Ave Maria.")

Tom glances sheepishly but sullenly at her averted figure and slumps at the table. The coffee is scalding hot; he sips it and gasps and spits it back in the cup. At his gasp, Amanda catches her breath and half turns. Then catches herself and turns back to window.

Tom blows on his coffee, glancing sidewise at his mother. She clears her throat. Tom clears his. He starts to rise. Sinks back down again, scratches his head, clears his throat again. Amanda coughs. Tom raises his cup in both hands to blow on it, his eyes staring over the rim of it at his mother for several moments. Then he slowly sets the cup down and awkwardly and hesitantly rises from the chair.

Tom: *(hoarsely)* Mother. I—I apologize. Mother. *(Amanda draws a quick, shuddering breath. Her face works grotesquely. She breaks into childlike tears.)* I'm sorry for what I said, for everything that I said, I didn't mean it.

AMANDA: *(sobbingly)* My devotion has made me a witch and so I make myself hateful to my children!

TOM: No, you *don't.*

35 AMANDA: I worry so much, don't sleep, it makes me nervous!

TOM: *(gently)* I understand that.

AMANDA: I've had to put up a solitary battle all these years. But you're my
right-hand bower! Don't fall down, don't fail!

TOM: *(gently)* I try, Mother.

AMANDA: *(with great enthusiasm)* Try and you will SUCCEED! *(The notion
makes her breathless.)* Why, you—you're just *full* of natural endow-
ments! Both of my children—they're *unusual* children! Don't you think I
know it? I'm so—*proud!* Happy and—feel I've—so much to be thankful
for but—Promise me one thing, son!

40 TOM: What, Mother?

AMANDA: Promise, son, you'll—never be a drunkard!

TOM: *(turns to her grinning)* I will never be a drunkard, Mother.

AMANDA: That's what frightened me so, that you'd be drinking! Eat a bowl
of Purina!

TOM: Just coffee, Mother.

45 AMANDA: Shredded wheat biscuit?

TOM: No. No, Mother, just coffee.

AMANDA: You can't put in a day's work on an empty stomach. You've got
ten minutes—don't gulp! Drinking too-hot liquids makes cancer of the
stomach. . . . Put cream in.

TOM: No, thank you.

AMANDA: To cool it.

50 TOM: No! No, thank you, I want it black.

AMANDA: I know, but it's not good for you. We have to do all that we can to
build ourselves up. In these trying times we live in, all that we have to
cling to is—each other. . . . That's why it's so important to—Tom, I—I
sent out your sister so I could discuss something with you. If you hadn't
spoken I would have spoken to you. *(Sits down.)*

TOM: *(gently)* What is it, Mother, that you want to discuss?

AMANDA: Laura!

Tom puts his cup down slowly.

(Legend On Screen: "Laura.")

(Music: "The Glass Menagerie.")

TOM: —Oh.—Laura . . .

55 AMANDA: *(touching his sleeve)* You know how Laura is. So quiet but—still
water runs deep! She notices things and I think she—broods about them.
(Tom looks up.) A few days ago I came in and she was crying.

TOM: What about?

AMANDA: You.

TOM: Me?

AMANDA: She has an idea that you're not happy here.

60 TOM: What gave her that idea?

AMANDA: What gives her any idea? However, you do act strangely. I—I'm not criticizing, understand *that!* I know your ambitions do not lie in the warehouse, that like everybody in the whole wide world—you've had to—make sacrifices, but—Tom—Tom—life's not easy, it calls for—Spartan endurance! There's so many things in my heart that I cannot describe to you! I've never told you but I—*loved* your father. . . .

TOM: *(gently)* I know that, Mother.

AMANDA: And you—when I see you taking after his ways! Staying out late—and—well, you *had* been drinking the night you were in that—terrifying condition! Laura says that you hate the apartment and that you go out nights to get away from it! Is that true, Tom?

TOM: No. You say there's so much in your heart that you can't describe to me. That's true of me, too. There's so much in my heart that I can't describe to *you!* So let's respect each other's—

65 AMANDA: But, why—*why*, Tom—are you always so *restless?* Where do you go to, nights?

TOM: I—go to the movies.

AMANDA: Why do you go to the movies so much, Tom?

TOM: I go to the movies because—I like adventure. Adventure is something I don't have much of at work, so I go to the movies.

AMANDA: But, Tom, you go to the movies *entirely* too *much!*

70 TOM: I like a lot of adventure.

Amanda looks baffled, then hurt. As the familiar inquisition resumes he becomes hard and impatient again. Amanda slips back into her querulous attitude toward him.

(Image On Screen: Sailing Vessel With Jolly Roger.)

AMANDA: Most young men find adventure in their careers.

TOM: Then most young men are not employed in a warehouse.

AMANDA: The world is full of young men employed in warehouses and offices and factories.

TOM: Do all of them find adventure in their careers?

75 AMANDA: They do or they do without it! Not everybody has a craze for adventure.

TOM: Man is by instinct a lover, a hunter, a fighter, and none of those instincts are given much play at the warehouse!

AMANDA: Man is by instinct! Don't quote instinct to me! Instinct is something that people have got away from! It belongs to animals! Christian adults don't want it!

TOM: What do Christian adults want, then, Mother?

AMANDA: Superior things! Things of the mind and the spirit! Only animals have to satisfy instincts! Surely your aims are somewhat higher than theirs! Than monkeys—pigs—

80 **Tom:**   I reckon they're not.

    Amanda: You're joking. However, that isn't what I wanted to discuss.

    Tom: *(rising)* I haven't much time.

    Amanda: *(pushing his shoulders)* Sit down.

    Tom: You want me to punch in red at the warehouse, Mother?

85 **Amanda:**   You have five minutes. I want to talk about Laura.

(Legend: "Plans And Provisions.")

    Tom: All right! What about Laura?

    Amanda: We have to be making plans and provisions for her. She's older than you, two years, and nothing has happened. She just drifts along doing nothing. It frightens me terribly how she just drifts along.

    Tom: I guess she's the type that people call home girls.

    Amanda: There's no such type, and if there is, it's a pity! That is unless the home is hers, with a husband!

90 **Tom:**   What?

    Amanda: Oh, I can see the handwriting on the wall as plain as I see the nose in front of my face! It's terrifying! More and more you remind me of your father! He was out all hours without explanation—Then *left! Goodbye!* And me with the bag to hold. I saw that letter you got from the Merchant Marine. I know what you're dreaming of. I'm not standing here blindfolded. Very well, then. Then *do* it! But not till there's somebody to take your place.

    Tom: What do you mean?

    Amanda: I mean that as soon as Laura has got somebody to take care of her, married, a home of her own, independent—why, then you'll be free to go wherever you please, on land, on sea, whichever way the wind blows! But until that time you've got to look out for your sister. I don't say me because I'm old and don't matter! I say for your sister because she's young and dependent. I put her in business college—a dismal failure! Frightened her so it made her sick to her stomach. I took her over to the Young People's League at the church. Another fiasco. She spoke to nobody, nobody spoke to her. Now all she does is fool with those pieces of glass and play those worn-out records. What kind of a life is that for a girl to lead!

    Tom: What can I do about it?

95 **Amanda:**   Overcome selfishness! Self, self, self is all that you ever think of! *(Tom springs up and crosses to get his coat. It is ugly and bulky. He pulls on a cap with earmuffs.)* Where is your muffler? Put your wool muffler on! *(He snatches it angrily from the closet and tosses it around his neck and pulls both ends tight.)* Tom! I haven't said what I had in mind to ask you.

    Tom: I'm too late to—

    Amanda: *(catching his arms—very importunately. Then shyly)* Down at the warehouse, aren't there some—nice young men?

    Tom: No!

AMANDA: There *must* be—*some* . . .
100 **TOM:** Mother—

Gesture.

AMANDA: Find out one that's clean-living—doesn't drink and—ask him out
for sister!
TOM: What?
AMANDA: For *sister!* To *meet!* Get *acquainted!*
TOM: *(stamping to door)* Oh, my *go-osh!*
105 **AMANDA:** Will you? *(He opens door. Imploringly.)* Will you? *(He starts
down.)* Will you? Will you, dear?
TOM: *(calling back)* YES!

*Amanda closes the door hesitantly and with a troubled but faintly hopeful
expression.*

(Screen Image: a glamour magazine cover.)

Spot Amanda at phone.

AMANDA: Ella Cartwright? This is Amanda Wingfield! How are you, honey?
How is that kidney condition? *(Count five.)* Horrors! *(Count five.)* You're
a Christian martyr, yes, honey, that's what you are, a Christian martyr!
Well, I just happened to notice in my little red book that your subscription
to the *Companion* has just run out! I knew that you wouldn't want to miss
out on the wonderful serial starting in this new issue. It's by Bessie Mae
Hopper, the first thing she's written since *Honeymoon for Three.* Wasn't
that a strange and interesting story? Well, this one is even lovelier, I believe. It has a sophisticated society background. It's all about the horsey
set on Long Island!

(Fade Out.)

SCENE V

(Legend On Screen: "Annunciation.") Fade with music.

*It is early dusk of a spring evening. Supper has just been finished in the
Wingfield apartment. Amanda and Laura in light colored dresses are removing dishes from the table, in the upstage area, which is shadowy, their
movements formalized almost as a dance or ritual, their moving forms as
pale and silent as moths.*

*Tom, in white shirt and trousers, rises from the table and crosses toward
the fire-escape.*

AMANDA: *(as he passes her)* Son, will you do me a favor?
TOM: What?

AMANDA: Comb your hair! You look so pretty when your hair is combed! *(Tom slouches on sofa with evening paper. Enormous caption "Franco Triumphs.")* There is only one respect in which I would like you to emulate your father.

TOM: What respect is that?

5 **AMANDA:**   The care he always took of his appearance. He never allowed himself to look untidy. *(He throws down the paper and crosses to fire-escape.)* Where are you going?

TOM: I'm going out to smoke.

AMANDA: You smoke too much. A pack a day at fifteen cents a pack. How much would that amount to in a month? Thirty times fifteen is how much, Tom? Figure it out and you will be astounded at what you could save. Enough to give you a night-school course in accounting at Washington U! Just think what a wonderful thing that would be for you, son!

Tom is unmoved by the thought.

TOM: I'd rather smoke. *(He steps out on landing, letting the screen door slam.)*

AMANDA: *(sharply)* I know! That's the tragedy of it. . . . *(Alone, she turns to look at her husband's picture.)*

(Dance Music: "All The World Is Waiting For The Sunrise!")

10 **TOM:**   *(to the audience)* Across the alley from us was the Paradise Dance Hall. On evenings in spring the windows and doors were open and the music came outdoors. Sometimes the lights were turned out except for a large glass sphere that hung from the ceiling. It would turn slowly about and filter the dusk with delicate rainbow colors. Then the orchestra played a waltz or a tango, something that had a slow and sensuous rhythm. Couples would come outside, to the relative privacy of the alley. You could see them kissing behind ash-pits and telephone poles. This was the compensation for lives that passed like mine, without any change or adventure. Adventure and change were imminent in this year. They were waiting around the corner for all these kids. Suspended in the mist over Berchtesgaden,[6] caught in the folds of Chamberlain's[7] umbrella—In Spain there was Guernica! But here there was only hot swing music and liquor, dance halls, bars, and movies, and sex that hung in the gloom like a chandelier and flooded the world with brief, deceptive rainbows. . . . All the world was waiting for bombardments!

Amanda turns from the picture and comes outside.

---

[6] A resort in West Germany, in the Bavarian Alps, site of Hitler's fortified retreat, the Berghof.

[7] (Arthur) Neville Chamberlain (1869-1940)—Conservative party Prime Minister of England (1937-1940) who advocated a policy of appeasement toward Hitler.

AMANDA: *(sighing)* A fire-escape landing's a poor excuse for a porch. *(She spreads a newspaper on a step and sits down, gracefully and demurely as if she were settling into a swing on a Mississippi veranda.)* What are you looking at?

TOM: The moon.

AMANDA: Is there a moon this evening?

TOM: It's rising over Garfinkel's Delicatessen.

15 **AMANDA:** So it is! A little silver slipper of a moon. Have you made a wish on it yet?

TOM: Um-hum.

AMANDA: What did you wish for?

TOM: That's a secret.

AMANDA: A secret, huh? Well, I won't tell mine either. I will be just as mysterious as you.

20 **TOM:** I bet I can guess what yours is.

AMANDA: Is my head so transparent?

TOM: You're not a sphinx.

AMANDA: No, I don't have secrets. I'll tell you what I wished for on the moon. Success and happiness for my precious children! I wish for that whenever there's a moon, and when there isn't a moon, I wish for it, too.

TOM: I thought perhaps you wished for a gentleman caller.

25 **AMANDA:** Why do you say that?

TOM: Don't you remember asking me to fetch one?

AMANDA: I remember suggesting that it would be nice for your sister if you brought home some nice young man from the warehouse. I think I've made that suggestion more than once.

TOM: Yes, you have made it repeatedly.

AMANDA: Well?

30 **TOM:** We are going to have one.

AMANDA: What?

TOM: A gentleman caller!

(The Annunciation Is Celebrated With Music.)

Amanda rises.

(Image On Screen: Caller With Bouquet.)

AMANDA: You mean you have asked some nice young man to come over?

TOM: Yep. I've asked him to dinner.

35 **AMANDA:** You really did?

TOM: I did!

AMANDA: You did, and did he—*accept?*

TOM: He did!

AMANDA: Well, well—well, well! That's—lovely!

40 **TOM:** I thought that you would be pleased.

AMANDA: It's definite, then?

Tom: Very definite.

Amanda: Soon?

Tom: Very soon.

45 **Amanda:** For heaven's sake, stop putting on and tell me some things, will you?

Tom: What things do you want me to tell you?

Amanda: Naturally I would like to know when he's *coming!*

Tom: He's coming tomorrow.

Amanda: *Tomorrow?*

50 **Tom:** Yep. Tomorrow.

Amanda: But, Tom!

Tom: Yes, Mother?

Amanda: Tomorrow gives me no time!

Tom: Time for what?

55 **Amanda:** Preparations! Why didn't you phone me at once, as soon as you asked him, the minute that he accepted? Then, don't you see, I could have been getting ready!

Tom: You don't have to make any fuss.

Amanda: Oh, Tom, Tom, Tom, of course I have to make a fuss! I want things nice, not sloppy! Not thrown together. I'll certainly have to do some fast thinking, won't I?

Tom: I don't see why you have to think at all.

Amanda: You just don't know. We can't have a gentleman caller in a pigsty! All my wedding silver has to be polished, the monogrammed table linen ought to be laundered! The windows have to be washed and fresh curtains put up. And how about clothes? We have to *wear* something, don't we?

60 **Tom:** Mother, this boy is no one to make a fuss over!

Amanda: Do you realize he's the first young man we've introduced to your sister? It's terrible, dreadful, disgraceful that poor little sister has never received a single gentleman caller! Tom, come inside! *(She opens the screen door.)*

Tom: What for?

Amanda: I want to ask you some things.

Tom: If you're going to make such a fuss, I'll call it off, I'll tell him not to come.

65 **Amanda:** You certainly won't do anything of the kind. Nothing offends people worse than broken engagements. It simply means I'll have to work like a Turk! We won't be brilliant, but we'll pass inspection. Come on inside. *(Tom follows, groaning.)* Sit down.

Tom: Any particular place you would like me to sit?

Amanda: Thank heavens I've got that new sofa! I'm also making payments on a floor lamp I'll have sent out! And put the chintz covers on, they'll brighten things up! Of course I'd hoped to have these walls re-papered. . . . What is the young man's name?

Tom: His name is O'Connor.

AMANDA: That, of course, means fish—tomorrow is Friday! I'll have that salmon loaf—with Durkee's dressing! What does he do? He works at the warehouse?

70 **TOM:** Of course! How else would I—

AMANDA: Tom, he—doesn't drink?

TOM: Why do you ask me that?

AMANDA: Your father *did!*

TOM: Don't get started on that!

75 **AMANDA:** He *does* drink, then?

TOM: Not that I know of!

AMANDA: Make sure, be certain! The last thing I want for my daughter's a boy who drinks!

TOM: Aren't you being a little premature? Mr. O'Connor has not yet appeared on the scene!

AMANDA: But will tomorrow. To meet your sister, and what do I know about his character? Nothing! Old maids are better off than wives of drunkards!

80 **TOM:** Oh, my God!

AMANDA: Be still!

TOM: *(leaning forward to whisper)* Lots of fellows meet girls whom they don't marry!

AMANDA: Oh, talk sensibly, Tom—and don't be sarcastic! *(She has gotten a hairbrush.)*

TOM: What are you doing?

85 **AMANDA:** I'm brushing that cow-lick down! What is this young man's position at the warehouse?

TOM: *(submitting grimly to the brush and the interrogation)* This young man's position is that of a shipping clerk, Mother.

AMANDA: Sounds to me like a fairly responsible job, the sort of a job *you* would be in if you just had more *get-up.* What is his salary? Have you got any idea?

TOM: I would judge it to be approximately eighty-five dollars a month.

AMANDA: Well—not princely, but—

90 **TOM:** Twenty more than I make.

AMANDA: Yes, how well I know! But for a family man, eighty-five dollars a month is not much more than you can just get by on. . . .

TOM: Yes, but Mr. O'Connor is not a family man.

AMANDA: He might be, mightn't he? Some time in the future?

TOM: I see. Plans and provisions.

95 **AMANDA:** You are the only young man that I know of who ignores the fact that the future becomes the present, the present the past, and the past turns into everlasting regret if you don't plan for it!

TOM: I will think that over and see what I can make of it.

AMANDA: Don't be supercilious with your mother! Tell me some more about this—what do you call him?

TOM: James D. O'Connor. The D. is for Delaney.

AMANDA: Irish on *both* sides! *Gracious!* And doesn't drink?

100 TOM: Shall I call him up and ask him right this minute?

AMANDA: The only way to find out about those things is to make discreet inquiries at the proper moment. When I was a girl in Blue Mountain and it was suspected that a young man drank, the girl whose attentions he had been receiving, if any girl *was*, would sometimes speak to the minister of his church, or rather her father would if her father was living, and sort of feel him out on the young man's character. That is the way such things are discreetly handled to keep a young woman from making a tragic mistake!

TOM: Then how did you happen to make a tragic mistake?

AMANDA: That innocent look of your father's had everyone fooled! He *smiled*—the world was *enchanted!* No girl can do worse than put herself at the mercy of a handsome appearance! I hope that Mr. O'Connor is not too good-looking.

TOM: No, he's not too good-looking. He's covered with freckles and hasn't too much of a nose.

105 AMANDA: He's not right-down homely, though?

TOM: Not right-down homely. Just medium homely, I'd say.

AMANDA: Character's what to look for in a man.

TOM: That's what I've always said, Mother.

AMANDA: You've never said anything of the kind and I suspect you would never give it a thought.

110 TOM: Don't be suspicious of me.

AMANDA: At least I hope he's the type that's up and coming.

TOM: I think he really goes in for self-improvement.

AMANDA: What reason have you to think so?

TOM: He goes to night school.

115 AMANDA: *(beaming)* Splendid! What does he do, I mean study?

TOM: Radio engineering and public speaking!

AMANDA: Then he has visions of being advanced in the world! Any young man who studies public speaking is aiming to have an executive job some day! And radio engineering? A thing for the future! Both of these facts are very illuminating. Those are the sort of things that a mother should know concerning any young man who comes to call on her daughter. Seriously or—not.

TOM: One little warning. He doesn't know about Laura. I didn't let on that we had dark ulterior motives. I just said, why don't you come have dinner with us? He said okay and that was the whole conversation.

AMANDA: I bet it was! You're eloquent as an oyster. However, he'll know about Laura when he gets here. When he sees how lovely and sweet and pretty she is, he'll thank his lucky stars he was asked to dinner.

120 TOM: Mother, you mustn't expect too much of Laura.

AMANDA: What do you mean?

TOM: Laura seems all those things to you and me because she's ours and we love her. We don't even notice she's crippled any more.

AMANDA: Don't say crippled! You know that I never allow that word to be used!

TOM: But face facts, Mother. She is and—that's not all—

125 **AMANDA:** What do you mean "not all"?

TOM: Laura is very different from other girls.

AMANDA: I think the difference is all to her advantage.

TOM: Not quite all—in the eyes of others—strangers—she's terribly shy and lives in a world of her own and those things make her seem a little peculiar to people outside the house.

AMANDA: Don't say peculiar.

130 **TOM:** Face the facts. She is.

(The Dance-hall Music Changes To A Tango That Has A Minor And Somewhat Ominous Tone.)

AMANDA: In what way is she peculiar—may I ask?

TOM: *(gently)* She lives in a world of her own—a world of—little glass ornaments, Mother. . . . *(Gets up. Amanda remains holding brush, looking at him, troubled.)* She plays old phonograph records and—that's about all—*(He glances at himself in the mirror and crosses to door.)*

AMANDA: *(sharply)* Where are you going?

TOM: I'm going to the movies. *(Out screen door.)*

135 **AMANDA:** Not to the movies, every night to the movies! *(Follows quickly to screen door.)* I don't believe you always go to the movies! *(He is gone. Amanda looks worriedly after him for a moment. Then vitality and optimism return and she turns from the door. Crossing to portieres.)* Laura! Laura! *(Laura answers from kitchenette.)*

LAURA: Yes, Mother.

AMANDA: Let those dishes go and come in front! *(Laura appears with dish towel. Gaily.)* Laura, come here and make a wish on the moon!

LAURA: *(entering)* Moon—moon?

AMANDA: A little silver slipper of a moon. Look over your left shoulder, Laura, and make a wish! *(Laura looks faintly puzzled as if called out of sleep. Amanda seizes her shoulders and turns her at an angle by the door.)* Now! Now, darling, *wish!*

140 **LAURA:** What shall I wish for, Mother?

AMANDA: *(her voice trembling and her eyes suddenly filling with tears)* Happiness! Good Fortune!

The violin rises and the stage dims out.

SCENE VI

(Image: High-School Hero.)

TOM: And so the following evening I brought Jim home to dinner. I had known Jim slightly in high school. In high school Jim was a hero. He had tremendous Irish good nature and vitality with the scrubbed and polished look of white chinaware. He seemed to move in a continual spotlight. He was a star in basketball, captain of the debating club, president of the senior class and the glee club and he sang the male lead in the annual light operas. He was always running or bounding, never just walking. He seemed always at the point of defeating the law of gravity. He was shooting with such velocity through his adolescence that you would logically expect him to arrive at nothing short of the White House by the time he was thirty. But Jim apparently ran into more interference after his graduation from Soldan. His speed had definitely slowed. Six years after he left high school he was holding a job that wasn't much better than mine.

(Image: Clerk.)

He was the only one at the warehouse with whom I was on friendly terms. I was valuable to him as someone who could remember his former glory, who had seen him win basketball games and the silver cup in debating. He knew of my secret practice of retiring to a cabinet of the washroom to work on poems when business was slack in the warehouse. He called me Shakespeare. And while the other boys in the warehouse regarded me with suspicious hostility, Jim took a humorous attitude toward me. Gradually his attitude affected the others, their hostility wore off and they also began to smile at me as people smile at an oddly fashioned dog who trots across their path at some distance.

I knew that Jim and Laura had known each other at Soldan, and I had heard Laura speak admiringly of his voice. I didn't know if Jim remembered her or not. In high school Laura had been as unobtrusive as Jim had been astonishing. If he did remember Laura, it was not as my sister, for when I asked him to dinner, he grinned and said, "You know, Shakespeare, I never thought of you as having folks!"

He was about to discover that I did. . . .

(Light Up Stage.)

(Legend On Screen: "The Accent Of A Coming Foot.")

Friday evening. It is about five o'clock of a late spring evening which comes "scattering poems in the sky."

A delicate lemony light is in the Wingfield apartment.

Amanda has worked like a Turk in preparation for the gentleman caller. The results are astonishing. The new floor lamp with its rose-silk shade is in place, a colored paper lantern conceals the broken light fixture in the ceiling, new billowing white curtains are at the windows, chintz covers are on chairs and sofa, a pair of new sofa pillows make their initial appearance.

Open boxes and tissue paper are scattered on the floor.

Laura stands in the middle with lifted arms while Amanda crouches before her, adjusting the hem of the new dress, devout and ritualistic. The

dress is colored and designed by memory. The arrangement of Laura's hair
is changed; it is softer and more becoming. A fragile, unearthly prettiness
has come out in Laura: she is like a piece of translucent glass touched by
light, given a momentary radiance, not actual, not lasting.

AMANDA: *(impatiently)* Why are you trembling?
LAURA: Mother, you've made me so nervous!
AMANDA: How have I made you nervous?
5   **LAURA:**   By all this fuss! You make it seem so important!
AMANDA: I don't understand you, Laura. You couldn't be satisfied with just
   sitting home, and yet whenever I try to arrange something for you, you
   seem to resist it. *(She gets up.)* Now take a look at yourself. No, wait! Wait
   just a moment—I have an idea!
LAURA: What is it now?

Amanda produces two powder puffs which she wraps in handkerchiefs
and stuffs in Laura's bosom.

LAURA: Mother, what are you doing?
AMANDA: They call them "Gay Deceivers"!
10   **LAURA:**   I won't wear them!
AMANDA: You will!
LAURA: Why should I?
AMANDA: Because, to be painfully honest, your chest is flat.
LAURA: You make it seem like we were setting a trap.
15   **AMANDA:**   All pretty girls are a trap, a pretty trap, and men expect them to
   be. *(Legend: "A Pretty Trap.")* Now look at yourself, young lady. This is
   the prettiest you will ever be! I've got to fix myself now! You're going to
   be surprised by your mother's appearance! *(She crosses through*
   portieres, humming gaily.)

Laura moves slowly to the long mirror and stares solemnly at herself.
   A wind blows the white curtains inward in a slow, graceful motion and
with a faint, sorrowful sighing.

AMANDA: *(offstage)* It isn't dark enough yet. *(She turns slowly before the*
   mirror with a troubled look.)

(Legend On Screen: "This Is My Sister: Celebrate Her With Strings!" Music.)

AMANDA: *(laughing, off)* I'm going to show you something. I'm going to
   make a spectacular appearance!
LAURA: What is it, Mother?
AMANDA: Possess your soul in patience—you will see! Something I've resur-
   rected from that old trunk! Styles haven't changed so terribly much after
   all. . . . *(She parts the portieres.)* Now just look at your mother! *(She wears*
   a girlish frock of yellowed voile with a blue silk sash. She carries a bunch
   of jonquils—the legend of her youth is nearly revived. Feverishly.) This is

the dress in which I led the cotillion. Won the cakewalk twice at Sunset Hill, wore one spring to the Governor's ball in Jackson! See how I sashayed around the ballroom, Laura? *(She raises her skirt and does a mincing step around the room.)* I wore it on Sundays for my gentlemen callers! I had it on the day I met your father—I had malaria fever all that spring. The change of climate from East Tennessee to the Delta—weakened resistance—I had a little temperature all the time—not enough to be serious—just enough to make me restless and giddy! Invitations poured in—parties all over the Delta!—"Stay in bed," said Mother, "you have fever!"—but I just wouldn't.—I took quinine but kept on going, going!—Evenings, dances!—Afternoons, long, long rides! Picnics—lovely!—So lovely, that country in May.—All lacy with dogwood, literally flooded with jonquils!—That was the spring I had the craze for jonquils. Jonquils became an absolute obsession. Mother said, "Honey, there's no more room for jonquils." And still I kept bringing in more jonquils. Whenever, wherever I saw them, I'd say, "Stop! Stop! I see jonquils!" I made the young men help me gather the jonquils! It was a joke, Amanda and her jonquils! Finally there were no more vases to hold them, every available space was filled with jonquils. No vases to hold them? All right, I'll hold them myself! And then I—*(She stops in front of the picture.) (Music)* met your father! Malaria fever and jonquils and then—this—boy. . . . *(She switches on the rose-colored lamp.)* I hope they get here before it starts to rain. *(She crosses upstage and places the jonquils in bowl on table.)* I gave your brother a little extra change so he and Mr. O'Connor could take the service car home.

20 **LAURA:**   *(with altered look)* What did you say his name was?

AMANDA: O'Connor.

LAURA: What is his first name?

AMANDA: I don't remember. Oh, yes, I do. It was—Jim!

Laura sways slightly and catches hold of a chair.

(Legend On Screen: "Not Jim!")

LAURA: *(faintly)* Not—Jim!

25 **AMANDA:**   Yes, that was it, it was Jim! I've never known a Jim that wasn't nice!

(Music: Ominous.)

LAURA: Are you sure his name is Jim O'Connor?

AMANDA: Yes. Why?

LAURA: Is he the one that Tom used to know in high school?

AMANDA: He didn't say so. I think he just got to know him at the warehouse.

30 **LAURA:**   There was a Jim O'Connor we both knew in high school—*(Then, with effort.)* If that is the one that Tom is bringing to dinner—you'll have to excuse me, I won't come to the table.

AMANDA: What sort of nonsense is this?

LAURA: You asked me once if I'd ever liked a boy. Don't you remember I showed you this boy's picture?

AMANDA: You mean the boy you showed me in the year book?

LAURA: Yes, that boy.

35 AMANDA: Laura, Laura, were you in love with that boy?

LAURA: I don't know, Mother. All I know is I couldn't sit at the table if it was him!

AMANDA: It won't be him! It isn't the least bit likely. But whether it is or not, you will come to the table. You will not be excused.

LAURA: I'll have to be, Mother.

AMANDA: I don't intend to humor your silliness, Laura. I've had too much from you and your brother, both! So just sit down and compose yourself till they come. Tom has forgotten his key so you'll have to let them in, when they arrive.

40 LAURA: *(panicky)* Oh, Mother—*you* answer the door!

AMANDA: *(lightly)* I'll be in the kitchen—busy!

LAURA: Oh, Mother, please answer the door, don't make me do it!

AMANDA: *(crossing into kitchenette)* I've got to fix the dressing for the salmon. Fuss, fuss—silliness!—over a gentleman caller!

Door swings shut. Laura is left alone.

(Legend: "Terror!")

She utters a low moan and turns off the lamp—sits stiffly on the edge of the sofa, knotting her fingers together.

(Legend On Screen: "The Opening Of A Door!")

Tom and Jim appear on the fire-escape steps and climb to landing. Hearing their approach, Laura rises with a panicky gesture. She retreats to the portieres.

The doorbell. Laura catches her breath and touches her throat. Low drums.

AMANDA: *(calling)* Laura, sweetheart! The door!

Laura stares at it without moving.

45 JIM: I think we just beat the rain.

TOM: Uh-huh. *(He rings again, nervously. Jim whistles and fishes for a cigarette.)*

AMANDA: *(very, very gaily)* Laura, that is your brother and Mr. O'Connor! Will you let them in, darling?

Laura crosses toward kitchenette door.

LAURA: *(breathlessly)* Mother—you go to the door!

Amanda steps out of kitchenette and stares furiously at Laura. She points imperiously at the door.

LAURA: Please, please!

50 **AMANDA:** *(in a fierce whisper)* What is the matter with you, you silly thing?

LAURA: *(desperately)* Please, you answer it, *please!*

AMANDA: I told you I wasn't going to humor you, Laura. Why have you chosen this moment to lose your mind?

LAURA: Please, please, please, you go!

AMANDA: You'll have to go to the door because I can't!

55 **LAURA:** *(despairingly)* I can't either!

AMANDA: Why?

LAURA: I'm *sick!*

AMANDA: I'm sick, too—of your nonsense! Why can't you and your brother be normal people? Fantastic whims and behavior! *(Tom gives a long ring.)* Preposterous goings on! Can you give me one reason—*(Calls out lyrically.)* COMING! JUST ONE SECOND!—why should you be afraid to open a door? Now you answer it, Laura!

LAURA: Oh, oh, oh . . . *(She returns through the portieres. Darts to the victrola and winds it frantically and turns it on.)*

60 **AMANDA:** Laura Wingfield, you march right to that door!

LAURA: Yes—yes, Mother!

A faraway, scratchy rendition of "Dardanella" softens the air and gives her strength to move through it. She slips to the door and draws it cautiously open. Tom enters with the caller, Jim O'Connor.

TOM: Laura, this is Jim. Jim, this is my sister, Laura.

JIM: *(stepping inside)* I didn't know that Shakespeare had a sister!

LAURA: *(retreating stiff and trembling from the door)* How—how do you do?

65 **JIM:** *(heartily extending his hand)* Okay!

Laura touches it hesitantly with hers.

JIM: Your hand's *cold*, Laura!

LAURA: Yes, well—I've been playing the victrola. . . .

JIM: Must have been playing classical music on it! You ought to play a little hot swing music to warm you up!

LAURA: Excuse me—I haven't finished playing the victrola. . . .

She turns awkwardly and hurries into the front room. She pauses a second by the victrola. Then catches her breath and darts through the portieres like a frightened deer.

70 **JIM:** *(grinning)* What was the matter?

TOM: Oh—with Laura? Laura is—terribly shy.

JIM: Shy, huh? It's unusual to meet a shy girl nowadays. I don't believe you ever mentioned you had a sister.

TOM: Well, now you know. I have one. Here is the *Post Dispatch.* You want a piece of it?

JIM: Uh-huh.

75 **TOM:** What piece? The comics?

JIM: Sports! *(Glances at it.)* Ole Dizzy Dean is on his bad behavior.

TOM: *(disinterested)* Yeah? *(Lights cigarette and crosses back to fire-escape door.)*

JIM: Where are *you* going?

TOM: I'm going out on the terrace.

80 **JIM:** *(goes after him)* You know, Shakespeare—I'm going to sell you a bill of goods!

TOM: What goods?

JIM: A course I'm taking.

TOM: Huh?

JIM: In public speaking! You and me, we're not the warehouse type.

85 **TOM:** Thanks—that's good news. But what has public speaking got to do with it?

JIM: It fits you for—executive positions!

TOM: Awww.

JIM: I tell you it's done a helluva lot for me.

(Image: Executive At Desk.)

TOM: In what respect?

90 **JIM:** In every! Ask yourself what is the difference between you an' me and men in the office down front? Brains?—No!—Ability?—No! Then what? Just one little thing—

TOM: What is that one little thing?

JIM: Primarily it amounts to—social poise! Being able to square up to people and hold your own on any social level!

AMANDA: *(offstage)* Tom?

TOM: Yes, Mother?

95 **AMANDA:** Is that you and Mr. O'Connor?

TOM: Yes, Mother.

AMANDA: Well, you just make yourselves comfortable in there.

TOM: Yes, Mother.

AMANDA: Ask Mr. O'Connor if he would like to wash his hands.

100 **JIM:** Aw—no—thank you—I took care of that at the warehouse. Tom—

TOM: Yes?

JIM: Mr. Mendoza was speaking to me about you.

TOM: Favorably?

JIM: What do you think?

105 **TOM:** Well—

JIM: You're going to be out of a job if you don't wake up.

Tom: I am waking up—
Jim: You show no signs.
Tom: The signs are interior.

(Image On Screen: The Sailing Vessel With Jolly Roger Again.)

110 **Tom:**   I'm planning to change. *(He leans over the rail speaking with quiet exhilaration. The incandescent marquees and signs of the first-run movie houses light his face from across the alley. He looks like a voyager.)* I'm right at the point of committing myself to a future that doesn't include the warehouse and Mr. Mendoza or even a night-school course in public speaking.
   Jim: What are you gassing about?
   Tom: I'm tired of the movies.
   Jim: Movies!
   Tom: Yes, movies! Look at them—*(A wave toward the marvels of Grand Avenue.)* All of those glamorous people—having adventures—hogging it all, gobbling the whole thing up! You know what happens? People go to the *movies* instead of *moving!* Hollywood characters are supposed to have all the adventures for everybody in America, while everybody in America sits in a dark room and watches them have them! Yes, until there's a war. That's when adventure becomes available to the masses! *Everyone's* dish, not only Gable's! Then the people in the dark room come out of the dark room to have some adventures themselves—Goody, goody—It's our turn now, to go to the South Sea Island—to make a safari—to be exotic, far-off—But I'm not patient. I don't want to wait till then. I'm tired of the *movies* and I am *about* to *move!*
115 **Jim:**   *(incredulously)* Move?
   Tom: Yes.
   Jim: When?
   Tom: Soon!
   Jim: Where? Where?

Theme three music seems to answer the question, while Tom thinks it over. He searches among his pockets.

120 **Tom:**   I'm starting to boil inside. I know I seem dreary, but inside—well, I'm boiling! Whenever I pick up a shoe, I shudder a little thinking how short life is and what I am doing!—Whatever that means. I know it doesn't mean shoes—except as something to wear on a traveler's feet! *(Finds paper.)* Look—
   Jim: What?
   Tom: I'm a member.
   Jim: *(reading)* The Union of Merchant Seamen.
   Tom: I paid my dues this month, instead of the light bill.
125 **Jim:**   You will regret it when they turn the lights off.
   Tom: I won't be here.

JIM: How about your mother?

TOM: I'm like my father. The bastard son of a bastard! See how he grins? And he's been absent going on sixteen years!

JIM: You're just talking, you drip. How does your mother feel about it?

130 **TOM:** Shhh—Here comes Mother! Mother is not acquainted with my plans!

AMANDA: *(enters portieres)* Where are you all?

TOM: On the terrace, Mother.

They start inside. She advances to them. Tom is distinctly shocked at her appearance. Even Jim blinks a little. He is making his first contact with girlish Southern vivacity and in spite of the night-school course in public speaking is somewhat thrown off the beam by the unexpected outlay of social charm.

Certain responses are attempted by Jim but are swept aside by Amanda's gay laughter and chatter. Tom is embarrassed but after the first shock Jim reacts very warmly. Grins and chuckles, is altogether won over.

(Image: Amanda As A Girl.)

AMANDA: *(coyly smiling, shaking her girlish ringlets)* Well, well, well, so this is Mr. O'Connor. Introductions entirely unnecessary. I've heard so much about you from my boy. I finally said to him, Tom—good gracious!— why don't you bring this paragon to supper? I'd like to meet this nice young man at the warehouse!—Instead of just hearing him sing your praises so much! I don't know why my son is so stand-offish—that's not Southern behavior! Let's sit down and—I think we could stand a little more air in here! Tom, leave the door open. I felt a nice fresh breeze a moment ago. Where has it gone? Mmm, so warm already! And not quite summer, even. We're going to burn up when summer really gets started. However, we're having—we're having a very light supper. I think light things are better fo' this time of year. The same as light clothes are. Light clothes an' light food are what warm weather calls fo'. You know our blood gets so thick during th' winter—it takes a while fo' us to *adjust* ou'selves!—when the season changes . . . It's come so quick this year. I wasn't prepared. All of a sudden—heavens! Already summer!—I ran to the trunk an' pulled out this light dress—Terribly old! Historical almost! But feels so good—so good an' co-ol, y'know. . . .

TOM: Mother—

135 **AMANDA:** Yes, honey?

TOM: How about—supper?

AMANDA: Honey, you go ask Sister if supper is ready! You know that Sister is in full charge of supper! Tell her you hungry boys are waiting for it. *(To Jim.)* Have you met Laura?

JIM: She—

AMANDA: Let you in? Oh, good, you've met already! It's rare for a girl as sweet an' pretty as Laura to be domestic! But Laura is, thank heavens, not only pretty but also very domestic. I'm not at all. I never was a bit. I never could make a thing but angel-food cake. Well, in the South we had so many servants. Gone, gone, gone. All vestiges of gracious living! Gone completely! I wasn't prepared for what the future brought me. All of my gentlemen callers were sons of planters and so of course I assumed that I would be married to one and raise my family on a large piece of land with plenty of servants. But man proposes—and woman accepts the proposal!—To vary that old, old saying a little bit—I married no planter! I married a man who worked for the telephone company!—that gallantly smiling gentleman over there! *(Points to the picture.)* A telephone man who—fell in love with long-distance!—Now he travels and I don't even know where!—But what am I going on for about my—tribulations? Tell me yours—I hope you don't have any! Tom?

140   **Tom:**   *(returning)* Yes, Mother?

    Amanda: Is supper nearly ready?

    Tom: It looks to me like supper is on the table.

    Amanda: Let me look—*(She rises prettily and looks through portieres.)* Oh, lovely—But where is Sister?

    Tom: Laura is not feeling well and says that she thinks she'd better not come to the table.

145   **Amanda:**   What?—Nonsense!—Laura? Oh, Laura!

    Laura: *(offstage, faintly)* Yes, Mother.

    Amanda: You really must come to the table. We won't be seated until you come to the table! Come in, Mr. O'Connor. You sit over there and I'll— Laura? Laura Wingfield! You're keeping us waiting, honey! We can't say grace until you come to the table!

The back door is pushed weakly open and Laura comes in. She is obviously quite faint, her lips trembling, her eyes wide and staring. She moves unsteadily toward the table.

(Legend: "Terror!")

Outside a summer storm is coming abruptly. The white curtains billow inward at the windows and there is a sorrowful murmur and deep blue dusk. Laura suddenly stumbles—She catches at a chair with a faint moan.

    Tom: Laura!

    Amanda: Laura! *(There is a clap of thunder.)* *(Legend: "Ah!")* *(Despairingly.)* Why, Laura, you *are* sick, darling! Tom, help your sister into the living room, dear! Sit in the living room, Laura—rest on the sofa. Well! *(To the gentleman caller.)* Standing over the hot stove made her ill!—I told her that it was just too warm this evening, but—*(Tom comes back in. Laura is on the sofa.)* Is Laura all right now?

150   **Tom:**   Yes.

    Amanda: What *is* that? Rain? A nice cool rain has come up! *(She gives the gentleman caller a frightened look.)* I think we may—have grace—now . . . *(Tom looks at her stupidly.)* Tom, honey—you say grace!

Tom: Oh . . . "For these and all thy mercies—" *(They bow their heads, Amanda stealing a nervous glance at Jim. In the living room Laura, stretched on the sofa, clenches her hand to her lips, to hold back a shuddering sob.)* God's Holy Name be praised—

(The Scene Dims Out.)

Scene VII

(A Souvenir.)

Half an hour later. Dinner is just being finished in the upstage area which is concealed by the drawn portieres.

    As the curtain rises Laura is still huddled upon the sofa, her feet drawn under her, her head resting on a pale blue pillow, her eyes wide and mysteriously watchful. The new floor lamp with its shade of rose-colored silk gives a soft, becoming light to her face, bringing out the fragile, unearthly prettiness which usually escapes attention. There is a steady murmur of rain, but it is slackening and stops soon after the scene begins; the air outside becomes pale and luminous as the moon breaks out.

    A moment after the curtain rises, the lights in both rooms flicker and go out.

Jim: Hey, there, Mr. Light Bulb!

Amanda laughs nervously.

(Legend: "Suspension Of A Public Service.")

Amanda: Where was Moses when the lights went out? Ha-ha. Do you know the answer to that one, Mr. O'Connor?

Jim: No, Ma'am, what's the answer?

Amanda: In the dark! *(Jim laughs appreciatively.)* Everybody sit still. I'll light the candles. Isn't it lucky we have them on the table? Where's a match? Which of you gentlemen can provide a match?

5 **Jim:** Here.

Amanda: Thank you, sir.

Jim: Not at all, Ma'am!

Amanda: I guess the fuse has burnt out. Mr. O'Connor, can you tell a burnt-out fuse? I know I can't and Tom is a total loss when it comes to mechanics. *(Sound: Getting Up: Voices Recede A Little To Kitchenette.)* Oh, be careful you don't bump into something. We don't want our gentleman caller to break his neck. Now wouldn't that be a fine howdy-do?

Jim: Ha-ha! Where is the fuse-box?

10 **Amanda:** Right here next to the stove. Can you see anything?

Jim: Just a minute.

Amanda: Isn't electricity a mysterious thing? Wasn't it Benjamin Franklin who tied a key to a kite? We live in such a mysterious universe, don't we?

Some people say that science clears up all the mysteries for us. In my opinion it only creates more! Have you found it yet?

JIM: No, Ma'am. All these fuses look okay to me.

AMANDA: Tom!

15   **TOM:**   Yes, Mother?

AMANDA: That light bill I gave you several days ago. The one I told you we got the notices about?

TOM: Oh.—Yeah.

(Legend: "Ha!")

AMANDA: You didn't neglect to pay it by any chance?

TOM: Why, I—

20   **AMANDA:**   Didn't! I might have known it!

JIM: Shakespeare probably wrote a poem on that light bill, Mrs. Wingfield.

AMANDA: I might have known better than to trust him with it! There's such a high price for negligence in this world!

JIM: Maybe the poem will win a ten-dollar prize.

AMANDA: We'll just have to spend the remainder of the evening in the nineteenth century, before Mr. Edison made the Mazda lamp!

25   **JIM:**   Candlelight is my favorite kind of light.

AMANDA: That shows you're romantic! But that's no excuse for Tom. Well, we got through dinner. Very considerate of them to let us get through dinner before they plunged us into everlasting darkness, wasn't it, Mr. O'Connor?

JIM: Ha-ha!

AMANDA: Tom, as a penalty for your carelessness you can help me with the dishes.

JIM: Let me give you a hand.

30   **AMANDA:**   Indeed you will not!

JIM: I ought to be good for something.

AMANDA: Good for something? *(Her tone is rhapsodic.) You?* Why, Mr. O'-Connor, nobody, *nobody's* given me this much entertainment in years— as you have!

JIM: Aw, now, Mrs. Wingfield!

AMANDA: I'm not exaggerating, not one bit! But Sister is all by her lonesome. You go keep her company in the parlor! I'll give you this lovely old candelabrum that used to be on the altar at the church of the Heavenly Rest. It was melted a little out of shape when the church burnt down. Lightning struck it one spring. Gypsy Jones was holding a revival at the time and he intimated that the church was destroyed because the Episcopalians gave card parties.

35   **JIM:**   Ha-ha.

AMANDA: And how about coaxing Sister to drink a little wine? I think it would be good for her! Can you carry both at once?

JIM: Sure. I'm Superman!

AMANDA: Now, Thomas, get into this apron!

The door of kitchenette swings closed on Amanda's gay laughter; the flickering light approaches the portieres.

Laura sits up nervously as he enters. Her speech at first is low and breathless from the almost intolerable strain of being alone with a stranger.

(The Legend: "I Don't Suppose You Remember Me At All!")

In her first speeches in this scene, before Jim's warmth overcomes her paralyzing shyness, Laura's voice is thin and breathless as though she has run up a steep flight of stairs.

Jim's attitude is gently humorous. In playing this scene it should be stressed that while the incident is apparently unimportant, it is to Laura the climax of her secret life.

JIM: Hello, there, Laura.

40 **LAURA:** *(faintly)* Hello. *(She clears her throat.)*

JIM: How are you feeling now? Better?

LAURA: Yes. Yes, thank you.

JIM: This is for you. A little dandelion wine. *(He extends it toward her with extravagant gallantry.)*

LAURA: Thank you.

45 **JIM:** Drink it—but don't get drunk! *(He laughs heartily. Laura takes the glass uncertainly; laughs shyly.)* Where shall I set the candles?

LAURA: Oh—oh, anywhere . . .

JIM: How about here on the floor? Any objections?

LAURA: No.

JIM: I'll spread a newspaper under to catch the drippings. I like to sit on the floor. Mind if I do?

50 **LAURA:** Oh, no.

JIM: Give me a pillow?

LAURA: What?

JIM: A pillow!

LAURA: Oh . . . *(Hands him one quickly.)*

55 **JIM:** How about you? Don't you like to sit on the floor?

LAURA: Oh—yes.

JIM: Why don't you, then?

LAURA: I—will.

JIM: Take a pillow! *(Laura does. Sits on the other side of the candelabrum. Jim crosses his legs and smiles engagingly at her.)* I can't hardly see you sitting way over there.

60 **LAURA:** I can—see you.

JIM: I know, but that's not fair, I'm in the limelight. *(Laura moves her pillow closer.)* Good! Now I can see you! Comfortable?

LAURA: Yes.

JIM: So am I. Comfortable as a cow. Will you have some gum?

Laura: No, thank you.

65 **Jim:**   I think that I will indulge, with your permission. *(Musingly unwraps it and holds it up.)* Think of the fortune made by the guy that invented the first piece of chewing gum. Amazing, huh? The Wrigley Building is one of the sights of Chicago.—I saw it summer before last when I went up to the Century of Progress. Did you take in the Century of Progress?

Laura: No, I didn't.

Jim: Well, it was quite a wonderful exposition. What impressed me most was the Hall of Science. Gives you an idea of what the future will be in America, even more wonderful than the present time is! *(Pause. Smiling at her.)* Your brother tells me you're shy. Is that right, Laura?

Laura: I—don't know.

Jim: I judge you to be an old-fashioned type of girl. Well, I think that's a pretty good type to be. Hope you don't think I'm being too personal—do you?

70 **Laura:**   *(hastily, out of embarrassment)* I believe I *will* take a piece of gum, if you—don't mind. *(Clearing her throat.)* Mr. O'Connor, have you—kept up with your singing?

Jim: Singing? Me?

Laura: Yes. I remember what a beautiful voice you had.

Jim: When did you hear me sing?

(Voice Offstage In The Pause.)

Voice (offstage):

O blow, ye winds, heigh-ho,
A-roving I will go!
I'm off to my love
With a boxing glove—
Ten thousand miles away!

Jim: You say you've heard me sing?

75 **Laura:**   Oh, yes! Yes, very often . . . I—don't suppose you remember me—at all?

Jim: *(smiling doubtfully)* You know I have an idea I've seen you before. I had that idea soon as you opened the door. It seemed almost like I was about to remember your name. But the name that I started to call you—wasn't a name! And so I stopped myself before I said it.

Laura: Wasn't it—Blue Roses?

Jim: *(springs up, grinning)* Blue Roses! My gosh, yes—Blue Roses! That's what I had on my tongue when you opened the door! Isn't it funny what tricks your memory plays? I didn't connect you with the high school somehow or other. But that's where it was; it was high school. I didn't even know you were Shakespeare's sister! Gosh, I'm sorry.

Laura: I didn't expect you to. You—barely knew me!

80 **Jim:**   But we did have a speaking acquaintance, huh?

LAURA: Yes, we—spoke to each other.

JIM: When did you recognize me?

LAURA: Oh, right away!

JIM: Soon as I came in the door?

85 LAURA: When I heard your name I thought it was probably you. I knew that Tom used to know you a little in high school. So when you came in the door—Well, then I was—sure.

JIM: Why didn't you *say* something, then?

LAURA: *(breathlessly)* I didn't know what to say, I was—too surprised!

JIM: For goodness' sakes! You know, this sure is funny!

LAURA: Yes! Yes, isn't it, though . . .

90 JIM: Didn't we have a class in something together?

LAURA: Yes, we did.

JIM: What class was that?

LAURA: It was—singing—Chorus!

JIM: Aw!

95 LAURA: I sat across the aisle from you in the Aud.

JIM: Aw.

LAURA: Mondays, Wednesdays and Fridays.

JIM: Now I remember—you always came in late.

LAURA: Yes, it was so hard for me, getting upstairs. I had that brace on my leg—it clumped so loud!

100 JIM: I never heard any clumping.

LAURA: *(wincing at the recollection)* To me it sounded like—thunder!

JIM: Well, well, well. I never even noticed.

LAURA: And everybody was seated before I came in. I had to walk in front of all those people. My seat was in the back row. I had to go clumping all the way up the aisle with everyone watching!

JIM: You shouldn't have been self-conscious.

105 LAURA: I know, but I was. It was always such a relief when the singing started.

JIM: Aw, yes, I've placed you now! I used to call you Blue Roses. How was it that I got started calling you that?

LAURA: I was out of school a little while with pleurosis. When I came back you asked me what was the matter. I said I had pleurosis—you thought I said Blue Roses. That's what you always called me after that!

JIM: I hope you didn't mind.

LAURA: Oh, no—I liked it. You see, I wasn't acquainted with many—people. . . .

110 JIM: As I remember you sort of stuck by yourself.

LAURA: I—I—never had much luck at—making friends.

JIM: I don't see why you wouldn't.

LAURA: Well, I—started out badly.

JIM: You mean being—

115 LAURA: Yes, it sort of—stood between me—

JIM: You shouldn't have let it!

LAURA: I know, but it did, and—

JIM: You were shy with people!

LAURA: I tried not to be but never could—

120 **JIM:** Overcome it?

LAURA: No, I—I never could!

JIM: I guess being shy is something you have to work out of kind of gradually.

LAURA: *(sorrowfully)* Yes—I guess it—

JIM: Takes time!

125 **LAURA:** Yes—

JIM: People are not so dreadful when you know them. That's what you have to remember! And everybody has problems, not just you, but practically everybody has got some problems. You think of yourself as having the only problems, as being the only one who is disappointed. But just look around you and you will see lots of people as disappointed as you are. For instance, I hoped when I was going to high school that I would be further along at this time, six years later, than I am now—You remember that wonderful write-up I had in *The Torch?*

LAURA: Yes! *(She rises and crosses to table.)*

JIM: It said I was bound to succeed in anything I went into! *(Laura returns with the annual.)* Holy Jeez! *The Torch!* (He accepts it reverently. They smile across it with mutual wonder. Laura crouches beside him and they begin to turn through it. Laura's shyness is dissolving in his warmth.)*

LAURA: Here you are in *Pirates of Penzance!*

130 **JIM:** *(wistfully)* I sang the baritone lead in that operetta.

LAURA: *(rapidly)* So—*beautifully!*

JIM: *(protesting)* Aw—

LAURA: Yes, yes—beautifully—beautifully!

JIM: You heard me?

135 **LAURA:** All three times!

JIM: No!

LAURA: Yes!

JIM: All three performances?

LAURA: *(looking down)* Yes.

140 **JIM:** Why?

LAURA: I—wanted to ask you to—autograph my program.

JIM: Why didn't you ask me to?

LAURA: You were always surrounded by your own friends so much that I never had a chance to.

JIM: You should have just—

145 **LAURA:** Well, I—thought you might think I was—

JIM: Thought I might think you was—what?

LAURA: Oh—

JIM: *(with reflective relish)* I was beleaguered by females in those days.

LAURA: You were terribly popular!

150 JIM: Yeah—

LAURA: You had such a—friendly way—

JIM: I was spoiled in high school.

LAURA: Everybody—liked you!

JIM: Including you?

155 LAURA: I—yes, I—I did, too—*(She gently closes the book in her lap.)*

JIM: Well, well, well!—Give me that program, Laura. *(She hands it to him. He signs it with a flourish.)* There you are—better late than never!

LAURA: Oh, I—what a—surprise!

JIM: My signature isn't worth very much right now. But some day—maybe— it will increase in value! Being disappointed is one thing and being discouraged is something else. I am disappointed but I'm not discouraged. I'm twenty-three years old. How old are you?

LAURA: I'll be twenty-four in June.

160 JIM: That's not old age!

LAURA: No, but—

JIM: You finished high school?

LAURA: *(with difficulty)* I didn't go back.

JIM: You mean you dropped out?

165 LAURA: I made bad grades in my final examinations. *(She rises and replaces the book and the program. Her voice strained.)* How is—Emily Meisenbach getting along?

JIM: Oh, that kraut-head!

LAURA: Why do you call her that?

JIM: That's what she was.

LAURA: You're not still—going with her?

170 JIM: I never see her.

LAURA: It said in the Personal Section that you were—engaged!

JIM: I know, but I wasn't impressed by that—propaganda!

LAURA: It wasn't—the truth?

JIM: Only in Emily's optimistic opinion!

175 LAURA: Oh—

(Legend: "What Have You Done Since High School?")

Jim lights a cigarette and leans indolently back on his elbows smiling at Laura with a warmth and charm which light her inwardly with altar candles. She remains by the table and turns in her hands a piece of glass to cover her tumult.

JIM: *(after several reflective puffs on a cigarette)* What have you done since high school? *(She seems not to hear him.)* Huh? *(Laura looks up.)* I said what have you done since high school, Laura?

LAURA: Nothing much.

JIM: You must have been doing something these six long years.

LAURA: Yes.

180 **JIM:** Well, then, such as what?

LAURA: I took a business course at business college—

JIM: How did that work out?

LAURA: Well, not very—well—I had to drop out, it gave me—indigestion—

Jim laughs gently.

JIM: What are you doing now?

185 **LAURA:** I don't do anything—much. Oh, please don't think I sit around doing nothing! My glass collection takes up a good deal of my time. Glass is something you have to take good care of.

JIM: What did you say—about glass?

LAURA: Collection I said—I have one—*(She clears her throat and turns away again, acutely shy.)*

JIM: *(abruptly)* You know what I judge to be the trouble with you? Inferiority complex! Know what that is? That's what they call it when someone low-rates himself! I understand it because I had it, too. Although my case was not so aggravated as yours seems to be. I had it until I took up public speaking, developed my voice, and learned that I had an aptitude for science. Before that time I never thought of myself as being outstanding in any way whatsoever! Now I've never made a regular study of it, but I have a friend who says I can analyze people better than doctors that make a profession of it. I don't claim that to be necessarily true, but I can sure guess a person's psychology, Laura! *(Takes out his gum.)* Excuse me, Laura. I always take it out when the flavor is gone. I'll use this scrap of paper to wrap it in. I know how it is to get it stuck on a shoe. Yep—that's what I judge to be your principal trouble. A lack of confidence in yourself as a person. You don't have the proper amount of faith in yourself. I'm basing that fact on a number of your remarks and also on certain observations I've made. For instance that clumping you thought was so awful in high school. You say that you even dreaded to walk into class. You see what you did? You dropped out of school, you gave up an education because of a clump, which as far as I know was practically non-existent! A little physical defect is what you have. Hardly noticeable even! Magnified thousands of times by imagination! You know what my strong advice to you is? Think of yourself as *superior* in some way!

LAURA: In what way would I think?

190 **JIM:** Why, man alive, Laura! Just look about you a little. What do you see? A world full of common people! All of 'em born and all of 'em going to die! Which of them has one-tenth of your good points! Or mine! Or anyone else's, as far as that goes—Gosh! Everybody excels in some one thing. Some in many! *(Unconsciously glances at himself in the mirror.)* All you've got to do is discover in *what!* Take me, for instance. *(He adjusts his tie at the mirror.)* My interest happens to lie in electro-dynamics. I'm taking a course in radio engineering at night school, Laura, on top of a

fairly responsible job at the warehouse. I'm taking that course and studying public speaking.

Laura: Ohhhh.

Jim: Because I believe in the future of television! *(Turning back to her.)* I
wish to be ready to go up right along with it. Therefore I'm planning to get
in on the ground floor. In fact, I've already made the right connections and
all that remains is for the industry itself to get underway! Full steam—*(His
eyes are starry.)* Knowledge—Zzzzzp! *Money*—Zzzzzp!—*Power!* That's
the cycle democracy is built on! *(His attitude is convincingly dynamic.
Laura stares at him, even her shyness eclipsed in her absolute wonder.
He suddenly grins.)* I guess you think I think a lot of myself!

Laura: No—o-o-o, I—

Jim: Now how about you? Isn't there something you take more interest in
than anything else?

195 **Laura:** Well, I do—as I said—have my—glass collection—

A peal of girlish laughter from the kitchen.

Jim: I'm not right sure I know what you're talking about. What kind of
glass is it?

Laura: Little articles of it, they're ornaments mostly! Most of them are little animals made out of glass, the tiniest little animals in the world.
Mother calls them a glass menagerie! Here's an example of one, if you'd
like to see it! This one is one of the oldest. It's nearly thirteen. *(He
stretches out his hand.) (Music: "The Glass Menagerie.")* Oh, be careful—if you breathe, it breaks!

Jim: I'd better not take it. I'm pretty clumsy with things.

Laura: Go on, I trust you with him! *(Places it in his palm.)* There now—
you're holding him gently! Hold him over the light, he loves the light! You
see how the light shines through him?

200 **Jim:** It sure does shine!

Laura: I shouldn't be partial, but he is my favorite one.

Jim: What kind of a thing is this one supposed to be?

Laura: Haven't you noticed the single horn on his forehead?

Jim: A unicorn, huh?

205 **Laura:** Mmm-hmmm!

Jim: Unicorns, aren't they extinct in the modern world?

Laura: I know!

Jim: Poor little fellow, he must feel sort of lonesome.

Laura: *(smiling)* Well, if he does he doesn't complain about it. He stays on
a shelf with some horses that don't have horns and all of them seem to get
along nicely together.

210 **Jim:** How do you know?

Laura: *(lightly)* I haven't heard any arguments among them!

Jim: *(grinning)* No arguments, huh? Well, that's a pretty good sign! Where
shall I set him?

LAURA: Put him on the table. They all like a change of scenery once in a while!

JIM: *(stretching)* Well, well, well, well—Look how big my shadow is when I stretch!

215 **LAURA:** Oh, oh, yes—it stretches across the ceiling!

JIM: *(crossing to door)* I think it's stopped raining. *(Opens fire-escape door.)* Where does the music come from?

LAURA: From the Paradise Dance Hall across the alley.

JIM: How about cutting the rug a little, Miss Wingfield?

LAURA: Oh, I—

220 **JIM:** Or is your program filled up? Let me have a look at it. *(Grasps imaginary card.)* Why, every dance is taken! I'll just have to scratch some out. *(Waltz Music: "La Golondrina.")* Ahhh, a waltz! *(He executes some sweeping turns by himself, then holds his arms toward Laura.)*

LAURA: *(breathlessly)* I—can't dance!

JIM: There you go, that inferiority stuff!

LAURA: I've never danced in my life!

JIM: Come on, try!

225 **LAURA:** Oh, but I'd step on you!

JIM: I'm not made out of glass.

LAURA: How—how—how do we start?

JIM: Just leave it to me. You hold your arms out a little.

LAURA: Like this?

230 **JIM:** A little bit higher. Right. Now don't tighten up, that's the main thing about it—relax.

LAURA: *(laughing breathlessly)* It's hard not to.

JIM: Okay.

LAURA: I'm afraid you can't budge me.

JIM: What do you bet I can't? *(He swings her into motion.)*

235 **LAURA:** Goodness, yes, you can!

JIM: Let yourself go, now, Laura, just let yourself go.

LAURA: I'm—

JIM: Come on!

LAURA: Trying!

240 **JIM:** Not so stiff—Easy does it!

LAURA: I know but I'm—

JIM: Loosen th' backbone! There now, that's a lot better.

LAURA: Am I?

JIM: Lots, lots better! *(He moves her about the room in a clumsy waltz.)*

245 **LAURA:** Oh, my!

JIM: Ha-ha!

LAURA: Goodness, yes you can!

JIM: Ha-ha-ha! *(They suddenly bump into the table, Jim stops.)* What did we hit on?

LAURA: Table.

250 **JIM:** Did something fall off it? I think—

LAURA: Yes.

JIM: I hope that it wasn't the little glass horse with the horn!

LAURA: Yes.

JIM: Aw, aw, aw. Is it broken?

255 **LAURA:** Now it is just like all the other horses.

JIM: It's lost its—

LAURA: Horn! It doesn't matter. Maybe it's a blessing in disguise.

JIM: You'll never forgive me. I bet that that was your favorite piece of glass.

LAURA: I don't have favorites much. It's no tragedy, Freckles. Glass breaks so easily. No matter how careful you are. The traffic jars the shelves and things fall off them.

260 **JIM:** Still I'm awfully sorry that I was the cause.

LAURA: *(smiling)* I'll just imagine he had an operation. The horn was removed to make him feel less—freakish! *(They both laugh.)* Now he will feel more at home with the other horses, the ones that don't have horns . . .

JIM: Ha-ha, that's very funny! *(Suddenly serious.)* I'm glad to see that you have a sense of humor. You know—you're—well—very different! Surprisingly different from anyone else I know! *(His voice becomes soft and hesitant with a genuine feeling.)* Do you mind me telling you that? *(Laura is abashed beyond speech.)* You make me feel sort of—I don't know how to put it! I'm usually pretty good at expressing things, but—This is something that I don't know how to say! *(Laura touches her throat and clears it— turns the broken unicorn in her hands.) (Even softer.)* Has anyone ever told you that you were pretty? *(Pause: Music.) (Laura looks up slowly, with wonder, and shakes her head.)* Well, you are! In a very different way from anyone else. And all the nicer because of the difference, too. *(His voice becomes low and husky. Laura turns away, nearly faint with the novelty of her emotions.)* I wish you were my sister. I'd teach you to have some confidence in yourself. The different people are not like other people, but being different is nothing to be ashamed of. Because other people are not such wonderful people. They're one hundred times one thousand. You're one times one! They walk all over the earth. You just stay here. They're common as—weeds, but—you—well, you're—*Blue Roses!*

(Image On Screen: Blue Roses.)

(Music Changes.)

LAURA: But blue is wrong for—roses . . .

JIM: It's right for you—You're—pretty!

265 **LAURA:** In what respect am I pretty?

JIM: In all respects—believe me! Your eyes—your hair—are pretty! Your hands are pretty! *(He catches hold of her hand.)* You think I'm making this up because I'm invited to dinner and have to be nice. Oh, I could do that! I could put on an act for you, Laura, and say lots of things without being very sincere. But this time I am. I'm talking to you sincerely. I happened to notice you had this inferiority complex that keeps you from feeling comfortable with people. Somebody needs to build your confidence up and make you proud instead of shy and turning away and—blushing—Somebody ought to—ought to—*kiss you, Laura! (His hand slips slowly up her arm to her shoulder.) (Music Swells Tumultuously.) (He suddenly turns her about and kisses her on the lips. When he releases her Laura sinks on the sofa with a bright, dazed look. Jim backs away and fishes in his pocket for a cigarette.) (Legend On Screen: "Souvenir.")* Stumble-john! *(He lights the cigarette, avoiding her look. There is a peal of girlish laughter from Amanda in the kitchen. Laura slowly raises and opens her hand. It still contains the little broken glass animal. She looks at it with a tender, bewildered expression.)* Stumble-john! I shouldn't have done that—That was way off the beam. You don't smoke, do you? *(She looks up, smiling, not hearing the question. He sits beside her a little gingerly. She looks at him speechlessly—waiting. He coughs decorously and moves a little farther aside as he considers the situation and senses her feelings, dimly, with perturbation. Gently.)* Would you—care for a—mint? *(She doesn't seem to hear him but her look grows brighter even.)* Peppermint—Life Saver? My pocket's a regular drug store—wherever I go . . . *(He pops a mint in his mouth. Then gulps and decides to make a clean breast of it. He speaks slowly and gingerly.)* Laura, you know, if I had a sister like you, I'd do the same thing as Tom, I'd bring out fellows—introduce her to them. The right type of boys of a type to—appreciate her. Only—well—he made a mistake about me. Maybe I've got no call to be saying this. That may not have been the idea in having me over. But what if it was? There's nothing wrong about that. The only trouble is that in my case—I'm not in a situation to do the right thing. I can't take down your number and say I'll phone. I can't call up next week and—ask for a date. I thought I had better explain the situation in case you misunderstood it and—hurt your feelings. . . . *(Pause. Slowly, very slowly, Laura's look changes, her eyes returning slowly from his to the ornament in her palm.)*

Amanda utters another gay laugh in the kitchen.

LAURA: *(faintly)* You—won't—call again?

JIM: No, Laura. I can't. *(He rises from the sofa.)* As I was just explaining, I've—got strings on me, Laura, I've—been going steady! I go out all the time with a girl named Betty. She's a home-girl like you, and Catholic, and Irish, and in a great many ways we—get along fine. I met her last summer on a moonlight boat trip up the river to Alton, on the *Majestic.* Well—right away from the start it was—love! *(Legend: Love!) (Laura sways slightly forward and grips the arm of the sofa. He fails to notice, now enrapt in his own comfortable being.)* Being in love has made a new man of me! *(Leaning stiffly forward, clutching the arm of the sofa, Laura struggles visibly with her storm. But Jim is oblivious, she is a long way off.)* The power of love is really pretty tremendous! Love is something that—changes the whole world, Laura! *(The storm abates a little and Laura leans back. He notices her again.)* It happened that Betty's aunt took sick, she got a wire and had to go to Centralia. So Tom—when he asked me to dinner—I naturally just accepted the invitation, not knowing that you—that he—that I—*(He stops awkwardly.)* Huh—I'm a stumble-john! *(He flops back on the sofa. The holy candles in the altar of Laura's face have been snuffed out! There is a look of almost infinite desolation. Jim glances at her uneasily.)* I wish that you would—say something. *(She bites her lip which was trembling and then bravely smiles. She opens her hand again on the broken glass ornament. Then she gently takes his hand and raises it level with her own. She carefully places the unicorn in the palm of his hand, then pushes his fingers closed upon it.)* What are you—doing that for? You want me to have him?—Laura? *(She nods.)* What for?

LAURA: A—souvenir . . .

She rises unsteadily and crouches beside the victrola to wind it up.

(Legend On Screen: "Things Have A Way Of Turning Out So Badly.")

(Or Image: "Gentleman Caller Waving Good-bye!—Gaily.")

At this moment Amanda rushes brightly back in the front room. She bears a pitcher of fruit punch in an old-fashioned cut-glass pitcher and a plate of macaroons. The plate has a gold border and poppies painted on it.

270 AMANDA: Well, well, well! Isn't the air delightful after the shower? I've made you children a little liquid refreshment. *(Turns gaily to the gentleman caller.)* Jim, do you know that song about lemonade?
　　　　　"Lemonade, lemonade
　　　　　Made in the shade and stirred with a spade—
　　　　　Good enough for any old maid!"

JIM: *(uneasily)* Ha-ha! No—I never heard it.

AMANDA: Why, Laura! You look so serious!

JIM: We were having a serious conversation.

AMANDA: Good! Now you're better acquainted!

275 JIM: *(uncertainly)* Ha-ha! Yes.

AMANDA: You modern young people are much more serious-minded than my generation. I was so gay as a girl!

JIM: You haven't changed, Mrs. Wingfield.

AMANDA: Tonight I'm rejuvenated! The gaiety of the occasion, Mr. O'Connor! *(She tosses her head with a peal of laughter. Spills lemonade.)* Oooo! I'm baptizing myself!

JIM: Here—let me—

280 AMANDA: *(setting the pitcher down)* There now. I discovered we had some maraschino cherries. I dumped them in, juice and all!

JIM: You shouldn't have gone to that trouble. Mrs. Wingfield.

AMANDA: Trouble, trouble? Why it was loads of fun! Didn't you hear me cutting up in the kitchen? I bet your ears were burning! I told Tom how outdone with him I was for keeping you to himself so long a time! He should have brought you over much, much sooner! Well, now that you've found your way, I want you to be a very frequent caller! Not just occasional but all the time. Oh, we're going to have a lot of gay times together! I see them coming! Mmm, just breathe that air! So fresh, and the moon's so pretty! I'll skip back out—I know where my place is when young folks are having a—serious conversation!

JIM: Oh, don't go out, Mrs. Wingfield. The fact of the matter is I've got to be going.

AMANDA: Going, now? You're joking! Why, it's only the shank of the evening, Mr. O'Connor!

285 JIM: Well, you know how it is.

AMANDA: You mean you're a young workingman and have to keep workingmen's hours. We'll let you off early tonight. But only on the condition that next time you stay later. What's the best night for you? Isn't Saturday night the best night for you workingmen?

JIM: I have a couple of time-clocks to punch, Mrs. Wingfield. One at morning, another one at night!

AMANDA: My, but you *are* ambitious! You work at night, too?

JIM: No, Ma'am, not work but—Betty! (*He crosses deliberately to pick up his hat. The band at the Paradise Dance Hall goes into a tender waltz.*)

290 AMANDA: Betty? Betty? Who's Betty! (*There is an ominous cracking sound in the sky.*)

JIM: Oh, just a girl. The girl I go steady with! (*He smiles charmingly. The sky falls.*)

(*Legend: "The Sky Falls."*)

AMANDA: (*a long-drawn exhalation*) Ohhhh . . . Is it a serious romance, Mr. O'Connor?

JIM: We're going to be married the second Sunday in June.

AMANDA: Ohhhh—how nice! Tom didn't mention that you were engaged to be married.

295 JIM: The cat's not out of the bag at the warehouse yet. You know how they are. They call you Romeo and stuff like that. (*He stops at the oval mirror to put on his hat. He carefully shapes the brim and the crown to give a discreetly dashing effect.*) It's been a wonderful evening, Mrs. Wingfield. I guess this is what they mean by Southern hospitality.

AMANDA: It really wasn't anything at all.

JIM: I hope it don't seem like I'm rushing off. But I promised Betty I'd pick her up at the Wabash depot, an' by the time I get my jalopy down there her train'll be in. Some women are pretty upset if you keep 'em waiting.

AMANDA: Yes, I know—The tyranny of women! (*Extends her hand.*) Goodbye, Mr. O'Connor. I wish you luck—and happiness—and success! All three of them, and so does Laura!—Don't you, Laura?

LAURA: Yes!

300 JIM: *(taking her hand)* Goodbye, Laura. I'm certainly going to treasure that souvenir. And don't you forget the good advice I gave you. *(Raises his voice to a cheery shout.)* So long, Shakespeare! Thanks again, ladies— Good night!

He grins and ducks jauntily out.

Still bravely grimacing, Amanda closes the door on the gentleman caller. Then she turns back to the room with a puzzled expression. She and Laura don't dare to face each other. Laura crouches beside the victrola to wind it.

AMANDA: *(faintly)* Things have a way of turning out so badly. I don't believe that I would play the victrola. Well, well—well—Our gentleman caller was engaged to be married! Tom!

TOM: *(from back)* Yes, Mother?

AMANDA: Come in here a minute. I want to tell you something awfully funny.

TOM: *(enters with macaroon and a glass of the lemonade)* Has the gentleman caller gotten away already?

305 AMANDA: The gentleman caller has made an early departure. What a wonderful joke you played on us!

TOM: How do you mean?

AMANDA: You didn't mention that he was engaged to be married.

TOM: Jim? Engaged?

AMANDA: That's what he just informed us.

310 TOM: I'll be jiggered! I didn't know about that.

AMANDA: That seems very peculiar.

TOM: What's peculiar about it?

AMANDA: Didn't you call him your best friend down at the warehouse?

TOM: He is, but how did I know?

315 AMANDA: It seems extremely peculiar that you wouldn't know your best friend was going to be married!

TOM: The warehouse is where I work, not where I know things about people!

AMANDA: You don't know things anywhere! You live in a dream; you manufacture illusions! *(He crosses to door.)* Where are you going?

TOM: I'm going to the movies.

AMANDA: That's right, now that you've had us make such fools of ourselves. The effort, the preparations, all the expense! The new floor lamp, the rug, the clothes for Laura! All for what? To entertain some other girl's fiancé! Go to the movies, go! Don't think about us, a mother deserted, an unmarried sister who's crippled and has no job! Don't let anything interfere with your selfish pleasure! Just go, go, go—to the movies!

320 TOM: All right, I will! The more you shout about my selfishness to me the quicker I'll go, and I won't go to the movies!

AMANDA: Go, then! Then go to the moon—you selfish dreamer!

Tom smashes his glass on the floor. He plunges out on the fire-escape, slamming the door. Laura screams—cut by door.

Dance-hall music up. Tom goes to the rail and grips it desperately, lifting his face in the chill white moonlight penetrating the narrow abyss of the alley.

(Legend On Screen: "And So Good-bye . . .")

Tom's closing speech is timed with the interior pantomime. The interior scene is played as though viewed through sound-proof glass. Amanda appears to be making a comforting speech to Laura who is huddled upon the sofa. Now that we cannot hear the mother's speech, her silliness is gone and she has dignity and tragic beauty. Laura's dark hair hides her face until at the end of the speech she lifts it to smile at her mother. Amanda's gestures are slow and graceful, almost dancelike, as she comforts the daughter. At the end of her speech she glances a moment at the father's picture—then withdraws through the portieres. At close of Tom's speech, Laura blows out the candles, ending the play.

TOM: I didn't go to the moon, I went much further—for time is the longest distance between two places—Not long after that I was fired for writing a poem on the lid of a shoe-box. I left Saint Louis. I descended the steps of this fire-escape for a last time and followed, from then on, in my father's footsteps, attempting to find in motion what was lost in space—I traveled around a great deal. The cities swept about me like dead leaves, leaves that were brightly colored but torn away from the branches. I would have stopped, but was pursued by something. It always came upon me unawares, taking me altogether by surprise. Perhaps it was a familiar bit of music. Perhaps it was only a piece of transparent glass. Perhaps I am walking along a street at night, in some strange city, before I have found companions. I pass the lighted window of a shop where perfume is sold. The window is filled with pieces of colored glass, tiny transparent bottles in delicate colors, like bits of a shattered rainbow. Then all at once my sister touches my shoulder. I turn around and look into her eyes . . . Oh, Laura, Laura, I tried to leave you behind me, but I am more faithful than I intended to be! I reach for a cigarette, I cross the street, I run into the movies or a bar, I buy a drink, I speak to the nearest stranger—anything that can blow your candles out! *(Laura bends over the candles.)*—for nowadays the world is lit by lightning! Blow out your candles, Laura—and so goodbye . . .

She blows the candles out.

(The Scene Dissolves.)

The Timeless World of a Play

Tennessee Williams

Carson McCullers concludes one of her lyric poems with the line: "Time, the endless idiot, runs screaming 'round the world." It is this continual rush of time, so violent that it appears to be screaming, that deprives our actual lives of so much dignity and meaning, and it is, perhaps more than anything else, the *arrest of time* which has taken place in a completed work of art that gives to certain plays their feeling of depth and significance. In the London notices of *Death of a Salesman* a certain notoriously skeptical critic made the remark that Willy Loman was the sort of man that almost any member of the audience would have kicked out of an office had he applied for a job or detained one for conversation about his troubles. The remark itself possibly holds some truth. But the implication that Willy Loman is consequently a character with whom we have no reason to concern ourselves in drama, reveals a strikingly false conception of what plays are. Contemplation is something that exists outside of time, and so is the tragic sense. Even in the actual world of commerce, there exists in some persons a sensibility to the unfortunate situations of others, a capacity for concern and compassion, surviving from a more tender period of life outside the present whirling wire-cage of business activity. Facing Willy Loman across an office desk, meeting his nervous glance and hearing his querulous voice, we would be very likely to glance at our wrist watch and our schedule of other appointments. We would not kick him out of the office, no, but we would certainly *ease* him out with more expedition than Willy had feebly hoped for. But suppose there had been no wrist watch or office clock, and suppose there had *not* been the schedule of pressing appointments, and suppose that we were not actually facing Willy across a desk—and facing a person is *not* the best way to *see* him!—suppose, in other words, that the meeting with Willy Loman had somehow occurred within a world *outside* of time. Then I think we would receive him with concern and kindness and even with respect. If the world of a play did not offer us this occasion to view its characters under that special condition of a *world without time,* then, indeed, the characters and occurrences of drama would become equally pointless, equally trivial, as corresponding meetings and happenings in life.

The classic tragedies of Greece had tremendous nobility. The actors wore great masks, movements were formal, dance-like, and the speeches had an epic quality which doubtless were as removed from the normal conversation of their contemporary society as they seem today. Yet they did not seem false to the Greek audiences: the magnitude of the events and the passions aroused by them did not seem ridiculously out of proportion to common experience. And I wonder if this was not because the Greek audiences knew, instinctively or by training, that the created world of a play is removed from that element which makes people *little* and their emotions fairly inconsequential.

Great sculpture often follows the lines of the human body: yet the repose of great sculpture suddenly transmutes those human lines to something that has an absoluteness, a purity, a beauty, which would not be possible in a living mobile form.

A play may be violent, full of motion: yet it has that special kind of repose which allows contemplation and produces the climate in which tragic importance is a possible thing, provided that certain modern conditions are met.

In actual existence the moments of love are succeeded by the moments of satiety and sleep. The sincere remark is followed by a cynical distrust. Truth is fragmentary, at best: we love and betray each other not in quite the same breath but in two breaths that occur in fairly close sequence. But the fact that passion occurred in *passing,* that it then declined into a more familiar sense of indifference, should not be regarded as proof of its inconsequence. And this is the very truth that drama wishes to bring us. . . .

Whether or not we admit it to ourselves, we are all haunted by a truly awful sense of impermanence. I have always had a particularly keen sense of this at New York cocktail parties, and perhaps that is why I drink the martinis almost as fast as I can snatch them from the tray. This sense is the febrile thing that hangs in the air. Horror of insincerity, of *not meaning,* overhangs these affairs like the cloud of cigarette smoke and the hectic chatter. This horror is the only thing, almost, that is left unsaid at such functions. All social functions involving a group of people not intimately known to each other are always under this shadow. They are almost always (in an unconscious way) like that last dinner of the condemned: where steak or turkey, whatever the doomed man wants, is served in his cell as a mockingly cruel reminder of what the great-big-little-transitory world had to offer.

In a play, time is arrested in the sense of being confined. By a sort of legerdemain, events are made to remain *events,* rather than being reduced so quickly to mere *occurrences.* The audience can sit back in a comforting dusk to watch a world which is flooded with light and in which emotion and action have a dimension and dignity that they would likewise have in real existence, if only the shattering intrusion of time could be locked out.

About their lives people ought to remember that when they are finished, everything in them will be contained in a marvelous state of repose which is the same as that which they unconsciously admired in drama. The rush is temporary. The great and only possible dignity of man lies in his power deliberately to choose certain moral values by which to live as steadfastly as if he, too, like a character in a play, were immured against the corrupting rush of time. Snatching the eternal out of the desperately fleeting is the great magic trick of human existence. As far as we know, as far as there exists any kind of empiric evidence, there is no way to beat the game of *being* against *non-being,* in which non-being is the predestined victor on realistic levels.

Yet plays in the tragic tradition offer us a view of certain moral values in violent juxtaposition. Because we do not participate, except as spectators, we can view them clearly, within the limits of our emotional equipment.

These people on the stage do not return our looks. We do not have to answer their questions nor make any sign of being in company with them, nor do we have to compete with their virtues nor resist their offenses. All at once, for this reason, we are able to *see* them! Our hearts are wrung by recognition and pity, so that the dusky shell of the auditorium where we are gathered anonymously together is flooded with an almost liquid warmth of unchecked human sympathies, relieved of self-consciousness, allowed to function. . . .

Men pity and love each other more deeply than they permit themselves to know. The moment after the phone has been hung up, the hand reaches for a scratch pad and scrawls a notation: "Funeral Tuesday at five, Church of the Holy Redeemer, don't forget flowers." And the same hand is only a little shakier than usual as it reaches, some minutes later, for a highball glass that will pour a stupefaction over the kindled nerves. Fear and evasion are the two little beasts that chase each other's tails in the revolving wire-cage of our nervous world. They distract us from feeling too much about things. Time rushes toward us with its hospital tray of infinitely varied narcotics, even while it is preparing us for its inevitably fatal operation. . . .

So successfully have we disguised from ourselves the intensity of our own feelings, the sensibility of our own hearts, that plays in the tragic tradition have begun to seem untrue. For a couple of hours we may surrender ourselves to a world of fiercely illuminated values in conflict, but when the stage is covered and the auditorium lighted, almost immediately there is a recoil of disbelief. "Well, well!" we say as we shuffle back up the aisle, while the play dwindles behind us with the sudden perspective of an early Chirico painting. By the time we have arrived at Sardi's, if not as soon as we pass beneath the marquee, we have convinced ourselves once more that life has as little resemblance to the curiously stirring and meaningful occurrences on the stage as a jingle has to an elegy of Rilke.

This modern condition of his theatre audience is something that an author must know in advance. The diminishing influence of life's destroyer, time, must be somehow worked into the context of his play. Perhaps it is a certain foolery, a certain distortion toward the grotesque, which will solve the problem for him. Perhaps it is only restraint, putting a mute on the strings that would like to break all bounds. But almost surely, unless he contrives in some way to relate the dimensions of his tragedy to the dimensions of a world in which time is *included*—he will be left among his magnificent debris on a dark stage, muttering to himself: "Those fools. . . . "

And if they could hear him above the clatter of tongues, glasses, chinaware, and silver, they would give him this answer: "But you have shown us a world not ravaged by time. We admire your innocence. But we have seen our photographs, past and present. Yesterday evening we passed our first wife on the street. We smiled as we spoke but we didn't really see her! It's too bad, but we know what is true and not true, and at 3 A.M. your disgrace will be in print!"

Lorraine Hansberry, 1930–1965

A Raisin in the Sun (1959)

CHARACTERS

(in order of appearance)

Ruth Younger
Walter Lee Younger
Travis Younger
Beneatha Younger
Lena Younger
Joseph Asagai
George Murchison
Mrs. Johnson
Karl Lindner
Bobo
Moving Men

Act I

SCENE ONE

The Younger living room would be a comfortable and well-ordered room if it were not for a number of indestructible contradictions to this state of being. Its furnishings are typical and undistinguished and their primary feature now is that they have clearly had to accommodate the living of too many people for too many years—and they are tired. Still, we can see that at some time, a time probably no longer remembered by the family (except perhaps for Mama), the furnishings of this room were actually selected with care and love and even hope—and brought to this apartment and arranged with taste and pride.

That was a long time ago. Now the once loved pattern of the couch upholstery has to fight to show itself from under acres of crocheted doilies and couch covers which have themselves finally come to be more important than the upholstery. And here a table or a chair has been moved to disguise the worn places in the carpet; but the carpet has fought back by showing its weariness, with depressing uniformity, elsewhere on its surface.

Weariness has, in fact, won in this room. Everything has been polished, washed, sat on, used, scrubbed too often. All pretenses but living itself have long since vanished from the very atmosphere of this room.

Moreover, a section of this room, for it is not really a room unto itself, though the landlord's lease would make it seem so, slopes backward to provide a small kitchen area, where the family prepares the meals that are eaten in the living room proper, which must also serve as dining room. The single window that has been provided for these "two" rooms is located in this kitchen area. The sole natural light the family may enjoy in the course of a day is only that which fights its way through this little window.

At left, a door leads to a bedroom which is shared by Mama and her daughter, Beneatha. At right, opposite, is a second room (which in the beginning of the life of this apartment was probably a breakfast room) which serves as a bedroom for Walter and his wife, Ruth.

Time: Sometime between World War II and the present.

Place: Chicago's Southside.

At Rise: It is morning dark in the living room. Travis is asleep on the make-down bed at center. An alarm clock sounds from within the bedroom at right, and presently Ruth enters from that room and closes the door behind her. She crosses sleepily toward the window. As she passes her sleeping son she reaches down and shakes him a little. At the window she raises the shade and a dusky Southside morning light comes in feebly. She fills a pot with water and puts it on to boil. She calls to the boy, between yawns, in a slightly muffled voice.

Ruth is about thirty. We can see that she was a pretty girl, even exceptionally so, but now it is apparent that life has been little that she expected, and disappointment has already begun to hang in her face. In a few years, before thirty-five even, she will be known among her people as a "settled woman."

She crosses to her son and gives him a good, final, rousing shake.

RUTH: Come on now, boy, it's seven thirty! *(Her son sits up at last, in a stupor of sleepiness.)* I say hurry up, Travis! You ain't the only person in the world got to use a bathroom! *(The child, a sturdy, handsome little boy of ten or eleven, drags himself out of the bed and almost blindly takes his towels and "today's clothes" from drawers and a closet and goes out to the bathroom, which is in an outside hall and which is shared by another family or families on the same floor. Ruth crosses to the bedroom door at right and opens it and calls in to her husband.)* Walter Lee! . . . It's after seven thirty! Lemme see you do some waking up in there now! *(She waits.)* You better get up from there, man! It's after seven thirty I tell you. *(She waits again.)* All right, you just go ahead and lay there and next thing you know Travis be finished and Mr. Johnson'll be in there and you'll be fussing and cussing round here like a madman! And be late too! *(She waits, at the end of patience.)* Walter Lee—it's time for you to GET UP!

She waits another second and then starts to go into the bedroom, but is apparently satisfied that her husband has begun to get up. She stops, pulls the door to, and returns to the kitchen area. She wipes her face with a moist cloth and runs her fingers through her sleep-disheveled hair in a vain effort and ties an apron around her housecoat. The bedroom door at right opens and her husband stands in the doorway in his pajamas, which are rumpled and mismated. He is a lean, intense young man in his middle thirties, inclined to quick nervous movements and erratic speech habits— and always in his voice there is a quality of indictment.

WALTER: Is he out yet?

RUTH: What you mean *out?* He ain't hardly got in there good yet.

WALTER: *(wandering in, still more oriented to sleep than to a new day)* Well, what was you doing all that yelling for if I can't even get in there yet? *(Stopping and thinking.)* Check coming today?

5 **RUTH:** They *said* Saturday and this is just Friday and I hopes to God you ain't going to get up here first thing this morning and start talking to me 'bout no money—'cause I 'bout don't want to hear it.

WALTER: Something the matter with you this morning?

RUTH: No—I'm just sleepy as the devil. What kind of eggs you want?

WALTER: Not scrambled. *(Ruth starts to scramble eggs.)* Paper come? *(Ruth points impatiently to the rolled up* Tribune *on the table, and he gets it and spreads it out and vaguely reads the front page.)* Set off another bomb yesterday.

RUTH: *(Maximum indifference.)* Did they?

10 **WALTER:** *(Looking up.)* What's the matter with you?

RUTH: Ain't nothing the matter with me. And don't keep asking me that this morning.

WALTER: Ain't nobody bothering you. *(Reading the news of the day absently again.)* Say Colonel McCormick is sick.

RUTH: *(Affecting tea-party interest.)* Is he now? Poor thing.

WALTER: *(Sighing and looking at his watch.)* Oh, me. *(He waits.)* Now what is that boy doing in that bathroom all this time? He just going to have to start getting up earlier. I can't be being late to work on account of him fooling around in there.

15 **RUTH:** *(Turning on him.)* Oh, no he ain't going to be getting up no earlier no such thing! It ain't his fault that he can't get to bed no earlier nights 'cause he got a bunch of crazy good-for-nothing clowns sitting up running their mouths in what is supposed to be his bedroom after ten o'clock at night . . .

WALTER: That's what you mad about, ain't it? The things I want to talk about with my friends just couldn't be important in your mind, could they?

He rises and finds a cigarette in her handbag on the table and crosses to the little window and looks out, smoking and deeply enjoying this first one.

RUTH: (*Almost matter of factly, a complaint too automatic to deserve emphasis.*) Why you always got to smoke before you eat in the morning?

WALTER: (*At the window.*) Just look at 'em down there . . . Running and racing to work . . . (*He turns and faces his wife and watches her a moment at the stove, and then, suddenly.*) You look young this morning, baby.

RUTH: (*Indifferently.*) Yeah?

20 **WALTER:** Just for a second—stirring them eggs. Just for a second it was—you looked real young again. (*He reaches for her; she crosses away. Then, drily.*) It's gone now—you look like yourself again!

RUTH: Man, if you don't shut up and leave me alone.

WALTER: (*Looking out to the street again.*) First thing a man ought to learn in life is not to make love to no colored woman first thing in the morning. You all some eeeevil people at eight o'clock in the morning.

Travis appears in the hall doorway, almost fully dressed and quite wide awake now, his towels and pajamas across his shoulders. He opens the door and signals for his father to make the bathroom in a hurry.

TRAVIS: (*Watching the bathroom.*) Daddy, come on! (*Walter gets his bathroom utensils and flies out to the bathroom.*)

RUTH: Sit down and have your breakfast, Travis.

25 **TRAVIS:** Mama, this is Friday. (*Gleefully.*) Check coming tomorrow, huh?

RUTH: You get your mind off money and eat your breakfast.

TRAVIS: (*Eating.*) This is the morning we supposed to bring the fifty cents to school.

RUTH: Well, I ain't got no fifty cents this morning.

TRAVIS: Teacher say we have to.

30 **RUTH:** I don't care what teacher say. I ain't got it. Eat your breakfast, Travis.

TRAVIS: I *am* eating.

RUTH: Hush up now and just eat!

The boy gives her an exasperated look for her lack of understanding, and eats grudgingly.

TRAVIS: You think Grandmama would have it?

RUTH: No! And I want you to stop asking your grandmother for money, you hear me?

35 **TRAVIS:** (*Outraged.*) Gaaaleee! I don't ask her, she just gimme it sometimes!

RUTH: Travis Willard Younger—I got too much on me this morning to be—

TRAVIS: Maybe Daddy—

RUTH: *Travis!*

The boy hushes abruptly. They are both quiet and tense for several seconds.

TRAVIS: *(Presently.)* Could I maybe go carry some groceries in front of the supermarket for a little while after school then?

40 **RUTH:** Just hush, I said. *(Travis jabs his spoon into his cereal bowl viciously, and rests his head in anger upon his fists.)* If you through eating, you can get over there and make up your bed.

The boy obeys stiffly and crosses the room, almost mechanically, to the bed and more or less folds the bedding into a heap, then angrily gets his books and cap.

TRAVIS: *(Sulking and standing apart from her unnaturally.)* I'm gone.

RUTH: *(Looking up from the stove to inspect him automatically.)* Come here. *(He crosses to her and she studies his head.)* If you don't take this comb and fix this here head, you better! *(Travis puts down his books with a great sigh of oppression, and crosses to the mirror. His mother mutters under her breath about his "slubbornness.")* 'Bout to march out of here with that head looking just like chickens slept in it! I just don't know where you get your slubborn ways . . . And get your jacket, too. Looks chilly out this morning.

TRAVIS: *(With conspicuously brushed hair and jacket.)* I'm gone.

RUTH: Get carfare and milk money—*(Waving one finger.)*—and not a single penny for no caps, you hear me?

45 **TRAVIS:** *(With sullen politeness.)* Yes'm.

He turns in outrage to leave. His mother watches after him as in his frustration he approaches the door almost comically. When she speaks to him, her voice has become a very gentle tease.

RUTH: *(Mocking; as she thinks he would say it.)* Oh, Mama makes me so mad sometimes, I don't know what to do! *(She waits and continues to his back as he stands stock-still in front of the door.)* I wouldn't kiss that woman good-bye for nothing in this world this morning! *(The boy finally turns around and rolls his eyes at her, knowing the mood has changed and he is vindicated; he does not, however, move toward her yet.)* Not for nothing in this world! *(She finally laughs aloud at him and holds out her arms to him and we see that it is a way between them, very old and practiced. He crosses to her and allows her to embrace him warmly but keeps his face fixed with masculine rigidity. She holds him back from her presently and looks at him and runs her fingers over the features of his face. With utter gentleness—.)* Now—whose little old angry man are you?

TRAVIS: *(The masculinity and gruffness start to fade at last.)* Aw gaalee— Mama . . .

RUTH: *(Mimicking.)* Aw—gaaaaalleeeee, Mama! *(She pushes him, with rough playfulness and finality, toward the door.)* Get on out of here or you going to be late.

TRAVIS: *(In the face of love, new aggressiveness.)* Mama, could I *please* go carry groceries?

50 **RUTH:** Honey, it's starting to get so cold evenings.

WALTER: *(Coming in from the bathroom and drawing a make-believe gun from a make-believe holster and shooting at his son.)* What is it he wants to do?

RUTH: Go carry groceries after school at the supermarket.

WALTER: Well, let him go . . .

TRAVIS: *(Quickly, to the ally.)* I *have* to—she won't gimme the fifty cents . . .

55 **WALTER:** *(To his wife only.)* Why not?

RUTH: *(Simply, and with flavor.)* 'Cause we don't have it.

WALTER: *(To Ruth only.)* What you tell the boy things like that for? *(Reaching down into his pants with a rather important gesture.)* Here, son—

He hands the boy the coin, but his eyes are directed to his wife's. Travis takes the money happily.

TRAVIS: Thanks, Daddy.

He starts out. Ruth watches both of them with murder in her eyes. Walter stands and stares back at her with defiance, and suddenly reaches into his pocket again on an afterthought.

WALTER: *(Without even looking at his son, still staring hard at his wife.)* In fact, here's another fifty cents . . . Buy yourself some fruit today—or take a taxicab to school or something!

60 **TRAVIS:** Whoopee—

He leaps up and clasps his father around the middle with his legs, and they face each other in mutual appreciation; slowly Walter Lee peeks around the boy to catch the violent rays from his wife's eyes and draws his head back as if shot.

WALTER: You better get down now—and get to school, man.

TRAVIS: *(At the door.)* O.K. Good-bye.

He exits.

WALTER: *(After him, pointing with pride.)* That's *my* boy. *(She looks at him in disgust and turns back to her work.)* You know what I was thinking 'bout in the bathroom this morning?

RUTH: No.

65 **WALTER:** How come you always try to be so pleasant!

RUTH: What is there to be pleasant 'bout!

WALTER: You want to know what I was thinking 'bout in the bathroom or not!

RUTH: I know what you thinking 'bout.

WALTER: *(Ignoring her.)* 'Bout what me and Willy Harris was talking about last night.

70 **RUTH:** *(Immediately—a refrain.)* Willy Harris is a good-for-nothing loud-mouth.

WALTER: Anybody who talks to me has got to be a good-for-nothing loud-mouth, ain't he? And what you know about who is just a good-for-nothing loudmouth? Charlie Atkins was just a "good-for-nothing loudmouth" too, wasn't he! When he wanted me to go in the dry-cleaning business with him. And now—he's grossing a hundred thousand a year. A hundred thou-sand dollars a year! You still call *him* a loudmouth!

RUTH: *(Bitterly.)* Oh, Walter Lee . . .

She folds her head on her arms over the table.

WALTER: *(Rising and coming to her and standing over her.)* You tired, ain't you? Tired of everything. Me, the boy, the way we live—this beat-up hole—everything. Ain't you? *(She doesn't look up, doesn't answer.)* So tired—moaning and groaning all the time, but you wouldn't do nothing to help, would you? You couldn't be on my side that long for nothing, could you?

RUTH: Walter, please leave me alone.

75 **WALTER:** A man needs for a woman to back him up . . .

RUTH: Walter—

WALTER: Mama would listen to you. You know she listen to you more than she do me and Bennie. She think more of you. All you have to do is just sit down with her when you drinking your coffee one morning and talking 'bout things like you do and—*(He sits down beside her and demon-strates graphically what he thinks her methods and tone should be.)*—you just sip your coffee, see, and say easy like that you been thinking 'bout that deal Walter Lee is so interested in, 'bout the store and all, and sip some more coffee, like what you saying ain't really that important to you—And the next thing you know, she be listening good and asking you questions and when I come home—I can tell her the details. This ain't no fly-by-night proposition, baby. I mean we figured it out, me and Willy and Bobo.

RUTH: *(With a frown.)* Bobo?

WALTER: Yeah. You see, this little liquor store we got in mind cost seventy-five thousand and we figured the initial investment on the place be 'bout thirty thousand, see. That be ten thousand each. Course, there's a couple of hundred you got to pay so's you don't spend your life just waiting for them clowns to let your license get approved—

80 **RUTH:** You mean graft?

WALTER: *(Frowning impatiently.)* Don't call it that. See there, that just goes to show you what women understand about the world. Baby, don't *nothing* happen for you in this world 'less you pay *somebody* off!

RUTH: Walter, leave me alone! *(She raises her head and stares at him vig-orously—then says, more quietly.)* Eat your eggs, they gonna be cold.

WALTER: *(Straightening up from her and looking off.)* That's it. There you are. Man say to his woman: I got me a dream. His woman say: Eat your eggs. *(Sadly, but gaining in power.)* Man say: I got to take hold of this here world, baby! And a woman will say: Eat your eggs and go to work. *(Passionately now.)* Man say: I got to change my life, I'm choking to death, baby! And his woman say—*(In utter anguish as he brings his fists down on his thighs.)*—Your eggs is getting cold!

RUTH: *(Softly.)* Walter, that ain't none of our money.

85 **WALTER:**   *(Not listening at all or even looking at her.)* This morning, I was lookin' in the mirror and thinking about it . . . I'm thirty-five years old, I been married eleven years and I got a boy who sleeps in the living room— *(Very, very quietly.)*—and all I got to give him is stories about how rich white people live . . .

RUTH: Eat your eggs, Walter.

WALTER: *(Slams the table and jumps up.)*—DAMN MY EGGS—DAMN ALL THE EGGS THAT EVER WAS!

RUTH: Then go to work.

WALTER: *(Looking up at her.)* See—I'm trying to talk to you 'bout my-self—*(Shaking his head with the repetition.)*—and all you can say is eat them eggs and go to work.

90 **RUTH:**   *(Wearily.)* Honey, you never say nothing new. I listen to you every day, every night and every morning, and you never say nothing new. *(Shrugging.)* So you would rather *be* Mr. Arnold than be his chauffeur. So—I would *rather* be living in Buckingham Palace.

WALTER: That is just what is wrong with the colored woman in this world . . . Don't understand about building their men up and making 'em feel like they somebody. Like they can do something.

RUTH: *(Drily, but to hurt.)* There *are* colored men who do things.

WALTER: No thanks to the colored woman.

RUTH: Well, being a colored woman, I guess I can't help myself none.

She rises and gets the ironing board and sets it up and attacks a huge pile of rough-dried clothes, sprinkling them in preparation for the ironing and then rolling them into tight fat balls.

95 **WALTER:**   *(Mumbling.)* We one group of men tied to a race of women with small minds!

His sister Beneatha enters. She is about twenty, as slim and intense as her brother. She is not as pretty as her sister-in-law, but her lean, almost intel-lectual face has a handsomeness of its own. She wears a bright-red flannel nightie, and her thick hair stands wildly about her head. Her speech is a mixture of many things; it is different from the rest of the family's insofar as education has permeated her sense of English—and perhaps the Mid-west rather than the South has finally—at last—won out in her inflection; but not altogether, because over all of it is a soft slurring and transformed use of vowels which is the decided influence of the Southside. She passes through the room without looking at either Ruth or Walter and goes to the outside door and looks, a little blindly, out to the bathroom. She sees that it has been lost to the Johnsons. She closes the door with a sleepy vengeance and crosses to the table and sits down a little defeated.

BENEATHA: I am going to start timing those people.

WALTER: You should get up earlier.

BENEATHA: *(Her face in her hands. She is still fighting the urge to go back to bed.)* Really—would you suggest dawn? Where's the paper?

WALTER: *(Pushing the paper across the table to her as he studies her almost clinically, as though he has never seen her before.)* You a horrible-looking chick at this hour.

100 **BENEATHA:** *(Drily.)* Good morning, everybody.

WALTER: *(Senselessly.)* How is school coming?

BENEATHA: *(In the same spirit.)* Lovely. Lovely. And you know, biology is the greatest. *(Looking up at him.)* I dissected something that looked just like you yesterday.

WALTER: I just wondered if you've made up your mind and everything.

BENEATHA: *(Gaining in sharpness and impatience.)* And what did I answer yesterday morning—and the day before that?

105 **RUTH:** *(From the ironing board, like someone disinterested and old.)* Don't be so nasty, Bennie.

BENEATHA: *(Still to her brother.)* And the day before that and the day before that!

WALTER: *(Defensively.)* I'm interested in you. Something wrong with that? Ain't many girls who decide—

WALTER AND BENEATHA: *(In unison.)*—"to be a doctor."

Silence.

WALTER: Have we figured out yet just exactly how much medical school is going to cost?

110 **RUTH:** Walter Lee, why don't you leave that girl alone and get out of here to work?

BENEATHA: *(Exits to the bathroom and bangs on the door.)* Come on out of there, please!

She comes back into the room.

WALTER: *(Looking at his sister intently.)* You know the check is coming tomorrow.

BENEATHA: *(Turning on him with a sharpness all her own.)* That money belongs to Mama, Walter, and it's for her to decide how she wants to use it. I don't care if she wants to buy a house or a rocket ship or just nail it up somewhere and look at it. It's hers. Not ours—*hers.*

WALTER: *(Bitterly.)* Now ain't that fine! You just got your mother's interest at heart, ain't you, girl? You such a nice girl—but if Mama got that money she can always take a few thousand and help you through school too—can't she?

115 **BENEATHA:**   I have never asked anyone around here to do anything for me!

WALTER: No! And the line between asking and just accepting when the time comes is big and wide—ain't it!

BENEATHA: *(With fury.)* What do you want from me, Brother—that I quit school or just drop dead, which!

WALTER: I don't want nothing but for you to stop acting holy 'round here. Me and Ruth done made some sacrifices for you—why can't you do something for the family?

RUTH: Walter, don't be dragging me in it.

120 **WALTER:**   You are in it—Don't you get up and go work in somebody's kitchen for the last three years to help put clothes on her back?

RUTH: Oh, Walter—that's not fair . . .

WALTER: It ain't that nobody expects you to get on your knees and say thank you, Brother; thank you, Ruth; thank you, Mama—and thank you, Travis, for wearing the same pair of shoes for two semesters—

BENEATHA: *(Dropping to her knees.)* Well—I *do*—all right?—thank everybody! And forgive me for ever wanting to be anything at all! *(Pursuing him on her knees across the floor.)* FORGIVE ME, FORGIVE ME, FORGIVE ME!

RUTH: Please stop it! Your mama'll hear you.

125 **WALTER:**   Who the hell told you you had to be a doctor? If you so crazy 'bout messing 'round with sick people—then go be a nurse like other women— or just get married and be quiet . . .

BENEATHA: Well—you finally got it said . . . It took you three years but you finally got it said. Walter, give up; leave me alone—it's Mama's money.

WALTER: *He was my father, too!*

BENEATHA: So what? He was mine, too—and Travis' grandfather—but the insurance money belongs to Mama. Picking on me is not going to make her give it to you to invest in any liquor stores—*(Underbreath, dropping into a chair.)*—and I for one say, God bless Mama for that!

WALTER: *(To Ruth.)* See—did you hear? Did you hear!

130 **RUTH:**   Honey, please go to work.

WALTER: Nobody in this house is ever going to understand me.

BENEATHA: Because you're a nut.

WALTER: Who's a nut?

BENEATHA: You—you are a nut. Thee is mad, boy.

135 **WALTER:**   *(Looking at his wife and his sister from the door, very sadly.)* The world's most backward race of people, and that's a fact.

BENEATHA: *(Turning slowly in her chair.)* And then there are all those prophets who would lead us out of the wilderness—*(Walter slams out of the house.)*—into the swamps!

RUTH: Bennie, why you always gotta be pickin' on your brother? Can't you be a little sweeter sometimes? *(Door opens, Walter walks in. He fumbles with his cap, starts to speak, clears his throat, looks everywhere but at Ruth. Finally:)*

WALTER: *(To Ruth.)* I need some money for carfare.

RUTH: *(Looks at him, then warms; teasing, but tenderly.)* Fifty cents? *(She goes to her bag and gets money.)* Here—take a taxi!

Walter exits. Mama enters. She is a woman in her early sixties, full-bodied and strong. She is one of those women of a certain grace and beauty who wear it so unobtrusively that it takes a while to notice. Her dark-brown face is surrounded by the total whiteness of her hair, and, being a woman who has adjusted to many things in life and overcome many more, her face is full of strength. She has, we can see, wit and faith of a kind that keeps her eyes lit and full of interest and expectancy. She is, in a word, a beautiful woman. Her bearing is perhaps most like the noble bearing of the women of the Hereros of Southwest Africa—rather as if she imagines that as she walks she still bears a basket or a vessel upon her head. Her speech, on the other hand, is as careless as her carriage is precise—she is inclined to slur everything—but her voice is perhaps not so much quiet as simply soft.

140 **MAMA:** Who that 'round here slamming doors at this hour?

She crosses through the room, goes to the window, opens it, and brings in a feeble little plant growing doggedly in a small pot on the window sill. She feels the dirt and puts it back out.

RUTH: That was Walter Lee. He and Bennie was at it again.

MAMA: My children and they tempers. Lord, if this little old plant don't get more sun than it's been getting it ain't never going to see spring again. *(She turns from the window.)* What's the matter with you this morning, Ruth? You looks right peaked. You aiming to iron all them things? Leave some for me. I'll get to 'em this afternoon. Bennie honey, it's too drafty for you to be sitting 'round half dressed. Where's your robe?

BENEATHA: In the cleaners.

MAMA: Well, go get mine and put it on.

145 **BENEATHA:** I'm not cold, Mama, honest.

MAMA: I know—but you so thin . . .

BENEATHA: *(Irritably.)* Mama, I'm not cold.

MAMA: *(Seeing the make-down bed as Travis has left it.)* Lord have mercy, look at that poor bed. Bless his heart—he tries, don't he?

She moves to the bed Travis has sloppily made up.

RUTH: No—he don't half try at all 'cause he knows you going to come along behind him and fix everything. That's just how come he don't know how to do nothing right now—you done spoiled that boy so.

150 **MAMA:** *(Folding bedding.)* Well—he's a little boy. Ain't supposed to know 'bout housekeeping. My baby, that's what he is. What you fix for his breakfast this morning?

RUTH: *(Angrily.)* I feed my son, Lena!

MAMA: I ain't meddling—(*Underbreath; busy-bodyish.*) I just noticed all last week he had cold cereal, and when it starts getting this chilly in the fall a child ought to have some hot grits or something when he goes out in the cold—

RUTH: (*Furious.*) I gave him hot oats—is that all right!

MAMA: I ain't meddling. (*Pause.*) Put a lot of nice butter on it? (*Ruth shoots her an angry look and does not reply.*) He likes lots of butter.

155 RUTH: (*Exasperated.*) Lena—

MAMA: (*To Beneatha. Mama is inclined to wander conversationally sometimes.*) What was you and your brother fussing 'bout this morning?

BENEATHA: It's not important, Mama.

She gets up and goes to look out at the bathroom, which is apparently free, and she picks up her towels and rushes out.

MAMA: What was they fighting about?

RUTH: Now you know as well as I do.

160 MAMA: (*Shaking her head.*) Brother still worrying hisself sick about that money?

RUTH: You know he is.

MAMA: You had breakfast?

RUTH: Some coffee.

MAMA: Girl, you better start eating and looking after yourself better. You almost thin as Travis.

165 RUTH: Lena—

MAMA: Un-hunh?

RUTH: What are you going to do with it?

MAMA: Now don't you start, child. It's too early in the morning to be talking about money. It ain't Christian.

RUTH: It's just that he got his heart set on that store—

170 MAMA: You mean that liquor store that Willy Harris want him to invest in?

RUTH: Yes—

MAMA: We ain't no business people, Ruth. We just plain working folks.

RUTH: Ain't nobody business people till they go into business. Walter Lee say colored people ain't never going to start getting ahead till they start gambling on some different kinds of things in the world—investments and things.

MAMA: What done got into you, girl? Walter Lee done finally sold you on investing.

175 RUTH: No, Mama, something is happening between Walter and me. I don't know what it is—but he needs something—something I can't give him any more. He needs this chance, Lena.

MAMA: (*Frowning deeply.*) But liquor, honey—

RUTH: Well—like Walter say—I spec people going to always be drinking themselves some liquor.

MAMA: Well—whether they drinks it or not ain't none of my business. But whether I go into business selling it to 'em *is,* and I don't want that on my ledger this late in life. *(Stopping suddenly and studying her daughter-in-law.)* Ruth Younger, what's the matter with you today? You look like you could fall over right there.

RUTH: I'm tired.

180 **MAMA:** Then you better stay home from work today.

RUTH: I can't stay home. She'd be calling up the agency and screaming at them, "My girl didn't come in today—send me somebody! My girl didn't come in!" Oh, she just have a fit . . .

MAMA: Well, let her have it. I'll just call her up and say you got the flu—

RUTH: *(Laughing.)* Why the flu?

MAMA: 'Cause it sounds respectable to 'em. Something white people get, too. They know 'bout the flu. Otherwise they think you been cut up or something when you tell 'em you sick.

185 **RUTH:** I got to go in. We need the money.

MAMA: Somebody would of thought my children done all but starved to death the way they talk about money here late. Child, we got a great big old check coming tomorrow.

RUTH: *(Sincerely, but also self-righteously.)* Now that's your money. It ain't got nothing to do with me. We all feel like that—Walter and Bennie and me—even Travis.

MAMA: *(Thoughtfully, and suddenly very far away.)* Ten thousand dollars—

RUTH: Sure is wonderful.

190 **MAMA:** Ten thousand dollars.

RUTH: You know what you should do, Miss Lena? You should take yourself a trip somewhere. To Europe or South America or someplace—

MAMA: *(Throwing up her hands at the thought.)* Oh, child!

RUTH: I'm serious. Just pack up and leave! Go on away and enjoy yourself some. Forget about the family and have yourself a ball for once in your life—

MAMA: *(Drily.)* You sound like I'm just about ready to die. Who'd go with me? What I look like wandering 'round Europe by myself?

195 **RUTH:** Shoot—these here rich white women do it all the time. They don't think nothing of packing up they suitcases and piling on one of them big steamships and—swoosh!—they gone, child.

MAMA: Something always told me I wasn't no rich white woman.

RUTH: Well—what are you going to do with it then?

MAMA: I ain't rightly decided. *(Thinking. She speaks now with emphasis.)* Some of it got to be put away for Beneatha and her schoolin'—and ain't nothing going to touch that part of it. Nothing. *(She waits several seconds, trying to make up her mind about something, and looks at Ruth a little tentatively before going on.)* Been thinking that we maybe could meet the notes on a little old two-story somewhere, with a yard where Travis could play in the summertime, if we use part of the insurance for a down payment and everybody kind of pitch in. I could maybe take on a little day work again, few days a week—

RUTH: *(Studying her mother-in-law furtively and concentrating on her ironing, anxious to encourage without seeming to.)* Well, Lord knows, we've put enough rent into this here rat trap to pay for four houses by now . . .

200 **MAMA:** *(Looking up at the words "rat trap" and then looking around and leaning back and sighing—in a suddenly reflective mood—)* "Rat trap"—yes, that's all it is. *(Smiling.)* I remember just as well the day me and Big Walter moved in here. Hadn't been married but two weeks and wasn't planning on living here no more than a year. *(She shakes her head at the dissolved dream.)* We was going to set away, little by little, don't you know, and buy a little place out in Morgan Park. We had even picked out the house. *(Chuckling a little.)* Looks right dumpy today. But Lord, child, you should know all the dreams I had 'bout buying that house and fixing it up and making me a little garden in the back—*(She waits and stops smiling.)* And didn't none of it happen.

Dropping her hands in a futile gesture.

RUTH: *(Keeps her head down, ironing.)* Yes, life can be a barrel of disappointments, sometimes.

MAMA: Honey, Big Walter would come in here some nights back then and slump down on the coach there and just look at the rug, and look at me and look at the rug and then back at me—and I'd know he was down then . . . really down. *(After a second very long and thoughtful pause; she is seeing back to times that only she can see.)* And then, Lord, when I lost that baby—little Claude—I almost thought I was going to lose Big Walter too. Oh, that man grieved hisself! He was one man to love his children.

RUTH: Ain't nothin' can tear at you like losin' your baby.

MAMA: I guess that's how come that man finally worked hisself to death like he done. Like he was fighting his own war with this here world that took his baby from him.

205 **RUTH:** He sure was a fine man, all right. I always liked Mr. Younger.

MAMA: Crazy 'bout his children! God knows there was plenty wrong with Walter Younger—hard-headed, mean, kind of wild with women—plenty wrong with him. But he sure loved his children. Always wanted them to have something—be something. That's where Brother gets all these notions, I reckon. Big Walter used to say, he'd get right wet in the eyes sometimes, lean his head back with the water standing in his eyes and say, "Seem like God didn't see fit to give the black man nothing but dreams—but He did give us children to make them dreams seem worth while." *(She smiles.)* He could talk like that, don't you know.

RUTH: Yes, he sure could. He was a good man, Mr. Younger.

MAMA: Yes, a fine man—just couldn't never catch up with his dreams, that's all.

Beneatha comes in, brushing her hair and looking up to the ceiling, where the sound of a vacuum cleaner has started up.

BENEATHA: What could be so dirty on that woman's rugs that she has to vacuum them every single day?

210 **RUTH:** I wish certain young women 'round here who I could name would take inspiration about certain rugs in a certain apartment I could also mention.

BENEATHA: *(Shrugging.)* How much cleaning can a house need, for Christ's sakes.

MAMA: *(Not liking the Lord's name used thus.)* Bennie!

RUTH: Just listen to her—just listen!

BENEATHA: Oh, God!

215 **MAMA:** If you use the Lord's name just one more time—

BENEATHA: *(A bit of a whine.)* Oh, Mama—

RUTH: Fresh—just fresh as salt, this girl!

BENEATHA: *(Drily.)* Well—if the salt loses its savor—

MAMA: Now that will do. I just ain't going to have you 'round here reciting the scriptures in vain—you hear me?

220 **BENEATHA:** How did I manage to get on everybody's wrong side by just walking into a room?

RUTH: If you weren't so fresh—

BENEATHA: Ruth, I'm twenty years old.

MAMA: What time you be home from school today?

BENEATHA: Kind of late. *(With enthusiasm.)* Madeline is going to start my guitar lessons today.

Mama and Ruth look up with the same expression.

225 **MAMA:** Your *what* kind of lessons?

BENEATHA: Guitar.

RUTH: Oh, Father!

MAMA: How come you done taken it in your mind to learn to play the guitar?

BENEATHA: I just want to, that's all.

230 **MAMA:** *(Smiling.)* Lord, child, don't you know what to get tired of this now—like you got tired of that little do with yourself? How long it going to be before you play-acting group you joined last year? *(Looking at Ruth.)* And what was it the year before that?

RUTH: The horseback-riding club for which she bought that fifty-five-dollar riding habit that's been hanging in the closet ever since!

MAMA: *(To Beneatha.)* Why you got to flit so from one thing to another, baby?

MAMA: *(Sharply.)* I just want to learn to play the guitar. Is there anything wrong with that?

MAMA: Ain't nobody trying to stop you. I just wonders sometimes why you has to flit so from one thing to another all the time. You ain't never done nothing with all that camera equipment you brought home—

235 **BENEATHA:** I don't flit! I—I experiment with different forms of expression—

RUTH: Like riding a horse?

BENEATHA: —People have to express themselves one way or another.

MAMA: What is it you want to express?

BENEATHA: *(Angrily.)* Me! *(Mama and Ruth look at each other and burst into raucous laughter.)* Don't worry—I don't expect you to understand.

240 **MAMA:** *(To change the subject.)* Who you going out with tomorrow night?

BENEATHA: *(With displeasure.)* George Murchison again.

MAMA: *(Pleased.)* Oh—you getting a little sweet on him?

RUTH: You ask me, this child ain't sweet on nobody but herself—*(Under breath.)* Express herself!

They laugh.

BENEATHA: Oh—I like George all right, Mama. I mean I like him enough to go out with him and stuff, but—

245 **RUTH:** *(For devilment.)* What does *and stuff* mean?

BENEATHA: Mind your own business.

MAMA: Stop picking at her now, Ruth. *(She chuckles—then a suspicious sudden look at her daughter as she turns in her chair for emphasis.)* What DOES it mean?

BENEATHA: *(Wearily.)* Oh, I just mean I couldn't ever really be serious about George. He's—he's so shallow.

RUTH: Shallow—what do you mean he's shallow? He's *Rich!*

250 **MAMA:** Hush, Ruth.

BENEATHA: I know he's rich. He knows he's rich, too.

RUTH: Well—what other qualities a man got to have to satisfy you, little girl?

BENEATHA: You wouldn't even begin to understand. Anybody who married Walter could not possibly understand.

MAMA: *(Outraged.)* What kind of way is that to talk about your brother?

255 **BENEATHA:** Brother is a flip—let's face it.

MAMA: *(To Ruth, helplessly.)* What's a flip?

RUTH: *(Glad to add kindling.)* She's saying he's crazy.

BENEATHA: Not crazy. Brother isn't really crazy yet—he—he's an elaborate neurotic.

MAMA: Hush your mouth!

260 **BENEATHA:** As for George. Well. George looks good—he's got a beautiful car and he takes me to nice places and, as my sister-in-law says, he is probably the richest boy I will ever get to know and I even like him sometimes—but if the Youngers are sitting around waiting to see if their little

Bennie is going to tie up the family with the Murchisons, they are wasting their time.

RUTH: You mean you wouldn't marry George Murchison if he asked you someday? That pretty, rich thing? Honey, I knew you was odd—

BENEATHA: No I would not marry him if all I felt for him was what I feel now. Besides, George's family wouldn't really like it.

MAMA: Why not?

BENEATHA: Oh, Mama—The Murchisons are honest-to-God-real-*live*-rich colored people, and the only people in the world who are more snobbish than rich white people are rich colored people. I thought everybody knew that. I've met Mrs. Murchison. She's a scene!

265 **MAMA:** You must not dislike people 'cause they well off, honey.

BENEATHA: Why not? It makes just as much sense as disliking people 'cause they are poor, and lots of people do that.

RUTH: *(A wisdom-of-the-ages manner. To Mama.)* Well, she'll get over some of this—

BENEATHA: Get over it? What are you talking about, Ruth? Listen, I'm going to be a doctor. I'm not worried about who I'm going to marry yet—if I ever get married.

MAMA AND RUTH: *If!*

270 **MAMA:** Now, Bennie—

BENEATHA: Oh, I probably will . . . but first I'm going to be a doctor, and George, for one, still thinks that's pretty funny. I couldn't be bothered with that. I am going to be a doctor and everybody around here better understand that!

MAMA: *(Kindly.)* 'Course you going to be a doctor, honey, God willing.

BENEATHA: *(Drily.)* God hasn't got a thing to do with it.

MAMA: Beneatha—that just wasn't necessary.

275 **BENEATHA:** Well—neither is God. I get sick of hearing about God.

MAMA: Beneatha!

BENEATHA: I mean it! I'm just tired of hearing about God all the time. What has He got to do with anything? Does he pay tuition?

MAMA: You 'bout to get your fresh little jaw slapped!

RUTH: That's just what she needs, all right!

280 **BENEATHA:** Why? Why can't I say what I want to around here, like everybody else?

MAMA: It don't sound nice for a young girl to say things like that—you wasn't brought up that way. Me and your father went to trouble to get you and Brother to church every Sunday.

BENEATHA: Mama, you don't understand. It's all a matter of ideas, and God is just one idea I don't accept. It's not important. I am not going out and be immoral or commit crimes because I don't believe in God. I don't even think about it. It's just that I get tired of Him getting credit for all the things the human race achieves through its own stubborn effort. There simply is no blasted God—there is only man and it is *he* who makes miracles!

Mama absorbs this speech, studies her daughter and rises slowly and crosses to Beneatha and slaps her powerfully across the face. After, there is only silence and the daughter drops her eyes from her mother's face, and Mama is very tall before her.

MAMA: Now—you say after me, in my mother's house there is still God. *(There is a long pause and Beneatha stares at the floor wordlessly. Mama repeats the phrase with precision and cool emotion.)* In my mother's house there is still God.

BENEATHA: In my mother's house there is still God.

A long pause.

285 **MAMA:** *(Walking away from Beneatha, too disturbed for triumphant posture. Stopping and turning back to her daughter.)* There are some ideas we ain't going to have in this house. Not long as I am at the head of this family.

BENEATHA: Yes, ma'am.

Mama walks out of the room.

RUTH: *(Almost gently, with profound understanding.)* You think you a woman, Bennie—but you still a little girl. What you did was childish—so you got treated like a child.

BENEATHA: I see. *(Quietly.)* I also see that everybody thinks it's all right for Mama to be a tyrant. But all the tyranny in the world will never put a God in the heavens!

She picks up her books and goes out. Pause.

RUTH: *(Goes to Mama's door.)* She said she was sorry.

290 **MAMA:** *(Coming out, going to her plant.)* They frightens me, Ruth. My children.

RUTH: You got good children, Lena. They just a little off sometimes—but they're good.

MAMA: No—there's something come down between me and them that don't let us understand each other and I don't know what it is. One done almost lost his mind thinking 'bout money all the time and the other done commence to talk about things I can't seem to understand in no form or fashion. What is it that's changing, Ruth.

RUTH: *(Soothingly, older than her years.)* Now . . . you taking it all too seriously. You just got strong-willed children and it takes a strong woman like you to keep 'em in hand.

MAMA: *(Looking at her plant and sprinkling a little water on it.)* They spirited all right, my children. Got to admit they got spirit—Bennie and Walter. Like this little old plant that ain't never had enough sunshine or nothing—and look at it . . .

She has her back to Ruth, who has had to stop ironing and lean against something and put the back of her hand to her forehead.

295 **RUTH:** *(Trying to keep Mama from noticing.)* You . . . sure . . . loves that little old thing, don't you? . . .

MAMA: Well, I always wanted me a garden like I used to see sometimes at the back of the houses down home. This plant is close as I ever got to having one. *(She looks out of the window as she replaces the plant.)* Lord, ain't nothing as dreary as the view from this window on a dreary day, is there? Why ain't you singing this morning, Ruth? Sing that "No Ways Tired." That song always lifts me up so—*(She turns at last to see that Ruth has slipped quietly to the floor, in a state of semiconsciousness.)* Ruth! Ruth honey—what's the matter with you . . . Ruth!

CURTAIN

SCENE TWO

It is the following morning; a Saturday morning, and house cleaning is in progress at the Youngers. Furniture has been shoved hither and yon and Mama is giving the kitchen-area walls a washing down. Beneatha, in dungarees, with a handkerchief tied around her face, is spraying insecticide into the cracks in the walls. As they work, the radio is on and a Southside disk-jockey program is inappropriately filling the house with a rather exotic saxophone blues. Travis, the sole idle one, is leaning on his arms, looking out of the window.

TRAVIS: Grandmama, that stuff Bennie is using smells awful. Can I go downstairs, please?

MAMA: Did you get all them chores done already? I ain't seen you doing much.

TRAVIS: Yes'm—finished early. Where did Mama go this morning?

300 **MAMA:** *(Looking at Beneatha.)* She had to go on a little errand.

The phone rings. Beneatha runs to answer it and reaches it before Walter, who has entered from bedroom.

TRAVIS: Where?

MAMA: To tend to her business.

BENEATHA: Haylo . . . *(Disappointed.)* Yes, he is. *(She tosses the phone to Walter, who barely catches it.)* It's Willie Harris again.

WALTER: *(As privately as possible under Mama's gaze.)* Hello, Willie. Did you get the papers from the lawyer? . . . No, not yet. I told you the mailman doesn't get here till ten-thirty . . . No, I'll come there . . . Yeah! Right away. *(He hangs up and goes for his coat.)*

305 **BENEATHA:** Brother, where did Ruth go?

WALTER: *(As he exits.)* How should I know!

TRAVIS: Aw come on, Grandma. Can I go outside?

MAMA: Oh, I guess so. You stay right in front of the house, though, and keep a good lookout for the postman.

TRAVIS: Yes'm. *(He darts into bedroom for stickball and bat, reenters, and sees Beneatha on her knees spraying under sofa with behind upraised. He edges closer to the target, takes aim, and lets her have it. She screams.)* Leave them poor little cockroaches alone, they ain't bothering you none! *(He runs as she swings the spraygun at him viciously and playfully.)* Grandma! Grandma!

310 **MAMA:** Look out there, girl, before you be spilling some of that stuff on that child!

TRAVIS: *(Safely behind the bastion of Mama.)* That's right—look out, now! *(He exits.)*

BENEATHA: *(Drily.)* I can't imagine that it would hurt him—it has never hurt the roaches.

MAMA: Well, little boys' hides ain't as tough as Southside roaches. You better get over there behind the bureau. I seen one marching out of there like Napoleon yesterday.

BENEATHA: There's really only one way to get rid of them, Mama—

315 **MAMA:** How?

BENEATHA: Set fire to this building! Mama, where did Ruth go?

MAMA: *(Looking at her with meaning.)* To the doctor, I think.

BENEATHA: The doctor? What's the matter. *(They exchange glances.)* You don't think—

MAMA: *(With her sense of drama.)* Now I ain't saying what I think. But I ain't never been wrong 'bout a woman neither.

The phone rings.

320 **BENEATHA:** *(At the phone.)* Hay-lo . . . *(Pause, and a moment of recognition.)* Well—when did you get back! . . . And how was it? . . . Of course I've missed you—in my way . . . This morning? No . . . house cleaning and all that and Mama hates it if I let people come over when the house is like this . . . You *have?* Well, that's different . . . What is it—Oh, what the hell, come on over . . . Right, see you then. *Arrivederci.*

She hangs up.

MAMA: *(Who has listened vigorously, as is her habit.)* Who is that you inviting over here with this house looking like this? You ain't got the pride you was born with!

BENEATHA: Asagai doesn't care how houses look, Mama—he's an intellectual.

MAMA: *Who?*

BENEATHA: Asagai—Joseph Asagai. He's an African boy I met on campus. He's been studying in Canada all summer.

325 **MAMA:** What's his name?

BENEATHA: Asagai, Joseph. As-sah-guy . . . He's from Nigeria.

MAMA: Oh, that's the little country that was founded by slaves way back . . .

BENEATHA: No, Mama—that's Liberia.

MAMA: I don't think I never met no African before.

330 **BENEATHA:**   Well, do me a favor and don't ask him a whole lot of ignorant questions about Africans. I mean, do they wear clothes and all that—

MAMA: Well, now, I guess if you think we so ignorant 'round here maybe you shouldn't bring your friends here—

BENEATHA: It's just that people ask such crazy things. All anyone seems to know about when it comes to Africa is Tarzan—

MAMA: *(Indignantly.)* Why should I know anything about Africa?

BENEATHA: Why do you give money at church for the missionary work?

335 **MAMA:**   Well, that's to help save people.

BENEATHA: You mean save them from *heathenism*—

MAMA: *(Innocently.)* Yes.

BENEATHA: I'm afraid they need more salvation from the British and the French.

Ruth comes in forlornly and pulls off her coat with dejection. They both turn to look at her.

RUTH: *(Dispiritedly.)* Well, I guess from all the happy faces—everybody knows.

340 **BENEATHA:**   You pregnant?

MAMA: Lord have mercy, I sure hope it's a little old girl. Travis ought to have a sister.

Beneatha and Ruth give her a hopeless look for this grandmotherly enthusiasm.

BENEATHA: How far along are you?

RUTH: Two months.

BENEATHA: Did you mean to? I mean did you plan it or was it an accident?

345 **MAMA:**   What do you know about planning or not planning?

BENEATHA: Oh, Mama.

RUTH: *(Wearily.)* She's twenty years old, Lena.

BENEATHA: Did you plan it, Ruth?

RUTH: Mind your own business.

350 **BENEATHA:**   It is my business—where is he going to live, on the *roof?* *(There is silence following the remark as the three women react to the sense of it.)* Gee—I didn't mean that, Ruth, honest. Gee, I don't feel like that at all. I—I think it is wonderful.

RUTH: *(Dully.)* Wonderful.

BENEATHA: Yes—really. *(There is a sudden commotion from the street and she goes to the window to look out.)* What on earth is going on out there? These kids. *(There are, as she throws open the window, the shouts* *of children rising up from the street. She sticks her head out to see better and calls out.)* TRAVIS! TRAVIS . . . WHAT ARE YOU DOING DOWN THERE? *(She sees.)* Oh Lord, they're chasing a rat!

Ruth covers her face with hands and turns away.

MAMA: *(Angrily.)* Tell that youngun to get himself up here, at once!

BENEATHA: TRAVIS . . . YOU COME UPSTAIRS . . . AT ONCE!

355 **RUTH:** *(Her face twisted.)* Chasing a rat. . . .

MAMA: *(Looking at Ruth, worried.)* Doctor say everything going to be all right?

RUTH: *(Far away.)* Yes—she says everything is going to be fine . . .

MAMA: *(Immediately suspicious.)* "She"—What doctor you went to?

Ruth just looks at Mama meaningfully and Mama opens her mouth to speak as Travis bursts in.

TRAVIS: *(Excited and full of narrative, coming directly to his mother.)* Mama, you should of seen the rat . . . Big as a cat, honest! *(He shows an exaggerated size with his hands.)* Gaaleee, that rat was really cuttin' and Bubber caught him with his heel and the janitor, Mr. Barnett, got him with a stick—and then they got him in a corner and—BAM! BAM! BAM!— and he was still jumping around and bleeding like everything too— there's rat blood all over the street—

Ruth reaches out suddenly and grabs her son without even looking at him and clamps her hand over his mouth and holds him to her. Mama crosses to them rapidly and takes the boy from her.

360 **MAMA:** You hush up now . . . talking all that terrible stuff. . . . *(Travis is staring at his mother with a stunned expression. Beneatha comes quickly and takes him away from his grandmother and ushers him to the door.)*

BENEATHA: You go back outside and play . . . but not with any rats. *(She pushes him gently out the door with the boy straining to see what is wrong with his mother.)*

MAMA: *(Worriedly hovering over Ruth.)* Ruth honey—what's the matter with you—you sick?

Ruth has her fists clenched on her thighs and is fighting hard to suppress a scream that seems to be rising in her.

BENEATHA: What's the matter with her, Mama?

MAMA: *(Working her fingers in Ruth's shoulders to relax her.)* She be all right. Women gets right depressed sometimes when they get her way. *(Speaking softly, expertly, rapidly.)* Now you just relax. That's right . . . just lean back, don't think 'bout nothing at all . . . nothing at all—

365 **RUTH:** I'm all right . . .

The glassy-eyed look melts and then she collapses into a fit of heavy sobbing. The bell rings.

BENEATHA: Oh, my God—that must be Asagai.

MAMA: *(To Ruth.)* Come on now, honey. You need to lie down and rest awhile . . . then have some nice hot food.

They exit, Ruth's weight on her mother-in-law. Beneatha, herself profoundly disturbed, opens the door to admit a rather dramatic-looking young man with a large package.

ASAGAI: Hello, Alaiyo—

BENEATHA: *(Holding the door open and regarding him with pleasure.)* Hello . . . *(Long pause.)* Well—come in. And please excuse everything. My mother was very upset about my letting anyone come here with the place like this.

370 ASAGAI: *(Coming into the room.)* You look disturbed too . . . Is something wrong?

BENEATHA: *(Still at the door, absently.)* Yes . . . we've all got acute ghettoitis. *(She smiles and comes toward him, finding a cigarette and sitting.)* So—sit down! No! Wait! *(She whips the spraygun off sofa where she had left it and puts the cushions back. At last perches on arm of sofa. He sits.)* So, how was Canada?

ASAGAI: *(A sophisticate.)* Canadian.

BENEATHA: *(Looking at him.)* Asagai, I'm very glad you are back.

ASAGAI: *(Looking back at her in turn.)* Are you really?

375 BENEATHA: Yes—very.

ASAGAI: Why?—you were quite glad when I went away. What happened?

BENEATHA: You went away.

ASAGAI: Ahhhhhhhh.

BENEATHA: Before—you wanted to be so serious before there was time.

380 ASAGAI: How much time must there be before one knows what one feels?

BENEATHA: *(Stalling this particular conversation. Her hands pressed together, in a deliberately childish gesture.)* What did you bring me?

ASAGAI: *(Handing her the package.)* Open it and see.

BENEATHA: *(Eagerly opening the package and drawing out some records and the colorful robes of a Nigerian woman.)* Oh, Asagai! . . . You got them for me! . . . How beautiful . . . and the records too! *(She lifts out the robes and runs to the mirror with them and holds the drapery up in front of herself.)*

ASAGAI: *(Coming to her at the mirror.)* I shall have to teach you how to drape it properly. *(He flings the material about her for the moment and stands back to look at her.)* Ah—Oh-pay-gay-day, oh-gbah-mu-shay. *(A Yoruba exclamation for admiration.)* You wear it well . . . very well . . . mutilated hair and all.

385 **BENEATHA:**   *(Turning suddenly.)* My hair—what's wrong with my hair?

ASAGAI: *(Shrugging.)* Were you born with it like that?

BENEATHA: *(Reaching up to touch it.)* No . . . of course not.

She looks back to the mirror, disturbed.

ASAGAI: *(Smiling.)* How then?

BENEATHA: You know perfectly well how . . . as crinkly as yours . . . that's how.

390 **ASAGAI:**   And it is ugly to you that way?

BENEATHA: *(Quickly.)* Oh, no—not ugly . . . *(More slowly, apologetically.)* But it's so hard to manage when it's, well—raw.

ASAGAI: And so to accommodate that—you mutilate it every week?

BENEATHA: It's not mutilation!

ASAGAI: *(Laughing aloud at her seriousness.)* Oh . . . please! I am only teasing you because you are so very serious about these things. *(He stands back from her and folds his arms across his chest as he watches her pulling at her hair and frowning in the mirror.)* Do you remember the first time you met me at school? . . . *(He laughs.)* You came up to me and you said—and I thought you were the most serious little thing I had ever seen—you said: *(He imitates her.)* "Mr. Asagai—I want very much to talk with you. About Africa. You see, Mr. Asagai, I am looking for my *identity!*"

He laughs.

395 **BENEATHA:**   *(Turning to him, not laughing.)* Yes—

Her face is quizzical, profoundly disturbed.

ASAGAI: *(Still teasing and reaching out and taking her face in his hands and turning her profile to him.)* Well . . . it is true that this is not so much a profile of a Hollywood queen as perhaps a queen of the Nile—*(A mock dismissal of the importance of the question.)* But what does it matter? Assimilationism is so popular in your country.

BENEATHA: *(Wheeling, passionately, sharply.)* I am not an assimilationist!

ASAGAI: *(The protest hangs in the room for a moment and Asagai studies her, his laughter fading.)* Such a serious one. *(There is a pause.)* So—you like the robes? You must take excellent care of them—they are from my sister's personal wardrobe.

BENEATHA: *(With incredulity.)* You—you sent all the way home—for me?

400 **ASAGAI:**   *(With charm.)* For you—I would do much more . . . Well, that is what I came for. I must go.

BENEATHA: Will you call me Monday?

ASAGAI: Yes . . . We have a great deal to talk about. I mean about identity and time and all that.

BENEATHA: Time?

ASAGAI: Yes. About how much time one needs to know what one feels.

405 **BENEATHA:** You see! You never understood that there is more than one kind of feeling which can exist between a man and a woman—or, at least, there should be.

ASAGAI: *(Shaking his head negatively but gently.)* No. Between a man and a woman there need be only one kind of feeling. I have that for you . . . Now even . . . right this moment . . .

BENEATHA: I know—and by itself—it won't do. I can find that anywhere.

ASAGAI: For a woman it should be enough.

BENEATHA: I know—because that's what it says in all the novels that men write. But it isn't. Go ahead and laugh—but I'm not interested in being someone's little episode in America or—*(With feminine vengeance.)*—one of them! *(Asagai has burst into laughter again.)* That's funny as hell, huh!

410 **ASAGAI:** It's just that every American girl I have known has said that to me. White—black—in this you are all the same. And the same speech, too!

BENEATHA: *(Angrily.)* Yuk, yuk, yuk!

ASAGAI: It's how you can be sure that the world's most liberated women are not liberated at all. You all talk about it too much!

Mama enters and is immediately all social charm because of the presence of a guest.

BENEATHA: Oh—Mama—this is Mr. Asagai.

MAMA: How do you do?

415 **ASAGAI:** *(Total politeness to an elder.)* How do you do, Mrs. Younger. Please forgive me for coming at such an outrageous hour on a Saturday.

MAMA: Well, you are quite welcome. I just hope you understand that our house don't always look like this. *(Chatterish.)* You must come again. I would love to hear all about—*(Not sure of the name.)*—your country. I think it's so sad the way our American Negroes don't know nothing about Africa 'cept Tarzan and all that. And all that money they pour into these churches when they ought to be helping you people over there drive out them French and Englishmen done taken away your land.

The mother flashes a slightly superior look at her daughter upon completion of the recitation.

ASAGAI: *(Taken aback by this sudden and acutely unrelated expression of sympathy.)* Yes . . . yes . . .

MAMA: *(Smiling at him suddenly and relaxing and looking him over.)* How many miles is it from here to where you come from?

ASAGAI: Many thousands.

420 **MAMA:** *(Looking at him as she would Walter.)* I bet you don't half look after yourself, being away from your mama either. I spec you better come 'round here from time to time to get yourself some decent homecooked meals . . .

ASAGAI: *(Moved.)* Thank you. Thank you very much. *(They are all quiet, then—)* Well . . . I must go. I will call you Monday, Alaiyo.

MAMA: What's that he call you?

ASAGAI: Oh—"Alaiyo." I hope you don't mind. It is what you would call a nickname, I think. It is a Yoruba word. I am a Yoruba.

MAMA: *(Looking at Beneatha.)* I—I thought he was from—*(Uncertain.)*

425   ASAGAI: *(Understanding.)* Nigeria is my country. Yoruba is my tribal origin—

BENEATHA: You didn't tell us what Alaiyo means . . . for all I know, you might be calling me Little Idiot or something . . .

ASAGAI: Well . . . let me see . . . I do not know how just to explain it . . . The sense of a thing can be so different when it changes languages.

BENEATHA: You're evading.

ASAGAI: No—really it is difficult . . . *(Thinking.)* It means . . . it means One for Whom Bread—Food—Is Not Enough. *(He looks at her.)* Is that all right?

430   BENEATHA: *(Understanding, softly.)* Thank you.

MAMA: *(Looking from one to the other and not understanding any of it.)* Well . . . that's nice . . . You must come see us again—Mr.—

ASAGAI: Ah-sah-guy . . .

MAMA: Yes . . . Do come again.

ASAGAI: Good-bye.

He exits.

435   MAMA: *(After him.)* Lord, that's a pretty thing just went out here! *(Insinuatingly, to her daughter.)* Yes, I guess I see why we done commence to get so interested in Africa 'round here. Missionaries my aunt Jenny!

She exits.

BENEATHA: Oh, Mama! . . .

She picks up the Nigerian dress and holds it up to her in front of the mirror again. She sets the headdress on haphazardly and then notices her hair again and clutches at it and then replaces the headdress and frowns at herself. Then she starts to wriggle in front of the mirror as she thinks a Nigerian woman might. Travis enters and stands regarding her.

TRAVIS: What's the matter, girl, you cracking up?

BENEATHA: Shut up.

She pulls the headdress off and looks at herself in the mirror and clutches at her hair again and squinches her eyes as if trying to imagine something. Then, suddenly, she gets her raincoat and kerchief and hurriedly prepares for going out.

MAMA: *(Coming back into the room.)* She's resting now. Travis, baby, run next door and ask Miss Johnson to please let me have a little kitchen cleanser. This here can is empty as Jacob's kettle.

440   TRAVIS: I just came in.

MAMA: Do as you told. *(He exits and she looks at her daughter.)* Where you going?

BENEATHA: *(Halting at the door.)* To become a queen of the Nile!

She exits in a breathless blaze of glory. Ruth appears in the bedroom doorway.

MAMA: Who told you to get up?

RUTH: Ain't nothing wrong with me to be lying in no bed for. Where did Bennie go?

445 **MAMA:** *(Drumming her fingers.)* Far as I could make out—to Egypt. *(Ruth just looks at her.)* What time is it getting to?

RUTH: Ten twenty. And the mailman going to ring that bell this morning just like he done every morning for the last umpteen years.

Travis comes in with the cleanser can.

TRAVIS: She say to tell you that she don't have much.

MAMA: *(Angrily.)* Lord, some people I could name sure is tight-fisted! *(Directing her grandson.)* Mark two cans of cleanser down on the list there. If she that hard up for kitchen cleanser, I sure don't want to forget to get her none!

RUTH: Lena—maybe the woman is just short on cleanser—

450 **MAMA:** *(Not listening.)*—Much baking powder as she done borrowed from me all these years, she could of done gone into the baking business!

The bell sounds suddenly and sharply and all three are stunned—serious and silent—mid-speech. In spite of all the other conversations and distractions of the morning, this is what they have been waiting for, even Travis, who looks helplessly from his mother to his grandmother. Ruth is the first to come to life again.

RUTH: *(To Travis.)* Get down them steps, boy!

Travis snaps to life and flies out to get the mail.

MAMA: *(Her eyes wide, her hand to her breast.)* You mean it done really come?

RUTH: *(Excited.)* Oh, Miss Lena!

MAMA: *(Collecting herself.)* Well . . . I don't know what we all so excited about 'round here for. We known it was coming for months.

455 **RUTH:** That's a whole lot different from having it come and being able to hold it in your hands . . . a piece of paper worth ten thousand dollars . . . *(Travis bursts back into the room. He holds the envelope high above his head, like a little dancer, his face is radiant and he is breathless. He moves to his grandmother with sudden slow ceremony and puts the envelope into her hands. She accepts it, and then merely holds it and looks at it.)* Come on! Open it . . . Lord have mercy, I wish Walter Lee was here!

TRAVIS: Open it, Grandmama!

MAMA: *(Staring at it.)* Now you all be quiet. It's just a check.

RUTH: Open it . . .

MAMA: *(Still staring at it.)* Now don't act silly . . . We ain't never been no people to act silly 'bout no money—

460 **RUTH:**   *(Swiftly.)* We ain't never had none before—OPEN IT!

Mama finally makes a good strong tear and pulls out the thin blue slice of paper and inspects it closely. The boy and his mother study it raptly over Mama's shoulders.

MAMA: Travis! *(She is counting off with doubt.)* Is that the right number of zeros?

TRAVIS: Yes'm . . . ten thousand dollars. Gaalee, Grandmama, you rich.

MAMA: *(She holds the check away from her, still looking at it. Slowly her face sobers into a mask of unhappiness.)* Ten thousand dollars. *(She hands it to Ruth.)* Put it away somewhere, Ruth. *(She does not look at Ruth; her eyes seem to be seeing something somewhere very far off.)* Ten thousand dollars they give you. Ten thousand dollars.

TRAVIS: *(To his mother, sincerely.)* What's the matter with Grandmama—don't she want to be rich?

465 **RUTH:**   *(Distractedly.)* You go on out and play now, baby. *(Travis exits. Mama starts wiping dishes absently, humming intently to herself. Ruth turns to her, with kind exasperation.)* You've gone and got yourself upset.

MAMA: *(Not looking at her.)* I spec if it wasn't for you all . . . I would just put that money away or give it to the church or something.

RUTH: Now what kind of talk is that. Mr. Younger would just be plain mad if he could hear you talking foolish like that.

MAMA: *(Stopping and staring off.)* Yes . . . he sure would. *(Sighing.)* We got enough to do with that money, all right. *(She halts then, and turns and looks at her daughter-in-law hard; Ruth avoids her eyes and Mama wipes her hands with finality and starts to speak firmly to Ruth.)* Where did you go today, girl?

RUTH: To the doctor.

470 **MAMA:**   *(Impatiently.)* Now, Ruth . . . you know better than that. Old Doctor Jones is strange enough in his way but there ain't nothing 'bout him make somebody slip and call him "she"—like you done this morning.

RUTH: Well, that's what happened—my tongue slipped.

MAMA: You went to see that woman, didn't you?

RUTH: *(Defensively, giving herself away.)* What woman you talking about?

MAMA: *(Angrily.)* That woman who—

Walter enters in great excitement.

475 **WALTER:**   Did it come?

MAMA: *(Quietly.)* Can't you give people a Christian greeting before you start asking about money?

WALTER: *(To Ruth.)* Did it come? *(Ruth unfolds the check and lays it quietly before him, watching him intently with thoughts of her own. Walter sits down and grasps it close and counts off the zeros.)* Ten thousand dollars—*(He turns suddenly, frantically to his mother and draws some papers out of his breast pocket.)* Mama—look. Old Willy Harris put everything on paper—

MAMA: Son—I think you ought to talk to your wife . . . I'll go on out and leave you alone if you want—

WALTER: I can talk to her later—Mama, look—

480 **MAMA:** Son—

WALTER: WILL SOMEBODY PLEASE LISTEN TO ME TODAY!

MAMA: *(Quietly.)* I don't 'low no yellin' in this house, Walter Lee, and you know it—*(Walter stares at them in frustration and starts to speak several times.)* And there ain't going to be no investing in no liquor stores.

WALTER: But, Mama, you ain't even looked at it.

MAMA: I don't aim to have to speak on that again.

A long pause.

485 **WALTER:** You ain't looked at it and you don't aim to have to speak on that again? You ain't even looked at it and *you* have decided—*(Crumpling his papers.)* Well, *you* tell that to my boy tonight when you put him to sleep on the living-room couch . . . *(Turning to Mama and speaking directly to her.)* Yeah—and tell it to my wife, Mama, tomorrow when she has to go out of here to look after somebody else's kids. And tell it to *me,* Mama, every time we need a new pair of curtains and I have to watch *you* go out and work in somebody's kitchen. Yeah, you tell me then!

Walter starts out.

RUTH: Where you going?

WALTER: I'm going out!

RUTH: Where?

WALTER: Just out of this house somewhere—

490 **RUTH:** *(Getting her coat.)* I'll come too.

WALTER: I don't want you to come!

RUTH: I got something to talk to you about, Walter.

WALTER: That's too bad.

MAMA: *(Still quietly.)* Walter Lee—*(She waits and he finally turns and looks at her.)* Sit down.

495 **WALTER:** I'm a grown man, Mama.

MAMA: Ain't nobody said you wasn't grown. But you still in my house and my presence. And as long as you are—you'll talk to your wife civil. Now sit down.

RUTH: *(Suddenly.)* Oh, let him go on out and drink himself to death! He makes me sick to my stomach! *(She flings her coat against him and exits to bedroom.)*

WALTER: *(Violently flinging the coat after her.)* And you turn mine too, baby! *(The door slams behind her.)* That was my biggest mistake—

MAMA: *(Still quietly.)* Walter, what is the matter with you?

500 **WALTER:** Matter with me? Ain't nothing the matter with *me!*

MAMA: Yes there is. Something eating you up like a crazy man. Something more than me not giving you this money. The past few years I been watching it happen to you. You get all nervous acting and kind of wild in the eyes—*(Walter jumps up impatiently at her words.)* I said sit there now, I'm talking to you!

WALTER: Mama—I don't need no nagging at me today.

MAMA: Seem like you getting to a place where you always tied up in some kind of knot about something. But if anybody ask you 'bout it you just yell at 'em and bust out the house and go out and drink somewheres. Walter Lee, people can't live with that. Ruth's a good, patient girl in her way— but you getting to be too much. Boy, don't make the mistake of driving that girl away from you.

WALTER: Why—what she do for me?

505 **MAMA:** She loves you.

WALTER: Mama—I'm going out. I want to go off somewhere and be by my-self for a while.

MAMA: I'm sorry 'bout your liquor store, son. It just wasn't the thing for us to do. That's what I want to tell you about—

WALTER: I got to go out, Mama—

He rises.

MAMA: It's dangerous, son.

510 **WALTER:** What's dangerous?

MAMA: When a man goes outside his home to look for peace.

WALTER: *(Beseechingly.)* Then why can't there never be no peace in this house then?

MAMA: You done found it in some other house?

WALTER: No—there ain't no woman! Why do women always think there's a woman somewhere when a man gets restless. *(Picks up the check.)* Do you know what this money means to me? Do you know what this money can do for us? *(Puts it back.)* Mama—Mama—I want so many things . . .

515 **MAMA:** Yes, son—

WALTER: I want so many things that they are driving me kind of crazy . . . Mama—look at me.

MAMA: I'm looking at you. You a good-looking boy. You got a job, a nice wife, a fine boy and—

WALTER: A job. *(Looks at her.)* Mama, a job? I open and close car doors all day long. I drive a man around in his limousine and say, "Yes, sir; no, sir; very good, sir; shall I take the Drive, sir?" Mama, that ain't no kind of job . . . that ain't nothing at all. *(Very quietly.)* Mama, I don't know if I can make you understand.

MAMA: Understand what, baby?

520 **WALTER:** *(Quietly.)* Sometimes it's like I can see the future stretched out in front of me—just plain as day. The future, Mama. Hanging over there at the edge of my days. Just waiting for me—a big, looming blank space— full of *nothing.* Just waiting for *me.* But it don't have to be. *(Pause. Kneeling beside her chair.)* Mama—sometimes when I'm downtown and I pass them cool, quiet-looking restaurants where them white boys are sitting back and talking 'bout things . . . sitting there turning deals worth millions of dollars . . . sometimes I see guys don't look much older than me—

MAMA: Son—how come you talk so much 'bout money?

WALTER: *(With immense passion.)* Because it is life, Mama!

MAMA: *(Quietly.)* Oh—*(Very quietly.)* So now it's life. Money is life. Once upon a time freedom used to be life—now it's money. I guess the world really do change . . .

WALTER: No—it was always money, Mama. We just didn't know about it.

525 **MAMA:** No . . . something has changed. *(She looks at him.)* You something new, boy. In my time we was worried about not being lynched and getting to the North if we could and how to stay alive and still have a pinch of dignity too . . . Now here come you and Beneatha—talking 'bout things we ain't never even thought about hardly, me and your daddy. You ain't satisfied or proud of nothing we done. I mean that you had a home; that we kept you out of trouble till you was grown; that you don't have to ride to work on the back of nobody's streetcar—You my children—but how different we done become.

WALTER: *(A long beat. He pats her hand and gets up.)* You just don't understand, Mama, you just don't understand.

MAMA: Son—do you know your wife is expecting another baby? *(Walter stands, stunned, and absorbs what his mother has said.)* That's what she wanted to talk to you about. *(Walter sinks down into a chair.)* This ain't for me to be telling—but you ought to know. *(She waits.)* I think Ruth is thinking 'bout getting rid of that child.

WALTER: *(Slowly understanding.)*—No—no—Ruth wouldn't do that.

MAMA: When the world gets ugly enough—a woman will do anything for her family. *The part that's already living.*

530 **WALTER:** You don't know Ruth, Mama, if you think she would do that.

Ruth opens the bedroom door and stands there a little limp.

RUTH: *(Beaten.)* Yes I would too, Walter. *(Pause.)* I gave her a five-dollar down payment.

There is total silence as the man stares at his wife and the mother stares at her son.

MAMA: *(Presently.)* Well—*(Tightly.)* Well—son, I'm waiting to hear you say something . . . *(She waits.)* I'm waiting to hear how you be your father's son. Be the man he was . . . *(Pause. The silence shouts.)* Your wife say she going to destroy your child. And I'm waiting to hear you talk like him and say we a people who give children life, not who destroys them— *(She rises.)* I'm waiting to see you stand up and look like your daddy and say we done give up one baby to poverty and that we ain't going to give up nary another one . . . I'm waiting.

WALTER: Ruth—*(He can say nothing.)*

MAMA: If you a son of mine, tell her! *(Walter picks up his keys and his coat and walks out. She continues, bitterly.)* You . . . you are a disgrace to your father's memory. Somebody get me my hat!

CURTAIN

Act II

SCENE ONE

Time: Later the same day.

At rise: Ruth is ironing again. She has the radio going. Presently Beneatha's bedroom door opens and Ruth's mouth falls and she puts down the iron in fascination.

RUTH: What have we got on tonight!

BENEATHA: *(Emerging grandly from the doorway so that we can see her thoroughly robed in the costume Asagai brought.)* You are looking at what a well-dressed Nigerian woman wears—*(She parades for Ruth, her hair completely hidden by the headdress; she is coquettishly fanning herself with an ornate oriental fan, mistakenly more like Butterfly than any Nigerian that ever was.)* Isn't it beautiful? *(She promenades to the radio and, with an arrogant flourish, turns off the good loud blues that is playing.)* Enough of this assimilationist junk! *(Ruth follows her with her eyes as she goes to the phonograph and puts on a record and turns and waits ceremoniously for the music to come up. Then, with a shout—)* OCOMOGOSIAY!

Ruth jumps. The music comes up, a lovely Nigerian melody. Beneatha listens, enraptured, her eyes far away—"back to the past." She begins to dance. Ruth is dumbfounded.

RUTH: What kind of dance is that?

BENEATHA: A folk dance.

5 **RUTH:** *(Pearl Bailey.)* What kind of folks do that, honey?

BENEATHA: It's from Nigeria. It's a dance of welcome.

RUTH: Who you welcoming?

BENEATHA: The men back to the village.

RUTH: Where they been?

10 **BENEATHA:** How should I know—out hunting or something. Anyway, they are coming back now . . .

Ruth: Well, that's good.

Beneatha: *(With the record.)*

Alundi, alundi
Alundi alunya
Jop pu a jeepua
Ang gu sooooooooooo

Ai yai yae . . .
Ayehaye—alundi . . .

Walter comes in during this performance; he has obviously been drinking. He leans against the door heavily and watches his sister, at first with distaste. Then his eyes look off—"back to the past"—as he lifts both his fists to the roof, screaming.

Walter: YEAH . . . AND ETHIOPIA STRETCH FORTH HER HANDS AGAIN! . . .

Ruth: *(Drily, looking at him.)* Yes—and Africa sure is claiming her own tonight. *(She gives them both up and starts ironing again.)*

15   **Walter:**   *(All in a drunken, dramatic shout.)* Shut up! . . . I'm digging them drums . . . them drums move me! . . . *(He makes his weaving way to his wife's face and leans in close to her.)* In my *heart of hearts—(He thumps his chest.)*—I am much warrior!

Ruth: *(Without even looking up.)* In your heart of hearts you are much drunkard.

Walter: *(Coming away from her and starting to wander around the room, shouting.)* Me and Jomo . . . *(Intently, in his sister's face. She has stopped dancing to watch him in this unknown mood.)* That's my man, Kenyatta. *(Shouting and thumping his chest.)* FLAMING SPEAR! HOT DAMN! *(He is suddenly in possession of an imaginary spear and actively spearing enemies all over the room.)* OCOMOGOSIAY . . .

Beneatha: *(To encourage Walter, thoroughly caught up with this side of him.)* OCOMOGOSIAY, FLAMING SPEAR!

Walter: THE LION IS WAKING . . . OWIMOWEH! *(He pulls his shirt open and leaps up on the table and gestures with his spear.)*

20   **Beneatha:**   OWIMOWEH!

Walter: *(On the table, very far gone, his eyes pure glass sheets. He sees what we cannot, that he is a leader of his people, a great chief, a descendant of Chaka, and that the hour to march has come.)* Listen, my black brothers—

Beneatha: OCOMOGOSIAY!

Walter: —Do you hear the waters rushing against the shores of the coastlands—

Beneatha: OCOMOGOSIAY!

25   **Walter:**   —Do you hear the screeching of the cocks in yonder hills beyond where the chiefs meet in council for the coming of the mighty war—

BENEATHA: OCOMOGOSIAY!

And now the lighting shifts subtly to suggest the world of Walter's imagination, and the mood shifts from pure comedy. It is the inner Walter speaking: the Southside chauffeur has assumed an unexpected majesty.

WALTER: —Do you hear the beating of the wings of the birds flying low
over the mountains and the low places of our land—
BENEATHA: OCOMOGOSIAY!
WALTER: —Do you hear the singing of the women, singing the war songs of
our fathers to the babies in the great houses? Singing the sweet war songs!
(The doorbell rings.) OH, DO YOU HEAR, MY BLACK BROTHERS!
30 **BENEATHA:**   *(Completely gone.)* We hear you, Flaming Spear—

Ruth shuts off the phonograph and opens the door. George Murchison enters.

WALTER: Telling us to prepare for the GREATNESS OF THE TIME! *(Lights
back to normal. He turns and sees George.)* Black Brother!

He extends his hand for the fraternal clasp.

GEORGE: Black Brother, hell!
RUTH: *(Having had enough, and embarrassed for the family.)* Beneatha,
you got company—what's the matter with you? Walter Lee Younger, get
down off that table and stop acting like a fool . . .

*Walter comes down off the table suddenly and makes a quick exit to the
bathroom.*

RUTH: He's had a little to drink . . . I don't know what her excuse is.
35 **GEORGE:**   *(To Beneatha.)* Look honey, we're going *to* the theatre—we're
not going to be *in* it . . . so go change, huh?

*Beneatha looks at him and slowly, ceremoniously, lifts her hands and
pulls off the headdress. Her hair is close-cropped and unstraightened.
George freezes mid-sentence and Ruth's eyes all but fall out of her head.*

GEORGE: What in the name of—
RUTH: *(Touching Beneatha's hair.)* Girl, you done lost your natural mind!
Look at your head!
GEORGE: What have you done to your head—I mean your hair!
BENEATHA: Nothing—except cut it off.
40 **RUTH:**   Now that's the truth—it's what ain't been done to it! You expect
this boy to go out with you with your head all nappy like that?
BENEATHA: *(Looking at George.)* That's up to George. If he's ashamed of
his heritage—
GEORGE: Oh, don't be so proud of yourself, Bennie—just because you look
eccentric.
BENEATHA: How can something that's natural be eccentric?

GEORGE: That's what being eccentric means—being natural. Get dressed.

45 **BENEATHA:**   I don't like that, George.

RUTH: Why must you and your brother make an argument out of everything people say?

BENEATHA: Because I hate assimilationist Negroes!

RUTH: Will somebody please tell me what assimila-who-ever means!

GEORGE: Oh, it's just a college girl's way of calling people Uncle Toms—but that isn't what it means at all.

50 **RUTH:**   Well, what does it mean?

BENEATHA: *(Cutting George off and staring at him as she replies to Ruth.)* It means someone who is willing to give up his own culture and submerge himself completely in the dominant, and in this case *oppressive* culture!

GEORGE: Oh, dear, dear, dear! Here we go! A lecture on the African past! On our Great West African Heritage! In one second we will hear all about the great Ashanti empires; the great Songhay civilizations; and the great sculpture of Bénin—and then some poetry in the Bantu—and the whole monologue will end with the word *heritage!* *(Nastily.)* Let's face it, baby, your heritage is nothing but a bunch of raggedy-assed spirituals and some grass huts!

BENEATHA: GRASS HUTS! *(Ruth crosses to her and forcibly pushes her toward the bedroom.)* See there . . . you are standing there in your splendid ignorance talking about people who were the first to smelt iron on the face of the earth! *(Ruth is pushing her through the door.)* The Ashanti were performing surgical operations when the English—*(Ruth pulls the door to, with Beneatha on the other side, and smiles graciously at George. Beneatha opens the door and shouts the end of the sentence defiantly at George.)*—were still tattooing themselves with blue dragons! *(She goes back inside.)*

RUTH: Have a seat, George. *(They both sit. Ruth folds her hands rather primly on her lap, determined to demonstrate the civilization of the family.)* Warm, ain't it? I mean for September. *(Pause.)* Just like they always say about Chicago weather: If it's too hot or cold for you, just wait a minute and it'll change. *(She smiles happily at this cliché of clichés.)* Everybody say it's got to do with them bombs and things they keep setting off. *(Pause.)* Would you like a nice cold beer?

55 **GEORGE:**   No, thank you. I don't care for beer. *(He looks at his watch.)* I hope she hurries up.

RUTH: What time is the show?

GEORGE: It's an eight-thirty curtain. That's just Chicago, though. In New York standard curtain time is eight forty.

He is rather proud of this knowledge.

RUTH: *(Properly appreciating it.)* You get to New York a lot?

GEORGE: *(Offhand.)* Few times a year.

60 **RUTH:**   Oh—that's nice. I've never been to New York.

Walter enters. We feel he has relieved himself, but the edge of unreality is still with him.

WALTER: New York ain't got nothing Chicago ain't. Just a bunch of hustling people all squeezed up together—being "Eastern."

He turns his face into a screw of displeasure.

GEORGE: Oh—you've been?
WALTER: *Plenty* of times.
RUTH: *(Shocked at the lie.)* Walter Lee Younger!
65 **WALTER:**   *(Staring her down.)* Plenty! *(Pause.)* What we got to drink in this house? Why don't you offer this man some refreshment. *(To George.)* They don't know how to entertain people in this house, man.
GEORGE: Thank you—I don't really care for anything.
WALTER: *(Feeling his head; sobriety coming.)* Where's Mama?
RUTH: She ain't come back yet.
WALTER: *(Looking Murchison over from head to toe, scrutinizing his carefully casual tweed sports jacket over cashmere V-neck sweater over soft eyelet shirt and tie, and soft slacks, finished off with white buckskin shoes.)* Why all you college boys wear them faggoty-looking white shoes?
70 **RUTH:**   Walter Lee!

George Murchison ignores the remark.

WALTER: *(To Ruth.)* Well, they look crazy as hell—white shoes, cold as it is.
RUTH: *(Crushed.)* You have to excuse him—
WALTER: No he don't! Excuse me for what? What you always excusing me for! I'll excuse myself when I needs to be excused! *(A pause.)* They look as funny as them black knee socks Beneatha wears out of here all the time.
RUTH: It's the college *style*, Walter.
75 **WALTER:**   Style, hell. She looks like she got burnt legs or something!
RUTH: Oh, Walter—
WALTER: *(An irritable mimic.)* Oh, Walter! Oh, Walter! *(To Murchison.)* How's your old man making out? I understand you all going to buy that big hotel on the Drive? *(He finds a beer in the refrigerator, wanders over to Murchison, sipping and wiping his lips with the back of his hand, and straddling a chair backwards to talk to the other man.)* Shrewd move. Your old man is all right, man. *(Tapping his head and half winking for emphasis.)* I mean he knows how to operate. I mean he thinks *big*, you know what I mean, I mean for a *home*, you know? But I think he's kind of running out of ideas now. I'd like to talk to him. Listen, man, I got some plans that could turn this city upside down. I mean think like he does. *Big*. Invest big, gamble big, hell, lose *big* if you have to, you know what I mean. It's hard to find a man on this whole Southside who understands my kind of thinking—you dig? *(He scrutinizes Murchison again, drinks*

his beer, squints his eyes and leans in close, confidential, man to man.) Me and you ought to sit down and talk sometimes, man. Man, I got me some ideas . . .

MURCHISON: *(With boredom.)* Yeah—sometimes we'll have to do that, Walter.

WALTER: *(Understanding the indifference, and offended.)* Yeah—well, when you get the time, man. I know you a busy little boy.

80 **RUTH:** Walter, please—

WALTER: *(Bitterly, hurt.)* I know ain't nothing in this world as busy as you colored college boys with your fraternity pins and white shoes . . .

RUTH: *(Covering her face with humiliation.)* Oh, Walter Lee—

WALTER: I see you all all the time—with the books tucked under your arms—going to your *(British A—a mimic.)* "clahsses." And for what! What the hell you learning over there? Filling up your heads—*(Counting off on his fingers.)*—with the sociology and the psychology—but they teaching you how to be a man? How to take over and run the world? They teaching you how to run a rubber plantation or a steel mill? Naw—just to talk proper and read books and wear them faggoty-looking white shoes . . .

GEORGE: *(Looking at him with distaste, a little above it all.)* You're all wacked up with bitterness, man.

85 **WALTER:** *(Intently, almost quietly, between the teeth, glaring at the boy.)* And you—ain't you bitter, man? Ain't you just about had it yet? Don't you see no stars gleaming that you can't reach out and grab? You happy?—You contented son-of-a-bitch—you happy? You got it made? Bitter? Man, I'm a volcano. Bitter? Here I am a giant—surrounded by ants! Ants who can't even understand what it is the giant is talking about.

RUTH: *(Passionately and suddenly.)* Oh, Walter—ain't you with nobody!

WALTER: *(Violently.)* No! 'Cause ain't nobody with me! Not even my own mother!

RUTH: Walter, that's a terrible thing to say!

Beneatha enters, dressed for the evening in a cocktail dress and earrings, hair natural.

GEORGE: Well—hey—*(Crosses to Beneatha; thoughtful, with emphasis, since this is a reversal.)* You look great!

90 **WALTER:** *(Seeing his sister's hair for the first time.)* What's the matter with your head?

BENEATHA: *(Tired of the jokes now.)* I cut it off, Brother.

WALTER: *(Coming close to inspect it and walking around her.)* Well, I'll be damned. So that's what they mean by the African bush . . .

BENEATHA: Ha ha. Let's go, George.

GEORGE: *(Looking at her.)* You know something? I like it. It's sharp. I mean it really is. *(Helps her into her wrap.)*

95 **RUTH:** Yes—I think so, too. *(She goes to the mirror and starts to clutch at her hair.)*

WALTER: Oh no! You leave yours alone, baby. You might turn out to have a pin-shaped head or something!

BENEATHA: See you all later.

RUTH: Have a nice time.

GEORGE: Thanks. Good night. *(Half out the door, he reopens it. To Walter.)* Good night, Prometheus!

Beneatha and George exit.

100 **WALTER:** *(To Ruth.)* Who is Prometheus?

RUTH: I don't know. Don't worry about it.

WALTER: *(In fury, pointing after George.)* See there—they get to a point where they can't insult you man to man—they got to go talk about something ain't nobody never heard of!

RUTH: How do you know it was an insult? *(To humor him.)* Maybe Prometheus is a nice fellow.

WALTER: Prometheus! I bet there ain't even no such thing! I bet that simple-minded clown—

105 **RUTH:** Walter—

She stops what she is doing and looks at him.

WALTER: *(Yelling.)* Don't start!

RUTH: Start what?

WALTER: Your nagging! Where was I? Who was I with? How much money did I spend?

RUTH: *(Plaintively.)* Walter Lee—why don't we just try to talk about it . . .

110 **WALTER:** *(Not listening.)* I been out talking with people who understand me. People who care about the things I got on my mind.

RUTH: *(Wearily.)* I guess that means people like Willy Harris.

WALTER: Yes, people like Willy Harris.

RUTH: *(With a sudden flash of impatience.)* Why don't you all just hurry up and go into the banking business and stop talking about it!

WALTER: Why? You want to know why? 'Cause we all tied up in a race of people that don't know how to do nothing but moan, pray and have babies!

The line is too bitter even for him and he looks at her and sits down.

115 **RUTH:** Oh, Walter . . . *(Softly.)* Honey, why can't you stop fighting me?

WALTER: *(Without thinking.)* Who's fighting you? Who even cares about you?

This line begins the retardation of his mood.

RUTH: Well—*(She waits a long time, and then with resignation starts to put away her things.)* I guess I might as well go on to bed . . . *(More or less to herself.)* I don't know where we lost it . . . but we have . . . *(Then, to him.)* I—I'm sorry about this new baby, Walter. I guess maybe I better go on and do what I started . . . I guess I just didn't realize how bad things was with us . . . I guess I just didn't really realize—*(She starts out to the bedroom and stops.)* You want some hot milk?

WALTER: Hot milk?

RUTH: Yes—hot milk.

120 **WALTER:**   Why hot milk?

RUTH: 'Cause after all that liquor you come home with you ought to have something hot in your stomach.

WALTER: I don't want no milk.

RUTH: You want some coffee then?

WALTER: No, I don't want no coffee. I don't want nothing hot to drink. *(Almost plaintively.)* Why you always trying to give me something to eat?

125 **RUTH:**   *(Standing and looking at him helplessly.)* What *else* can I give you, Walter Lee Younger?

She stands and looks at him and presently turns to go out again. He lifts his head and watches her going away from him in a new mood which began to emerge when he asked her "Who even cares about you?"

WALTER: It's been rough, ain't it, baby? *(She hears and stops but does not turn around and he continues to her back.)* I guess between two people there ain't never as much understood as folks generally thinks there is. I mean like between me and you—*(She turns to face him.)* How we gets to the place where we scared to talk softness to each other. *(He waits, thinking hard himself.)* Why you think it got to be like that? *(He is thoughtful, almost as a child would be.)* Ruth, what is it gets into people ought to be close?

RUTH: I don't known, honey. I think about it a lot.

WALTER: On account of you and me, you mean? The way things are with us. The way something done come down between us.

RUTH: There ain't so much between us, Walter . . . Not when you come to me and try to talk to me. Try to be with me . . . a little even.

130 **WALTER:**   *(Total honesty.)* Sometimes . . . sometimes . . . I don't even know how to try.

RUTH: Walter—

WALTER: Yes?

RUTH: *(Coming to him, gently and with misgiving, but coming to him.)* Honey . . . life don't have to be like this. I mean sometimes people can do things so that things are better . . . You remember how we used to talk when Travis was born . . . about the way we were going to live . . . the kind of house . . . *(She is stroking his head.)* Well, it's all starting to slip away from us . . .

He turns her to him and they look at each other and kiss, tenderly and hungrily. The door opens and Mama enters—Walter breaks away and jumps up. A beat.

WALTER: Mama, where have you been?

135 **MAMA:** My—them steps is longer than they used to be. Whew! *(She sits down and ignores him.)* How you feeling this evening, Ruth?

Ruth shrugs, disturbed at having been interrupted and watching her husband knowingly.

WALTER: Mama, where have you been all day?

MAMA: *(Still ignoring him and leaning on the table and changing to more comfortable shoes.)* Where's Travis?

RUTH: I let him go out earlier and he ain't come back yet. Boy, is he going to get it!

WALTER: Mama!

140 **MAMA:** *(As if she has heard him for the first time.)* Yes, son?

WALTER: Where did you go this afternoon?

MAMA: I went downtown to tend to some business that I had to tend to.

WALTER: What kind of business?

MAMA: You know better than to question me like a child, Brother.

145 **WALTER:** *(Rising and bending over the table.)* Where were you, Mama? *(Bringing his fists down and shouting.)* Mama, you didn't go do something with that insurance money, something crazy?

The front door opens slowly, interrupting him, and Travis peeks his head in, less than hopefully.

TRAVIS: *(To his mother.)* Mama, I—

RUTH: "Mama I" nothing! You're going to get it, boy! Get on in that bedroom and get yourself ready!

TRAVIS: But I—

MAMA: Why don't you all never let the child explain hisself.

150 **RUTH:** Keep out of it now, Lena.

Mama clamps her lips together, and Ruth advances toward her son menacingly.

RUTH: A thousand times I have told you not to go off like that—

MAMA: *(Holding out her arms to her grandson.)* Well—at least let me tell him something. I want him to be the first one to hear . . . Come here, Travis. *(The boy obeys, gladly.)* Travis—*(She takes him by the shoulder and looks into his face.)*—you know that money we got in the mail this morning?

TRAVIS: Yes'm—

MAMA: Well—what you think your grandmama gone and done with that money?

155 **TRAVIS:** I don't know, Grandmama.

MAMA: *(Putting her finger on his nose for emphasis.)* She went out and she bought you a house! *(The explosion comes from Walter at the end of the revelation and he jumps up and turns away from all of them in a* *fury. Mama continues, to Travis.)* You glad about the house? It's going to be yours when you get to be a man.

TRAVIS: Yeah—I always wanted to live in a house.

MAMA: All right, gimme some sugar then—*(Travis puts his arms around her neck as she watches her son over the boy's shoulder. Then, to Travis, after the embrace.)* Now when you say your prayers tonight, you thank God and your grandfather—'cause it was him who give you the house—in his way.

RUTH: *(Taking the boy from Mama and pushing him toward the bedroom.)* Now you get out of here and get ready for your beating.

160 **TRAVIS:** Aw, Mama—

RUTH: Get on in there—*(Closing the door behind him and turning radiantly to her mother-in-law.)* So you went and did it!

MAMA: *(Quietly, looking at her son with pain.)* Yes, I did.

RUTH: *(Raising both arms classically.)* PRAISE GOD! *(Looks at Walter a moment, who says nothing. She crosses rapidly to her husband.)* Please, honey—let me be glad . . . you be glad too. *(She has laid her hands on his shoulders, but he shakes himself free of her roughly, without turning to face her.)* Oh, Walter . . . a home . . . *a home. (She comes back to Mama.)* Well—where is it? How big is it? How much it going to cost?

MAMA: Well—

165 **RUTH:** When we moving?

MAMA: *(Smiling at her.)* First of the month.

RUTH: *(Throwing back her head with jubilance.) Praise God!*

MAMA: *(Tentatively, still looking at her son's back turned against her and Ruth.)* It's—it's a nice house too . . . *(She cannot help speaking directly to him. An imploring quality in her voice, her manner, makes her almost like a girl now.)* Three bedrooms—nice big one for you and Ruth. . . . Me and Beneatha still have to share our room, but Travis have one of his own—and *(With difficulty.)* I figure if the—new baby—is a boy, we could get one of them double-decker outfits . . . And there's a yard with a little patch of dirt where I could maybe get to grow me a few flowers . . . And a nice big basement . . .

RUTH: Walter honey, be glad—

170 **MAMA:** *(Still to his back, fingering things on the table.)* 'Course I don't want to make it sound fancier than it is . . . It's just a plain little old house—but it's made good and solid—and it will be *ours*. Walter Lee—it makes a difference in a man when he can walk on floors that belong to *him* . . .

RUTH: Where is it?

MAMA: *(Frightened at this telling.)* Well—well—it's out there in Clybourne Park—

Ruth's radiance fades abruptly, and Walter finally turns slowly to face his mother with incredulity and hostility.

RUTH: Where?

MAMA: *(Matter-of-factly.)* Four o six Clybourne Street, Clybourne Park.

175 **RUTH:** Clybourne Park? Mama, there ain't no colored people living in Clybourne Park.

MAMA: *(Almost idiotically.)* Well, I guess there's going to be some now.

WALTER: *(Bitterly.)* So that's the peace and comfort you went out and bought for us today!

MAMA: *(Raising her eyes to meet his finally.)* Son—I just tried to find the nicest place for the least amount of money for my family.

RUTH: *(Trying to recover from the shock.)* Well—well—'course I ain't one never been 'fraid of no crackers, mind you—but—well, wasn't there no other houses nowhere?

180 **MAMA:** Them houses they put up for colored in them areas way out all seem to cost twice as much as other houses. I did the best I could.

RUTH: *(Struck senseless with the news, in its various degrees of goodness and trouble, she sits a moment, her fists propping her chin in thought, and then she starts to rise, bringing her fists down with vigor, the radiance spreading from cheek to cheek again.)* Well—well!—All I can say is—if this is my time in life—MY TIME—to say good-bye—*(And she builds with momentum as she starts to circle the room with an exuberant, almost tearfully happy release.)*—to these Goddamned cracking walls!—*(She pounds the walls.)*—and these marching roaches!—*(She wipes at an imaginary army of marching roaches.)*—and this cramped little closet which ain't now or never was no kitchen! . . . then I say it loud and good, HALLELUJAH! AND GOOD-BYE MISERY . . . I DON'T NEVER WANT TO SEE YOUR UGLY FACE AGAIN! *(She laughs joyously, having practically destroyed the apartment, and flings her arms up and lets them come down happily, slowly, reflectively, over her abdomen, aware for the first time perhaps that the life therein pulses with happiness and not despair.)* Lena?

MAMA: *(Moved, watching her happiness.)* Yes, honey?

RUTH: *(Looking off.)* Is there—is there a whole lot of sunlight?

MAMA: *(Understanding.)* Yes, child, there's a whole lot of sunlight.

Long pause.

185 **RUTH:** *(Collecting herself and going to the door of the room Travis is in.)* Well—I guess I better see 'bout Travis. *(To Mama.)* Lord, I sure don't feel like whipping nobody today!

She exits.

MAMA: *The mother and son are left alone now and the mother waits a long time, considering deeply, before she speaks.)* Son—you—you understand what I done, don't you? *(Walter is silent and sullen.)* I—I just seen my family falling apart today . . . just falling to pieces in front of my eyes . . . We couldn't of gone on like we was today. We was going backwards 'stead of forwards—talking 'bout killing babies and wishing each other was dead . . . When it gets like that in life—you just got to do something different, push on out and do something bigger . . . *(She waits.)* I wish you say something, son . . . I wish you'd say how deep inside you you think I done the right thing—

WALTER: *(Crossing slowly to his bedroom door and finally turning there and speaking measuredly.)* What you need me to say you done right for? *You* the head of this family. You run our lives like you want to. It was your money and you did what you wanted with it. So what you need for me to say it was all right for? *(Bitterly, to hurt her as deeply as he knows is possible.)* So you butchered up a dream of mine—you—who always talking 'bout your children's dreams . . .

MAMA: Walter Lee—

He just closes the door behind him. Mama sits alone, thinking heavily.

CURTAIN

SCENE TWO

Time: Friday night. A few weeks later.

At rise: Packing crates mark the intention of the family to move. Beneatha and George come in, presumably from an evening out again.

GEORGE: O.K. . . . O.K., whatever you say . . . *(They both sit on the couch. He tries to kiss her. She moves away.)* Look, we've had a nice evening; let's not spoil it, huh? . . .

He again turns her head and tries to nuzzle in and she turns away from him, not with distaste but with momentary lack of interest; in a mood to pursue what they were talking about.

190 **BENEATHA:** I'm *trying* to talk to you.

GEORGE: We always talk.

BENEATHA: Yes—and I love to talk.

GEORGE: *(Exasperated; rising.)* I know it and I don't mind it sometimes . . . I want you to cut it out, see—The moody stuff, I mean. I don't like it. You're a nice-looking girl . . . all over. That's all you need, honey, forget the atmosphere. Guys aren't going to go for the atmosphere— they're going to go for what they see. Be glad for that. Drop the Garbo routine. It doesn't go with you. As for myself, I want a nice—*(Groping.)*— simple *(Thoughtfully.)*—sophisticated girl . . . not a poet—O.K.?

He starts to kiss her, she rebuffs him again and he jumps up.

BENEATHA: Why are you angry, George?

195 **GEORGE:** Because this is stupid! I don't go out with you to discuss the nature of "quiet desperation" or to hear all about your thoughts—because
   the world will go on thinking what it thinks regardless—

BENEATHA: Then why read books? Why go to school?

GEORGE: *(With artificial patience, counting on his fingers.)* It's simple.
   You read books—to learn facts—to get grades—to pass the course—to get
   a degree. That's all—it has nothing to do with thoughts.

A long pause.

BENEATHA: I see. *(He starts to sit.)* Good night, George.

*George looks at her a little oddly, and starts to exit. He meets Mama com-
ing in.*

GEORGE: Oh—hello, Mrs. Younger.

200 **MAMA:** Hello, George, how you feeling?

GEORGE: Fine—fine, how are you?

MAMA: Oh, a little tired. You know them steps can get you after a day's
   work. You all have a nice time tonight?

GEORGE: Yes—a fine time. A fine time.

MAMA: Well, good night.

205 **GEORGE:** Good night. *(He exits. Mama closes the door behind her.)*

MAMA: Hello, honey. What you sitting like that for?

BENEATHA: I'm just sitting.

MAMA: Didn't you have a nice time?

BENEATHA: No.

210 **MAMA:** No? What's the matter?

BENEATHA: Mama, George is a fool—honest. *(She rises.)*

MAMA: *(Hustling around unloading the packages she has entered with.
   She stops.)* Is he, baby?

BENEATHA: Yes.

Beneatha makes up Travis' bed as she talks.

MAMA: You sure?

215 **BENEATHA:** Yes.

MAMA: Well—I guess you better not waste your time with no fools.

*Beneatha looks up at her mother, watching her put groceries in the refrig-
erator. Finally she gathers up her things and starts into the bedroom. At
the door she stops and looks back at her mother.*

BENEATHA: Mama—

MAMA: Yes, baby—

BENEATHA: Thank you.

220 **MAMA:** For what?

BENEATHA: For understanding me this time.

She exits quickly and the mother stands, smiling a little, looking at the place where Beneatha just stood. Ruth enters.

RUTH: Now don't you fool with any of this stuff, Lena—
MAMA: Oh, I just thought I'd sort a few things out. Is Brother here?
RUTH: Yes.
225 **MAMA:** *(With concern.)* Is he—
RUTH: *(Reading her eyes.)* Yes.

Mama is silent and someone knocks on the door. Mama and Ruth exchange weary and knowing glances and Ruth opens it to admit the neighbor, Mrs. Johnson, who is a rather squeaky wide-eyed lady of no particular age, with a newspaper under her arm.

MAMA: *(Changing her expression to acute delight and a ringing cheerful greeting.)* Oh—hello there, Johnson.
JOHNSON: *(This is a woman who decided long ago to be enthusiastic about EVERYTHING in life and she is inclined to wave her wrist vigorously at the height of her exclamatory comments.)* Hello there, yourself! H'you this evening, Ruth?
RUTH: *(Not much of a deceptive type.)* Fine, Mis' Johnson, h'you?
230 **JOHNSON:** Fine. *(Reaching out quickly, playfully, and patting Ruth's stomach.)* Ain't you starting to poke out none yet! *(She mugs with delight at the over-familiar remark and her eyes dart around looking at the crates and packing preparation; Mama's face is a cold sheet of endurance.)* Oh, ain't we getting ready round here, though! Yessir! Lookathere! I'm telling you the Youngers is really getting ready to "move on up a little higher!"—Bless God!
MAMA: *(A little drily, doubting the total sincerity of the Blesser.)* Bless God.
JOHNSON: He's good, ain't He?
MAMA: Oh yes, He's good.
JOHNSON: I mean sometimes He works in mysterious ways . . . but He works, don't He!
235 **MAMA:** *(The same.)* Yes, he does.
JOHNSON: I'm just sooooo happy for y'all. And this here child—*(About Ruth.)* looks like she could just pop open with happiness, don't she. Where's the rest of the family?
MAMA: Bennie's gone to bed—
JOHNSON: Ain't no . . . *(The implication is pregnancy.)* sickness done hit you—I hope . . . ?
MAMA: No—she just tired. She was out this evening.
240 **JOHNSON:** *(All is a coo, an emphatic coo.)* Aw—ain't that lovely. She still going out with the little Murchison boy?
MAMA: *(Drily.)* Ummmm huh.

JOHNSON: That's lovely. You sure got lovely children, Younger. Me and Isaiah talks all the time 'bout what fine children you was blessed with. We
sure do.

MAMA: Ruth, give Mis' Johnson a piece of sweet potato pie and some milk.

JOHNSON: Oh honey, I can't stay hardly a minute—I just dropped in to see
if there was anything I could do. *(Accepting the food easily.)* I guess y'all
seen the news what's all over the colored paper this week . . .

245   MAMA: No—didn't get mine yet this week.

JOHNSON: *(Lifting her head and blinking with the spirit of catastrophe.)*
You mean you ain't read 'bout them colored people that was bombed out
their place out there?

*Ruth straightens with concern and takes the paper and reads it. Johnson
notices her and feeds commentary.*

JOHNSON: Ain't it something how bad these here white folks is getting here
in Chicago! Lord, getting so you think you right down in Mississippi! *(With
a tremendous and rather insincere sense of melodrama.)* 'Course I think
it's wonderful how our folks keeps on pushing out. You hear some of these
Negroes round here talking 'bout how they don't go where they ain't
wanted and all that—but not me, honey! *(This is a lie.)* Wilhemenia
Othella Johnson goes anywhere, any time she feels like it! *(With head
movement for emphasis.)* Yes I do! Why if we left it up to these here crackers, the poor niggers wouldn't have nothing—*(She clasps her hand over
her mouth.)* Oh, I always forgets you don't 'low that word in your house.

MAMA: *(Quietly, looking at her.)* No—I don't 'low it.

JOHNSON: *(Vigorously again.)* Me neither! I was just telling Isaiah yesterday when he come using it in front of me—I said, "Isaiah, it's just like Mis'
Younger says all the time—"

250   MAMA: Don't you want some more pie?

JOHNSON: No—no thank you; this was lovely. I got to get on over home and
have my midnight coffee. I hear some people say it don't let them sleep but
I finds I can't close my eyes right lessen I done had that laaaast cup of coffee . . . *(She waits. A beat. Undaunted.)* My Goodnight coffee, I calls it!

MAMA: *(With much eye-rolling and communication between herself and
Ruth.)* Ruth, why don't you give Mis' Johnson some coffee.

Ruth gives Mama an unpleasant look for her kindness.

JOHNSON: *(Accepting the coffee.)* Where's Brother tonight?

MAMA: He's lying down.

255   JOHNSON: MMmmmmm, he sure gets his beauty rest, don't he? Good-looking
man. Sure is a good-looking man! *(Reaching out to pat Ruth's stomach
again.)* I guess that's how we keep on having babies around here. *(She
winks at Mama.)* One thing 'bout Brother, he always know how to have a
good time. And soooooo ambitious! I bet it was his idea y'all moving out to

Clybourne Park. Lord—I bet this time next month y'all's names will have been in the papers plenty—*(Holding up her hands to mark off each word of the headline she can see in front of her.)* "NEGROES INVADE CLYBOURNE PARK—BOMBED!"

MAMA: *(She and Ruth look at the woman in amazement.)* We ain't exactly moving out there to get bombed.

JOHNSON: Oh, honey—you know I'm praying to God every day that don't nothing like that happen! But you have to think of life like it is—and these here Chicago peckerwoods is some baaaad peckerwoods.

MAMA: *(Wearily.)* We done thought about all that Mis' Johnson.

Beneatha comes out of the bedroom in her robe and passes through to the bathroom. Mrs. Johnson turns.

JOHNSON: Hello there, Bennie!

260 **BENEATHA:**   *(Crisply.)* Hello, Mrs. Johnson.

JOHNSON: How is school?

BENEATHA: *(Crisply.)* Fine, thank you. *(She goes out.)*

JOHNSON: *(Insulted.)* Getting so she don't have much to say to nobody.

MAMA: The child was on her way to the bathroom.

265 **JOHNSON:**   I know—but sometimes she act like ain't got time to pass the time of day with nobody ain't been to college. Oh—I ain't criticizing her none. It's just—you know how some of our young people gets when they get a little education. *(Mama and Ruth say nothing, just look at her.)* Yes—well. Well, I guess I better get on home. *(Unmoving.)* 'Course I can understand how she must be proud and everything—being the only one in the family to make something of herself. I know just being a chauffeur ain't never satisfied Brother none. He shouldn't feel like that, though. Ain't nothing wrong with being a chauffeur.

MAMA: There's plenty wrong with it.

JOHNSON: What?

MAMA: Plenty. My husband always said being any kind of a servant wasn't a fit thing for a man to have to be. He always said a man's hands was made to make things, or to turn the earth with—not to drive nobody's car for 'em—or—*(She looks at her own hands.)* carry they slop jars. And my boy is just like him—he wasn't meant to wait on nobody.

JOHNSON: *(Rising, somewhat offended.)* Mmmmmmmmm. The Youngers is too much for me! *(She looks around.)* You sure one proud-acting bunch of colored folks. Well—I always thinks like Booker T. Washington said that time—"Education has spoiled many a good plow hand"—

270 **MAMA:**   Is that what old Booker T. said?

JOHNSON: He sure did.

MAMA: Well, it sounds just like him. The fool.

JOHNSON: *(Indignantly.)* Well—he was one of our great men.

MAMA: Who said so?

275 **JOHNSON:** *(Nonplussed.)* You know, me and you ain't never agreed about some things, Lena Younger. I guess I better be going—

RUTH: *(Quickly.)* Good night.

JOHNSON: Good night. Oh—*(Thrusting it at her.)* You can keep the paper! *(With a trill.)* 'Night.

MAMA: Good night, Mis' Johnson.

Mrs. Johnson exits.

RUTH: If ignorance was gold . . .

280 **MAMA:** Shush. Don't talk about folks behind their backs.

RUTH: You do.

MAMA: I'm old and corrupted. *(Beneatha enters.)* You was rude to Mis' Johnson, Beneatha, and I don't like it at all.

BENEATHA: *(At her door.)* Mama, if there are two things we, as a people, have got to overcome, one is the Klu Klux Klan—and the other is Mrs. Johnson. *(She exits.)*

MAMA: Smart aleck.

The phone rings.

285 **RUTH:** I'll get it.

MAMA: Lord, ain't this a popular place tonight.

RUTH: *(At the phone.)* Hello—Just a minute. *(Goes to door.)* Walter, it's Mrs. Arnold. *(Waits. Goes back to the phone. Tense.)* Hello. Yes, this is his wife speaking . . . He's lying down now. Yes . . . well, he'll be in tomorrow. He's been very sick. Yes—I know we should have called, but we were so sure he'd be able to come in today. Yes—yes, I'm very sorry. Yes . . . Thank you very much. *(She hangs up. Walter is standing in the doorway of the bedroom behind her.)* That was Mrs. Arnold.

WALTER: *(Indifferently.)* Was it?

RUTH: She said if you don't come in tomorrow that they are getting a new man . . .

290 **WALTER:** Ain't that sad—ain't that crying sad.

RUTH: She said Mr. Arnold has had to take a cab for three days . . . Walter, you ain't been to work for three days! *(This is a revelation to her.)* Where you been, Walter Lee Younger? *(Walter looks at her and starts to laugh.)* You're going to lose your job.

WALTER: That's right . . . *(He turns on the radio.)*

RUTH: Oh, Walter, and with your mother working like a dog every day—

A steamy, deep blues pours into the room.

WALTER: That's sad too—Everything is sad.

295 **MAMA:** What you been doing for these three days, son?

WALTER: Mama—you don't know all the things a man what got leisure can find to do in this city . . . What's this—Friday night? Well—Wednesday I borrowed Willy Harris' car and I went for a drive . . . just me and myself and I drove and drove . . . Way out . . . way past South Chicago, and I parked the car and I sat and looked at the steel mills all day long. I just sat in the car and looked at them big black chimneys for hours. Then I drove back and I went to the Green Hat. *(Pause.)* And Thursday—Thursday I borrowed the car again and I got in it and I pointed it the other way and I drove the other way—for hours—way, way up to Wisconsin, and I looked at the farms. I just drove and looked at the farms. Then I drove back and I went to the Green Hat. *(Pause.)* And today—today I didn't get the car. Today I just walked. All over the Southside. And I looked at the Negroes and they looked at me and finally I just sat down on the curb at Thirty-ninth and South Parkway and I just sat there and watched the Negroes go by. And then I went to the Green Hat. You all sad? You all depressed? And you know where I am going right now—

Ruth goes out quietly.

Mama: Oh, Big Walter, is this the harvest of our days?

Walter: You know what I like about the Green Hat? I like this little cat they got there who blows a sax . . . He blows. He talks to me. He ain't but 'bout five feet tall and he's got a conked head and his eyes is always closed and he's all music—

Mama: *(Rising and getting some papers out of her handbag.)* Walter—

300 **Walter:** And there's this other guy who plays the piano . . . and they got a sound. I mean they can work on some music . . . They got the best little combo in the world in the Green Hat . . . You can just sit there and drink and listen to them three men play and you realize that don't nothing matter worth a damn, but just being there—

Mama: I've helped do it to you, haven't I, son? Walter I been wrong.

Walter: Naw—you ain't never been wrong about nothing, Mama.

Mama: Listen to me, now. I say I been wrong, son. That I been doing to you what the rest of the world been doing to you. *(She turns off the radio.)* Walter—*(She stops and he looks up slowly at her and she meets his eyes pleadingly.)* What you ain't never understood is that I ain't got nothing, don't own nothing, ain't never really wanted nothing that wasn't for you. There ain't nothing as precious to me . . . There ain't nothing worth holding on to, money, dreams, nothing else—if it means—if it means it's going to destroy my boy. *(She takes an envelope out of her handbag and puts it in front of him and he watches her without speaking or moving.)* I paid the man thirty-five hundred dollars down on the house. That leaves sixty-five hundred dollars. Monday morning I want you to take this money and take three thousand dollars and put it in a savings account for Beneatha's medical schooling. The rest you put in a checking account—with your name on it. And from now on any penny that come out of it or that go in it is for you to look after. For you to decide. *(She drops her hands a little helplessly.)* It ain't much, but it's all I got in the world and I'm putting it in your hands. I'm telling you to be the head of this family from now on like you supposed to be.

WALTER: *(Stares at the money.)* You trust me like that, Mama?

305 **MAMA:** I ain't never stop trusting you. Like I ain't never stop loving you.

She goes out, and Walter sits looking at the money on the table. Finally, in a decisive gesture, he gets up, and, in mingled joy and desperation, picks up the money. At the same moment, Travis enters for bed.

TRAVIS: What's the matter, Daddy? You drunk?

WALTER: *(Sweetly, more sweetly than we have ever known him.)* No, Daddy ain't drunk. Daddy ain't going to never be drunk again. . . .

TRAVIS: Well, good night, Daddy.

The Father has come from behind the couch and leans over, embracing his son.

WALTER: Son, I feel like talking to you tonight.

310 **TRAVIS:** About what?

WALTER: Oh, about a lot of things. About you and what kind of man you going to be when you grow up. . . . Son—son, what do you want to be when you grow up?

TRAVIS: A bus driver.

WALTER: *(Laughing a little.)* A what? Man, that ain't nothing to want to be!

TRAVIS: Why not?

WALTER: 'Cause, man—it ain't big enough—you know what I mean.

315 **TRAVIS:** I don't know then. I can't make up my mind. Sometimes Mama asks me that too. And sometimes when I tell her I just want to be like you—she says she don't want me to be like that and sometimes she says she does . . .

WALTER: *(Gathering him up in his arms.)* You know what, Travis? In seven years you going to be seventeen years old. And things is going to be very different with us in seven years, Travis. . . . One day when you are seventeen I'll come home—home from my office downtown somewhere—

TRAVIS: You don't work in no office, Daddy.

WALTER: No—but after tonight. After what your daddy gonna do tonight, there's going to be offices—a whole lot of offices. . . .

320 **TRAVIS:** What you gonna do tonight, Daddy?

WALTER: You wouldn't understand yet, son, but your daddy's gonna make a transaction . . . a business transaction that's going to change our lives. . . . That's how come one day when you 'bout seventeen years old I'll come home and I'll be pretty tired, you know what I mean, after a day of conferences and secretaries getting things wrong the way they do . . . 'cause an executive's life is hell, man—*(The more he talks the farther away he gets.)* And I'll pull the car up on the driveway . . . just a plain black Chrysler, I think, with white walls—no—black tires. More elegant. Rich people don't have to be flashy . . . though I'll have to get something a little sportier for Ruth—maybe a Cadillac convertible to do her shopping in. . . . And I'll come up the steps to the house and the gardener will be clipping away at the hedges and he'll say, "Good evening, Mr. Younger." And I'll say, "Hello, Jefferson, how are you this evening?" And I'll go inside and Ruth will come downstairs and meet me at the door and we'll kiss each other and she'll take my arm and we'll go up to your room to see you sitting on the floor with the catalogues of all the great schools in America around you. . . . All the great schools in the world! And—and I'll say, all right son—it's your seventeenth birthday, what is it you've decided? . . . Just tell me where you want to go to school and you'll *go*. Just tell me, what it is you want to be—and you'll *be* it. . . . Whatever you want to be—Yessir! *(He holds his arms open for Travis.)* You just name it, son . . . *(Travis leaps into them.)* and I hand you the world!

Walter's voice has risen in pitch and hysterical promise and on the last line he lifts Travis high.

(Blackout)

Scene Three

Time: Saturday, moving day, one week later.

    Before the curtain rises, Ruth's voice, a strident, dramatic church alto, cuts through the silence.

    It is, in the darkness, a triumphant surge, a penetrating statement of expectation: "Oh, Lord, I don't feel no ways tired! Children, oh, glory hallelujah!"

    As the curtain rises we see that Ruth is alone in the living room, finishing up the family's packing. It is moving day. She is nailing crates and tying cartons. Beneatha enters, carrying a guitar case, and watches her exuberant sister-in-law.

Ruth: Hey!

Beneatha: *(Putting away the case.)* Hi.

Ruth: *(Pointing at a package.)* Honey—look in that package there and see what I found on sale this morning at the South Center. *(Ruth gets up and moves to the package and draws out some curtains.)* Lookahere—hand-turned hems!

325 **Beneatha:**   How do you know the window size out there?

Ruth: *(Who hadn't thought of that.)* Oh—Well, they bound to fit something in the whole house. Anyhow, they was too good a bargain to pass up. *(Ruth slaps her head, suddenly remembering something.)* Oh, Bennie—I meant to put a special note on that carton over there. That's your mama's good china and she wants 'em to be very careful with it.

Beneatha: I'll do it.

Beneatha finds a piece of paper and starts to draw large letters on it.

RUTH: You know what I'm going to do soon as I get in that new house?
BENEATHA: What?
330 **RUTH:**   Honey—I'm going to run me a tub of water up to here . . . (*With her fingers practically up to her nostrils.*) And I'm going to get in it—and I am going to sit . . . and sit . . . and sit in that hot water and the first person who knocks to tell *me* to hurry up and come out—
BENEATHA: Gets shot at sunrise.
RUTH: (*Laughing happily.*) You said it, sister! (*Noticing how large Beneatha is absent-mindedly making the note.*) Honey, they ain't going to read that from no airplane.
BENEATHA: (*Laughing herself.*) I guess I always think things have more emphasis if they are big, somehow.
RUTH: (*Looking up at her and smiling.*) You and your brother seem to have that as a philosophy of life. Lord, that man—done changed so 'round here. You know—you know what we did last night? Me and Walter Lee?
335 **BENEATHA:**   What?
RUTH: (*Smiling to herself.*) We went to the movies. (*Looking at Beneatha to see if she understands.*) We went to the movies. You know the last time me and Walter went to the movies together?
BENEATHA: No.
RUTH: Me neither. That's how long it been. (*Smiling again.*) But we went last night. The picture wasn't much good, but that didn't seem to matter. We went—and we held hands.
BENEATHA: Oh, Lord!
340 **RUTH:**   We held hands—and you know what?
BENEATHA: What?
RUTH: When we come out of the show it was late and dark and all the stores and things was closed up . . . and it was kind of chilly and there wasn't many people on the streets . . . and we was still holding hands, me and Walter.
BENEATHA: You're killing me.

Walter enters with a large package. His happiness is deep in him; he cannot keep still with his new-found exuberance. He is singing and wiggling and snapping his fingers. He puts his package in a corner and puts a phonograph record, which he has brought in with him, on the record player. As the music, soulful and sensuous, comes up he dances over to Ruth and tries to get her to dance with him. She gives in at last to his raunchiness and in a fit of giggling allows herself to be drawn into his mood. They dip and she melts into his arms in a classic, body-melding "slow drag."

BENEATHA: (*Regarding them a long time as they dance, then drawing in her breath for a deeply exaggerated comment which she does not particularly mean.*) Talk about—oldddddddddd-fashioneddddddd—Negroes!

345 **WALTER:**   *(Stopping momentarily.)* What kind of Negroes?

He says this in fun. He is not angry with her today, nor with anyone. He starts to dance with his wife again.

BENEATHA: Old-fashioned.

WALTER: *(As he dances with Ruth.)* You know, when these *New Negroes* have their convention—*(Pointing at his sister.)*—that is going to be the chairman of the Committee on Unending Agitation. *(He goes on dancing, then stops.)* Race, race, race! . . . Girl, I do believe you are the first person in the history of the entire human race to successfully brainwash yourself. *(Beneatha breaks up and he goes on dancing. He stops again, enjoying his tease.)* Damn, even the N double A C P takes a holiday sometimes! *(Beneatha and Ruth laugh. He dances with Ruth some more and starts to laugh and stops and pantomimes someone over an operating table.)* I can just see that chick someday looking down at some poor cat on an operating table and before she starts to slice him, she says . . . *(Pulling his sleeves back maliciously.)* "By the way, what are your views on civil rights down there? . . ."

He laughs at her again and starts to dance happily. The bell sounds.

BENEATHA: Sticks and stones may break my bones but . . . words will never hurt me!

Beneatha goes to the door and opens it as Walter and Ruth go on with the clowning. Beneatha is somewhat surprised to see a quiet-looking middle-aged white man in a business suit holding his hat and a briefcase in his hand and consulting a small piece of paper.

MAN: Uh—how do you do, miss. I am looking for a Mrs.—*(He looks at the slip of paper.)* Mrs. Lena Younger? *(He stops short, struck dumb at the sight of the oblivious Walter and Ruth.)*

350 **BENEATHA:**   *(Smoothing her hair with slight embarrassment.)* Oh—yes, that's my mother. Excuse me *(She closes the door and turns to quiet the other two.)* Ruth! Brother! *(Enunciating precisely but soundlessly: "There's a white man at the door!" They stop dancing, Ruth cuts off the phonograph, Beneatha opens the door. The man casts a curious quick glance at all of them.)* Uh—come in please.

MAN: *(Coming in.)* Thank you.

BENEATHA: My mother isn't here just now. Is it business?

MAN: Yes . . . well, of a sort.

WALTER: *(Freely, the Man of the House.)* Have a seat. I'm Mrs. Younger's son. I look after most of her business matters.

Ruth and Beneatha exchange amused glances.

355 **MAN:**   *(Regarding Walter, and sitting.)* Well—My name is Karl Lindner . . .

WALTER: *(Stretching out his hand.)* Walter Younger. This is my wife—*(Ruth nods politely.)*—and my sister.

LINDNER: How do you do.

WALTER: *(Amiably, as he sits himself easily on a chair, leaning forward on his knees with interest and looking expectantly into the newcomer's face.)* What can we do for you, Mr. Lindner!

LINDNER: *(Some minor shuffling of the hat and briefcase on his knees.)* Well—I am a representative of the Clybourne Park Improvement Association—

360 WALTER: *(Pointing.)* Why don't you sit your things on the floor?

LINDNER: Oh—yes. Thank you. *(He slides the briefcase and hat under the chair.)* And as I was saying—I am from the Clybourne Park Improvement Association and we have had it brought to our attention at the last meeting that you people—or at least your mother—has bought a piece of residential property at—*(He digs for the slip of paper again.)*—four o six Clybourne Street . . .

WALTER: That's right. Care for something to drink? Ruth, get Mr. Lindner a beer.

LINDNER: *(Upset for some reason.)* Oh—no, really. I mean thank you very much, but no thank you.

RUTH: *(Innocently.)* Some coffee?

365 LINDNER: Thank you, nothing at all.

Beneatha is watching the man carefully.

LINDNER: Well, I don't know how much you folks know about our organization. *(He is a gentle man; thoughtful and somewhat labored in his manner.)* It is one of these community organizations set up to look after—oh, you know, things like block upkeep and special projects and we also have what we call our New Neighbors Orientation Committee . . .

BENEATHA: *(Drily.)* Yes—and what do they do?

LINDNER: *(Turning a little to her and then returning the main force to Walter.)* Well—it's what you might call a sort of welcoming committee, I guess. I mean they, we—I'm the chairman of the committee—go around and see the new people who move into the neighborhood and sort of give them the lowdown on the way we do things out in Clybourne Park.

BENEATHA: *(With appreciation of the two meanings, which escape Ruth and Walter.)* Un-huh.

370 LINDNER: And we also have the category of what the association calls—*(He looks elsewhere.)*—uh—special community problems . . .

BENEATHA: Yes—and what are some of those?

WALTER: Girl, let the man talk.

LINDNER: *(With understated relief.)* Thank you. I would sort of like to explain this thing in my own way. I mean I want to explain to you in a certain way.

WALTER: Go ahead.

375 LINDNER: Yes. Well. I'm going to try to get right to the point. I'm sure we'll all appreciate that in the long run.

BENEATHA: Yes.

WALTER: Be still now!

LINDNER: Well—

RUTH: *(Still innocently.)* Would you like another chair—you don't look comfortable.

380 **LINDNER:** *(More frustrated than annoyed.)* No, thank you very much. Please. Well—to get right to the point I—*(A great breath, and he is off at last.)* I am sure you people must be aware of some of the incidents which have happened in various parts of the city when colored people have moved into certain areas—*(Beneatha exhales heavily and starts tossing a piece of fruit up and down in the air.)* Well—because we have what I think is going to be a unique type of organization in American community life—not only do we deplore that kind of thing—but we are trying to do something about it. *(Beneatha stops tossing and turns with a new and quizzical interest to the man.)* We feel—*(gaining confidence in his mission because of the interest in the faces of the people he is talking to.)*—we feel that most of the trouble in this world, when you come right down to it—*(He hits his knee for emphasis.)*—most of the trouble exists because people just don't sit down and talk to each other.

RUTH: *(Nodding as she might in church, pleased with the remark.)* You can say that again, mister.

LINDNER: *(More encouraged by such affirmation.)* Then we don't try hard enough in this world to understand the other fellow's problem. The other guy's point of view.

RUTH: Now that's right.

Beneatha and Walter merely watch and listen with genuine interest.

LINDNER: Yes—that's the way we feel out in Clybourne Park. And that's why I was elected to come here this afternoon and talk to you people. Friendly like, you know, the way people should talk to each other and see if we couldn't find some way to work this thing out. As I say, the whole business is a matter of *caring* about the other fellow. Anybody can see that you are a nice family of folks, hard working and honest I'm sure. *(Beneatha frowns slightly, quizzically, her head tilted regarding him.)* Today everybody knows what it means to be on the outside of *something*. And of course, there is always somebody who is out to take advantage of people who don't always understand.

385 **WALTER:** What do you mean?

LINDNER: Well—you see our community is made up of people who've worked hard as the dickens for years to build up that little community. They're not rich and fancy people; just hard-working, honest people who don't really have much but those little homes and a dream of the kind of community they want to raise their children in. Now, I don't say we are perfect and there is a lot wrong in some of the things they want. But you've got to admit that a man, right or wrong, has the right to want to have the neighborhood he lives in a certain kind of way. And at the moment the overwhelming majority of our people out there feel that people get along better, take more of a common interest in the life of the community, when they share a common background. I want you to believe me when I tell you that race prejudice simply doesn't enter into it. It is a matter of the people of Clybourne Park believing, rightly or wrongly, as I say, that for the happiness of all concerned that our Negro families are happier when they live in their *own* communities.

BENEATHA: *(With a grand and bitter gesture.)* This, friends, is the Welcoming Committee!

WALTER: *(Dumbfounded, looking at Lindner.)* Is this what you came marching all the way over here to tell us?

LINDNER: Well, now we've been having a fine conversation. I hope you'll hear me all the way through.

390 **WALTER:** *(Tightly.)* Go ahead, man.

LINDNER: You see—in the face of all the things I have said, we are prepared to make your family a very generous offer . . .

BENEATHA: Thirty pieces and not a coin less!

WALTER: Yeah?

LINDNER: *(Putting on his glasses and drawing a form out of the briefcase.)* Our association is prepared, through the collective effort of our people, to buy the house from you at a financial gain to your family.

395 **RUTH:** Lord have mercy, ain't this the living gall!

WALTER: All right, you through?

LINDNER: Well, I want to give you the exact terms of the financial arrangement—

WALTER: We don't want to hear no exact terms of no arrangements. I want to know if you got any more to tell us 'bout getting together?

LINDNER: *(Taking off his glasses.)* Well—I don't suppose that you feel . . .

400 **WALTER:** Never mind how I feel—you got any more to say 'bout how people ought to sit down and talk to each other? . . . Get out of my house, man.

He turns his back and walks to the door.

LINDNER: *(Looking around at the hostile faces and reaching and assembling his hat and briefcase.)* Well—I don't understand why you people are reacting this way. What do you think you are going to gain by moving into a neighborhood where you just aren't wanted and where some elements—well—people can get awful worked up when they feel that their whole way of life and everything they've ever worked for is threatened.

WALTER: Get out.

LINDNER: *(At the door, holding a small card.)* Well—I'm sorry it went like this.

WALTER: Get out.

405 **LINDNER:** *(Almost sadly regarding Walter.)* You just can't force people to change their hearts, son.

He turns and puts his card on a table and exits. Walter pushes the door to with stinging hatred, and stands looking at it. Ruth just sits and Beneatha just stands. They say nothing. Mama and Travis enter.

MAMA: Well—this all the packing got done since I left out of here this morning. I testify before God that my children got all the energy of the *dead!* What time the moving men due?

BENEATHA: Four o'clock. You had a caller, Mama.

She is smiling, teasingly.

MAMA: Sure enough—who?

BENEATHA: *(Her arms folded saucily.)* The Welcoming Committee.

Walter and Ruth giggle.

410 **MAMA:**   *(Innocently.)* Who?

BENEATHA: The Welcoming Committee. They said they're sure going to be glad to see you when you get there.

WALTER: *(Devilishly.)* Yeah, they said they can't hardly wait to see your face.

Laughter.

MAMA: *(Sensing their facetiousness.)* What's the matter with you all?

WALTER: Ain't nothing the matter with us. We just telling you 'bout the gentleman who came to see you this afternoon. From the Clybourne Park Improvement Association.

415 **MAMA:**   What he want?

RUTH: *(In the same mood as Beneatha and Walter.)* To welcome you, honey.

WALTER: He said they can't hardly wait. He said the one thing they don't have, that they just *dying* to have out there is a fine family of fine colored people! *(To Ruth and Beneatha.)* Ain't that right!

RUTH: *(Mockingly.)* Yeah! He left his card—

BENEATHA: *(Handing card to Mama.)* In case.

Mama reads and throws it on the floor—understanding and looking off as she draws her chair up to the table on which she has put her plant and some sticks and some cord.

420 **MAMA:**   Father, give us strength. *(Knowingly—and without fun.)* Did he threaten us?

BENEATHA: Oh—Mama—they don't do it like that any more. He talked Brotherhood. He said everybody ought to learn how to sit down and hate each other with good Christian fellowship.

She and Walter shake hands to ridicule the remark.

MAMA: *(Sadly.)* Lord, protect us . . .

RUTH: You should hear the money those folks raised to buy the house from us. All we paid and then some.

BENEATHA: What they think we going to do—eat 'em?

425 **RUTH:** No, honey, marry 'em.

MAMA: *(Shaking her head.)* Lord, Lord, Lord . . .

RUTH: Well—that's the way the crackers crumble. *(A beat.)* Joke.

BENEATHA: *(Laughingly noticing what her mother is doing.)* Mama, what are you doing?

MAMA: Fixing my plant so it won't get hurt none on the way . . .

430 **BENEATHA:** Mama, you going to take *that* to the new house?

MAMA: Un-huh—

BENEATHA: That raggedy-looking old thing?

MAMA: *(Stopping and looking at her.)* It expresses ME!

RUTH: *(With delight, to Beneatha.)* So there, Miss Thing!

Walter comes to Mama suddenly and bends down behind her and squeezes her in his arms with all his strength. She is overwhelmed by the suddenness of it and, though delighted, her manner is like that of Ruth and Travis.

435 **MAMA:** Look out now, boy! You make me mess up my thing here!

WALTER: *(His face lit, he slips down on his knees beside her, his arms still about her.)* Mama . . . you know what it means to climb up in the chariot?

MAMA: *(Gruffly, very happy.)* Get on away from me now . . .

RUTH: *(Near the gift-wrapped package, trying to catch Walter's eye.)* Psst—

WALTER: What the old song say, Mama . . .

440 **RUTH:** Walter—Now?

She is pointing at the package.

WALTER: *(Speaking the lines, sweetly, playfully, in his mother's face.)*
    I got wings . . . you got wings . . .
    All God's Children got wings . . .

MAMA: Boy—get out of my face and do some work . . .

WALTER:
    When I get to heaven gonna put on my wings,
    Gonna fly all over God's heaven . . .

BENEATHA: *(Teasingly, from across the room.)* Everybody talking 'bout heaven ain't going there!

445 **WALTER:** *(To Ruth, who is carrying the box across to them.)* I don't know, you think we ought to give her that . . . Seems to me she ain't been very appreciative around here.

MAMA: *(Eyeing the box, which is obviously a gift.)* What is that?

WALTER: *(Taking it from Ruth and putting it on the table in front of Mama.)* Well—what you all think? Should we give it to her?

RUTH: Oh—she was pretty good today.

MAMA: I'll good you—

She turns her eyes to the box again.

450 **BENEATHA:** Open it, Mama.

She stands up, looks at it, turns and looks at all of them, and then presses her hands together and does not open the package.

WALTER: *(Sweetly.)* Open it, Mama. It's for you. *(Mama looks in his eyes. It is the first present in her life without its being Christmas. Slowly she opens her package and lifts out, one by one, a brand-new sparkling set of gardening tools. Walter continues, prodding.)* Ruth made up the note— read it . . .

MAMA: *(Picking up the card and adjusting her glasses.)* "To our own Mrs. Miniver—Love from Brother, Ruth and Beneatha." Ain't that lovely . . .

TRAVIS: *(Tugging at his father's sleeve.)* Daddy, can I give her mine now?

WALTER: All right, son. *(Travis flies to get his gift.)*

455 **MAMA:** Now I don't have to use my knives and forks no more . . .

WALTER: Travis didn't want to go in with the rest of us, Mama. He got his own. *(Somewhat amused.)* We don't know what it is . . .

TRAVIS: *(Racing back in the room with a large hatbox and putting it in front of his grandmother.)* Here!

MAMA: Lord have mercy, baby. You done gone and bought your grand-mother a hat!

TRAVIS: *(Very proud.)* Open it!

She does and lifts out an elaborate, but very elaborate, wide gardening hat, and all the adults break up at the sight of it.

460 **RUTH:** Travis, honey, what is that?

TRAVIS: *(Who thinks it is beautiful and appropriate.)* It's a gardening hat! Like the ladies always have on in the magazines when they work in their gardens.

BENEATHA: *(Giggling fiercely.)* Travis—we were trying to make Mama Mrs. Miniver—not Scarlett O'Hara!

MAMA: *(Indignantly.)* What's the matter with you all! This here is a beau-tiful hat! *(Absurdly.)* I always wanted me one just like it!

She pops it on her head to prove it to her grandson, and the hat is ludi-crous and considerably oversized.

RUTH: Hot dog! Go, Mama!

465 **WALTER:** *(Doubled over with laughter.)* I'm sorry, Mama—but you look like you ready to go out and chop you some cotton sure enough!

They all laugh except Mama, out of deference to Travis' feelings.

MAMA: *(Gathering the boy up to her.)* Bless your heart—this is the prettiest hat I ever owned—*(Walter, Ruth and Beneatha chime in—noisily, festively and insincerely congratulating Travis on his gift.)* What are we all standing around here for? We ain't finished packin' yet. Bennie, you ain't packed one book.

The bell rings.

BENEATHA: That couldn't be the movers . . . it's not hardly two good yet—

Beneatha goes into her room. Mama starts for door.

WALTER: *(Turning, stiffening.)* Wait—wait—I'll get it.

He stands and looks at the door.

MAMA: You expecting company, son?
470 **WALTER:** *(Just looking at the door.)* Yeah—yeah . . .

Mama looks at Ruth, and they exchange innocent and unfrightened glances.

MAMA: *(Not understanding.)* Well, let them in, son.
BENEATHA: *(From her room.)* We need some more string.
MAMA: Travis—you run to the hardware and get me some string cord.

Mama goes out and Walter turns and looks at Ruth. Travis goes to a dish for money.

RUTH: Why don't you answer the door, man?
475 **WALTER:** *(Suddenly bounding across the floor to embrace her.)* 'Cause sometimes it hard to let the future begin! *(Stooping down in her face.)*
    I got wings! You got wings!
    All God's children got wings!
(He crosses to the door and throws it open. Standing there is a very slight little man in a not too prosperous business suit and with haunted frightened eyes and a hat pulled down tightly, brim up, around his forehead. Travis passes between the men and exits. Walter leans deep in the man's face, still in his jubilance.)
    When I get to heaven gonna put on my wings,
    Gonna fly all over God's heaven . . .
(The little man just stares at him.)
    Heaven—
(Suddenly he stops and looks past the little man into the empty hallway.)
    Where's Willy, man?
BOBO: He ain't with me.
WALTER: *(Not disturbed.)* Oh—come on in. You know my wife.
BOBO: *(Dumbly, taking off his hat.)* Yes—h'you, Miss Ruth.
RUTH: *(Quietly, a mood apart from her husband already, seeing Bobo.)* Hello, Bobo.

480 **WALTER:** You right on time today . . . Right on time. That's the way! *(He slaps Bobo on his back.)* Sit down . . . lemme hear.

Ruth stands stiffly and quietly in back of them, as though somehow she senses death, her eyes fixed on her husband.

BOBO: *(His frightened eyes on the floor, his hat in his hands.)* Could I please get a drink of water, before I tell you about it, Walter Lee?

Walter does not take his eyes off the man. Ruth goes blindly to the tap and gets a glass of water and brings it to Bobo.

WALTER: There ain't nothing wrong, is there?

BOBO: Lemme tell you—

WALTER: Man—didn't nothing go wrong?

485 **BOBO:** Lemme tell you—Walter Lee. *(Looking at Ruth and talking to her more than to Walter.)* You know how it was. I got to tell you how it was. I mean first I got to tell you how it was all the way . . . I mean about the money I put in, Walter Lee . . .

WALTER: *(With taut agitation now.)* What about the money you put in?

BOBO: Well—it wasn't much as we told you—me and Willy—*(He stops.)* I'm sorry, Walter. I got a bad feeling about it. I got a real bad feeling about it . . .

WALTER: Man, what you telling me about all this for? . . . Tell me what happened in Springfield . . .

BOBO: Springfield.

490 **RUTH:** *(Like a dead woman.)* What was supposed to happen in Springfield?

BOBO: *(To her.)* This deal that me and Walter went into with Willy—Me and Willy was going to go down to Springfield and spread some money 'round so's we wouldn't have to wait so long for the liquor license . . . That's what we were going to do. Everybody said that was the way you had to do, you understand, Miss Ruth?

WALTER: Man—what happened down there?

BOBO: *(A pitiful man, near tears.)* I'm trying to tell you, Walter.

WALTER: *(Screaming at him suddenly.)* THEN TELL ME, GOD-DAMMIT . . . WHAT'S THE MATTER WITH YOU?

495 **BOBO:** Man . . . I didn't go to no Springfield, yesterday.

WALTER: *(Halted, life hanging in the moment.)* Why not?

BOBO: *(The long way, the hard way to tell.)* 'Cause I didn't have no reasons to . . .

WALTER: Man, what are you talking about!

BOBO: I'm talking about the fact that when I got to the train station yesterday morning—eight o'clock like we planned . . . Man—*Willy didn't never show up.*

500 **WALTER:** Why . . . where was he . . . where is he?

BOBO: That's what I'm trying to tell you . . . I don't know . . . I waited six hours . . . I called his house . . . and I waited . . . six hours . . . I waited in that train station six hours . . . *(Breaking into tears.)* That was all the extra money I had in the world . . . *(Looking up at Walter with the tears running down his face.)* Man, *Willy is gone.*

WALTER: Gone, what you mean Willy is gone? Gone where? You mean he went by himself. You mean he went off to Springfield by himself—to take care of getting the license—*(Turns and looks anxiously at Ruth.)* You mean maybe he didn't want too many people in on the business down there? *(Looks to Ruth again, as before.)* You know Willy got his own ways. *(Looks back to Bobo.)* Maybe you was late yesterday and he just went on down there without you. Maybe—maybe—he's been callin' you at home tryin' to tell you what happened or something. Maybe—maybe— he just got sick. He's somewhere—he's got to be somewhere. We just got to find him—me and you got to find him. *(Grabs Bobo senselessly by the collar and starts to shake him.)* We got to!

BOBO: *(In sudden angry, frightened agony.)* What's the matter with you, Walter! *When a cat take off with your money he don't leave you no road maps!*

WALTER: *(Turning madly, as though he is looking for Willy in the very room.)* Willy! . . . Willy . . . don't do it . . . Please don't do it . . . Man, not with that money . . . Man, please, not with that money . . . Oh, God . . . Don't let it be true . . . *(He is wandering around, crying out for Willy and looking for him or perhaps for help from God.)* Man . . . I trusted you . . . Man, I put my life in your hands . . . *(He starts to crumple down on the floor as Ruth just covers her face in horror. Mama opens the door and comes into the room, with Beneatha behind her.)* Man . . . *(He starts to pound the floor with his fists, sobbing wildly.)* THAT MONEY IS MADE OUT OF MY FATHER'S FLESH—

505 **BOBO:** *(Standing over him helplessly.)* I'm sorry, Walter . . . *(Only Walter's sobs reply. Bobo puts on his hat.)* I had my life staked on this deal, too . . .

He exits.

MAMA: *(To Walter.)* Son—*(She goes to him, bends down to him, talks to his bent head.)* Son . . . Is it gone? Son, I gave you sixty-five hundred dollars. Is it gone? All of it? Beneatha's money too?

WALTER: *(Lifting his head slowly.)* Mama . . . I never . . . went to the bank at all . . .

MAMA: *(Not wanting to believe him.)* You mean . . . your sister's school money . . . you used that too . . . Walter? . . .

WALTER: Yessss! All of it . . . It's all gone . . .

There is total silence. Ruth stands with her face covered with her hands; Beneatha leans forlornly against a wall, fingering a piece of red ribbon from the mother's gift. Mama stops and looks at her son without recognition and then, quite without thinking about it, starts to beat him senselessly in the face. Beneatha goes to them and stops it.

510 **BENEATHA:** Mama!

Mama stops and looks at both of her children and rises slowly and wanders vaguely, aimlessly away from them.

MAMA: I seen . . . him . . . night after night . . . come in . . . and look at that rug . . . and then look at me . . . the red showing in his eyes . . . the veins moving in his head . . . I seen him grow thin and old before he was forty . . . working and working and working like somebody's old horse . . . killing himself . . . and you—you give it all away in a day—*(She raises her arms to strike him again.)*

BENEATHA: Mama—

MAMA: Oh, God . . . *(She looks up to Him.)* Look down here—and show me the strength.

BENEATHA: Mama—

515 **MAMA:** *(Folding over.)* Strength . . .

BENEATHA: *(Plaintively.)* Mama . . .

MAMA: Strength!

CURTAIN

Act III

An hour later.

    At curtain, there is a sullen light of gloom in the living room, gray light not unlike that which began the first scene of Act One. At left we can see Walter within his room, alone with himself. He is stretched out on the bed, his shirt out and open, his arms under his head. He does not smoke, he does not cry out, he merely lies there, looking up at the ceiling, much as if he were alone in the world.

    In the living room Beneatha sits at the table, still surrounded by the now almost ominous packing crates. She sits looking off. We feel that this is a mood struck perhaps an hour before, and it lingers now, full of the empty sound of profound disappointment. We see on a line from her brother's bedroom the sameness of their attitudes. Presently the bell rings and Beneatha rises without ambition or interest in answering. It is Asagai, smiling broadly, striding into the room with energy and happy expectation and conversation.

ASAGAI: I came over . . . I had some free time. I thought I might help with the packing. Ah, I like the look of packing crates! A household in preparation for a journey! It depresses some people . . . but for me . . . it is another feeling. Something full of the flow of life, do you understand? Movement, progress . . . It makes me think of Africa.

BENEATHA: Africa!

ASAGAI: What kind of a mood is this? Have I told you how deeply you move me?

BENEATHA: He gave away the money, Asagai . . .

5 **ASAGAI:**   Who gave away what money?

BENEATHA: The insurance money. My brother gave it away.

ASAGAI: Gave it away?

BENEATHA: He made an investment! With a man even Travis wouldn't have trusted with his most worn-out marbles.

ASAGAI: And it's gone?

10 **BENEATHA:**   Gone!

ASAGAI: I'm very sorry . . . And you, now?

BENEATHA: Me? . . . Me? . . . Me, I'm nothing . . . Me. When I was very small . . . we used to take our sleds out in the wintertime and the only hills we had were the ice-covered stone steps of some houses down the street. And we used to fill them in with snow and make them smooth and slide down them all day . . . and it was very dangerous, you know . . . far too steep . . . and sure enough one day a kid named Rufus came down too fast and hit the sidewalk and we saw his face just split open right there in front of us . . . And I remember standing there looking at his bloody open face thinking that was the end of Rufus. But the ambulance came and they took him to the hospital and they fixed the broken bones and they sewed it all up . . . and the next time I saw Rufus he just had a little line down the middle of his face . . . I never got over that . . .

ASAGAI: What?

BENEATHA: That that was what one person could do for another, fix him up—sew up the problem, make him all right again. That was the most marvelous thing in the world . . . I wanted to do that. I always thought it was the one concrete thing in the world that a human being could do. Fix up the sick, you know—and make them whole again. This was truly being God . . .

15 **ASAGAI:**   You wanted to be God?

BENEATHA: No—I wanted to cure. It used to be so important to me. I wanted to cure. It used to matter. I used to care. I mean about people and how their bodies hurt . . .

ASAGAI: And you've stopped caring?

BENEATHA: Yes—I think so.

ASAGAI: Why?

20 **BENEATHA:**   *(Bitterly.)* Because it doesn't seem deep enough, close enough to what ails mankind! It was a child's way of seeing things—or an idealist's.

ASAGAI: Children see things very well sometimes—and idealists even better.

BENEATHA: I know that's what you think. Because you are still where I left off. You with all your talk and dreams about Africa! You still think you can patch up the world. Cure the Great Sore of Colonialism—*(Loftily, mocking it.)* with the Penicillin of Independence—!

ASAGAI: Yes!

BENEATHA: Independence *and then what?* What about all the crooks and thieves and just plain idiots who will come into power and steal and plunder the same as before—only now they will be black and do it in the name of the new Independence—WHAT ABOUT THEM?!

25 **ASAGAI:**   That will be the problem for another time. First we must get there.

BENEATHA: And where does it end?

ASAGAI: End? Who even spoke of an end? To life? To living?

BENEATHA: An end to misery! To stupidity! Don't you see there isn't any real progress, Asagai, there is only one large circle that we march in, around and around, each of us with our own little picture in front of us— our own little mirage that we think is the future.

ASAGAI: That is the mistake.

30 **BENEATHA:**   What?

ASAGAI: What you just said—about the circle. It isn't a circle—it is simply a long line—as in geometry, you know, one that reaches into infinity. And because we cannot see the end—we also cannot see how it changes. And it is very odd but those who see the changes—who dream, who will not give up—are called idealists . . . and those who see only the circle—we call *them* the "realists"!

BENEATHA: Asagai, while I was sleeping in that bed in there, people went out and took the future right out of my hands! And nobody asked me, no-body consulted me—they just went out and changed my life!

ASAGAI: Was it your money?

BENEATHA: What?

35 **ASAGAI:**   Was it your money he gave away?

BENEATHA: It belonged to all of us.

ASAGAI: But did you earn it? Would you have had it at all if your father had not died?

BENEATHA: No.

ASAGAI: Then isn't there something wrong in a house—in a world—where all dreams, good or bad, must depend on the death of a man? I never thought to see *you* like this, Alaiyo. You! Your brother made a mistake and you are grateful to him so that now you can give up the ailing human race on account of it! You talk about what good is struggle, what good is any-thing! Where are we all going and why are we bothering!

40 **BENEATHA:**   AND YOU CANNOT ANSWER IT!

ASAGAI: *(Shouting over her.) I LIVE THE ANSWER! (Pause.)* In my village at home it is the exceptional man who can even read a newspaper . . . or who ever sees a book at all. I will go home and much of what I will have to say will seem strange to the people of my village. But I will teach and work and things will happen, slowly and swiftly. At times it will seem that nothing changes at all . . . and then again the sudden dramatic events which make history leap into the future. And then quiet again. Retrogres-sion even. Guns, murder, revolution. And I even will have moments when

I wonder if the quiet was not better than all that death and hatred. But I will look about my village at the illiteracy and disease and ignorance and I will not wonder long. And perhaps . . . perhaps I will be a great man . . . I mean perhaps I will hold on to the substance of truth and find my way always with the right course . . . and perhaps for it I will be butchered in my bed some night by the servants of empire . . .

BENEATHA: *The martyr!*

ASAGAI: *(He smiles.)* . . . or perhaps I shall live to be a very old man, respected and esteemed in my new nation . . . And perhaps I shall hold office and this is what I'm trying to tell you, Alaiyo: Perhaps the things I believe now for my country will be wrong and outmoded, and I will not understand and do terrible things to have things my way or merely to keep my power. Don't you see that there will be young men and women—not British soldiers then, but my own black countrymen—to step out of the shadows some evening and slit my then useless throat? Don't you see they have always been there . . . that they always will be. And that such a thing as my own death will be an advance? They who might kill me even . . . actually replenish all that I was.

BENEATHA: Oh, Asagai, I know all that.

45 ASAGAI: Good! Then stop moaning and groaning and tell me what you plan to do.

BENEATHA: Do?

ASAGAI: I have a bit of a suggestion.

BENEATHA: What?

ASAGAI: *(Rather quietly for him.)* That when it is all over—that you come home with me—

50 BENEATHA: *(Staring at him and crossing away with exasperation.)* Oh—Asagai—at this moment you decide to be romantic!

ASAGAI: *(Quickly understanding the misunderstanding.)* My dear, young creature of the New World—I do not mean across the city—I mean across the ocean: home—to Africa.

BENEATHA: *(Slowly understanding and turning to him with murmured amazement.)* To Africa?

ASAGAI: Yes! . . . *(Smiling and lifting his arms playfully.)* Three hundred years later the African Prince rose up out of the seas and swept the maiden back across the middle passage over which her ancestors had come—

BENEATHA: *(Unable to play.)* To—to Nigeria?

55 ASAGAI: Nigeria. Home. *(Coming to her with genuine romantic flippancy.)* I will show you our mountains and our stars; and give you cool drinks from gourds and teach you the old songs and the ways of our people—and, in time, we will pretend that—*(Very softly.)*—you have only been away for a day. Say that you'll come—*(He swings her around and takes her full in his arms in a kiss which proceeds to passion.)*

BENEATHA: *(Pulling away suddenly.)* You're getting me all mixed up—

ASAGAI: Why?

BENEATHA: Too many things—too many things have happened today. I must sit down and think. I don't know what I feel about anything right this minute.

She promptly sits down and props her chin on her fist.

ASAGAI: *(Charmed.)* All right, I shall leave you. No—don't get up. *(Touching her, gently, sweetly.)* Just sit awhile and think . . . Never be afraid to sit awhile and think. *(He goes to door and looks at her.)* How often I have looked at you and said, "Ah—so this is what the New World hath finally wrought . . ."

He exits. Beneatha sits on alone. Presently Walter enters from his room and starts to rummage through things, feverishly looking for something. She looks up and turns in her seat.

60 **BENEATHA:** *(Hissingly.)* Yes—just look at what the New World hath wrought! . . . Just look! *(She gestures with bitter disgust.)* There he is! *Monsieur le petit bourgeois noir*—himself! There he is—Symbol of a Rising Class! Entrepreneur! Titan of the system! *(Walter ignores her completely and continues frantically and destructively looking for something and hurling things to floor and tearing things out of their place in his search. Beneatha ignores the eccentricity of his actions and goes on with the monologue of insult.)* Did you dream of yachts on Lake Michigan, Brother? Did you see yourself on that Great Day sitting down at the Conference Table, surrounded by all the mighty bald-headed men in America? All halted, waiting, breathless, waiting for your pronouncements on industry? Waiting on you—Chairman of the Board! *(Walter finds what he is looking for—a small piece of white paper—and pushes it in his pocket and puts on his coat and rushes out without ever having looked at her. She shouts after him.)* I look at you and I see the final triumph of stupidity in the world!

The door slams and she returns to just sitting again. Ruth comes quickly out of Mama's room.

RUTH: Who was that?

BENEATHA: Your husband.

RUTH: Where did he go?

BENEATHA: Who knows—maybe he has an appointment at U.S. Steel.

65 **RUTH:** *(Anxiously, with frightened eyes.)* You didn't say nothing bad to him, did you?

BENEATHA: Bad? Say anything bad to him? No—I told him he was a sweet boy and full of dreams and everything is strictly peachy keen, as the ofay kids say!

Mama enters from her bedroom. She is lost, vague, trying to catch hold, to make some sense of her former command of the world, but it still eludes her. A sense of waste overwhelms her gait; a measure of apology rides on her shoulders. She goes to her plant, which has remained on the table, looks at it, picks it up and takes it to the window sill and sits it outside, and she stands and looks at it a long moment. Then she closes the window, straightens her body with effort and turns around to her children.

MAMA: Well—ain't it a mess in here, though? (*A false cheerfulness, a beginning of something.*) I guess we all better stop moping around and get some work done. All this unpacking and everything we got to do. (*Ruth raises her head slowly in response to the sense of the line; and Beneatha in similar manner turns very slowly to look at her mother.*) One of you all better call the moving people and tell 'em not to come.

RUTH: Tell 'em not to come?

MAMA: Of course, baby. Ain't no need in 'em coming all the way here and having to go back. They charges for that too. (*She sits down, fingers to her brow, thinking.*) Lord, ever since I was a little girl, I always remembers people saying, "Lena—Lena Eggleston, you aims too high all the time. You needs to slow down and see life a little more like it is. Just slow down some." That's what they always used to say down home—"Lord, that Lena Eggleston is a high-minded thing. She'll get her due one day!"

70 RUTH: No, Lena . . .

MAMA: Me and Big Walter just didn't never learn right.

RUTH: Lena, no! We gotta go. Bennie—tell her . . . (*She rises and crosses to Beneatha with her arms outstretched. Beneatha doesn't respond.*) Tell her we can still move . . . the notes ain't but a hundred and twenty-five a month. We got four grown people in this house—we can work . . .

MAMA: (*To herself.*) Just aimed too high all the time—

RUTH: (*Turning and going to Mama fast—the words pouring out with urgency and desperation.*) Lena—I'll work . . . I'll work twenty hours a day in all the kitchens in Chicago . . . I'll strap my baby on my back if I have to and scrub all the floors in America and wash all the sheets in America if I have to—but we got to MOVE! We got to get OUT OF HERE!

Mama reaches out absently and pats Ruth's hand.

75 MAMA: No—I sees things differently now. Been thinking 'bout some of the things we could do to fix this place up some. I seen a second-hand bureau over on Maxwell Street just the other day that could fit right there. (*She points to where the new furniture might go. Ruth wanders away from her.*) Would need some new handles on it and then a little varnish and it look like something brand-new. And—we can put up them new curtains in the kitchen . . . Why this place be looking fine. Cheer us all up so that we forget trouble ever come . . . (*To Ruth.*) And you could get some nice

screens to put up in your room round the baby's bassinet . . . *(She looks at both of them, pleadingly.)* Sometimes you just got to know when to give up some things . . . and hold on to what you got. . . .

Walter enters from the outside, looking spent and leaning against the door, his coat hanging from him.

MAMA: Where you been, son?

WALTER: *(Breathing hard.)* Made a call.

MAMA: To who, son?

WALTER: To The Man. *(He heads for his room.)*

80 **MAMA:** What man, baby?

WALTER: *(Stops in the door.)* The Man, Mama. Don't you know who The Man is?

RUTH: Walter Lee?

WALTER: *The Man.* Like the guys in the streets say—The Man. Captain Boss—Mistuh Charley . . . Old Cap'n Please Mr. Bossman . . .

BENEATHA: *(Suddenly.)* Lindner!

85 **WALTER:** That's right! That's good. I told him to come right over.

BENEATHA: *(Fiercely, understanding.)* For what? What do you want to see him for!

WALTER: *(Looking at his sister.)* We going to do business with him.

MAMA: What you talking 'bout, son?

WALTER: Talking 'bout life, Mama. You all always telling me to see life like it is. Well—I laid in there on my back today . . . and I figured it out. Life just like it is. Who gets and who don't get. *(He sits down with his coat on and laughs.)* Mama, you know it's all divided up. Life is. Sure enough. Between the takers and the "tooken." *(He laughs.)* I've figured it out finally. *(He looks around at them.)* Yeah. Some of us always getting "tooken." *(He laughs.)* People like Willy Harris, they don't never get "tooken." And you know why the rest of us do? 'Cause we all mixed up. Mixed up bad. We get to looking 'round for the right and the wrong; and we worry about it and cry about it and stay up nights trying to figure out 'bout the wrong and the right of things all the time . . . And all the time, man, them takers is out there operating, just taking and taking. Willy Harris? Shoot—Willy Harris don't even count. He don't even count in the big scheme of things. But I'll say one thing for old Willy Harris . . . he's taught me something. He's taught me to keep my eye on what counts in this world. Yeah— *(Shouting out a little.)* Thanks, Willy!

90 **RUTH:** What did you call that man for, Walter Lee?

WALTER: Called him to tell him to come on over to the show. Gonna put on a show for the man. Just what he wants to see. You see, Mama, the man came here today and he told us that them people out there where you want us to move—well they so upset they willing to pay us *not* to move! *(He laughs again.)* And—and oh, Mama—you would of been proud of the way me and Ruth and Bennie acted. We told him to get out . . . Lord have mercy! We told the man to get out! Oh, we was some proud folks this afternoon, yeah. *(He lights a cigarette.)* We were still full of that old-time stuff . . .

RUTH: *(Coming toward him slowly.)* You talking 'bout taking them people's money to keep us from moving in that house?

WALTER: I ain't just talking 'bout it, baby—I'm telling you that's what's going to happen!

BENEATHA: Oh, God! Where is the bottom! Where is the real honest-to-God bottom so he can't go any farther!

95 **WALTER:** See—that's the old stuff. You and that boy that was here today. You all want everybody to carry a flag and a spear and sing some marching songs, huh? You wanna spend your life looking into things and trying to find the right and the wrong part, huh? Yeah. You know what's going to happen to that boy someday—he'll find himself sitting in a dungeon, locked in forever—and the takers will have the key! Forget it, baby! There ain't no causes—there ain't nothing but taking in this world, and he who takes most is smartest—and it don't make a damn bit of difference *how.*

MAMA: You making something inside me cry, son. Some awful pain inside me.

WALTER: Don't cry, Mama. Understand. That white man is going to walk in that door able to write checks for more money than we ever had. It's important to him and I'm going to help him . . . I'm going to put on the show, Mama.

MAMA: Son—I come from five generations of people who was slaves and sharecroppers—but ain't nobody in my family never let nobody pay 'em no money that was a way of telling us we wasn't fit to walk the earth. We ain't never been that poor. *(Raising her eyes and looking at him.)* We ain't never been that—dead inside.

BENEATHA: Well—we are dead now. All the talk about dreams and sunlight that goes on in this house. It's all dead now.

100 **WALTER:** What's the matter with you all! I didn't make this world! It was give to me this way! Hell, yes, I want me some yachts someday! Yes, I want to hang some real pearls 'round my wife's neck. Ain't she supposed to wear no pearls? Somebody tell me—tell me, who decides which women is suppose to wear pearls in this world. I tell you I am a *man*—and I think my wife should wear some pearls in this world!

This last line hangs a good while and Walter begins to move about the room. The word "Man" has penetrated his consciousness; he mumbles it to himself repeatedly between strange agitated pauses as he moves about.

MAMA: Baby, how you going to feel on the inside?

WALTER: Fine! . . . Going to feel fine . . . a man . . .

MAMA: You won't have nothing left then, Walter Lee.

WALTER: *(Coming to her.)* I'm going to feel fine, Mama. I'm going to look that son-of-a-bitch in the eyes and say—*(He falters.)*—and say, "All right, Mr. Lindner—*(He falters even more.)*—that's *your* neighborhood out there! You got the right to keep it like you want! You got the right to have it like you want! Just write the check and—the house is yours." And—and I am going to say—*(His voice almost breaks.)* "And you—you people just put the money in my hand and you won't have to live next to this bunch of stinking niggers! . . ." *(He straightens up and moves away from his mother, walking around the room.)* And maybe—maybe I'll just get down on my black knees . . . *(He does so; Ruth and Bennie and Mama watch him in frozen horror.)* "Captain, Mistuh, Bossman—*(Groveling and grinning and wringing his hands in profoundly anguished imitation of the slow-witted movie stereotype.)* A-hee-hee-hee! Oh, yassuh boss! Yasssssuh! Great white—*(Voice breaking, he forces himself to go on.)*—Father, just gi' ussen de money, fo' God's sake, and we's—we's ain't gwine come out deh and dirty up yo' white folks neighborhood . . ." *(He breaks down completely.)* And I'll feel fine! Fine! FINE! *(He gets up and goes into the bedroom.)*

105 **BENEATHA:** That is not a man. That is nothing but a toothless rat.

MAMA: Yes—death done come in this here house. *(She is nodding, slowly, reflectively.)* Done come walking in my house on the lips of my children. You what supposed to be my beginning again. You—what supposed to be my harvest. *(To Beneatha.)* You—you mourning your brother?

BENEATHA: He's no brother of mine.

MAMA: What you say?

BENEATHA: I said that that individual in that room is no brother of mine.

110 **MAMA:** That's what I thought you said. You feeling like you better than he is today? *(Beneatha does not answer.)* Yes? What you tell him a minute ago? That he wasn't a man? Yes? You give him up for me? You done wrote his epitaph too—like the rest of the world? Well, who give you the privilege?

BENEATHA: Be on my side for once! You saw what he just did, Mama! You saw him—down on his knees. Wasn't it you who taught me to despise any man who would do that? Do what he's going to do?

MAMA: Yes—I taught you that. Me and your daddy. But I thought I taught you something else too . . . I thought I taught you to love him.

BENEATHA: Love him? There is nothing left to love.

MAMA: There is *always* something left to love. And if you ain't learned that, you ain't learned nothing. *(Looking at her.)* Have you cried for that boy today? I don't mean for yourself and for the family 'cause we lost the money. I mean for him: what he been through and what it done to him. Child, when do you think is the time to love somebody the most? When they done good and made things easy for everybody? Well then, you ain't through learning—because that ain't the time at all. It's when he's at his lowest and can't believe in hisself 'cause the world done whipped him so! When you starts measuring somebody, measure him right, child, measure him right. Make sure you done taken into account what hills and valleys he come through before he got to wherever he is.

Travis bursts into the room at the end of the speech, leaving the door open.

115 **TRAVIS:** Grandmama—the moving men are downstairs! The truck just pulled up.

MAMA: *(Turning and looking at him.)* Are they, baby? They downstairs?

She sighs and sits. Lindner appears in the doorway. He peers in and knocks lightly, to gain attention, and comes in. All turn to look at him.

LINDNER: *(Hat and briefcase in hand.)* Uh—hello . . .

Ruth crosses mechanically to the bedroom door and opens it and lets it swing open freely and slowly as the lights come up on Walter within, still in his coat, sitting at the far corner of the room. He looks up and out through the room to Lindner.

RUTH: He's here.

A long minute passes and Walter slowly gets up.

LINDNER: *(Coming to the table with efficiency, putting his briefcase on the table and starting to unfold papers and unscrew fountain pens.)* Well, I certainly was glad to hear from you people. *(Walter has begun the trek out of the room, slowly and awkwardly, rather like a small boy, passing the back of his sleeve across his mouth from time to time.)* Life can really be so much simpler than people let it be most of the time. Well—with whom do I negotiate? You, Mrs. Younger, or your son here? *(Mama sits with her hands folded on her lap and her eyes closed as Walter advances. Travis goes closer to Lindner and looks at the papers curiously.)* Just some official papers, sonny.

120 **RUTH:** Travis, you go downstairs—

MAMA: *(Opening her eyes and looking into Walter's.)* No. Travis, you stay right here. And you make him understand what you doing, Walter Lee. You teach him good. Like Willy Harris taught you. You show where our five generations done come to. *(Walter looks from her to the boy, who grins at him innocently.)* Go ahead, son—*(She folds her hands and closes her eyes.)* Go ahead.

WALTER: *(At last crosses to Lindner, who is reviewing the contract.)* Well, Mr. Lindner. *(Beneatha turns away.)* We called you—*(There is a profound, simple groping quality in his speech.)*—because, well, me and my family *(He looks around and shifts from one foot to the other.)* Well—we are very plain people . . .

LINDNER: Yes—

WALTER: I mean—I have worked as a chauffeur most of my life—and my wife here, she does domestic work in people's kitchens. So does my mother. I mean—we are plain people . . .

125   **LINDNER:**   Yes, Mr. Younger—

WALTER: *(Really like a small boy, looking down at his shoes and then up at the man.)* And—uh—well, my father, well, he was a laborer most of his life. . . .

LINDNER: *(Absolutely confused.)* Uh, yes—yes, I understand. *(He turns back to the contract.)*

WALTER: *(A beat; staring at him.)* And my father—*(With sudden intensity.)* My father almost *beat a man to death* once because this man called him a bad name or something, you know what I mean?

LINDNER: *(Looking up, frozen.)* No, no, I'm afraid I don't—

130   **WALTER:**   *(A beat. The tension hangs; then Walter steps back from it.)* Yeah. Well—what I mean is that we come from people who had a lot of *pride.* I mean—we are very proud people. And that's my sister over there and she's going to be a doctor—and we are very proud—

LINDNER: Well—I am sure that is very nice, but—

WALTER: What I am telling you is that we called you over here to tell you that we are very proud and that this—*(Signaling to Travis.)* Travis, come here. *(Travis crosses and Walter draws him before him facing the man.)* This is my son, and he makes the sixth generation our family in this country. And we have all thought about your offer—

LINDNER: Well, good . . . good—

WALTER: And we have decided to move into our house because my father— my father—he earned it for us brick by brick. *(Mama has her eyes closed and is rocking back and forth as though she were in church, with her head nodding the Amen yes.)* We don't want to make no trouble for nobody or fight no causes, and we will try to be good neighbors. And that's *all* we got to say about that. *(He looks the man absolutely in the eyes.)* We don't want your money. *(He turns and walks away.)*

135   **LINDNER:**   *(Looking around at all of them.)* I take it then—that you have decided to occupy . . .

BENEATHA: That's what the man said.

LINDNER: *(To Mama in her reverie.)* Then I would like to appeal to you, Mrs. Younger. You are older and wiser and understand things better I am sure . . .

MAMA: I am afraid you don't understand. My son said we was going to move and there ain't nothing left for me to say. *(Briskly.)* You know how these young folks is nowadays, mister. Can't do a thing with 'em! *(As he opens his mouth, she rises.)* Good-bye.

LINDNER: *(Folding up his materials.)* Well—if you are that final about it . . . there is nothing left for me to say. *(He finishes, almost ignored by the family, who are concentrating on Walter Lee. At the door Lindner halts and looks around.)* I sure hope you people know what you're getting into.

He shakes his head and exits.

140 **RUTH:** *(Looking around and coming to life.)* Well, for God's sake—if the moving men are here—LET'S GET THE HELL OUT OF HERE!

MAMA: *(Into action.)* Ain't it the truth! Look at all this here mess. Ruth, put Travis' good jacket on him . . . Walter Lee, fix your tie and tuck your shirt in, you look like somebody's hoodlum! Lord have mercy, where is my plant? *(She flies to get it amid the general bustling of the family, who are deliberately trying to ignore the nobility of the past moment.)* You all start on down . . . Travis child, don't go empty-handed . . . Ruth, where did I put that box with my skillets in it? I want to be in charge of it myself . . . I'm going to make us the biggest dinner we ever ate tonight . . . Beneatha, what's the matter with them stockings? Pull them things up, girl . . .

The family starts to file out as two moving men appear and begin to carry out the heavier pieces of furniture, bumping into the family as they move about.

BENEATHA: Mama, Asagai asked me to marry him today and go to Africa—

MAMA: *(In the middle of her getting-ready activity.)* He did? You ain't old enough to marry nobody—*(Seeking the moving men lifting one of her chairs precariously.)* Darling, that ain't no bale of cotton, please handle it so we can sit in it again! I had that chair twenty-five years . . .

The movers sigh with exasperation and go on with their work.

BENEATHA: *(Girlishly and unreasonably trying to pursue the conversation.)* To go to Africa, Mama—be a doctor in Africa . . .

145 **MAMA:** *(Distracted.)* Yes, baby—

WALTER: *Africa!* What he want you to go to Africa for?

BENEATHA: To practice there . . .

WALTER: Girl, if you don't get all them silly ideas out your head! You better marry yourself a man with some loot . . .

BENEATHA: *(Angrily, precisely as in the first scene of the play.)* What have you got to do with who I marry!

150 **WALTER:** Plenty. Now I think George Murchison—

BENEATHA: *George Murchison!* I wouldn't marry him if he was Adam and I was Eve!

Walter and Beneatha go out yelling at each other vigorously and the anger is loud and real till their voices diminish. Ruth stands at the door and turns to Mama and smiles knowingly.

MAMA: *(Fixing her hat at last.)* Yeah—they something all right, my children . . .

RUTH: Yeah—they're something. Let's go, Lena.

MAMA: *(Stalling, starting to look around at the house.)* Yes—I'm coming. Ruth—

155 **RUTH:** Yes?

MAMA: *(Quietly, woman to woman.)* He finally come into his manhood today, didn't he? Kind of like a rainbow after the rain . . .

RUTH: *(Biting her lip lest her own pride explode in front of Mama.)* Yes, Lena.

Walter's voice calls for them raucously.

WALTER: *(Off stage.)* Y'all come on! These people charges by the hour, you know!

MAMA: *(Waving Ruth out vaguely.)* All right, honey—go on down. I be down directly.

Ruth hesitates, then exits. Mama stands, at last alone in the living room, her plant on the table before her as the lights start to come down. She looks around at all the walls and ceilings and suddenly, despite herself, while the children call below, a great heaving thing rises in her and she puts her fist to her mouth to stifle it, takes a final desperate look, pulls her coat about her, pats her hat and goes out. The lights dim down. The door opens and she comes back in, grabs her plant, and goes out for the last time.

CURTAIN

Historical Perspective on *A Raisin in the Sun*

Loften Mitchell

Lorraine Hansberry, a Chicagoan, had written poetry and reviewed plays for *Freedom*, an uptown journal. She had started working on a number of plays, but never completed any. One night she sat working on a family play; then she became annoyed with it, flung the pages into the air, and they scattered over the floor. Her husband, Robert Nemiroff, got on his hands and knees and picked up page after page. He carefully arranged these and placed them on a desk. Miss Hansberry later said that was a turning point in her career. She sat down and completed the play.

That play was *A Raisin in the Sun*. She drew the title from Langston Hughes' book of poetry, *Montage of a Dream Deferred:*

> *What happens to a dream deferred?*
> *Does it dry up like a raisin in the sun?*
> *Does it fester like an old sore and run,*
> *Or, does it explode?*

One night the Nemiroffs entertained music publisher Philip Rose and his actress-wife, Doris Belack. They talked about Lorraine's writing, and as the evening progressed, she read her play. The Roses were impressed. The next morning Philip called Lorraine and told her he wanted to option her play.

Lorraine laughed when she told the story. She said: "I told Phil I'd take his money and keep it."

Mr. Rose wasn't laughing. They drew up legal documents and he had an option on *A Raisin in the Sun.* Then he really went to work. He contacted Sidney Poitier, who agreed to star in the play. He went out and signed Lloyd Richards to serve as director, then began a series of backers' auditions.

Everybody everyplace had criticisms of the work. Mr. Rose tried to get co-producers, but he was turned down. Finally, David Cogan, an accountant, agreed to join Mr. Rose. Money began to come in, never in any great amounts. Mr. Rose wasn't discouraged. He put his company into rehearsals without knowing where he would open the show. He held some run-throughs in New York City, then got a house in Boston.

Off the show went to Boston, where it opened to good reviews. The company went on to Philadelphia, where more good reviews followed. The Shuberts remembered they had told Mr. Rose they would arrange a New York house for him if he did well on the road. Mr. Rose took the show on to Chicago, where its success was repeated. And then New York saw it on March 11, 1959, and the critics sang.

A Raisin in the Sun not only won the Critics Circle Award; it made money. And it projected its cast members beautifully. Sidney Poitier—and later Ossie Davis—Ruby Dee, Claudia McNeil, Diana Sands, Ivan Dixon, Louis Gossett, Lonne Elder III, Douglas Turner and director Lloyd Richards made notable contributions to this moving family drama.

A Raisin in the Sun created controversy offstage, too. Negroes got tired of hearing whites say: "Even though I'm of such-and-such background, I could identify with that Negro family." And some Negroes answered, bluntly: "Yes, I could also identify with the Nazi victims and the victims of the potato-famine." Then—someone accused the play of being too much like O'Casey's *Juno and the Paycock.* Right behind that accusation came another—that it was really a Jewish play with a Negro cast and that is why it did so well. And there were Negroes who became angry because critics said the play really said nothing about the Negro plight, that it was not an angry play, and they lauded the playwright for showing "balance" in her writing.

Then there were Negro intellectuals who felt whites had "patronized" the play. They declared no urban Negro would do what Miss Hansberry's hero did—give thousands of dollars at one time to a man whose address he didn't know. Those intellectuals claimed that, had this been a "white" play, the critics would have questioned that fact. But since it was a Negro hero, it was overlooked.

A Raisin in the Sun crystallized the era Negro playwrights began to call the "nots." The critics said *In Splendid Error* was *not* a message play, *Trouble in Mind* was *not* vindictive, *Take a Giant Step,* was *not* just about Negroes, *Simply Heavenly* was *not* an angry play, *A Land Beyond the River* was *not* a propaganda play, and *A Raisin in the Sun* was *not* a Negro play. In other words, black playwrights were being praised for *not* making white people uncomfortable in the theatre. Black playwrights began to worry about their work.

But they were being produced and Negro actors were working. They worked, too, in integrated hits such as Sammy Davis' *Mr. Wonderful* and in Lena Horne's *Jamaica.* Everyone saw great things in store for black artists. The American Society of African Culture held a writers' conference at the Henry Hudson Hotel in 1959, and in looking back over the decade, everyone admitted that the decade which began as the fearful fifties had developed into one of optimism and output.

The millennium was here! Loudly proclaimed was the Second Black Renaissance.

Credits